COMPUTER SCIENCE
IN K–12

An A to Z handbook on teaching programming

Edited by
Shuchi Grover, Ph.D.

Edfinity

For permissions and any information related to this book write to: hello@edfinity.com

All photos are credited to the article author(s) unless otherwise noted.

Book design: Robert Vizzini
Cover art: Julie Alice Chappell
Proofreader: Pamela Hunt

About the cover art: *The Electric Blue Butterfly, Circuit Board Insect has been thoughtfully fabricated from discarded and obsolete computer and circuit board components including a tiny glass optical component from a computer camera device. Circuit board patterns are repeated on his wings as delicate wing veins. Each one of my Computer Bugs is a one off, original artwork...there are no two alike. It is my hope that my Upcycled Insect Artworks help to highlight the dangers of planned obsolescence and raise awareness of e-waste in the natural environment.*
— Artist, Julie Alice Campbell

ISBN 978-1-7346627-0-2 Paperback Color Print
ISBN 978-1-7346627-1-9 Paperback Black and White Print
ISBN 978-1-7346627-2-6 Hardcover

Edfinity
Palo Alto, CA 94306 U.S.A.
e-mail: hello@edfinity.com

Printed in the United States of America.

To the memory of my father, D.C. Grover. A publisher for close to 65 years, he was immersed in a world of books and scholarly literature all his life. As a progressive thinker and ardent supporter of education and educators, he prodded me for years to take the learning from my research and create a book for teachers. The vision for this handbook was born out of that encouragement.

Contents

Contents

Acknowledgments

Writing this book has been an exhausting but exhilarating experience. I profusely thank each and every individual who has been a part of this journey.

The book is testimony to the amazing "Computer Science for All" community in the US (especially) and around the world. It would not have come together had it not been for my wonderful co-authors who so willingly jumped on board! I was humbled and elated with every 'yay' that I got from all the authors and co-authors. Phil B, Miles B, Shannon C, Katharine C, Paul C, Jill D, Debbie F, Katrina F, Baker F, Steven F, Dan G, Joanna G, Matthias H, Maya I, Yasmin K, Richard K, Todd L, Tia M, Frieda M, Jens M, Josh P, Kelly P, Kathryn R, Jennifer R, Vicky S, Sue S, Jessica S, Carla S, Juha S, Jakita T, Bryan T, Rebecca V, Jane W, Dave W, JonAlf D-W, David W, Aman Y and Mike Z — my heartfelt thanks to each one of you for joining me on this amazing ride, and your incredible generosity for the greater good.

My heartfelt thanks also to those who contributed examples in and/or shaped various chapters— Colby Tofel-Grehl, Chris Oban, Dawn duPriest, Emmanual Schanzer, Irene Lee, Jared O'Leary, and Jens Mönig, as well as those acknowledged in individual chapters.

A special thank you to Mark Guzdial for his gracious and enthusiastic agreement to write the Foreword that provides a wonderful backdrop to this book.

To Bill Marsland, Carrie MacDonald, Jeanie Smith, Josh Paley, Maureen Willis, Smita Kolhatkar, Stan Vong, Tinu Hu, Xander Piper and all the CS teachers who have welcomed me over the years to their elementary, middle, and high school CS classrooms - thank you!

My gratitude to Robert Vizzini and Pamela Hunt for their patience and assistance with layout and editing of book chapters.

A big thank you to Julie Alice Chappell in Portsmouth, England, for her stunning artwork that she permitted me to use for the book cover.

Finally, a heartfelt thanks to my family for their support. My late father prodded me for years to publish my dissertation as a book for teachers everywhere. My mother and sisters are a constant source of encouragement. My sons, Sid and Sam, helped me with topic ideas and chapter discussions. Saving the best for last— my extra-huge thanks to my husband, Shivram. He is my font of strength who has supported me every single step of the way. Without his daily nudges and non-trivial assistance with production, this book would have remained a pipe-dream.

This book has been 8 years in the making. The seeds of what makes this book stand apart from any other— the synthesis of content, practices, and pedagogy—were sown during my Ph.D. at Stanford University while designing an introductory programming curriculum for middle grades with guidance from my advisors Roy Pea and Steve Cooper. I am eternally grateful for their valuable mentorship that put me on this rewarding and gratifying path of studying the teaching and learning of computing and programming in K-12 classrooms.

Contributors

Editor and Co-Author

Shuchi Grover is a senior research scientist at Looking Glass Ventures and a visiting scholar at Stanford University. Her research is focused on teaching and learning of computer science, computational thinking, and programming in schools. She has been working with children and programming since 2001, first in informal afterschool settings, and then in classrooms. Her current research encompasses the design of curricula and assessments for all levels of preK-12 CS education, as well as the integration of computing and coding in STEM and other subjects. She has led, and continues to lead, several large research projects (often in collaboration with universities and research organizations) with grants from the US National Science Foundation and other federal agencies. She also consults globally on projects related to K-12 CS, programming, and computational thinking education. The vision for a guide book for teachers encompassing both content and pedagogy took shape during her doctoral studies at Stanford University, which involved creating an introductory programming curriculum that drew on learnings from research in CS education as well as the learning sciences. In addition to publishing her research in leading academic journals, Shuchi is active in teacher outreach. She regularly collaborates with K-12 CS teachers and authors articles aimed at wider audiences beyond the research community. Over the past decade, she has served on the National K-12 Computer Science Framework team, taskforces of the Computer Science Teachers' Association, the ACM Education Advisory Committee (2018-present), and the editorial board of the ACM Transactions on Computing Education (2015-present).

Shuchi's educational journey includes undergraduate and graduate degrees in computer science, an Ed.M. in Technology in Education from Harvard University, and a Ph.D. in Learning Sciences and Technology Design from Stanford University. She lives in Palo Alto, California, where she loves to crochet and garden in her spare time. [*@shuchig, https://www.shuchigrover.com*]

Contributors

Dr. Aman Yadav is a Professor of Educational Psychology and Educational Technology at Michigan State University with extensive experience in research, evaluation, and teacher professional development. His areas of expertise include computer science education, problem-based learning, and online learning. His work has been published in a number of leading journals. [*@yadavaman, http://www.amanyadav.org*]

Baker Franke is a curriculum writer, professional development facilitator, and research and evaluation manager for Code.org. Prior to Code.org Baker taught high school computer science at the University of Chicago Laboratory Schools, and was vice-president of the Chicago chapter of CSTA. He enjoys neither piña coladas nor getting caught in the rain.

Bryan Twarek is Director of Education for the Computer Science Teachers Association, where he manages CSTA's student and teacher standards and develops programs to improve the equitable teaching and learning of K-12 computer science. Previously, he directed computer science policy, curriculum, and professional development for the San Francisco public schools. [*@btwarek*]

Carla Agard-Strickland is the Digital Development Manager at UChicago STEM Education. An experienced mathematics teacher and curriculum developer, she works with elementary teachers to integrate computer science into their existing mathematics instruction. Carla brings an Afro-Caribbean perspective and a passion for equitable, high-quality instruction to her work in education. [*@CisforCarla*]

Dan Garcia is a UC Berkeley EECS Teaching Professor. A "CSforALL" national leader, he is also an ACM Distinguished Educator, ACM Distinguished Speaker, and SIGCSE Vice-Chair. His APCSP-endorsed Beauty and Joy of Computing (BJC) course has reached 650 teachers worldwide, and at UC Berkeley has shattered CS gender enrollment records.

David Wolber is a Professor of Computer Science at the University of San Francisco. He is the lead author of the book "App Inventor 2: Create your own Android apps", and he runs the site *appinventor.org*.

David Weintrop is an Assistant Professor of Teaching & Learning, Policy & Leadership in the College of Education with a joint appointment in the College of Information Studies at the University of Maryland. His research focuses on the design, implementation, and evaluation of accessible, engaging, and equitable computational learning environments.

Dr. Deborah A. Fields is an associate research professor at Utah State University. Her research focuses on understanding and supporting students making creative artifacts and online communities where children share such artifacts in ways that create intersections between their interests, communities, and identities.

Frieda McAlear, (Inupiaq) MRes, is the Senior Research Associate at the Kapor Center. Frieda co-founded the Women of Color in Computing Collaborative (WOCCC) and she is a founding partner in the Expanding Computer Science for Native American Girls project, a partnership between the WOCCC and the American Indian Science and Engineering Society.

Jakita Thomas is a Philpott Westpoint Stevens Associate Professor of Computer Science and Software Engineering at Auburn University. She directs the CUltuRally & SOcially Relevant (CURSOR) Computing Lab. She is a recipient of the NSF's Faculty Early Career Development Award and the Presidential Early Career Award for Scientists and Engineers.

Jane Waite has worked in industry as a developer, as a K-5 teacher and is now a researcher and teacher trainer. She has researched the use of the MicroBit, PRIMM, Semantic Waves and teaching K-5 programming. She is a Teaching Fellow and PhD student at Queen Mary University of London. [*@janewaite*]

Jennifer Rosato is the Director of the National Center for Computer Science Education and an Assistant Professor of Computer Information Systems at the College of St. Scholastica. She co-leads the Mobile CSP and CSAwesome projects as wells as pre-service and in-service computer science teacher education programs.

Contributors

Jens Mönig is a researcher at SAP and makes interactive programming environments. He is fanatical about visual coding blocks. Jens is the architect and lead programmer of UC Berkeley's "Snap! Build Your Own Blocks" programming language used in the introductory "Beauty and Joy of Computing" curriculum.

Dr. Jessica Solyom is an Assistant Research Professor in the School of Social Transformation and Associate Director of the Center for Gender Equity in Science and Technology at Arizona State University. She is an expert in the areas of racial justice, indigenous epistemologies, critical race theory, race and racism in education, and equity and inclusion.

Jill Denner is a Senior Research Scientist at Education, Training, Research, a non-profit organization in California. She does applied research and evaluation with a focus on broadening participation in computing and other STEM fields, and has developed several after-school programs that engage children and their families in computer science.

Joanna Goode is the Sommerville Knight Professor of Education at the University of Oregon. Formerly a high school computer science teacher, Joanna's research examines how computing education practices and policies can broaden participation for girls and minoritized students. She is a co-creator of the Exploring Computer Science program.

JonAlf Dyrland-Weaver has been teaching high school computer science for 14 years and is currently a teacher and Director of Computer Science at Stuyvesant High School in NYC. His passion for both teaching and computer science is largely the fault of fellow author Mike Zamansky.

Josh Paley teaches computer science at Gunn High School in Palo Alto, CA. He holds a BS in Mathematics and Computer Science and a MS in Applied Mathematics from UIUC. He was a Summer Lecturer at the University of California, Berkeley. He wants to eat some fish and chips.

Juha Sorva is Senior University Lecturer at Aalto University, Finland. His research interests include the learning and teaching of introductory programming, learners' understandings of programming concepts, instructional design in ebooks, and program visualization. His other interests include Diet Coke and the word "partridge."

Katharine Childs works in the research team at Raspberry Pi Foundation and holds an MSc in Computing in Education from Nottingham Trent University. An ex-teacher and network manager, she is interested in helping students learn about computing in real-world contexts and spoke about this in her TEDx talk "Coding the Hairy Toe" [@IAmKatharineC]

Kathryn Rich is a doctoral candidate in Educational Psychology and Educational Technology at Michigan State University and a mathematics and computer science curriculum developer at UChicago STEM Education. She works with elementary teachers to integrate technology into instruction. She holds degrees in mathematics and learning sciences. [@KatietheCurious; katiethecurious.com]

Professor Katrina Falkner is Interim Executive Dean for the Faculty of Engineering, Computer and Mathematical Sciences, The University of Adelaide, and Leads research and programs at the Computer Science Education Research Group (CSER). In 2014 she launched a national K-12 Digital Technologies program, providing free online training to Australian teachers.

Kelly Powers is a Teacher in Residence at Cornell Tech working in NYC schools as a Computational Thinking and Computer Science Coach. Kelly works to bring a program of rigor and joy to all schools. Kelly is currently coaching teachers at PS86 in the Bronx developing their CT/CS K-6 pathway.

Matthias Hauswirth leads the Lugano Computing Education Research Lab (luce.inf.usi.ch) at USI Università della Svizzera italiana in Switzerland. He loves Swiss chocolate, teaching and research in programming languages and CS education, and contributing to high school programming textbooks and training programs for future computer science high school teachers.

Maya Israel is an associate professor of educational technology at the University of Florida. Her research focuses on supporting students with disabilities and other struggling learners' meaningful engagement in K-12 computer science as well as on Universal Design for Learning (UDL).

Mike Zamansky has been teaching CS for thirty years. He is the architect of the highly regarded CS program at Stuyvesant High School, the inspiration for The Academy for Software Engineering, and is known as "the Godfather of CS Education." Mike runs Hunter College's CS teacher certification and undergraduate honors CS programs.

Miles Berry is principal lecturer in computing education at the University of Roehampton. A former teacher and head teacher, he was part of the team who created England's national curriculum for computing. He serves on the boards of Computing At School, the CSTA and England's National Centre for Computing Education. *@mberry*, *milesberry.net*

Paul Curzon, a Professor of Computer Science, Queen Mary University of London, cofounded the inspirational cs4fn/Teaching London Computing projects, was awarded the IEEE Taylor L Booth award for Education "for outstanding contributions to the rebirth of computer science as a school subject" and coauthored "The Power of Computational Thinking".

Philip Bagge is a computing school teacher and inspector for Hampshire in the UK. He enjoys exploring new methods of teaching computing science and trying them out in his classes. Phil believes that the real sweet spot in teaching programming lie where educational and computing research are both taken into account. Phil authors the code-it.co.uk resources.

Dr. Rebecca Vivian is a Researcher at the Computer Science Education Research Group (CSER) at The University of Adelaide, with a BEd(Prim)(Hons) and PhD(Education). Her research covers CS education, learning sciences and technology-enhanced learning. She trains teachers in K-12 CS education and is passionate about engaging future generations in STEM. *@RebeccaVivian*

Contributors

Richard Kick teaches high school mathematics and computer science with BS and MS degrees from UIUC and Chicago State University. He taught AP Computer Science using Pascal, C++, and Java. He wrote C++ code at Fermilab, and was a College Board reader, table and question leader, and test development committee member.

Shannon Campe is a Program Manager at Education, Training, Research (ETR) - a non-profit health equity organization. The focus of her research and evaluation is on increasing diversity in STEM with an emphasis on computing. She has designed, managed, and taught students involved in multiple in- and after-school computing programs.

Steven Floyd is a doctoral candidate in Curriculum Studies at Western University and an Education Officer with Ontario's Ministry of Education. Steven has taught high school computer science since 2003 and is a winner of the CSTA's Award for Teaching Excellence in Computer Science.

Sue Sentance is Chief Learning Officer at the Raspberry Pi Foundation, UK. Her research interests include programming education, teacher professional learning and physical computing. She is a teacher and teacher educator and currently has a leading role in a government-funded programme to bring high-quality computing education to all schools in England. [*@suesentance*]

Tia Madkins is assistant professor in the College of Education and faculty research affiliate with the Population Research Center at The University of Texas at Austin. Her research focuses on how preservice and inservice teachers engage equity pedagogies to transform STEAM + computing learning environments for intersectionally minoritized students. (*tmadkins@austin.utexas.edu*, *@ProfTiaMadkins*)

Todd Lash is a research associate with the Creative Technology Research Lab (CTRL) were he studies ways to increase equity in and access to high-quality computer science education for all students and instructional strategies that address the challenges faced by struggling learners engaged in computer science education activities.

Vicky Sedgwick has been teaching elementary and middle school CS for ten years and is currently teaching 4th-6th grade CS at a private school in the Los Angeles area. Vicky was a standards writer on the 2017 CSTA K–12 Computer Science Standards and the 2020 Standards for CS Teachers.

Yasmin Kafai is professor at the University of Pennsylvania. She is a learning designer and researcher of online tools, projects and communities to promote computational making, crafting, and creativity. She helped develop and research the programming language Scratch and an electronic textile curriculum. Kafai earned a doctorate from Harvard University.

Foreword

Inventing Computing Education in Schools

Introducing computing into schools requires invention and research. Computer science is still new, as academic disciplines go. For most of the first 50 years of computer science as a field, students studying it were adults in higher education—undergraduates, scientists, or engineers—who had decided for themselves to learn about these powerful technologies and how they were shaped.

In K–12 schools, we teach computer science to children for whom computing is ever present but rarely considered. Many children have smart phones or gaming devices, but few ask how they are made. The task of teaching these students, who are not asking for the knowledge and skills, is much different than in higher education: Schoolteachers have to motivate students to engage with computer science. Although advised by standards, many teachers have to choose what knowledge and which skills are worth it for their students to learn.

In the 1960s, when the first computer science classes and degrees were created and offered in higher education, teachers were the inventors of the field. They were mathematicians and engineers who had developed the new computing technology. Most postsecondary teachers of computer science today have received academic training in the new discipline of computer science. The ACM SIGCSE Technical Symposium annually gathers over 1,500 of these experts who focus on how to teach computer science to undergraduates.

In contrast, most computing teachers in schools worldwide have far less expertise in computer science. Few of them in the United States have any formal education in computer science, though most have earned a certification to teach business, career, or vocational classes. They have expertise in teaching, but they may not have expertise with computing or programming.

Our challenges in preparing schoolteachers for computer science classes are very different from those we have faced in the history of computing education. We have to provide teachers with the knowledge of the subject matter of computer science. We also have to provide teachers with pedagogical content knowledge, or the knowledge of how to teach computing to children.

Worldwide, we are literally inventing computing education in schools as we go along. This book represents the cutting edge of that effort. The authors of this book are among the world's leaders in thinking about what to teach about computer science in schools and how to teach it.

Foreword

Why Teach Computer Science in Schools?

Different contexts (countries, states, districts, or schools) have different reasons for teaching computer science to K–12 (primary and secondary school) children. I start from thinking about these reasons in terms of three definitions.

- Computer science was originally defined in a 1967 letter in the journal *Science* as the study of computers and all the phenomena associated with them.[1]

- Computing is a broader umbrella concept that includes information systems, computer engineering, and software engineering, as well as computer science.

- Programming refers to reading and writing a notation that is specific enough to control a computer's process at some point in the future.

We can use these definitions to tease out what we want students to know. Do we want students to know computer science, or, more broadly, computing? Do we want students to learn job skills in computer science, or computing skills that they can use in their future jobs? Is programming useful in itself as a job skill, or to support learning in computer science or computing? If we want students to gain skills in the broad umbrella of computing, do we have to include programming? Or is programming itself a useful tool for supporting learning and literacy?

Rafi Santo, Sara Vogel, and Dixie Ching published a paper last year describing a range of visions that drive teachers' desire to teach computing education.[2] I recommend reading the entire report. Following are a quotes describing teachers' rationales:

- "We should teach CS because we need to promote a more diverse tech workforce."

- "We should teach CS because it will allow youth to solve problems in their community through technology."

- "Being a good citizen in the 21st century will include digital citizenship."

- "Computing may provide our youth with more and better career opportunities to choose from."

The teachers' use of "CS" and "computing" are mostly compatible with the definitions I offer. We may use these rationales to explore what we want students to learn.

---

[1] Newell, A., Perlis, A. J., & Simon, H. A. (1967). Computer science. *Science*, 157(3795), 1373–1374. DOI: 10.1126/science.157.3795.1373-b

[2] Santo, R., Vogel, S., & Ching, D. (2019). CS for What? Diverse visions of computer science education in practice. *CSforALL*. https://academicworks.cuny.edu/gc_pubs/562/

- If we are trying to influence the workforce or give students career opportunities, we are likely aiming at students learning job skills, whether concrete programming skills or social skills like teamwork.

- If we want students to solve problems with technology, programming is going to be one of the target skills because it's the most powerful and flexible medium for technological invention.

- Digital citizenship is closer to general computing skills than any specific computer science or programming skills.

Our first question has to be what we want the students to know, and why. Then we can define what our computing teachers need to know so they can embark on design and experimentation in their classrooms to achieve the learning goals.

What Do Computing Teachers Need to Know?

The point of this book is to serve as a guide for computing teachers about what they need to know to achieve their learning goals. Dr. Shuchi Grover is a world leader in research on integrating computing into primary and secondary classrooms. She has gathered some of the top experts in integrating programming, computing, and computer science into schools who present many reasons for teaching these important subjects. They recognize a range of expectations for computing teachers depending on where, what, and whom they are teaching.

Several chapters here help teachers learn and teach programming skills, such as data structures and modularity. The book also contains chapters on more general computing skills, like creativity and planning. It's much harder for computer science teachers to find guidance on how to teach computer science. This book provides that critical and too-rare knowledge, with chapters on worked examples and pair programming, among other pedagogical techniques.

This collection represents the best of how we (researchers, developers, and teachers of computing) think about what computing teachers need to know. The whole field of computing education is an exciting combination of design and experimentation. Computer science is new, computing education is newer, and our efforts to make the power of computing available to all students through schools have just started. I have no doubt that all computing educators will find this book useful in their own classrooms. These authors are explorers and pioneers, and they offer what they have learned to inform your own pioneering practice.

—**Mark Guzdial,** *Professor, University of Michigan*

Preface

When you learn, teach. When you get, give. —Maya Angelou

This handbook, which strives to embody Maya Angelou's enduring quote, is *for* **teachers** and *by* **teachers and researchers** steeped in computer science (CS) education. The authors of each chapter have generously shared what we know and have learned about teaching introductory programming from classroom experience as well as research in the field. We have also shared concrete examples as well as abstract principles distilled from research studies (our own as well as those of others) and years of experience in teaching CS concepts and practices and working with pedagogies in introductory computer science classrooms. Ultimately, we want this book to be an **essential, enduring, practical guide for K–12 teachers for teaching introductory programming**.

Quis? Quid? Ubi? Quibus Auxiliis? Cur? Quomodo? Quando?

Taking a leaf from the playbook of philosophers, thinkers, theologians, rhetoricians of old, and teachers of today, I have organized the introduction to this book by *who, what, where, with what, why, how*, and *when* (with some custom rearrangement of the order). Having worked as an educator and education researcher for 20 years, I have always found the **why** to be the most rewarding place to begin a scientific or literary argument.

WHY THIS BOOK?

Learning to code is the cool new thing in K–12 schools worldwide. Computer science, coding, and computational thinking are shaking up formal school education everywhere. Long considered the domain of tertiary education (or informal, interest-driven learning for the few who were fortunate to have access to it), coding is now reaching school classrooms in a concerted attempt to educate every learner this new-age foundational skill. In doing so, we also democratize learning by providing every student with the necessary skills to compete and succeed in a world driven by computing.

However, there is a Dickensian "best of times, worst of times" shade to this boom in K–12 CS education. On the one hand, excitement surrounds the introduction of programming to students at all grade levels from elementary to high school. There is enthusiasm among children and parents about learning this skill that demystifies computing for a generation that was born in a world of smartphones and the internet. On the other hand, there is widespread anxiety and confusion among schools, teachers and administrators about teacher preparation for teaching CS and programming to all students at all grade levels. What should be taught? How should it be taught at various grade levels? What do students typically struggle to learn? How can we support all learners, including those with learning difficulties? How can we make the classroom a fair, inclusive, and learner-centered environment for students from diverse genders, ethnicities, cultures, prior experiences, and backgrounds? These are questions CS schoolteachers wrestle with, **regardless of country or context**.

It comes as news to no one that there is a huge need to build teacher capacity to teach this subject. Several teachers tasked—or courageously stepping forward—to take on the mantle of teaching programming have never learned or taught CS or programming before. Often, they have only a few days of basic training on programming aligned closely to the curriculum they are expected to teach. Often, such training provides them only a cursory experience with the curriculum as learners themselves. As much as we must laud the passion of K–12 CS teachers who identify with this reality, we must also recognize that we need to do better by our teachers and students. We must provide a robust foundation for computer science, and especially programming, to those teaching programming in classrooms.

As anyone associated with formal education knows, teaching is not just about access to a curriculum but also about having **knowledge and understanding of what needs to be taught and how it should be taught**—both content knowledge and pedagogical knowledge specific to that content. The phrase **pedagogical content knowledge** (PCK) is used to describe this crucial combination of content and teaching knowledge for teachers. This book aims to help current and aspiring K-12 CS teachers build both content knowledge and PCK related to teaching introductory programming.

FOR WHOM AND BY WHOM?

The audience for this book is *any K–12 CS teacher anywhere*. Every curious teacher who is preparing to teach, or is already teaching, computer science (and especially programming) in school classrooms worldwide can benefit from this book. The ideas presented here are foundational. They transcend programming languages as well as geographical and other classroom contexts. The book is also helpful for teachers and curriculum designers who may be keen to learn what topics to teach, how to teach them, and of what student struggles and difficulties they should be mindful.

This book is indirectly also for your students who will learn with and from you. My hope is that through you, the reader, this work will reach countless school-going children between the ages of 5 and 18 worldwide.

Teachers wrote this book—40 teachers, to be precise, who are either full-time classroom teachers in schools and colleges, teacher trainers, or teachers who combine teaching of programming with curriculum design and research. These authors represent classrooms in the United States, Canada, UK, Finland, Switzerland, Germany, and Australia. They bring an unparalleled breadth and depth of experience and knowledge gleaned from research, curriculum design, and/or classroom practice at the elementary, middle, high school, and college levels. Although the ideas in all the chapters aim to inform teaching at all grade bands, some are more relevant for certain grade bands than others. For example, the chapters on recursion and data structures are more relevant for secondary teachers because those topics are not taught in primary grades. Chapters also reflect the authors' own experiences and expertise. Although some chapters may have examples that lean toward one grade band more than others (a reflection of the authors' own experiences), they share ideas that are relevant at **all** grade levels.

WHAT THIS BOOK IS ABOUT (AND WHAT IT IS NOT)

Computer science and programming are unique subjects and topics of study in many ways, perhaps due to the need to cover the abstractness as well as the concreteness that the study of programming encapsulates. On the one hand, foundational ideas and concepts, such as algorithms, logic, operators and expressions, variables and data structures, and repetition and recursion, underlie much of what we hope for students to learn in an introductory programming experience. On the other hand, programming needs to be situated and taught in the context of a programming language. Over the course of their study, a learner will ideally (and likely) encounter multiple forms of programming in a multitude of programming languages. Several *constructs* share conceptual similarity with those in other languages even though they may differ in the name or exact implementation. What this book aims to cover are those *underlying ideas* that are foundational to most introductory programming in classrooms. These fundamentals are concretized through examples in specific programming languages that the authors favor or, quite simply, are familiar with from their teaching or research. The hope is that you will benefit from all the examples regardless of the programming language in which they are situated and abstract these fundamental ideas that underpin programming in general.

Preface

▶ A–Z of Teaching Programming (12 Pedagogies, 14 Concepts and Practices)

A unique feature of this book is the A-to-Z ground it covers related to teaching introductory programming, embodied in its alphabetical organization. The book comprises 26 chapters that cover the most fundamental concepts and practices and well-researched pedagogies related to introductory programming in K–12 computer science. Table 1 presents an alternate table of contents organized by chapter type.

Table 1. Alternate table of contents by chapter type—concept, practice, or pedagogy

Concept	Algorithms
	Data Structures
	Events
	JavaScript, Python, Scratch, or Something Else? Navigating the Bustling World of Introductory Programming Languages
	Modularity With Methods and Functions
	Operators and Expressions
	Repetition and Recursion
	Selection With Conditionals
	Variables
	X-ing Boundaries With Physical Computing
Practice	Before You Program, Plan!
	Knowledge, Skills, Attitudes, and Beliefs: Learning Goals for Introductory Programming
	Testing and Debugging
	Yay, My Program Works! Beyond Working Code...Good Habits of Programming
Pedagogy	Creative Coding
	Feedback With Formative Check-Ins
	Guided Exploration With Unplugged Activities
	Hard Fun with Hands-On Constructionist Project-Based Learning
	Integrating Programming Into Other Subjects
	Learner-Centered and Culturally Relevant Pedagogy
	Naïve Conceptions of Novice Programmers
	Peer Collaboration and Pair Programming
	Questions and Inquiry
	Universal Design for Learning
	Worked Examples and Other Scaffolding Strategies
	Zestful Learning

Concepts represent the basic topics of understanding that relate to the semantics of creating programs, whereas ***practices*** encapsulate the pragmatics and strategies that students must learn hand-in-hand with concepts to create programs. Together these programming concepts and practices encompass the ***what to teach*** that are addressed in 14 chapters. How to teach (***pedagogy*** of programming) is covered in the other 12 chapters. The pedagogy chapters draw on over 30 years of research in teaching introductory programming as well as in the learning sciences on ***how children learn*** and ***how to design for learning*** keeping cognitive as well as socioemotional and sociocultural learning goals in mind.

> **A note on pedagogy chapters:** Although there is consensus in the field on the ways in which students struggle when learning programming, it is important to recognize the diversity in schools of thought on pedagogy. Researchers enjoy healthy debate on these approaches. However, they all agree that student learning must be scaffolded and that student autonomy and teacher-provided scaffolds must be balanced. These approaches tend to diverge (to varying degrees) in how much scaffolding to provide and the manner in which it should be provided. This book presents all these views with equanimity in chapters on creative coding, constructionist project-based learning, guided exploration with unplugged activities, worked examples and other scaffolding strategies, universal design for learning, and zestful learning. The goal is to make teachers aware of all these approaches, and we hope that they will find their own sweet spot that works for them and their learners.

It is also worth stating at the outset that this book approaches computer science education through the lens of the imperative programming paradigm as embodied by languages like Scratch, Java, and C/C++ . Although many of the issues and questions we discuss through the book are pertinent regardless of the choice of programming environment, functional programming deals with foundational concepts like data, functions-as-variables, and state in fundamentally different ways. Our discussion of some issues may therefore not be applicable to introductory programming classes taught through the lens of functional programming and/or the use of functional programming languages.

▶ What This Book Is Not About

This book is not a programming primer—it does not teach someone to program. It is designed to ***teach a teacher to teach programming***. It does not provide a single prescribed curriculum or sequence of lesson plans for teaching introductory programming. Several curricular sequences have been developed and made available for various grade levels. This book aims to be a guide; to help teachers venturing into the world of CS teaching to build a foundational understanding of computer science specifically as it relates to introductory programming, no matter what curriculum or grade level they teach.

While choosing the 26 ideas that are most crucial for the K–12 introductory programming teacher, I had to make some hard choices. Some other concepts were also considered as candidates but had to be dropped (or perhaps saved for a second volume of this book!). Topics such as databases and objects, for example, may be part of advanced high school learning but are not typically included in introductory programming in K–12. Other computing topics such as binary numbers and memory as they relate to introductory programming are also more typical of the undergraduate CS curriculum rather than programming in primary and secondary school education.

Lastly, computer science is a not just about programming. Although learning to program is central to (and often a very large, or the only, part of an introductory CS curriculum, other CS topics cover aspects of computer hardware, networks, and the societal and ethical impacts of computing This book does not cover those topics. It focuses entirely on the teaching and learning of introductory programming.

HOW TO USE THE BOOK

If you are a teacher new or relatively new to teaching programming, you should read this book in its entirety—it will provide you with an enduring foundation of what you are teaching and how to teach it. If you are a teacher who has been teaching programming for some time, you too will benefit from this book. It is my hope that despite your experience, you, too, will discover new ideas and enjoy several 'aha' moments from the many examples and pedagogical tips and ideas shared here.

Preface

The chapters are designed to be accessible and friendly to all teachers spanning K–12 education. Although many of them draw on research, they are not written like research articles but rather aim to be practical and actionable reading for teachers.

▶ Sequence of Chapters

The 26 chapters in this book are alphabetically sequenced, and as such, concepts, practices, and pedagogies are not chunked together. You may read the book in any order (hopefully *after reading the Foreword and this Preface*). However, here are some additional guidelines.

Pedagogy chapters are relevant to teaching any concept or practice. A few "umbrella" chapters have an overarching quality in the sense that they are connected to every other concept, practice, and pedagogy chapter in the book. It would help you to read these first. These include

- **Chapter 11, Knowledge, Skills, Attitudes, and Beliefs: Learning Goals for Introductory Programming**. This chapter gives a broad overview of what teaching programming is all about, or what it is we hope for students to come away with through their introductory programming learning experience, in terms of disciplinary knowledge and skills, and otherwise.

- **Chapter 10, JavaScript, Python, Scratch, or Something Else? Navigating the Bustling World of Introductory Programming Languages**. This chapter examines the many choices of K-12 programming languages and shares guidance on how these tools may influence the learning experience for students at various age/grade levels.

- **Chapter 14, Naïve Conceptions of Novice Programmers**. This chapter discusses naïve student conceptions of programming that impede their learning of specific concepts, as well as programming in general. It mainly deals with the student difficulties that have motivated many of us to devote years of research on pedagogy and how to teach specific topics or programming more generally.

- **Chapter 6. Feedback With Formative Check-Ins**. Formatively assessing student learning frequently as part of the learning is crucial regardless of programming concept or pedagogy.

Other than these overarching chapters, each chapter attempts to stay faithful to a single topic. However, several ideas are referenced in chapters other than the one dedicated to the idea in question. For example, **Chapter 22, Variables,** references ideas related to **Chapter 15, Operators and Expressions**. All chapters help make these connections by pointing to other chapters wherever and whenever relevant.

▶ Chapter Structure

Most chapters roughly follow the same arc.

- The chapter begins with an **introduction** that defines the concept, practice, or pedagogy along with specific examples to support a basic understanding of the topic.

- The introductory section is followed by **concrete classroom ideas and examples** that target various grade levels and are situated in the context of different block- and text-based programming environments. Even if you are a teacher who uses only block-based programming in the classroom, the text-based examples will be useful, and vice versa.

- Most chapters end with a section on **research and readings** and a **bibliography**. These closing sections provide pointers to interested teachers on where they can find readings to dig deeper, should they choose to do so. The bibliography reflects research that the authors have drawn on to guide the assertions, suggestions, and cautions made by the authors in the chapter. This could be seminal research in the field on the topic or research conducted by the authors themselves.

- Most concepts or practices chapters discuss what trips up students or **common mistakes students make** related to the specific topic. Several concepts chapters end with a section on **what to watch out for** that is dedicated to student difficulties. (This section is in lieu of or in addition to a Readings and Research section.)

▶ Writing Conventions

This book is intended for teachers in any country or on any continent. The ideas transcend geographical and cultural boundaries. Although the chapters are written by authors from the United States, Canada, UK, Switzerland, Finland, Germany, and Australia, it is written predominantly by US teachers and researchers. As such, the language reflects terms and phrases commonly used in the US. K–12 refers to basic primary and secondary (pre-college/university) education. The following table helps explain how children's ages typically map to the various grade bands and school levels—elementary, middle, and high—used in the book.

(K–12) School Level I	School Level II	Grades	Ages (Years)
Elementary/Primary	Lower Elementary	K–2	5–7
	Upper Elementary	3–5	8–10
Secondary	Middle	6–8	11–13
	High	9–12	14–17

> Key ideas in chapters are highlighted using callout boxes like this one. This convention is also used for tips and cautionary notes, as well as quotes from noted people in the field.

This book is rich with many examples using actual code snippets in popular block-based and text-based languages used in K–12 settings, like Scratch, Snap!, Python, and JavaScript. Scratch examples may appear in current or previous version of Scratch. They work to exemplify an idea, regardless of version. If code phrases are used in the text, they are written in a monospace `Courier` font. These include names of `variables`, `constructs`, and names of `blocks` or `events` in block-based languages.

WHEN/WHERE TO USE THIS BOOK

This book may be used as a text in K–12 CS teacher-training programs or as a reference for in-service teachers who can read it over a summer or winter break and/or refer to it as a handy handbook throughout the year. To paraphrase Dr. Seuss, you may use this book *"here or there or anywhere!"*

In closing, I want to thank you for undertaking the important task of teaching school children computer science and programming, no matter where you are in your journey as a teacher of programming in schools. As Grace Hopper (who was a Rear Admiral in the US Navy and one of the nation's first computer scientists and programmers), famously said, *"..programming is more than an important practical art. It is also a gigantic undertaking in the foundations of knowledge."*

Happy reading, happy learning, and happy teaching!

—Shuchi Grover, Ph.D.

Algorithms

Shuchi Grover

INTRODUCTION

Welcome to the exciting world of computer programming with A for Algorithms!

Algorithms are precise step-by-step plans or procedures to meet an end goal or to solve a problem; algorithmic thinking is the skill involved in developing an algorithm.

In a sense, algorithms are conceptual "blueprints" for procedures that can be implemented as computer programs in a programming language. Computer code can be thought of as incarnations of various algorithms written in a specific language to be interpreted and executed by a machine.

Algorithms are the bedrock of programs. Algorithmic thinking implicitly underpins all programming, because every program is essentially a special form of algorithm that is encoded so that it can be executed on the computer.

> *"Would you tell me, please, which way I ought to go from here?"*
> *"That depends a good deal on where you want to get to," said the Cat.*
> *– Lewis Carroll (1865)*
> *Alice's Adventures In Wonderland*

> Instructions given to computers ("computer programs") must be written in a programming language that the computer understands (see example in Figure 1). They must be precise - there is no margin for the interpretation that humans are capable of.

```
Step 1: Let n be the decimal number.
Step 2: Let b be the number, initially 0, that
        becomes our answer. (We'll compose
        the binary number from right to left.)

Step 3: Repeat the following substeps until n
        becomes 0:
    Step 3a: Divide n by 2, letting the result
             be d and the remainder be r.
    Step 3b: Append the remainder, r, as
             the leftmost digit of b.
    Step 3c: Let d be the new value of n.
```

```java
// function to convert decimal to binary
static void decToBinary(int n)
{
    // array to store binary number
    int[] binaryNum = new int[1000];

    // counter for binary array
    int i = 0;
    while (n > 0)
    {
    // storing remainder in binary array
        binaryNum[i] = n % 2;
        n = n / 2;
        i++;
    }

    // printing binary array in reverse order
    for (int j = i - 1; j >= 0; j--)
            System.out.print(binaryNum[j];
}
```

Figure 1. An algorithm for converting from a decimal number to a binary number written for a human versus a program that expresses the algorithm in Java for the computer to execute.

ALGORITHMS ARE PROCEDURAL ABSTRACTIONS

Abstraction is another fundamental idea in programming (that also happens to start with the letter "A"!). Many believe it to be the cornerstone of computer science. Abstraction is the process of removing physical, spatial, or temporal details or attributes in the study of objects or systems to focus attention on details of greater importance or relevance. It is a means to simplify, manage, and distill a complex system to its salient attributes. Abstraction is also the process of generalization (or parameterization), which allows us to create a solution that works correctly for a range of inputs. Programming a computer essentially involves dealing with layers of abstractions. The programming language (such as Java, Python, C++, or Scheme) in which we code is an abstraction that hides the complexity of performing operations in machine language, which is the set of primitive instructions in the computer's working memory. In fact, machine language is also an abstraction that hides the details of ultimately carrying out the instructions and steps in 0s and 1s in the computer's circuitry. And the computer itself is a physical machine, which is a complex network of wires and integrated circuits that follow the laws of physics and generate patterns of electrical and magnetic activity.

> *In designing a program to carry out some task, the programmer thinks only in terms of the subject domain and the highest levels (of abstraction) that exists for the programming system. The fact that these are in turn represented at a lower level (and that in turn at a still lower level) is only of secondary relevance. For someone designing a program or piece of hardware at one of the lower levels, the subject domain is the next higher level itself.* —Winograd & Flores, 1987

In this sense, it is more precise to state that an algorithm is an abstract description of a computational procedure. Take a look at the everyday examples of algorithms in Figure 2, and note the details that have been "abstracted away" in each algorithm. Google Maps does not care about the many details of the route from the origin to the destination. Which is the scenic route? Which route takes you past the most gas (petrol) stations? Which route is better given the day of the week? A crochet pattern does not care which color the yarn is or what material it is (cotton, wool, acrylic, bamboo, or silk). The brownie recipe does not care what brand the flour is or in which country you're baking the brownie. The assembly instructions you received along with your unassembled furniture package do not care how old you are and what kind of screwdriver or hammer you use or in what room you assemble the desk. It may well be that in a similar algorithm that achieves a different end goal, such details may be relevant and therefore be part of the instructions. However, these details are clearly irrelevant in the examples shown.

▶ Multiple Solutions to the Same Problem

> Students may (correctly) intuit that not all algorithms are born equal and that one computational approach to solving a problem may indeed be preferable to another —perhaps because it is more reliable, more robust to varied inputs, or more efficient. A crucial aspect of learning programming (and, more broadly, understanding computer science) is gaining an appreciation for the fact that different algorithms can get you to an end goal, or simply put, there are often multiple solutions to a problem.

Google Maps showcases a simple everyday example. Alternate routes are better or worse than others based on different criteria—time taken, construction on roadways, mode of travel (by car, bicycle, public transportation, or on foot), distance traveled, time of day, or highway tolls. Which option you select may be based on one of these criteria or on something as personal as a specific route taking you past a take-out diner where you might want to stop to pick up dinner. Some algorithmic solutions for programming may be different only superficially, but in some cases, the difference may be significant based on various criteria such as time taken to execute, memory resource allocation in the computer, and so on - these are nontrivial differences that are extremely important in practice, and should be presented as such to students. The many searching and sorting algorithms that exist (some of which are discussed later in this chapter) vary greatly in efficiency.

▶ Examples of Algorithms in Everyday Life

Several everyday activities involve algorithms, including cooking recipes, instructions to assemble an item of furniture, knitting and crochet instructions (that are often encoded in symbolic language), or a route specified by Google Maps. Figure 2 shows many different types of algorithms that humans interpret and act on.

You may use these examples in your classroom as an introduction to the notion of algorithms.

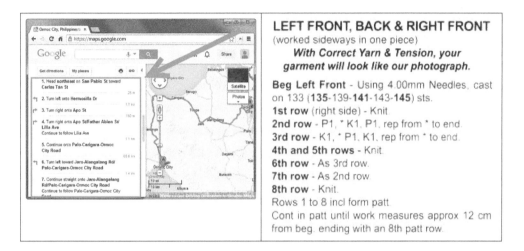

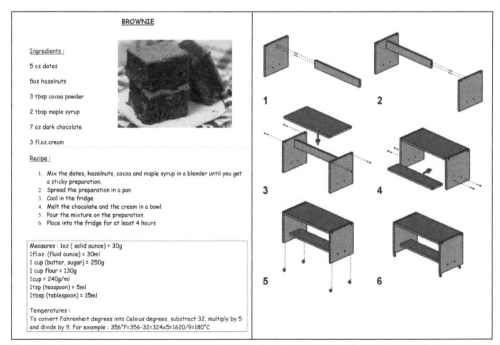

Figure 2. Google Maps, knitting patterns, recipes, and furniture assembly instructions are just some examples of the several algorithms we encounter in everyday life.

CHARACTERISTICS AND COMPONENTS OF ALGORITHMS

According to Donald Knuth, the father of algorithmic analysis in computer science, in addition to algorithms being a finite set of instructions for solving a specific type of problem (the idea of **accuracy** is implicit), algorithms, in general, are defined by the following characteristics:

- **Finiteness**: An algorithm must always terminate after a finite number of steps.

- **Definiteness**: Each step of an algorithm must be precisely defined; the actions to be carried out must be rigorously and unambiguously specified for each case.

- **Input**: An algorithm has zero or more inputs, which are quantities given to it initially before the algorithm begins or dynamically as the algorithm runs.

- **Output**: An algorithm generally has one or more outputs: products of the execution of the algorithm that have a specified relation to the inputs.

- **Effectiveness**: An algorithm is also generally expected to be effective, in the sense that its operations must all be sufficiently basic so that they can in principle be done exactly and in a finite length of time by someone using pencil and paper.

> With these features of algorithms in mind, pick your classroom examples wisely. Cookbook recipe examples are popular but their usefulness is limited in a programming classroom. Although recipes presumably have the qualities of finiteness, input, and output, they notoriously lack definiteness.

Algorithms describe a process articulated as a set of steps to be carried out in sequence from the starting point to the end goal. Most algorithms that students encounter in primary and secondary programming curricula involve three basic building blocks—*sequence*, *selection*, and *repetition*. Steps in an algorithm follow a sequence; however, there could be set(s) of actions that are **repeated** (see **Chapter 18**) and/or conditionals (see **Chapter 19**), which are decision-making checkpoints that make the algorithm select one set of actions or another. (Note: Event triggers can break sequential execution, and/or result in parallel execution of multiple code chunks. More on this in **Chapter 5**.)

Figure 3 describes the steps to be taken when administering emergency CPR. Can you identify these three elements?

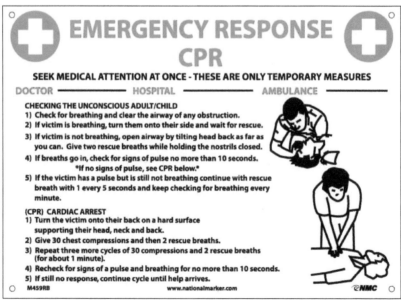

Figure 3. The algorithm for CPR: Can you identify sequence, selection, and repetition?

TEACHING IDEAS

Teaching algorithms in the classroom can involve having students create algorithms, enact algorithms, convert algorithms into code, and evaluate different algorithms to solve the same problem. These activities may be done using examples and ways that are suitable for grade and age level.

Creating Algorithms. Teaching algorithmic thinking in the context of programming must involve helping learners create a precise set of instructions that can be programmed. This idea of consciously planning before programming and creating a sketch of the program solution as an algorithm is a key step and is dealt with in **Chapter 2 (Before You Program, Plan!)**. The sketch or outline of the program solution can be created in plain text, pseudocode, a flowchart, or even a storyboard (especially for younger learners).

Enacting Algorithms. Students at all grade levels must be encouraged to enact or try out a set of instructions for solving a problem. This can be done on pen and paper, a pair activity (such as the *Guess My Number* algorithm described in **Chapter 2**), or even a physical activity in the classroom with groups of students enacting an algorithm (such as a sorting algorithm).

> *An algorithm must be seen to be believed, and the best way to learn what an algorithm is all about is to try it. The reader should always take pencil and paper and work through an example of each algorithm immediately upon encountering it in the text.* —Donald Knuth in *The Art of Computer Programming, Volume 1*

Converting Existing Algorithms From Pseudocode Into Code. Pseudocode is the description of an algorithm written in an informal language (such as natural language) that does not involve syntax of a programming language. **Chapter 2** shares examples of pseudocode from elementary grades. For middle and high school grades especially, learning how to express an algorithm in pseudocode is a useful skill.

Students should experience moving from pseudocode to a program. For example, check out the algorithm in Wikipedia for calculating whether a given year is a leap year (Figure 4a), and see how easy it is to go from the leap year algorithm to creating a program in any programming language (Figure 4b). This example was used successfully as an exercise with middle school students who used the algorithm to code the program in Scratch. Students felt empowered in being able to code an "algorithm" found on Wikipedia. (The leap year algorithm also provided the opportunity to introduce the *modulo* operator.)

Comparing Algorithms. Articulating multiple solutions to problems, comparing two or more given solutions to problems, and evaluating their effectiveness against given criteria are a useful class of activities to help students understand this key aspect of computational and algorithmic solutions.

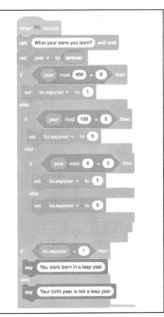

Algorithm [edit]

The following pseudocode determines whether a year is a *leap year* or a *common year* in the Gregorian calendar (and in the proleptic Gregorian calendar before 1582). The *year* variable being tested is the integer representing the number of the year in the Gregorian calendar.

if (*year* is not divisible by 4) **then** (it is a common year)
else if (*year* is not divisible by 100) **then** (it is a leap year)
else if (*year* is not divisible by 400) **then** (it is a common year)
else (it is a leap year)

Figure 4a and b. Leap year algorithm from https://en.wikipedia.org/wiki/Leap_year and a Scratch program version of the algorithm to determine whether a given year is a leap year

▶ Ideas for Primary Grades

Algorithmic thinking can be taught from the earliest grades. Spatial navigation activities that require detailing the steps to get from a starting point to a destination are a great way to get kids started (Figure 5). Stories are also a great way to introduce algorithms because they have an inherent (logical) order and sequence (Figure 6). Unplugged (non-programming/non-digital) navigation activities such as story cards can be used to have students specify the sequence of steps that represent a solution to a goal.

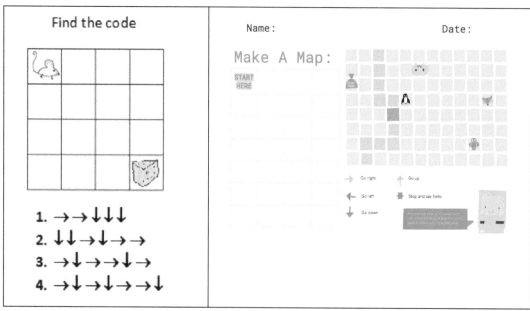

Figure 5. Navigational activities for teaching algorithmic thinking

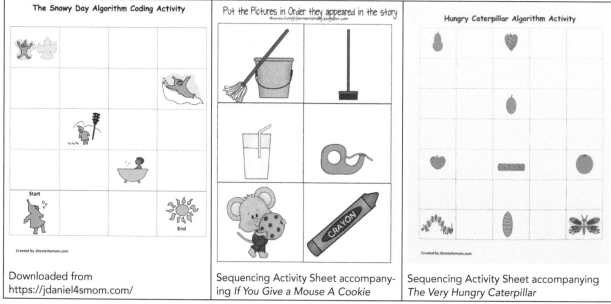

Figure 6. Leveraging stories for teaching algorithmic thinking

Digital tools such as Lightbot Jr. and Kodable have a variety of maze-like puzzles to engage students in algorithmic thinking to navigate 2-D spaces. ScratchJr is a programming environment that allows children to make creative artifacts (programs) while also fostering algorithmic thinking skills. **Chapter 2** on planning before programming and **Chapter 3, Creative Coding** provide more ideas on how to foster learning of algorithms in younger grades. Programming environments can be used to sequence everyday activities. The "Make a block" functionality in environments like Scratch and Snap! can be leveraged to create blocks (with no code inside them necessarily) and provided to students to sequence (Figure 7b).

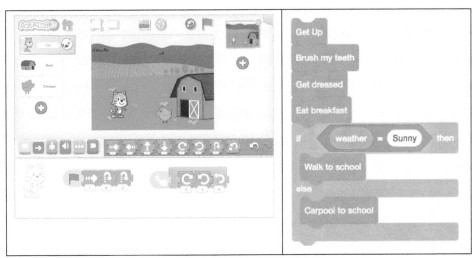

Figure 7a. ScratchJr for creating simple stories to foster algorithmic thinking; **Figure 7b.** Scratch blocks created to mimic everyday activities that students can snap into sequence

In upper elementary (and middle) grades, using "turtle geometry" to draw shapes is an engaging way to teach sequence and algorithms. Logo, created by Seymour Papert and his colleagues, was one of the earliest programming languages designed with children in mind. It aimed to teach algorithmic and "procedural thinking" by providing visual feedback to learners about the outcome of executing the sequence of steps in the program. The language allowed students to create amazing geometric shapes using a basic set of commands such as forward, right, left, and repeat. (See Figures 8 and 9.) This "low floor" all but eliminated barriers to getting started with creating visual artifacts through programming. Papert's goal was to provide a tool for children to grasp powerful ideas of mathematics through turtle geometry. However, these design principles for introducing algorithmic thinking have since been incorporated in several new-age programming environments such as Scratch, Snap!, and App Inventor.

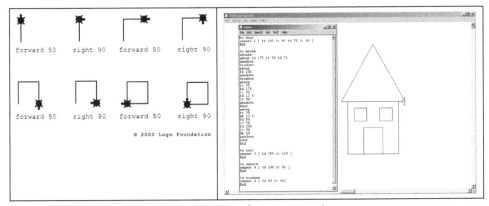

Figure 8. Simple shapes drawn using a simple set of Logo commands

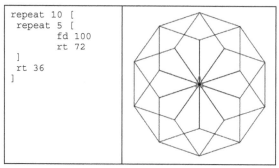

```
repeat 10 [
 repeat 5 [
        fd 100
        rt 72
 ]
 rt 36
]
```

Figure 9. Complex shapes drawn using a simple set of Logo commands (source: http://milesberry.net)

▶ Ideas for Secondary Grades

By the middle grades, students should be able to create stories and maze-like puzzles that have elements of sequence, repetition, and selection. Stories, games, and geometric artwork that students create as a form of creative expression are effective in the middle grades for fostering algorithmic thinking.

▶ Writing Algorithms in Pseudocode (or Other Forms)

Having students think through the algorithm before coding is an essential skill, as shown in the next chapter on planning before programming. Algorithms can be written in natural language or something between natural language and code (pseudocode) or in other forms such as flowcharts. See **Chapter 2** for examples of pseudocode that students could be encouraged to write, such as the *Guess My Number* game and finding the average of a set of numbers.

▶ Comparing Algorithms

Design and study of algorithms can get more sophisticated at the high school level. In addition to creating programs as described earlier, students should engage more seriously in comparing and evaluating algorithms for efficiency (in terms of speed or memory used) or even elegance and simplicity. As Donald Knuth puts it, *"we want 'good' algorithms in some loosely defined aesthetic sense. One criterion . . . is the length of time taken to perform the algorithm. . . Other criteria are adaptability of the algorithm to computers, its simplicity and elegance, etc."*

Students should be encouraged to compare algorithms based on given criteria. An example from AP Computer Science Principles (an advanced CS course for high school students in the US) is shown in Figure 9. Besides offering the answer, have your students discuss if the algorithms differ in any way in terms of efficiency (number of addition operations, or number of variables needed, etc.).

13. There are 32 students standing in a classroom. Two different algorithms are given for finding the average height of the students.

Algorithm A

Step 1: All students stand.

Step 2: A randomly selected student writes his or her height on a card and is seated.

Step 3: A randomly selected standing student adds his or her height to the value on the card, records the new value on the card, and is seated. The previous value on the card is erased.

Step 4: Repeat step 3 until no students remain standing.

Step 5: The sum on the card is divided by 32. The result is given to the teacher.

Algorithm B

Step 1: All students stand.

Step 2: Each student is given a card. Each student writes his or her height on the card.

Step 3: Standing students form random pairs at the same time. Each pair adds the numbers written on their cards and writes the result on one student's card; the other student is seated. The previous value on the card is erased.

Step 4: Repeat step 3 until one student remains standing.

Step 5: The sum on the last student's card is divided by 32. The result is given to the teacher.

Which of the following statements is true?

(A) Algorithm A always calculates the correct average, but Algorithm B does not.

(B) Algorithm B always calculates the correct average, but Algorithm A does not.

(C) Both Algorithm A and Algorithm B always calculate the correct average.

(D) Neither Algorithm A nor Algorithm B calculates the correct average.

Figure 10. Comparing algorithms (Source: AP Computer Science Principles guidelines from College Board— https://apcentral.collegeboard.org/pdf/ap-computer-science-principles-course-and-exam-description-0.pdf)

▶ Sorting and Searching Algorithms in High School Computer Science

Computer science involves finding efficient algorithms to do mundane tasks like sorting lots of objects (names, numbers, or other compound objects) or searching for a particular name from a large list of names. Sorting is the process of placing objects in order. Keeping things sorted helps with **search** and retrieval (and there are several different sorting algorithms that are efficient in different situations). Think of how much easier it would be to announce the lowest and highest scores on a test if you had a sorted—as opposed to an unsorted—list of scores for the class. Sorting and searching algorithms are subjects of extensive study by computer scientists. It's so amazing that an innovative web search algorithm was the seed that revolutionized the 21st century and grew into Google, one of the biggest organizations on this planet today!

Several algorithms for searching are well known in computer science. One of the simplest algorithms is *linear search*, in which a search is done sequentially through a data set to find the matching value. Binary search is another example of a search algorithm where the search is accomplished by continually dividing the data set into two distinct subsets to locate the matching value. It works most efficiently if the data are sorted or ordered. (Check out the *Guess My Number* algorithm in **Chapter 2** as an example of a binary search.) Figure 10 shows the pseudocode for linear and binary search algorithms designed to look for a target in a list. Discuss with students which of the two is more efficient in terms of speed, and why. What if the list is unsorted?

Linear Search Algorithm	Binary Search Algorithm
``FOR EACH item in List
{
    IF (item = target)
        DISPLAY "Found target!"

}
``` | ```low ← 0
high ← N // N is the number of items in List
middle ← item (low+high)/2
REPEAT UNTIL (middle = target OR low > high)
{
    IF (target < middle)
        high ← middle - 1
    IF (target > middle)
        low ← middle + 1
    middle ← item (low+high)/2
}
IF (middle = target)
    DISPLAY "Found target!"
ELSE
    DISPLAY "Target not in list"
``` |

Figure 11. Pseudocode for linear and binary search algorithms

Popular sorting algorithms include bubble sort, insertion sort, quick sort, merge sort, bucket sort, and radix sort. Among these, *bubble sort* is the most basic for sorting a set of values. It works by going through the set and comparing two adjacent values at once, then swapping those values if necessary. *Did you notice that the previous sentence loosely described the algorithm for a bubble sort?*

The algorithm shown below describes how an *insertion sort* works. It is easy to see which of these two algorithms is more efficient—having students count the number of comparisons in each drives the point home well.

1. Start with the second element.
2. Pick the element next to the already-sorted sequence, and insert it to the correct place—move every element of the already-sorted sequence, which has a higher value than the element being sorted, one place right, and then put the element into the gap (correct place within the sequence).
3. While the array/list contains any unsorted elements GOTO: 2.

> Wikipedia has visualizations of these algorithms for small sets of numbers. Have students explore these visualizations, write the pseudocode, enact the algorithm, and discuss which algorithm is better suited for which situation.

Sorting algorithms lend themselves well to physical enactment in the classroom. All you need are cards of numbers or names for students to hold (to represent different values to be sorted) and you have the makings of a lively kinesthetic activity in the classroom. You can also provide students with pen-and-paper exercises for enacting different algorithms and detailing the state of the list with every interim iteration of the algorithm.

Also check out the **CS Unplugged** curriculum (https://classic.csunplugged.org/sorting-algorithms/) in which children as young as 8 and 10 years of age compare different methods for sorting, and see how one method can perform the task much more quickly than another one.

Finally, students can analyze and compare the various algorithms by actually coding them as programs that perform sort and search on various kinds of data of various sizes.

COMPUTABILITY AND THE LIMITATIONS OF ALGORITHMS

Students' understanding of algorithms in primary and secondary years is centered on the belief that the problem being tackled has a solution. It is important, however, for high school students to appreciate the idea of computability and realize the limits of algorithms and computation. For example, there are **undecidable problems**, a class of decision problems for which it is impossible to construct an algorithm that always leads to a correct yes or no answer. The halting problem is probably one of the most well-known undecidable problems. It states that no algorithm can correctly determine whether arbitrary programs eventually halt when run. Another class of problems is considered **intractable** because they are essentially infeasible to implement computationally even though they may have an algorithm that solves the problem. Such problems can be solved in theory—given large but finite resources, especially time—but in practice, any solution takes too many resources to be useful. Problems that deal with exponential growth, such as the Wheat and Chessboard problem (based on an ancient Indian tale), are examples of intractable problems. The idea of intractable problems is used in cryptography; it is the reason we are asked to create passwords that are a minimum length and contain a mix of letters, characters, and numbers—a brute force solution (i.e., trying out every combination) to crack such a password will presumably take an inordinate amount of computing resources. Heuristics, or **heuristic algorithms**, are used instead to solve intractable problems. These are essentially algorithms that are not the optimal solution, but they produce a feasible and close-to-correct solution to a problem. Examples of heuristic algorithms include the shortest path algorithms for solving problems like the famous Traveling Salesman problem (TSP).

RESEARCH AND READINGS

Seymour Papert of the MIT Media Lab is credited with the use of turtle geometry to teach young learners procedural and algorithmic thinking in the context of drawing geometrical shapes. Several examples presented in this chapter have been drawn from the author's doctoral dissertation work at Stanford University, where she worked with students in middle grades to help them learn programming in Scratch and also strong computational thinking skills including algorithmic thinking. The CS Unplugged activities shared in this chapter are drawn from the work of Tim Bell and colleagues in New Zealand. Donald Knuth is touted to be the father of algorithmic theory and is credited with calling computer science the "study of algorithms." He won the Turing Award (basically the Nobel Prize for computer science) in 1974. His multivolume text on algorithms, *The Art of Computer Programming*, is considered a defining treatise on computer science, algorithms, and programming.

Wikipedia is a great resource for many of the ideas in this chapter including basic information on classic problems such as the halting problem, TSP, and the Wheat and Chessboard problem.

BIBLIOGRAPHY

Bell, T. C., Witten, I. H., & Fellows, M. (1998). Computer Science Unplugged: Off-line activities and games for all ages. Computer Science Unplugged.

Grover, S. (2014). *Foundations for advancing computational thinking: Balanced designs for deeper learning in an online computer science course for middle school students.* (Doctoral dissertation, Stanford University).

Knuth, D. E. (1968). *The art of computer programming, Vol. 1: Fundamental algorithms.* Addison-Wesley.

Knuth, D. E. (2011). The *art of computer programming,* Volumes 1–4A boxed set. Addison-Wesley Professional.

Papert, S. (1980). *Mindstorms: Children, computers, and powerful ideas.* Basic Books, Inc.

Winograd, T. F., & Flores, F. (1987). *Understanding computers and cognition: A new foundation for design.* Ablex Publishing.

ALGORITHMS

Before You Program, Plan!

Philip Bagge and Shuchi Grover

INTRODUCTION

Weeks of programming can save you hours of planning.
– Anonymous

The thought processes required to create, maintain, and explain a plan to get to a goal are vital in most human endeavours, and programming is no exception. Planning before programming involves formulating and defining the algorithm that will need to be implemented to meet the objective of the program. Algorithms can be visually articulated as sequences of steps written in a natural language or pseudocode or a flowchart or sequences of drawings as in a storyboard. Articulating a set of instructions—in any form—greatly aids students in the process of translating those instructions into whichever programming language they are using, and seeing a roadmap for their code to achieve the goal.

Planning is also closely intertwined with the idea of decomposition—a key aspect of computational thinking or problem solving. Decomposition entails deconstructing a big problem into its functional subparts and modules for ease of solving.

For software engineers, planning before creating a program or a software system can be tremendously beneficial. It gives the coders foresight into problems they might face, defines the functional subparts that can be implemented by a collaborative team, can reveal weaknesses in their potential system, and makes the actual exercise of programming easier because they have intuition and a mental model for the key aspects of the program or system.

The remainder of this chapter discusses planning in terms of different levels of abstraction in the course of programming and presents ideas for planning through several examples.

▶ Levels of Planning

Drawing the work of Michal Armoni as well as Jane Waite (and colleagues), we believe that students must understand planning at the four levels of programming development, or four levels of abstraction.

- Problem level
- Algorithm level
- Program level
- Program Execution level

The Problem level identifies what the goal of the program is, its audience, as well as high level constructs like the input to the program, and the desired form of the output. This is essentially the 'idea' level when a student thinks of a project they want to create.

The Algorithm level is where the idea becomes a detailed plan or algorithm using algorithmic elements such as sequence, repetition, and selection (see **Chapter 1, Algorithms**). The algorithm could convey other aspects of the program, including data and objects, initialization, appearance, as well as structural design, in the case of a physical computing project (where the code is combined to work with electronics).

The **Program level** involves translating the algorithm into code using a specific programming language.

The **Program Execution level** reacts to how the code behaves when it is run on a machine or digital device. This stage involves changing the code in order to fix bugs that are encountered.

▶ Linear, Iterative, or Decomposed Planning Progression

One usually naturally progresses from Problem to Algorithm to Program to Program Execution levels (Figure 1a), However, the process is often iterative and does not follow a strict linear order. For example, a bug identified during the Program Execution level might require revisiting the Program, Algorithm or Problem level to change features of the algorithm or code, thus creating a more iterative, cyclical process (Figure 1b).

Some programming projects, especially those that are very modular (such as games) can also benefit from a more decomposed use of the levels of abstraction. This is where students write an algorithm to solve a self-contained part of a project before converting this into code and testing it. Students repeat this process until all parts of the project are complete (Figure 1c).

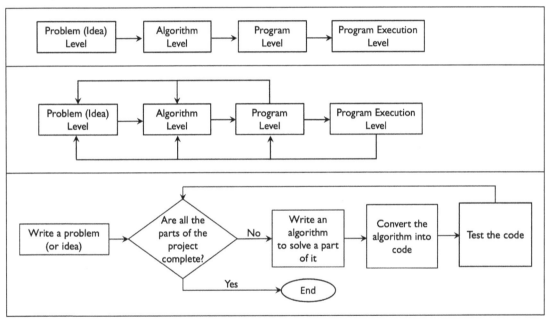

Figure 1a, b, and c. Linear, iterative, and decomposed planning processes

TEACHING PLANNING

This rest of the chapter is going to focus on the Problem (or idea) level and the Algorithm level, which collectively we can describe as *planning before programming*.

▶ Problem (or Idea) Level

"If you can't write it down in English, you can't code it"—Peter Halpern, Brooklyn, New York

Our youngest students might express the problem or idea verbally. This is an example of a 6-year-old expressing their Problem level orally to their teacher before coding in ScratchJr.

"I want to make a zoo. When you touch the animals, they make their noise and move around."

A good follow-up question would be, "Are you making that for your classmates or for younger/older children?" This query would start students thinking about audience at the Problem level stage.

The Problem level plan might include a simple diagram that pupils use as an aid to verbalize their ideas or to support a written description of the goals of the program. Figure 2 shows a picture created by a 9-year-old alongside a written description of the algorithm in plain English before designing and programming a game in Scratch.

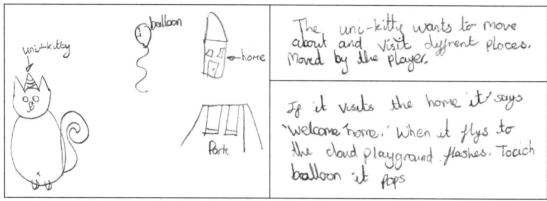

Figure 2. A diagram along with written descriptions of the program goals and algorithm

This level can simply be a brief but clear written problem statement in a student's own words. It could include varying levels of detail. For example,

- *Create a program that records your steps over a day (or a week).*

- *Make a program that calculates the average of a set of test scores that are given to the program one by one.*

- *Create a "maze" game where a user must help a mouse go through a maze to the cheese (goal). The mouse will get 5 lives meaning they can touch the wall of the maze a maximum of five times. The mouse returns to the starting point when it touches the wall a 6th time.*

- *Write a program that turns miles into kilometers. You will need to ask the user to input a number (for miles). You will then divide that number by 0.62 and print the result.*

> It is advisable for the Problem (or idea) level to not use programming language or refer to algorithmic and programming constructs such as selection or repetition.

Figure 3 shows an example of a 10-year-old student's problem level plan in which all ideas are expressed independently of programming constructs but rather in relation to the effects they want to see in their game.

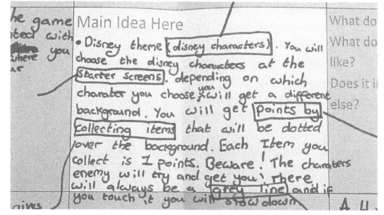

Figure 3. Problem (or idea) level planning is done independently of programming constructs

▶ Algorithm Level

▶ Algorithm

Probably the most crucial and difficult element in planning before programming is turning an idea or problem statement into an algorithm (see **Chapter 1** to learn more about algorithms). If students have not seen a variety of algorithms modeled before, then their ability to construct one will be severely limited.

Students need to understand that an algorithm is written for another human to understand and that there is no formal language of algorithms, but students need to be precise and avoid ambiguity.

Algorithms Do Not Involve Code or Code Constructs

Students must understand the crucial distinction between writing an algorithm and writing code. While the former is typically expressed for humans to interpret, writing code involves using a programming language for a machine to interpret and act on. For example, in the Python programming language, a count-controlled loop can only be written as

```
for i in range(4):
    print("Hello World")
```

However, a human can express a count-controlled loop in many ways: do this four times, loop four times, repeat four lots, and so on. A human can use any language or symbols that another human would interpret as a count-controlled loop. Writing an algorithm using `for i in range(4):` might actually obscure the meaning if the reader has no knowledge of Python.

When demonstrating how to write an algorithm, teachers should avoid expressing it in terms of programming language blocks or constructs, although it could be a close phrase. For example, they could use the word 'display' instead of 'print' or 'say' to suggest showing an output on the screen. Or in the case of the "maze" game above, they might say, "*keep checking how many lives are left*" instead of "repeat until no lives left". When talking about a sprite in the Algorithm level, they might refer to a character or avatar. This helps to underline for the student that they are in the planning stage rather than the programming stage.

> Thinking in terms of algorithms rather than code benefits students in that algorithms are designed to be "programming language agnostic". This enables the implementation of universal algorithmic constructs in any programming language.

Linguistic Guidelines for Articulating Algorithms

Students should be taught simple rules for expressing algorithms (see **Chapter 1, Algorithms**).These rules could be formal as for pseudocode. Younger students could use simple sentences in natural language. However, they should be taught how to use a new line to express a next step, or ways of chunking different actions and commands for repeating steps or conditionals (through the use of parentheses or bullets). Although optional, these make more complex algorithms easier to read and comprehend. The **Problem/ Program Decomposition for Planning** section of this chapter shares several illustrative examples.

Figure 4 shows an algorithm a 9-year-old wrote to plan how their Scratch game will end. They have used a mixture of non-Scratch language such as loop alongside Scratch language such as `forever`. They have not used indentation but have put separate ideas on separate lines. They have not defined which color will trigger the end of the game— that is perhaps a detail left for the Program level. This is not uncommon, especially for smaller programs with few actions, as is the case in elementary grades.

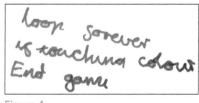

Figure 4.

For written algorithms, algorithmic grammar and conventions are useful and should be modeled and encouraged because they aid clarity, reduce error, and make it easier to convert algorithms into code. One such example of a planning algorithm is shared below (in the Problem/Program Decomposition for Planning section) for a program aimed at calculating the average test score for a class of students. It demonstrates levels of planning and writing of algorithms as well as the use of pseudocode.

Flowchart Algorithms

Some programming projects benefit from being planned using flowchart topography. Flowcharts can be useful for novice programmers to think through aspects of decision-making. There is a learning curve associated with using flowcharts, however. Educators working with younger pupils have to weigh the benefits of simplifying the flow of control versus the extra time needed to introduce the new shapes and what they mean. Flowcharts could be combined with pictures of code blocks as shown in Figure 5 to help bridge the Algorithm and Program levels for younger students early in their learning of programming.

Flowcharts as a planning tool are much more useful where there is a single flow of control such as the clock programming project (Figure 5) and less useful where projects have multiple flows of control as exemplified by many gaming projects. Parallelism in environments like Scratch also makes it difficult for students to draw flowcharts depicting concurrently executed actions.

If teachers decide to use flowcharts, students always benefit from being given exemplar projects and questions that require them to read and interpret the algorithm or completion flowcharts where only a small part of the algorithm needs to be completed.

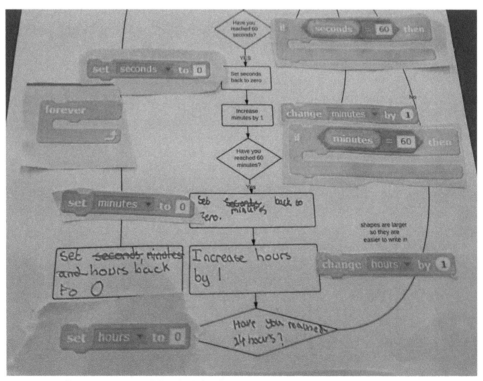

Figure 5. In this project most of the clock flowchart algorithm was provided, but the 10-year old students, working in similar ability pairs, had to spot the pattern, complete the algorithm, and work out which Scratch code blocks match to which parts of the algorithm.

PROBLEM/PROGRAM DECOMPOSITION FOR PLANNING

Decomposition, a key skill in programming and computational thinking, is about breaking down a problem, algorithm, program solution, process, or software system into subparts or subproblems to make the problem easier to solve. It is a way of dealing with complexity—something a lot of computer science concerns itself with—because the separate parts can then be understood, solved, developed, and evaluated separately. Decomposition is also closely related to the idea of modularity and breaking down a solution into functional units. It could also take the form of developing multiple parts of a solution part by part (e.g., designing a game level by level).

Decomposition is a way of thinking about problems, algorithms, artifacts, processes, and systems in terms of their parts. The parts can then be understood, solved, developed, and evaluated separately, which makes complex problems easier to solve and large systems easier to design (and maintain). Not surprisingly, as programming practices go, there is a lot of overlap between decomposition and planning. Oftentimes decomposition happens along functional subpieces of the problem or program. Functional decomposition introduces modularity as functional subparts or "modules" of the program are identified and coded, and can often lead to reuse of the modules.

Decomposition would typically aid the Algorithm level of planning. Here are a few examples demonstrating how planning involves functional decomposition (drawn from Grover's doctoral dissertation research).

Example 1: *Guess My Number* game where the computer decides on a number and you as the player of the game have to guess it. To keep it simple, one could first code a version of the game that requires guessing a number between 1 and 10. Learners can plan the algorithm by thinking in terms of splitting the problem into broad tasks such as

1. Player 1 (could be the computer) initially decides (or "thinks of") on a number (the Magic Number).

2. Player 2 tries to guess the magic number and is told whether it's right or wrong.

3. Keep track of the number of tries.

4. A correct guess ends the game or Player 2 runs out of a given number of tries.

In addition to this broad breakdown, one of the first things students could be encouraged to do is to think of what you know and what is unknown at the beginning of the game—what the knowns and the unknowns are (à la Pólya[1]'s guide to problem solving discussed in some more detail in **Chapter 17, Questions and Inquiry**).

Known: (1) a magic number and (2) the number of tries for Player 2.

Unknown: What numbers Player 2 will guess; and whether Player 2 will get the magic number within the number of tries (say, three tries).

What to keep track of: How many tries left.

---

[1] ***How to Solve It*** (1945) is a small volume by mathematician George Pólya that describes methods of problem solving. His simple method used mainly in mathematics contexts works well for planning of algorithmic and programming solutions as well—

How to Solve It suggests the following steps when solving a mathematical problem:

1. First, you have to **understand the problem**.
2. After understanding, **make a plan**.
3. **Carry out the plan**.
4. **Look back** on your work. How could it be better?

Pólya further advises: "If you can't solve a problem, then there is an easier problem you can solve: find it." Or: "If you cannot solve the proposed problem, try to first solve some related problem. Could you imagine a more accessible related problem?"
(Source: https://en.wikipedia.org/wiki/How_to_Solve_It)

The following broad breakdown leads to the following algorithm:

1. The computer decides on a number.

2. Player enters a guess for the number.

3. Check if player guessed the right number.

    3.1 If yes, say "Yay, you guessed it!"; game over.

    3.2 If no, you are asked to guess again.

4. Repeat Steps 2 and 3, keeping track of the number of tries.

5. (After incorrect guess on third try, you say "Sorry, you're out of attempts."

Here's an algorithm with a more explicit use of an if-else language.

1. The computer decides on a number.

2. Enter a guess for the number.

3. Check if your friend has guessed it correctly.

    3.1 If yes,

        3.1.1."Yay, you guessed it!"; game over.

    3.2 Else

        3.2.1 You ask her to guess again.

        EndIf

4. Repeat Steps 2 and 3, keeping track of the number of tries.

5. After incorrect guess on third try, you say "Sorry, you're out of attempts."

Example 2: Pseudocode for calculating the average score of a set of scores by breaking down the algorithm into the functional pieces of the algorithm.

```
// Initialization
1.1 Set [AverageScore] to 0
1.2 Set [SumOfScores] to 0
1.3 Set [NumOfScores] to 0
1.4 Set [CurrentScore] to 0

2. Ask teacher for number of students in her class
3. Set [NumOfScores] to what teacher inputs
// Loop through all the scores and aggregate a running Sum
4. Loop [NumOfScores] times
{
        4.1 Ask next score
        4.2 Put it into [CurrentScore]
        4.3 Increase [SumofScores] by [CurrentScore]
}
// Calculate the average by dividing the sum with the number of scores
5. Calculate [AverageScore] as [SumOfScores] / [NumOfScores]
6. Print [AverageScore]
```

Example 3: Kayla is saving money to buy a new bicycle. Kayla has six uncles. On Kayla's birthday, each uncle gave her money to help her buy the bicycle. To figure out if she has enough money to buy the bicycle, Kayla decides to create a program. In this case, students can think of the broad algorithm as having three parts.

Part A: Getting to know the cost of the bicycle

Part B: Totaling the gift money from the six uncles

Part C: Checking to see if Kayla has enough money to buy the bicycle

These distinct functional parts are shown in the final Scratch code below.

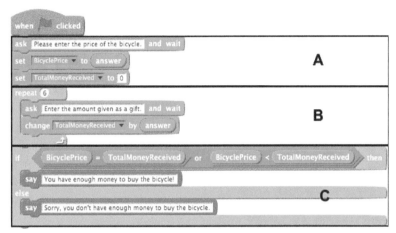

Part A is about getting to know the cost of the bicycle; Part B totals the gift money from the six uncles; and Part C checks if Kayla has enough money to buy the bicycle.

▶ Planning the Starting State of the Program: Initialization

Initialization ensures that a program always starts with (and is returned to) an initial starting position before being run again. Typically, this might involve ensuring that variables are reset to their starting value on program commencement. Many block-based programming languages like Scratch and Snap! don't require the programmer to set an initial value before a variable can be used. The following scenario is common in introductory programming classrooms. Asking questions about initialization in the planning stage can help reduce errors and the amount of debugging needed.

A 9-year-old created a simple mathematics quiz in Scratch. She has added a point every time the user gets a question right in their quiz. The first time they run this program, it will work perfectly. Scratch variables default to 0 when first used so the points given will be correct. The second time they run the code, points from the previous time the program was run will be carried over.

Another type of initialization needed is of program 'state'—the initial setup of the program. This is needed in game design, for example, where characters need to start in a set location on the screen. Gamers call these spawn points. Drawing spawn points on a diagram or describing where they may appear are two possible ways students can plan for this type of initialization.

Teachers need to include initialization in their curricula, provide good examples of it in their worked examples, and ask questions of students about this during their planning phases.

▶ Planning Involving Objects

Objects are all the separate parts of our program. In Python it might be a window, a function, variables, or a list. In Scratch this might be a sprite, backgrounds, a build-your-own-block procedure, a list, or a variable. If we are using a microcontroller such as the Micro:bit or Crumble or a prototyping computer such as the Raspberry Pi, then this might include physical objects such as wires, buzzers, lights, or resistors. In essence objects are all the parts we think we might need to turn that initial idea into a plan.

Asking students to think about the objects they might need before they start to convert some of these into algorithms is an essential part of the planning process. There are often many programming solutions to the same problem or idea. Asking students to list all the objects they might need for different solutions and giving them time to discuss these with a partner is an efficient method of encouraging them to explore solution diversity before converting one solution or one set of objects into an algorithm.

Appearance Design

What can the student do to make their project more pleasing to the target audience? Have they thought about who they are writing their program for? What will it look or feel like? What colors or graphics will it use? Does it have a genre that it fits into? Not all projects will necessitate appearance design, but those that do will benefit from appearance design thinking before construction. It can be tempting to ignore this aspect, but there is some evidence that it contributes to a student's long-term appreciation of programming.

Structural Design

Though for all intents and purposes our modern computers provide an almost unlimited playground for our novice programmer, the inclusion of electronics severely limits choice. Learning to work within these constraints is an important aspect of planning. Microcontrollers such as the Micro:bit or prototyping computers such as the Raspberry Pi have a limited number of easily accessed inputs and outputs. Drawing a diagram to show where all the wiring will attach and which ports will be used before connecting things together and programming ensures that a plan is viable (Figure 6).

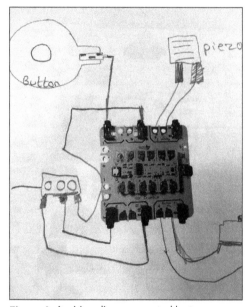

Figure 6. A wiring diagram created by two 10-year olds to go with their independent electronic project that uses the Crumble microcontroller with a Crumble playground attachment. Note how this first phase of structural design uses real objects rather than electrical symbols, including a photocopy of the board.

THINGS TO WATCH OUT FOR

▶ Teaching With the Four Levels of Abstraction

Not all projects need students to work at all the levels. Typically, many teachers articulate the problem and ask pupils to complete the other levels. However, it is valuable for students to spent time at the Algorithm level that they can go on to the Program and Program Execution levels. Alternatively, they could select the nearest matching ideas level from similar alternatives, encouraging closer examination and discussion. Students can also be provided with a working program and goal statement, and asked to complete the algorithm focusing on a particular aspect such as writing in pseudocode, initialization, object identification, appearance design, or structural design.

Phasing in Planning Features

Although there is nearly always merit in students describing their Problem level in one form or another, it is possible to overdo aspects of the Algorithm level for simple projects, especially where students are mainly using block-based programming languages and simpler programming constructs. Once pupils are creating more complex programs or using constructs such as selection, variables, or procedures/functions, then a detailed Algorithm level is essential. An expert educator will gradually introduce planning and design elements as they become important, depending on the genre and complexity of the project.

▶ Student Aversion to Planning as an Exercise

Students are often averse to spending time thinking about and expressing a plan for their program. They'd much rather jump right into coding. With the fun factor being a big part of introductory block-based programming environments, having to plan their program delay the fun part of the process for the student. However, teachers can help students appreciate that the time invested in planning ultimately helps them avoid many frustrations later. The quote at the start of the chapter is something that programmers have learned from experience. Research shows that planning before programming and thinking through the algorithm (or what is referred to as 'top-down programming') improves learning outcomes. Having a roadmap of the program and how it achieves its goal also helps students to better communicate and present their project to an audience.

It may be worthwhile to display posters and quotes on planning in the classroom to serve as a reminder to students. That aside, you can do the following to encourage planning before programming:

- Model good planning
- Make use of the four levels of abstraction
- Use different language for different levels
- Break up planning into smaller chunks for younger learners
- Explain and model initialization
- Decompose planning and plan to decompose

BIBLIOGRAPHY

Armoni, M. (2013). On teaching abstraction in computer science to novices. *Journal of Computers in Mathematics and Science Teaching, 32*(3), 265–284.

Bentley, J. (2016). *Programming pearls.* (25th printing). Addison-Wesley Professional.

Grover, S. (2014). *Foundations for advancing computational thinking: Balanced designs for deeper learning in an online computer science course for middle school students* (Doctoral dissertation, Stanford University).

Pólya, G.(1945) *How to Solve It*, Princeton University Press, Princeton.

Waite, J. L., Curzon, P., Marsh, W., Sentance, S., & Hadwen-Bennett, A. (2018). Abstraction in action: K–5 teachers' uses of levels of abstraction, particularly the design level, in teaching programming. *International Journal of Computer Science Education in Schools, 2*(1), 14–40.

Creative Coding

Miles Berry

INTRODUCTION: WHAT IS CREATIVE CODING?

"Creative coding" is a pedagogy centered on the expression of pupils' own original ideas through the medium of code. Creative coding can best be understood through its five characteristics: making, originality, quality, fluency, and culture.

▶ Making

Creative coding means that a pupil has not only *thought* creatively but has actually made something that expresses that thinking. A literal interpretation of creativity demands that something be *created*, that imagination is given *expression* in some medium or another: in this present context, that means code. The great insight at the heart of Seymour Papert's theory of constructionism is that pupils learn not just through experience and experiment, or through reading, listening, and discussing, but also, and particularly effectively, in making things for themselves and for others to see.

"Digital making" has come to include physical computing (see **Chapter 24, X-ing Boundaries with Physical Computing**) alongside software and digital artifacts. Many teachers report pupils finding robotics or other hardware-based projects highly motivating, although it's certainly not the case that all physical computing projects are creative ones.

▶ Originality

Ken Robinson defines creativity as the process of having original ideas that have value. In creative coding, pupils have ample scope to develop programs that take their own ideas as a starting point. All too often, teachers seem to feel obliged to provide detailed, step-by-step instructions or narrowly specified problems, neither of which offer much opportunity for pupils' own original thinking. Alternative approaches, in which pupils receive a more open design brief, or perhaps just some time and support to work on their own independent projects, offer much more scope for original, imaginative, or innovative work.

▶ Quality

In teaching creative coding, teachers should encourage pupils to strive for their best possible work and emphasize an expectation of quality in every aspect of what pupils do. Although the *ideas* in creative coding should come from pupils themselves, teachers have a role to play in providing constructive, critical feedback on what each pupil makes.

▶ Fluency

Alongside the need to emphasize quality in the outputs of pupils' work, creative coding should also seek to develop fluency in the medium. Howard Gardner argues for a distinction between the original or novel behavior seen in young children and that which occurs where an individual has achieved mastery in the field in which they work. Coder Dojo's founder Bill Liao argues that code is like poetry: the fluency in language that writing poetry demands should be mirrored in an equivalent fluency with code.

Csikszentmihalyi argues that creativity is as much a cultural and social process as a psychological one. For creativity to flourish, there needs to be the right social environment: one in which experimentation or play is valued, one in which collaboration is encouraged, and one where feedback is sought, given, and acted on. The genuinely original is rare: in almost all cases the creative coder builds on the work of others, and thus a culture that acknowledges this seems important, too. In programming, the multilayered nature of abstraction makes it all but impossible to create something *without* drawing on others' work, for example: open source code, programming libraries, languages, APIs, or hardware.

STRENGTHS OF THE CREATIVE CODING APPROACH

A more creative approach to programming education that emphasizes making, originality, quality, fluency, and culture has many strengths.

Creative programming is situated firmly within the constructionist paradigm that characterised Papert's work with Logo. For many students, this is motivating, because there's a clear sense of achievement when things go well—an "I made this!" moment. When things go less well, pupils are more likely to persevere with the frustrations of debugging or discovering techniques for themselves. Many computing teachers, especially in higher education, report the gap between writing short problems that solve set problems and developing complete software projects. There are good reasons for this, but creative coding can give pupils the direct experience of working on larger projects. Emphasizing the creation of digital artifacts locates coding with traditionally "creative" subjects in school, such as art, design, technology, and many of the pedagogic approaches that are used in these subjects can be effectively applied in coding. The links with this creative side of the school curriculum can be further strengthened though projects where pupils apply their coding skills in these other domains.

When we move the focus in programming from solving set problems or responding to narrow design briefs to more open-ended, interest-driven tasks, pupils seem far more willing to find things out for themselves, developing curiosity and a willingness to experiment. They have a clear idea of what they want the computer to do (because they have thought of this for themselves) and then persevere in the process of making this happen. When pupils can choose their own projects to work on, programming can become much more pleasurable, because the chosen task is one that they are genuinely interested in, with consequent intrinsic motivation in overcoming difficulties encountered. Working on open-ended projects also gives pupils experience in managing complex projects for themselves, with the chance to apply computational thinking concepts at a level of abstraction above that of programming.

Creative coding places an emphasis on the quality of pupils' work, encouraging each to strive for excellence. Too often, an exercise- or problem-based approach to programming education leads to pupils developing answers that just work, that is, that give the right answer when given the test data or that satisfy the requirements of the design brief. Creative coding goes further than this, with pupils, independently or in response to feedback, refining user interfaces, refactoring code with more efficient algorithms, generalizing or extending their work, or providing narrative commentary so others can better understand their work.

Both Seymour Papert and Mitchell Resnick of the MIT Media Lab (the founders of Logo and Scratch, respectively) argued for the need for "high ceilings" in programming languages and environments designed with young people in mind (see **Chapter 10** on introductory programming languages). Pupils' increasing mastery of, and fluency in, a programming language takes them toward this ceiling. Programming education provides an introduction to the language, addressing the foundational constructs of the language such as sequence, selection and iteration, input, output, and simple data structures. However, these subjects are often taught in isolation, with little sense of how the fluent programmer weaves these constructs together. Pupils emerge having, for example, "done Scratch" but without any real sense of mastery over the language, of being able to express their own ideas through this medium. By analogy with language teaching, it's not enough to know the numbers, colors, and days of the week, nor is it sufficient to know the grammar and be able to translate simple sentences. Our aim should be holding conversations and extended, original writing. The building blocks of a language are useful only when they're used to build something.

Creative coding demands a creative culture in the classroom. A creative classroom culture can provide an even richer experience for pupils who already know one another and can work together on shared projects. A classroom culture that emphasizes the collaborative nature of creative work again provides a more authentic experience of software development than individual tasks ever could. Pair programming is a common software development method with the benefits of efficiency and quality of code, but when applied in the classroom it also appears to improve students' learning and motivation. (Also see **Chapter 11, Knowledge, Skills, Attitudes, and Beliefs; Chapter 16, Peer Collaboration and Pair Programming**; and **Chapter 26, Zestful Learning** for more detailed ideas on creating a supportive and collaborative classroom culture.)

EXAMPLES

Any programming language and environment can be used for the creative approach advocated for here, although some lend themselves more readily for a learner-led, exploratory approach than others, whereas some do seem more oriented toward the creation of more evidently creative artifacts than others. In addition to the examples here, mention should be made of Processing, particularly in its browser-based p5.js incarnation (https://p5js.org/) for new media art, and Sonic Pi, a Ruby-based live coding platform for performing algorithmic music (https://sonic-pi.net/). You can find examples that use these platforms in **Chapter 9, Integration Into Other Subjects**.

▶ Creative Coding With ScratchJr in Primary School

With young children (say between ages 5 and 8) in the lower primary grades, ScratchJr embodies many of the ideas of creative coding. In ScratchJr, students construct programs as sequences of blocks that snap together from left to right. With icons instead of text on blocks, ScratchJr is accessible to children for whom reading isn't yet easy. Although ScratchJr comes with a library of sprites and backgrounds so that young pupils can get started with coding straight away, it's easy for pupils to create their own characters and backgrounds, using a simple editor on screen or drawing them on paper and importing them into the program using the tablet's camera. It's also easy to record audio, so that characters can speak, although there's support for displaying text, too. ScratchJr is deliberately limited in scope: There aren't any user-defined variables, input is limited to clicking individual sprites, and there's no IF-THEN selection construct.

ScratchJr lends itself to open-ended creative storytelling rather than the more carefully sequenced problem-solving approach adopted by many other early coding apps. In the classroom context, teachers might link ScratchJr to any topic pupils are learning, for example, asking pupils to create a short animation about pirates, and then leaving it to children's own imagination as to what story they choose to tell. Being able to import pencil-and-paper drawings opens up more creative possibilities: Pupils can design characters and settings in traditional media, and perhaps write a story, before animating this in ScratchJr. Much of the most creative work in ScratchJr happens outside the classroom, where children simply play with ScratchJr, in much the same way as they may play with paints or construction toys, letting unfettered imagination take the lead in what they design or build (see Figure 1).

Figure 1. Screenshot of a ScratchJr project on a kindergartener's "My family" project

▶ Creative Coding With Scratch in Middle School

With older children (say 8- to 12-year-olds) in upper primary or middle school, Scratch itself provides an unrivalled set of tools, and, crucially, a community of other young people, for creative coding.

Like ScratchJr, Scratch is a block-based programming language that lends itself to two particularly fertile areas of creative coding: animations and games. Though the programming constructs that animations draw on can be more limited (e.g., there's rarely a need for input, selection statements, or variables), for pupils working independently, that can make things more accessible and allow them to give other elements of their program the creative attention they deserve. Again, teachers can choose to link animation projects explicitly to other curriculum topics, while still allowing pupils room to make the resulting artifacts distinctively their own. Game programming typically does draw on a wide range of programming constructs, including sequence, selection, repetition, input, output, and variables (see Figure 2). As with animation, this activity can be linked to curriculum topics: The distinction between a game and an interactive simulation is more to do with objectives than with the coding and media skills involved. Two further areas for creative coding in Scratch are worth mentioning here: turtle graphics and MIDI audio composition, both of which use additional library blocks in the current version of Scratch.

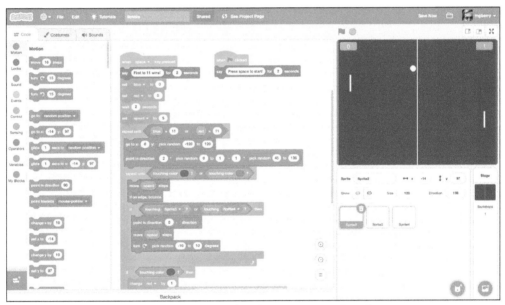

Figure 2. The classic computer game, Pong, is a favorite among young Scratch programmers

▶ Creative Coding With Python in High School

Students around age 13 and up (especially in high school) who have already learned to program in a block-based language such as Scratch might find themselves ready to move on to a more traditional, text-based language, in which programs are written rather than built. Many possibilities are available here, and teachers might need to balance the autonomy that a creative computing approach grants students with a desire to provide inspiration, instruction, and support in the classroom. Students learning independently might pursue projects for the web, Apple or Android devices, gaming, animation, or other domains, each of which might suggest its own best choice of language. On the other hand, as a teaching language for all students working together in a class, Python has much to commend it: the path from Scratch to Python is a well-trodden one; excellent teaching materials are available; and it's a language which can be applied to interesting, creative projects across a range of domains, from gaming and animation to data science and AI.

With text-based programming environments, a little more effort is needed if students are to benefit from the sense of—perhaps initially only peripheral—participation in a community (as is the case with the popular block-based programming environments): finding an audience for their work, getting support when faced with problems, and finding inspiration in the work of others. In school, teachers can do much to facilitate this sense of creative coding taking place within a community of more or less knowledgeable others. Afterschool coding clubs are one approach, but much can be done within lessons, too, providing shared portfolios of students' work, creating a wiki or forum for peer-to-peer support, and establishing a culture of collaboration on joint projects. Beyond the school, students should start learning to look for solutions to problems on sites such as Stack Overflow, progressing to posting clear questions there themselves if their searches come up empty, and perhaps providing solutions to others' problems themselves or refining the solutions offered by others. Students should learn to use GitHub, too, reading, understanding, and editing the work of others, and uploading the ongoing development of their own project work for others to see.

As students start to learn Python, it can be helpful to draw on some of the ideas for projects that they might already have encountered through creative coding in block-based programming environments. For example, turtle graphics is well supported in both languages, allowing pupils to take creative, geometric art produced in Scratch or Snap! and translate their code into the syntax of Python's turtle graphics library (see Figure 3a and 3b). The Python turtle commands include a number not available in Scratch, and so students can extend their algorithmic art further, or further still in Processing's Python mode. Media computation is rich territory for creative coding. Python provides libraries for manipulating images and audio samples, and music composition using samples is possible through Georgia Tech's EarSketch environment (earsketch.gatech.edu). Although game development is easy in many block-based environments, the step up to Python is a large one. Students might enjoy working initially in the medium of old-school, text-based adventures to compose their own interactive fiction, either in base Python or through the Tale library. For faster paced, interactive gaming, the Pygame library provides the needed tools and is a good motivator for developing some fluency in object-oriented programming. For students more interested in animation, Pygame is also a good toolkit, but the open source 3-D animation toolkit Blender uses Python as its scripting language.

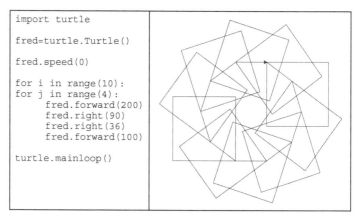

Figure 3a and 3b. Python's turtle graphics library for creative coding in a text-based language

CAVEATS

There are some potential downsides to creative coding as an approach to programming, and educators would be wise to think through how the impact of these might be minimized. The pragmatic approach is likely to be the inclusion of some open-ended projects where pupils' creativity and autonomy is to the fore, alongside other, more conventional scaffolded methods (such as those described in **Chapter 23, Worked Examples and Scaffolding Strategies**).

One of the principal dangers of a creative approach to programming is that the focus moves, almost inevitably, from learning to making. Proponents of constructionism argue that pupils learn through making, and there can be little doubt that pupils pick up ways of doing things or independently find solutions to the problems they encounter in creative projects. For them, however, and sometimes for their teachers, the focus is often on the completion of a product rather than the acquisition of defined skills, knowledge, and understanding that accompanies the production process (as detailed in **Chapter 11, Knowledge, Skills, Attitudes, and Beliefs**). There's also a danger that the knowledge and skills acquired can be biased: if all a pupil ever makes are animations, then, as indicated earlier, there's little scope for them to develop a *comprehensive grasp* of key constructs of computer programming. It's also possible that content acquisition happens in a rather ad hoc sequence, without a particularly firm foundation: students might *seem* adept at advanced coding using, for example, the Pygame libraries without having the accompanying general understanding of the object-oriented programming on which their game draws.

There's also a danger that those who've only experienced a creative approach to programming are left with misconceptions (see **Chapter 14, Naïve Conceptions of Novice Programmers**) or perhaps miss out on the general application of ideas or constructs learned in specific contexts—programs don't *always* involve moving characters around a stage; variables can be used to store more than just game scores; lists can be used for purposes other than inventories or high-score tables; Scratch inputs don't *have* to be dealt with using a `when the w key is pressed` block; and there are more ways to decompose a problem than creating multiple sprites or through broadcast and receive blocks.

Some in the education research community argue that minimally guided approaches to education, in which we might well include creative coding, are less efficient and effective than scaffolded learning approaches. It is perhaps hard enough for a pupil to master the semantics and the syntax of coding without the additional cognitive load of designing something creative. Perhaps, instead, teachers should focus on providing a good grounding in the fundamentals of programming, and only when these have been mastered might their students go on to apply these skills to their own original projects.

> The pragmatic teacher is likely to balance pedagogical approaches, using scaffolded approaches to explain the concepts that pupils would not discover for themselves alongside providing the time and space for them to apply these in creative, pupil-led projects.

One cause of pupils' frustrations—and it should be admitted, failures—in independent, creative project work is that their ambition can often exceed their capabilities. Pupils already familiar with the high-quality output of commercial animation or game studios, or that of much more experienced peers from the Scratch community or GitHub, may come to creative work with some wonderful, imaginative ideas of what they want their programs to do but no real idea of how to do this. Ambition is a noble thing, but the gap between what pupils can do and what they want to do is often too great. Their teachers play a role here in encouraging pupils to be more realistic about their project ideas, of starting with something more realistically achievable, and for introducing agile ideas like "breakable toys" (programs built for the purpose of learning) and the "minimum viable product."

BIBLIOGRAPHY

Csikszentmihalyi, M. (2006). A systems perspective on creativity. In J. Henry (Ed.) *Creative management and development*. London, Sage Publications.

Gardner, H. (1993). *Multiple intelligences*: The theory in practice. Basic Books.

Kirschner, P. A., Sweller, J., & Clark, R. E. (2006). Why minimal guidance during instruction does not work: An analysis of the failure of constructivist, discovery, problem-based, experiential, and inquiry-based teaching. *Educational Psychologist, 41*(2), 75–86.

Papert, S., & Harel, I. (1991). Situating constructionism. *Constructionism, 36*(2), 1–11.

Robinson, K. (2011). *Out of our minds*. Tantor Media, Incorporated.

Data Structures

Baker Franke and Richard Kick

INTRODUCTION: THE WHAT AND WHY OF DATA STRUCTURES

Programs often work with data—they store, retrieve, and manipulate it. This is done with a single data object or aggregations of data objects. Although **variables** store only one value at a time (see **Chapter 22, Variables**), programmers commonly need access to larger collections of data values that are conceptually related. For example, a program may provide access to all names of students in a particular classroom, maintain a list of songs to be played for a family event, store the salaries of employees, or store and access a collection of map locations to be visited on some trip. A sophisticated program may need to maintain a collection of complex, multivariable objects or even a collection of collections!

> Though it is (surprisingly) difficult to find a common definition that all textbook writers use to define the term *data structure*, it is clear that the study of **data structures** is associated with the principles, logic, and trade-offs associated with the organization, storage, retrieval, and modification of data collections.

A Concrete Example: Lists

Introductory students, at almost any grade level, can program with, and reason about, simple data structures. The most common data structure students learn first is a **List**.[1] Most programming languages and environments allow programmers to create and maintain lists of values, and they are typically understandable for all computer science students after a relatively short period of study.

In this chapter we focus almost exclusively on lists, highlighting important features and concepts pertinent to most data structures. As you might imagine, many other well-known and well-studied data structures exist besides lists—stacks, queues, heaps, trees, graphs, sets, maps, dictionaries, hash tables. In advanced courses in computer science, data structures and analysis of them can get quite complex (and fun!).

WHY DATA STRUCTURES ARE NEEDED (AND INTERESTING!)

Both the *organization* of a collection of data values and the associated *functionality* for the storage, retrieval, and manipulation of those values are *crucial* to the effectiveness of a program. Making programs more effective in terms of correctness, speed, or usefulness to the user is inherently of interest to the programmer.

What's especially interesting about data structures is that there are *trade-offs* that programmers must consider when creating, using, and implementing them. Think about the amount of storage required, the time needed to access individual data elements, and the ability to add, remove, and arrange values in the data structure. The choices a

---

[1] We capitalize List in this instance as a proper noun because it is a formal name for the concept of a list that carries some common understandings about its properties and functionality in programming.

programmer makes are highly dependent on the program's intended purpose and expected use. Sometimes solutions require a great deal of creativity.

Beyond working correctly, when discussing trade-offs in data structures, we typically talk about *efficiency*. Efficiency is considered in terms of both *memory*—efficient use of the computer's memory to store data values—and *speed*—the efficient use of computing cycles to retrieve or modify the data in the collection. Data structures are thus inextricably linked with algorithms at some level, and their study often goes hand in hand.

In the remainder of the chapter, we explain key ideas about data structures and intertwine strategies and ideas for teaching those ideas about data structures, including the use of everyday real-world examples, unplugged kinesthetic activities, and working with visualizations.

TEACHING IDEAS

▶ Introducing the Need for Data Structures

The need for data structures often arises in the K–12 classroom after studying and using variables for some time. As students consider large collections of data, using individual variables for each new data element becomes impractical.

For example, imagine a student is trying to write a program to help them remember the names of famous computer scientists. In the program, you are prompted to type the full name of some computer scientist, and the program tells you whether what you typed matches the name of some computer scientist:

```
Type someone's name: Ada Hopper
> NO! That is not a famous computer scientist. Try again.

Type someone's name: Grace Hopper
> YES! Grace Hopper is a famous computer scientist!
```

Armed with only knowledge of variables, students may be tempted to create a large number of variables, one for each name they want to recount.

```
var person1 = "Grace Hopper"
var person2 = "Alan Turing"
var person3 = "Ada Lovelace"
...
var person44 = "Donald Knuth"
var person45 = "Frances Allen"
```

Worse, the code to check dozens of variables for a particular value is clunky, hard to read, and difficult to maintain. It might look like a long series of if/else-if statements:

```
var name = userInput("Type someone's name:")
if (name == person1) display "YES! " + person1 + " is a famous..."
else if (name == person2) display "YES! " + person2 + " is a famous..."
else if (name == person3) display "YES! " + person3 + " is a famous..."
else if (name == person4) ...
...
else display "NO! That is not a famous computer scientist. Try again"
```

With the code above, to add a new name to the program, you'd have to change and add code in at least two places. You'd much rather be able to write code that contains all the names you want in a list and for the list to have some simple functionality for checking to see if it contains a particular value. (The following code follows JavaScript syntax, but several helper functions and other extraneous code are omitted. A simple list in JavaScript is called an *array* and uses the square bracket [ ] notation.)

```
var list = ["Grace Hopper","Alan Turing",
            "Ada Lovelace",...,"Donald Knuth","Frances Allen"];
    var name = userInput("Type someone's name:");

    if(list.includes(name))
      display("YES! " + name + " is a famous...");
    else
        display("NO! That is not a famous computer scientist...");
```

In the code above, the **data structure** is a list of strings of computer scientists' names. The **functionality** of the list is the method includes, which, we assume, returns TRUE if the list includes a value equal to the value stored in the variable name, and FALSE otherwise. Unlike the previous variables-only solution, now if we want to add a name to the program, we simply have to add to the list of names—the rest of the code will still do the job!

However, not all programming languages have such functionality built into the available data structures. You might need to write your own code to iteratively compare each element in a list to the value you are searching for.

```
        var list = ["Grace Hopper","Alan Turing",
                    "Ada Lovelace",....,"Donald Knuth","Frances Allen"]
        var name = userInput("Type someone's name:")

        var found_name = FALSE;
        for(var i=0; i<list.length; i++){
            if(list[i] == name) found_name = TRUE;
        }

        if(found_name)
            display "YES! " + name + " is a famous..."
        else
            display "NO! That is not a famous computer scientist..."
```

The code above uses a form of *linear search* to find whether the name the user entered is in the list. A loop iteratively checks each value in the list, one by one, for the name. If the name is found, then the Boolean found_name is set to TRUE. When the loop is over, if found_name is FALSE, it means that the code got through the entire loop without ever entering the if-statement that sets the variable to true—the name wasn't found in the list. Notice, however, that every value of the list is checked *no matter what*. If the name we're looking for is first in the list, the code is still going to check every one of the other values (one might say, needlessly).

This example is an interesting case of the interplay between data structures and algorithms. Notice that depending on what your program is trying to do, whether you write it yourself or whether the language has built-in function like includes, knowing exactly how the code works might be important. If this same technique were applied to a scenario where the list had 450 million values instead of 45, then *how* your code, or the includes method, goes about answering true or false might have consequences on your program's speed.

▶ The Relationship Between Variables and Data Structures

You can also see from the earlier example how `list` is used as a variable in the program. But rather than holding a single value, it is a reference to a *collection* of data values. This a place of potential confusion for early programmers. You can think of a variable as the simplest data structure. After all, variables allow for the storage, retrieval, and manipulation of individual data values. However, as a programming language feature, what variables *really* allow you to do is give names to memory locations where values are stored. In the case of a data structure (i.e., a collection of data values), a single variable allows you to give a name to the location in memory where the collection is stored. We address this concept in more depth later.

Some instructors might leverage their students' mental model of variables as individual data storage containers and describe data structures as collections of variables. Furthermore, they might describe a data structure as a *different type* of variable that simply holds lots of data values, or variables. As you'll see in upcoming examples, there is some value to this mental model.

Also notice that a single "bin" in the list like `list [2]` is essentially a variable. You can store, retrieve, and modify its value just like any other variable; it just happens to be a variable that belongs to a larger collection of values. Thus, students might be helped by thinking about `list` as a variable that refers to variables.

▶ Visualizing Lists

Lists are usually *indexed* collections, like a sequence of numbered bins, and are typically visualized in a few different ways, but you'll notice some commonalities (Table 1).

> Helping students visualize data structures is a key pedagogical strategy for helping them understand this concept.

Table 1. Visualizing lists and showing students how data lists are stored

Several block-based environments provide a visual representation of the list right on screen.	**list** 1 Ada Lovelace 2 Alan Turing 3 Grace Hopper 4 ... 5 ... 6 ... + length 45 =
Visualization might be provided as part of the debugging tools in a programming environment (BlueJ).[2]	cS_Test1 : CS_Test private String[] list Inspect / Get Show static fields Close list : String[] int length 45 Inspect / Get [0] "Ada Lovelace" [1] "Alan Turing" [2] "Grace Hopper" [3] ". . ." [4] ". . ." [5] ". . ." [6] ". . ." Show static fields Close

continued on next page

---

[2] Note that this visualization is not strictly accurate. It shows the array storing strings. The array would actually contain references to string objects, and the strings would be stored somewhere else. This level of detail is usually not discussed at the introductory level.

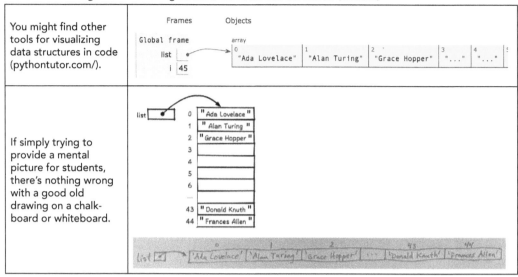

You might find other tools for visualizing data structures in code (pythontutor.com/).	Frames / Objects visualization with Global frame: list, i 45, and array "Ada Lovelace", "Alan Turing", "Grace Hopper", "...", "..."
If simply trying to provide a mental picture for students, there's nothing wrong with a good old drawing on a chalkboard or whiteboard.	list 0 "Ada Lovelace" 1 "Alan Turing" 2 "Grace Hopper" 3 4 5 6 ... 43 "Donald Knuth" 44 "Frances Allen"

Languages come with built-in syntax for accessing elements in the list by its index. For example, many languages use square brackets to indicate a list index as seen above. Thus list[2] would refer to the value stored at index 2 in the list. Scratch and Snap! provide a block for this, like so: item 2 of list ▾

Note that for lists in most languages, the first index is 0; however, for some (as in Scratch), the first index is 1.

▶ Example Project Ideas for Introducing Lists

Like the earlier computer scientist quiz, lists can be introduced at various grade levels through fun examples.

▶ Elementary School

Although lists are a more advanced idea than those introduced in primary grades, the 'About Me' quiz project presented here is a simple example shared on the Scratch wiki website.

▶ Middle School (Scratch or Python)

Below are a couple of interesting examples that show how lists can be used to introduce the idea of data structures in middle school.

The introductory project I did with my students at school using lists was for them to create an "About Me" quiz. The project had two lists. One was called Questions, and the other was called Answers.

In the questions they had to add three items to the list in question form.
For example,
What is my favorite food?
What is my pet's name?
What month was I born?

The Answers list held the answers in order.
pizza
Shadow
July

The main loop would repeat until the length of questions < 1 and ask Item 1 of the questions. The user would answer and the if-then-else beneath would check for correct or incorrect. If it was incorrect, we used a join block to say, good try but the answer is Item 1 of the answers.

Delete Item 1 of questions.

That continues to loop until all the items are deleted. It was a pretty simple and fun project.

1. **Random Sentence Generator** (possible Language Arts class tie-in): Create four lists for nouns, verbs, adverbs, and adjectives. Fill the lists with either, or a combination of, predefined words and user-entered words. With those lists you can start to get creative.

    a. Create a random sentence from a short combination of the words: For example (the Python code fragment assumes lists have been created and filled with values)

    ```
    # generate 4 random numbers in range of
    # 0 to current length of appropriate list
    n = randrange(0, len(nouns))
    vrb = randrange(0, len(verbs))
    adv = randrange(0, len(adverbs))
    adj = randrange(0, len(adjectives))
    # display 4 randomly chosen words as a sentence
    print nouns[n], verbs[vrb], adverbs[adv], adjectives[adj],"!"
    ```

    b. Make a randomized MadLibs by plugging randomly chosen words in to a larger piece of text. This example uses a "format string" and the random.choice feature of Python to shorten some of the code.

    ```
    print("Four score and seven years ago our _%ss_ _%s_ on this continent, a
    _%s_ nation, _%s_ in Liberty, and dedicated to the proposition that all _%ss_
    are created equal."%
         (random.choice(nouns),
         random.choice(verbs),
         random.choice(adjectives),
                     random.choice(verbs),
         random.choice(nouns)
         )
    )
    ```

2. **Object-Picking Game in Block-Based Visual Environments.** Create a game (in Scratch, Snap!, App Inventor, or Alice) that involves asking the user to specify objects they like, saving those choices in a list, and then moving about among levels to pick objects that have been asked for. Once all the desired objects have been picked, the user gets a reward. This game can be made simple or complex by adding more choices, adding different levels and backgrounds, or adding new characters that try to get to the object before the user can.

▶ High School (Java)

High school students often use the Java programming language (e.g., if they are preparing to take the AP Computer Science A exam in the United States). One project idea that students may enjoy is to explore various works of literature and compare word usage in those works. This is also an excellent example of how to integrate programming into language arts. Check out **Chapter 9, Integration Into School Subjects** for many other examples.

Text file versions of great literature can be found online at the Gutenberg Project. For example

- *The Tragedy of Hamlet*: http://www.gutenberg.org/cache/epub/2265/pg2265.txt

- *The Adventures of Huckleberry Finn*: https://www.gutenberg.org/files/76/76-0.txt

Many students study these classics in English class, and they can experience the use of computer science to better understand other academic fields. The use of lists, in particular the ArrayList, could help students perform the following tasks related to selected literature:

DATA STRUCTURES

1. Create a list of all words used in the chosen work of literature.

2. Count the word that is most frequently used.

3. Calculate the words that are shortest and longest.

4. Calculate the average length of the words used in the text.

5. **Advanced:** For every word in the text, make a list of the words that most frequently come after it. This is actually trickier than it might sound but leads to very fun results. You can use these lists to randomly generate texts that "sound like" the original.

Students should be encouraged to generate their own questions about the literature that they would like to explore. They should also have discussions of advanced data structures available in the Java libraries (such as Set and Map) that may be helpful with their explorations.

Lastly, **Nifty Assignments** (nifty.stanford.edu) contains a trove of fun assignments, many of which involve the use of lists in very interesting and novel contexts. Nifty Assignments is a resource created *mostly* by college instructors for mostly college instructors, but many are completely appropriate for high school students. A K–12 version of Nifty Assignments was created and lives under the auspices of the Computer Science Teachers Association (CSTA). Although CSTA Nifty Assignments is newer, as of this writing, it already contains two very nifty applications of lists. Check it out at **nifty.csteachers.org**.

PEDAGOGICAL STRATEGIES FOR TEACHING DATA STRUCTURES

In addition to the several ideas presented in the chapter, including visualizing lists, motivating the need for lists, and using fun examples for using lists, a few additional strategies for teaching data structures in the school classroom follow.

▶ Connect to Everyday Examples

It goes without saying that connecting data structures to everyday examples that are relevant to your students' lives is a good idea. Not to be hyperbolic, but once you and your students begin to consider data in terms of *how it might be structured to enable computing applications*, you begin to see the world in new ways. From how your kitchen cabinets are organized (or not), to student schedules and gradebooks, to a play log for a sports contest, to choreography in a dance routine, to coordinates on a map—*all* are potential areas to mine for student interest. Find something that will work for your students, and use it.

▶ Inquiry-Based Methods and Concept Invention

As mentioned earlier, so many premade libraries of data structures exist, with lots of built-in functionality that make it possible to use data structures without really understanding them. The authors of this chapter believe strongly in helping students understand the real insights and genius that underlie data structures and algorithms.

Process-Oriented Guided Inquiry Learning (POGIL, pogil.org) provides some good patterns for instruction that work well for teaching data structures, especially the notion of **concept invention**, which is generally constructivist in nature and goes like this: Given what your students currently know, present them with a use case or problem that falls just outside their domain knowledge. For example, if students know about arrays in Java, then they know that they must declare how many elements the array will have (the number of bins) before any values can be stored in it. Problem: What if that array becomes completely filled with values at some point during the running of the program, but you need to add one more element? You don't want the program to crash. How would you solve this problem? This is a common use case in real applications that needs to be handled.

This problem has in fact been solved in a variety of ways. Library-provided data structures handle the problem behind the scenes using (what have now) become conventional practices. By asking students to **invent** how they would solve the problem is both respectful of their intelligence and much more memorable when a canonical solution is presented. Students will likely come up with a variety of solutions to these common problems, and it's also useful to have students compare their solutions with those of their peers.

A reason this strategy is effective is that computer science problem-solving is very creative. Whether you're trying to solve a problem on your own or in an interview for a software engineering job, the **process of problem-solving** that you experience is the most important building block for your skills. By having students repeatedly engage in that problem-solving process, you're building their capacity to develop novel solutions to problems as well as maintaining the ethos of computer science as a creative intellectual endeavor underpinned by tenacity.

▶ Kinesthetic/Unplugged Activities

Here we present two different ways to think about lists—arrays and linked lists—in which we weave in things you might also have your students do to learn. The examples with students do double duty to both explain some concepts about data structures to the reader as well as promote thinking about classroom activities. Meta!

A list is typically thought of as a sequence of values— a first value, a second value, and so on until the last value. To help students better understand the concept of a list, it can be helpful for students to physically form lists featuring themselves as data elements in a variety of ways and to manipulate the lists to motivate discussions about the trade-offs related to data structure decisions. Here are two contrasting examples.

1. **Array:** Create squares next to each other on the floor of the classroom with tape or nonpermanent markers. Have students line up on spots on the floor that are marked with location numbers (indices). This layout can be described as what many computer languages refer to as an **array** of values. You can use the indices to access a particular student in the list of students (Figure 1).

Figure 1. Students physically enacting an array in the classroom

2. **Linked Lists:** Have students all stand up with about 5 feet of separation between them (something more than arm's length). Designate one of the students as the starting student. Have that student point to a second student. Have the second student point to a third student. Continue having each selected student pointing to a student not yet pointed to until all students except the last student are pointing to another student in the group. Have the last student point to the ground (Figure 2). Ask students how a particular student can be accessed. Help students realize that accessing a student requires beginning with the starting student and following the path of pointing students until the desired student is found. Have students add students to the list by changing the target of the points. Describe this list as a **linked list**. Discuss the trade-offs associated with this data structure.

Figure 2. Students physically enacting a linked list in the classroom

In both instances, it may be useful to also discuss with students the desired functionality and how these would be implemented in each of these two types of lists. You could use a concept invention approach (see above) to discuss solutions to various functions a list should support such as

- **Create** a new empty list that we can use in our program
- **Add** a value to the list
- **Remove** a value from the list
- **Get** a value from within the list
- **Find** whether a value exists in the list

In addition, we might also want to have students think about what happens when we use those operations in different scenarios. For example, what happens if we want to **add** a value

- To the **front** of the list?
- To **back** of the list?
- Somewhere in the **middle** of the list?

Similarly, discuss what happens when we remove an item. What if we wish to swap two items? Such a discussion may also include examples of how different languages treat this growing and shrinking of a data structure through addition and removal of elements from lists.

THINGS TO WATCH OUT FOR!

▶ Overloaded Terminology

It's important to differentiate between underlying concepts that are similar between languages and the actual terms used within the nomenclature of specific languages—different words can mean the same thing, depending on the language. Words like *list* and *array* are sometimes used interchangeably even though these terms do have more precise definitions. A "map" in Java is basically the same as a "dictionary" in Python, and other languages call the same thing an "associative array."

Sometimes, even official documents are loose with verbiage. For example, the AP CS Principles framework in the United States defines a list as *"an ordered sequence of elements."* The word *ordered* is problematic here. An "ordered list" in computer science typically means that the data elements themselves have some inherent property that lends them to being orderable, and that an "ordered list" means the elements are stored "in order." For example, a list of names might be listed in alphabetical order, a list of numbers might be listed in numerical order, and so on. In the case of this AP CS Principles definition, though, "ordered sequence" is meant to imply only that the list is indexed and the elements are stored linearly such that there is a notion of a "first element," a "second element," and so on.

▶ Abstract Concepts Versus Concrete Language Features

When teaching about data structures with students, it can be easy to get lost in the abstractions at play. It's also easy to accidentally get tangled up in or cause misconceptions due to overloaded terminology. Using precise language at times is going to be a useful teaching strategy to disambiguate ideas.

For example, the notion of a *list* is itself an abstract concept. In real life, of course, we use the word list to mean everything from our grocery list, to a to-do list, to a directory listing. And the abstract notion of a list is useful for reasoning about possible uses in a computer program. Lists of data are quite useful after all! However, it turns out that you could go about writing code in many ways to *implement* a list in a program, for example, the array versus linked list implementations described previously.

> The distinction between the **abstract** concept of a data structure, its purpose, and its primary functionality and the concrete **implementation** of it is probably among the more advanced topics you'll encounter in a high school computer science course. However, the distinction between an abstract data structure and its implementation is fundamental to advanced studies of algorithms and data structures.

Which brings us to a related potential point of confusion: **Different programming languages provide different kinds of built-in functionality related to data structures**. Some languages, such as C, offer only the most basic features necessary for building more advanced structures (caveat coming). You have to write a lot of code to *make* the functionality happen. Other languages like Python and JavaScript have a lot of functionality "built in" to the language. For younger students, languages like Scratch also have much of the functionality built in. A third option is to use well known "libraries" that contain data structures and functions for common use cases that ship with these languages; this is common for languages like C. Though the core language has only the most fundamental elements, you can import libraries into your program for your own use, so you don't have to write common routines from scratch every time.

However, is there ever a case where you might *not* want to use a library? One good reason is for student learning. Libraries are abstract—their entire purpose in a *professional* context is to *hide* complicated implementation details so that the programmer can focus on higher-order problems; it's presumed the professionals have already learned the principles that undergird these libraries. To use and reuse data structures from common libraries is considered good professional practice because it helps reduce program development time and likely reduces bugs and errors associated with data structure functions. Your students should definitely use them . . . *eventually*.

▶ Using Data Structures Versus Creating Them

When learning for the first time, however, you might not want to *hide* how things work. It can be useful to develop a rationale for the need for libraries organically as you usher students through a series of problems involving data structures. This will allow students to see the patterns for themselves and better appreciate what the library functions are doing. (See the earlier linear search example.) Rather than starting students out with fully formed data structures from libraries, you might have them grapple with programming the same functionality using only the built-in features of the language to more deeply understand, and develop intuitions about, the source of some of the trade-offs they'll have to think about later.

It is often helpful to use examples that illuminate some of the potential trade-offs associated with the use of particular data structure implementations. For example, implementations of lists often hide the details of growing and shrinking the data structure. Consider the implications associated with various implementations in terms of memory and processing efficiency. As with all foundational ideas related to programming, it is important that students learn the deeper concept of data organization and data structures, their usefulness for different algorithmic needs, and the potential trade-offs associated with various types of implementation.

DATA STRUCTURES

Events

Jennifer Rosato and David Wolber

INTRODUCTION: PROGRAMMING THE "WHEN"

Computers were originally designed to compute—to take in data, process it, and generate some output. Many of today's computational devices, however, perform tasks that make them more like event-response machines: reacting to the user touching a button on a phone screen, displaying location information from a GPS satellite, or notifying that a text from a friend has arrived.

Programming languages like Python and Java were designed for the traditional computational model and provide library "callback" code on top of the language to deal with such user interfaces and external events. Unfortunately, the add-ons are sophisticated and tend to preclude beginners, so most beginning lessons in these languages involve the students creating command-line "terminal" programs.

However, newer block-based drag-and-drop programming environments like Scratch, MIT App Inventor, Snap!, and Thunkable are based on the event-response model.

> **Event-based coding** features include built-in constructs for coding interactive behaviors like "When the button is clicked, Pac-Man jumps." These constructs significantly ease the task of event-response coding compared to traditional languages, which require complex "callback" procedures to be set up.

The visual nature of these languages is key to their popularity in school settings, but the event-handling nature is also a key factor in why beginners are able to build interesting apps with user interfaces, sensors, and databases. Because beginners can build complete, real-world applications, the programming classroom is truly alive! Students are highly motivated to create apps and programs that respond to external actions, and that pumps life into their learning. The "events-first" approach can thus also provide beginners with a broader understanding of software development than they get in a traditional classroom. They get hands-on experience with sensors, user interfaces, user testing, and multiuser shared data apps—exposure that is helpful when they revisit the topics in later courses based on traditional languages. As a teacher, you can thus introduce a much broader set of topics including user interface design, databases, and usability testing.

Most of the examples and ideas in this chapter draw on the authors' extensive experiences in teaching introductory programming with event-based languages and leading the development of teaching platforms (appinventor.org and mobile-csp.org) that use the MIT App Inventor programming environment. This chapter discusses event-based programming and techniques for teaching it inspired by their experiences to motivate beginning students to build real-world, engaging projects and truly democratize the coding world.

SETTING THE STAGE

The first task in coding with an event-based language is typically to create the user interface. Scratch, for example, uses the *stage* metaphor—projects are initiated by drawing or finding sprites for the stage, and programs run in a browser window (Figure 1a). In contrast, the App Inventor and Thunkable programs run on a mobile phone or tablet, so the design is centered on screens with components such as buttons, images, labels, maps, and sensors. You test and run your programs directly on a device, as shown in Figure 1b. Thunkable runs on both Android and iOS devices, whereas App Inventor runs only on Android (a cross-platform version is in development).

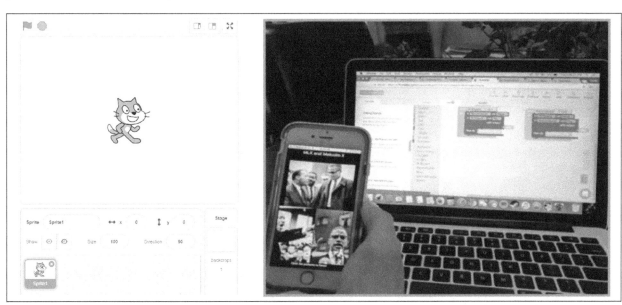

Figure 1a and b. Scratch programs run on a stage (a); App Inventor and Thunkable apps run on mobile devices (b)

The components and events available for Scratch and Snap! revolve around sprite activity, whereas App Inventor and Thunkable have a much more extensive tool set, including most of the functionality of a mobile device.

EVENT HANDLERS

Consider the simple soundboard app, *I Have a Dream*, shown in Figure 2. Clicking the lower-left button plays a speech by Martin Luther King, whereas clicking the lower-right button plays a speech by Malcolm X. Creating this simple app in Python or Java would not be easy, because coding when `Button is clicked` would require a fair amount of complex coding.

Event-based coding environments combine a user interface designer and a fundamental construct, *the event* handler, which simplifies the task of specifying the interactive behavior of the user interface. **An event handler is a "callback" procedure that specifies what should happen when a specific event occurs.**

Event handlers differ from other procedures in that whereas you call a procedure from within the app, you don't explicitly call an event handler. Instead, event handlers are **"triggered"** by an external event initiated by the user or system.

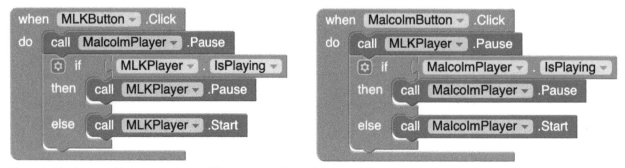

Figure 2. The *I Have a Dream* app plays a different speech for each button click

The outer when blocks in the code of Figure 2 specify the events of clicking the buttons. The inner blocks specify what should happen when the events occur. An event handler includes both the outer when block and its inner contents (the response). When the MLKButton is clicked, a speech by Malcolm X is paused and a speech by MLK is initiated if it isn't already playing or paused if it is. The opposite happens when the MalcolmButton is clicked.

In Scratch, the start of a program is triggered the when green flag clicked event. In Figure 3, two procedures—resetScreen and polygon—are called from the when green flag clicked event. resetScreen clears the screen and initializes the program to its starting state, and the polygon procedure draws a polygon of a given size and number of sides.

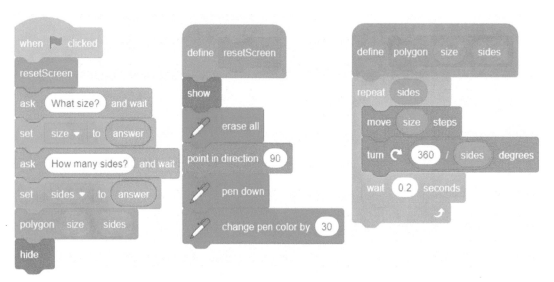

Figure 3. The start of a Scratch program is triggered by the when green flag clicked event

▶ Coding an Event Handler

when blocks are predefined constructs provided by event-based languages. The programmer can click on any component to see all of its blocks. In Figure 4, the programmer has clicked on the Texting1 component in App Inventor to display its blocks, including its one when block, the when Texting1.MessageReceived block at the top.

To code an event handler, the programmer drags the when block into the code screen and proceeds to code the response to the event by placing blocks within it.

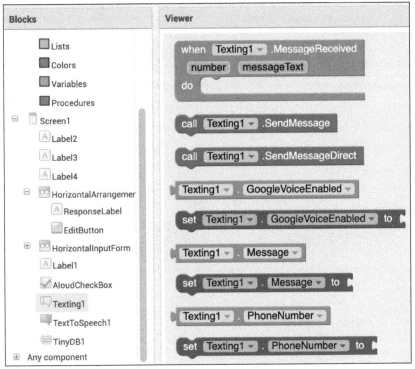

Figure 4. Adding events handlers for program components (or objects) in App Inventor

▶ Coding Complex Events

Events include more than just button clicks. In general, an event is something from the external world that happens *to the program or app* and fits into one of the following categories:

- User interface—a button click, mouse drag, keyboard key press
- Communications—an incoming SMS text message
- Location—a GPS signal triggered by the phone's location changing
- Database—a web database reporting that shared data has changed
- Web—an API sending data to the device
- Sensor—an accelerometer or other device sensor reporting activity
- Sprite events—two game characters colliding

Figure 5 shows some examples of when blocks for various event types from App Inventor, Thunkable, Scratch, and Snap!.

Each of these events is triggered by something happening to a device or within the app. Students may struggle with events that are triggered not by user actions but instead by the system. The event LocationSensor.LocationChanged in App Inventor (Figure 5a), for instance, is triggered when the device is moved and includes information about the new location. You can use this event handler to code geo-aware apps similar to the Find My iPhone app that helps the user to find the location of their iPhone.

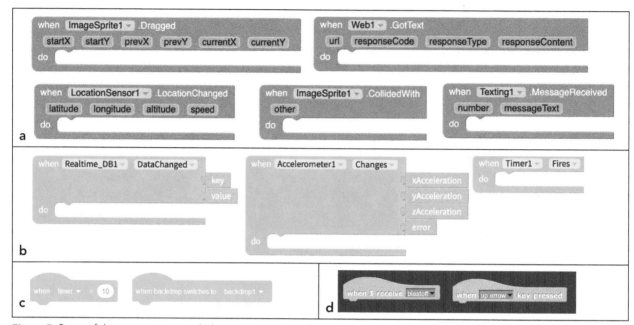

Figure 5. Some of the many events to which an app can respond (in MIT App Inventor (a), Thunkable (b), Scratch (c), and Snap! (d))

The `Realtime_DB.DataChanged` event in Thunkable (Figure 5b) is triggered when one app instance (user) posts data to the database. The event is triggered in all of the other app instances so they can update their local data and user interface (and so the users can see the posts of others). This event handler makes it possible to create social apps—chat, games, and so on—with shared data, something not generally in the realm of the beginner using traditional languages.

The `Timer.Fires` event in Thunkable (Figure 5b) is a special one in that it is triggered by the "event" of the passing of time. It is like an alarm clock, and you can set properties for how often it should trigger. `Timer.Fires` event handlers are used to code animated behaviors, such as a sprite moving a few pixels across the screen every few milliseconds.

Scratch and Snap! provide a way to broadcast programmer-defined messages that behave like events. One part of your code can broadcast a message, and other parts of the code can respond to it within a `when I receive` event like the `when I receive blastoff` event shown in Figure 5 (c and d).

▶ Event Parameters

Another area of difficulty for students learning events can be event parameters. Making connections to how parameters are used in procedures can be helpful for students, however. (See **Chapter 13, Modularity with Methods and Functions**). The events shown in Figure 4 are more complex than the button click and include additional information about the event (see the orangish and greenish subblocks). The additional information blocks for an event are called *event parameters*.

Event parameters provide information about an event that has occurred.

The set of components and events provided by languages like App Inventor, and the uniform manner of coding responses to them, puts amazing power into the hands of beginners. For students who never expected to code apps, it is like being given a magical power!

Figure 6 shows code created by a beginning programming student in high school. Can you tell what it does?

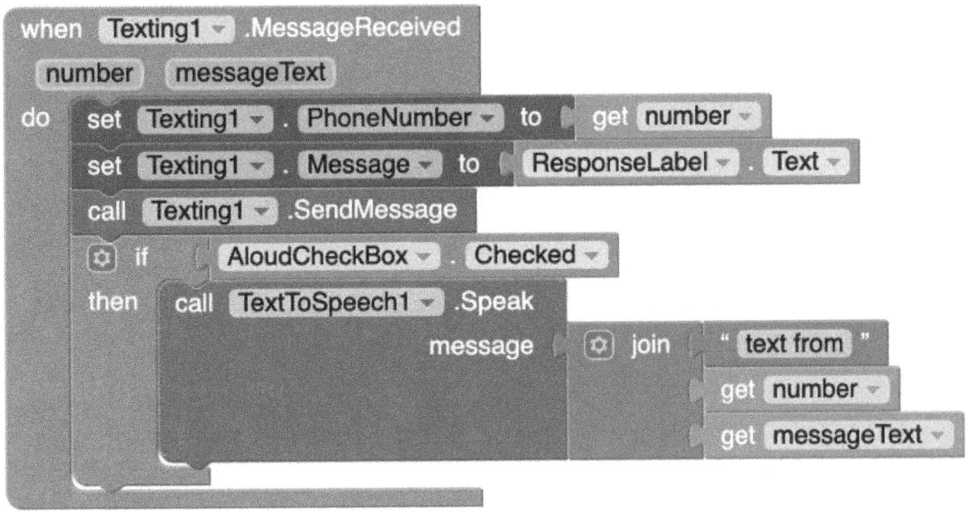

Figure 6. Event Handler for a "No Text While Driving" app

The No Text While Driving app (Figure 6) was created by a student who took note of the many car accidents that were occurring because of distracted drivers. Though he was in his first weeks of learning to code, he was able to create a powerful app: in this case, one that speaks incoming texts aloud and autoresponds to the text with a custom message, such as, "Sorry, I'm driving now."

In this example, when Texting1.MessageReceived event is triggered anytime a text message is received by the phone, and it has two event parameters, number and messageText, which appear as orangish ovals within the when block. "number" is the phone number of the device from which the incoming text came, and messageText is the actual text of the message. The coder can click these parameters to access get blocks that use the event information. In the response code shown, a get number block is used both to set the phone number for the autoresponse and as part of the words spoken aloud by the TextToSpeech component.

▶ Watch out! Understand the Event Queue

As students create more complex projects that respond to multiple events, it is important they understand how events are processed. In most languages, events are placed in a queue as they occur. The program executes the entire event handler for the "current event" before moving on to the next one. The user interface is not updated and is "frozen" until all the code in the event handler is completed.

Consider the Scratch blocks shown in Figure 7:

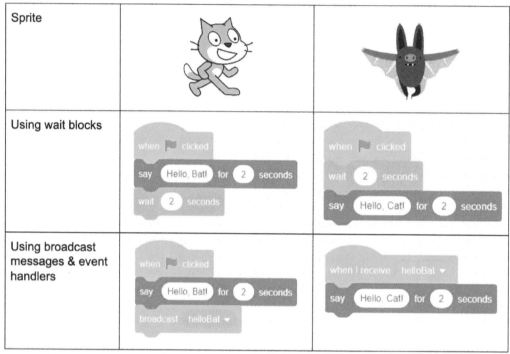

Figure 7. The same behavior in different ways with Scratch

TEACHING WITH EVENT-BASED LANGUAGES

Unlike most beginning Python or Java lessons and projects, event-driven projects start with designing the user interface, then determining the events that will trigger actions in the program and how the program should respond to each event. Here are a few tips and guidelines to aid the teaching process and scaffolding students' understanding of events.

1. **Encourage creativity in designing the user interface (UI).** Because work begins with the visual, students are able to connect their artistic and design interests with the world of code. The act of drawing, discovering media on the web, and graphically laying out the components is fun and motivating. Students aren't just learning to code; they're learning how to make their "pictures" interactive. This visual-first experience has been shown to motivate many art and design students to pursue computer science.

   It is important to give students time to be creative and explore designing user interfaces so that they develop an understanding of the options available. We encourage students to explore the extensive public galleries available and also assign scavenger hunt activities where students search for various components and behaviors within coding environments.

   > **Tip:** Be careful—students can get caught up in selecting/drawing images and styling if you don't provide time guidelines for them to move onto writing code.

2. **Paper prototyping.** Designing the UI can happen in the programming environment itself, or it can be planned out ahead of time on paper. Paper prototyping is especially helpful to use on days when computers are not available or when the UI is more complex. It also allows students to quickly share their project ideas and UIs and to gather feedback from classmates. Paper prototypes are often referred to as mock-ups or storyboards, and many templates are available online.

3. **Unplugged activities to explain events.** Helping students understand the events available, when you would want to use particular user interface components and events, and how to code the response to them is more challenging than the visual UI development. Unplugged activities are helpful for introducing students to the concept of events and event handlers. We've used activities such as *Simon Says* or this variation from Microsoft's Minecraft curriculum to help: https://minecraft.makecode.com/courses/csintro/events/unplugged-1.

4. **Alternative programming approaches.** Showing two versions of an application that uses event-based and non-event-based approaches for the same task can help students recognize and choose programming options. For example, in Scratch (Figure 7), one way to plan a conversation between two sprites is to use wait blocks and timing. Another way is to use broadcast messages, where a sprite can send a message out to all other sprites, who can then respond to that event handler when they receive the message.

5. **Event-based pseudocode.** Pseudocoding—designing the algorithms for a program prior to coding it—is an important technique for students to learn. Event-based languages don't have a single "recipe" broken down into parts. Instead they have multiple algorithms corresponding to each event that will be handled.

6. **Explore existing programs.** To scaffold students' abilities to plan event-driven programs, let them play with some existing programs and then deconstruct the user interface components, the events, and the algorithms for the event handlers. When they start a new program, try running a completed version for the students and then asking them to identify the UI components, events, and event-handler algorithms.

Event	Algorithm
`Texting1.MessageReceived`	1. Send the custom reply back to the sender of the text 2. Concatenate information from the text 3. Speak the text information aloud
`SubmitButton.Click`	2. Store the new message in the database
`Screen.Open`	1. Bring the custom message from the database

Figure 8. Listing events and algorithmic responses

Tip: When students are planning their own programs, ask guiding questions such as "How will the user know what to do?" or "How will the user tell the program to do X?" so that students can explain their thinking about the program events and event handlers. One step that students often forget is to make sure the UI provides feedback to the user once it has responded to an event.

The first step is thus to have students list all the events to which their program will respond. They can then write a phrase or sentence in pseudocode to describe what the response should be. Figure 8 provides an example from the Mobile CSP curriculum and includes an image of the UI with component types and a table of the corresponding event handlers and their algorithms for the *I Have a Dream* app, the first one they build in the course.

▶ Debugging and Usability Testing

Debugging a program that responds to multiple events is challenging. Because there is not a single thread of control, it is difficult to simulate events based on time or location or know if they're being triggered. For this reason, it is especially important to emphasize small code-test iterations and debugging techniques.

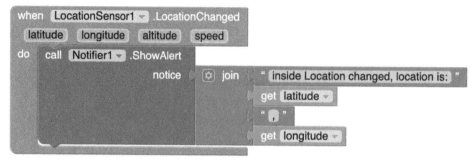

Figure 9. Use alerts to test if an event is being invoked

The beginner coder's favorite line is, of course, "It's not working." Emphasize the importance of rolling things back to determine what is happening, even going back to, "is the event even being triggered?" Encourage the age-old technique of temporarily adding `print` statements just for debugging, either by adding an extra label and setting the label's text or by using `Notifier` components like the one shown in Figure 9, which lets the programmer know the `LocationChanged` event has occurred and the value of the event parameters.

Because event-based languages allow beginners to create complete programs with user interfaces, you can also introduce them to usability testing, a crucial skill that is too often ignored in education. We require students to have others test their apps and model the "think-aloud" approach in which the tester talks as they navigate the app while the programmer remains silent (no matter how hard it is). Inevitably, students are amazed that the tester invokes events in a different order than they expected and often gets confused on how to proceed. They learn, however, how important early feedback loops are to any endeavor.

THINGS TO WATCH OUT FOR!

See the code snippet in Figure 10 from Code.org's AppLab. On first glance, you might expect this event handler to cause the sprite to move in an up-and-down motion on each click. When you run it, however, the sprite won't move at all when the click occurs. The reason is that the sprite's location property is changed internally, up 10, then down 10, but the user interface isn't updated until the entire event handler completes. The app's user sees no movement! It is important to show such examples to students to help them understand how events are dealt with internally.

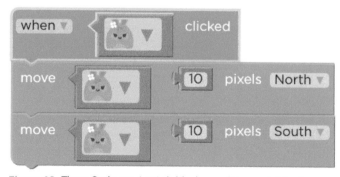

Figure 10. These Code.org AppLab blocks result in no visible change

It is also helpful to understand how each language's event model deals with multiple event handlers for a particular event. In Scratch and Code.org's Sprite Lab, programmers can create multiple event handlers for the same event (e.g., when green flag clicked), and they will all be executed in parallel. (This feature often leads to code fragmentation, which is not a desirable habit of programming—see **Chapter 25, Yay, My Program Works! Beyond Working Code...Developing Good Habits of Programming**). App Inventor and Thunkable do not allow more than one event handler for each event. In App Inventor, the blocks code will include a red "x" icon, indicating an error, in the event handler (Figure 11).

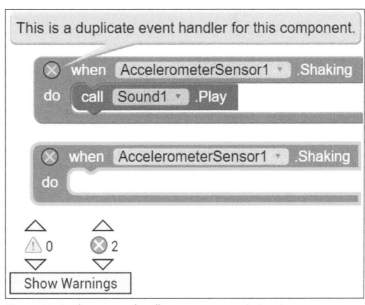

Figure 11. Duplicate event handlers cause an error in App Inventor

Understanding how the event processing works is key to helping students debug their programs. It is also a great exercise in understanding the behavior of a complex system.

BIBLIOGRAPHY

Hoffman, B., Morelli, R., & Rosato, J. (2019). Student engagement is key to broadening participation in CS. In *Proceedings of the 50th ACM Technical Symposium on Computer Science Education* (pp. 1123-–1129).

Turbak, F., Sherman, M., Martin, F., Wolber, D., & Pokress, S. C. (2014). Events-first programming in APP inventor. *Journal of Computing Sciences in Colleges*, 29(6), 81-–89.

Wolber, D. (2011). App inventor and real-world motivation. In *Proceedings of the 42nd ACM Technical Symposium On on Computer Computer Science Education* (pp. 601-–606).

Wolber, D., Abelson, H., & Friedman, M. (2015). Democratizing computing with app inventor. *GetMobile: Mobile Computing and Communications*, 18(4), 53-–58.

Feedback Through Formative Check-ins

Shuchi Grover, Vicky Sedgwick, & Kelly Powers

INTRODUCTION: WHAT AND WHY OF FORMATIVE FEEDBACK?

Formative feedback refers to formal and informal assessment moves or procedures that teachers employ in an effort to make inferences about what their students know and can do during their routine classroom learning. This is seen as assessment *for* learning (as opposed to assessment *of* learning, which is the more summative view of assessment). The overarching objective of the formative assessment process is not to assign a performance grade to a student but rather to supply reliable evidence to the teacher and student that could be used to enhance students' learning.

Computer science teachers can informally assess students in several ways, for example, a show of hands in response to a question; students' expressions of frustration, disengagement, or joy during a coding task; and informal conversations with students as they code and debug their programs. However, education literature makes the case for formal methods of feedback collection as well. Groundbreaking classroom research in the late 1990s by Paul Black and Dylan Wiliam showed that formative assessment in the classroom improves student learning.

Formative assessment is a process that involves both teachers and learners, and is characterized by the following:

1. When teachers implement formative assessment as a process in collaboration with their students, it can result in powerful learning,

2. Formative assessment as a process operates as a feedback loop and involves teachers making adjustments to their instruction based on evidence they collect while student learning is developing and providing students with feedback that helps them advance their learning, and

3. Students are equal stakeholders in the process and participate through peer and self-assessment.

Extending the idea elucidated in the third point above, a key part of the formative assessment process is the involvement of learners in the assessment process. In addition to peer and self-assessment, formative feedback to the learner (distinct from feedback to the

> The formative feedback loop is not complete until learners have clarity on gaps in their understanding—what they have and have not understood.

teacher) is essential.

Formative feedback benefits both the teacher and the student by making a student aware of what they need to work on and by making the teacher aware of adjustments (if necessary) to teaching activities and pacing. It alerts teachers to students' prior knowledge, as well as possible misconceptions. It lets teachers know which students have understood the ideas well and those who may need extra help or support in their learning. The teacher may infer from a quick autogradable quiz that most students did not understand how to construct nested conditionals, or they may discover through a short open-ended programming exercise what the students are passionate about outside of school. Formative assessments may also serve to reveal that students may have weak prior preparation in a topic in a related subject like mathematics that she had taken for granted and that may be impacting their ability to construct Boolean expressions that use arithmetic and relational operators.

> Peter Drucker famously said, **"What's measured improves."** Formative assessment allows teachers to see what students are thinking; this in turn helps them identify student difficulties. The ability to recognize and address errors in students' thinking through the use of formative assessment is extremely important in that one can improve only what one measures.

Brigid Barron and Linda Darling-Hammond assert in their book on project-based learning that robust assessments for deeper and meaningful learning must include "intellectually ambitious performance assessments" that define the tasks students will undertake in ways that allow them to learn and apply the desired concepts and skills in disciplined ways; "create guidance for students' efforts in the form of evaluation tools such as assignment guidelines and rubrics that define what constitutes good work"; and frequently use formative assessments to guide feedback to students and teachers' instructional decisions throughout the process.

TYPES OF FORMATIVE ASSESSMENT

Grover's work on assessments in introductory programming suggests that there needs to be multiple forms— or "systems"—of assessment to get a holistic and multifaceted view of student learning. Which assessments should be used when is a matter of choice for the teacher, where the class is in the learning schedule, what students might enjoy, the time available in a period or unit, the time taken (some forms are time-consuming to score whereas others provide near-instant feedback), the time available for the teacher (to grade and such), and modality (pen and paper, online, or in a programming environment). Table 1 details types of formative assessment with examples of various forms of each type as well as features and pros and cons of each type. The remainder of this chapter provides illustrative examples useful examples of each type.

Table 1. Types of formative assessment with examples, features, pros and cons

Assessment Type	Examples / Details
Programming Assignments • *Engaging and motivating* • *Usually time-consuming to score (and subjective)* • *Do not provide quick feedback* • *Must be accompanied with rubrics for teachers and students* *Modality: programming environment*	• Open-ended programming assignment • Open project with specific criteria • **Example 1: My Project** has at least two sprites engaging in a conversation. • **Example 2: My Project** uses blocks to change the appearance to match different backdrops in a story. • Closed-ended programming assignment with a desired end goal • Complete a partially coded programming project

continued on next page

Table 1. Types of formative assessment with examples, features, pros and cons *(continued)*

Assessment Type	Examples / Details

Quizzes: Multiple Choice (MC) & Fixed Answer
• *Usually autogradable*
• *Good for quick feedback on student understanding*
• *Can surface learner difficulties*
• *More test-like and not very engaging for students*
Modality: pen-paper or online
	• Present code snippets that require students to demonstrate code-comprehension skills. For example,
	  • A program with "fill-in-the-blank" slots (fixed response or options to choose from for the blanks)
	  • Analyzing and comparing programs
	  • Determining whether a piece of code meets its goal
	  • Multiple-choice options to fix a piece of buggy code
	  • Multiple-choice options for an expression for a conditional/loop
	• Present a programming requirement in text
	  • Multiple-choice options to pick the correct coding solution or aspects of the solution

Quizzes: Innovative Item Types • *Usually autogradable* • *Can surface learner difficulties* • *Good for quick feedback* • *More engaging than multiple-choice items* *Modality: pen-paper or online*	• Parson's problems or puzzles (rearranging provided code blocks or commands in correct sequence) • Hotspot items • Unit-tested coding (autograded) • Match options in two columns
Quizzes: Open Response Types • *Not autogradable* • *Provide good insights into learner understanding* • *Time-consuming and subjective to score* *Modality: pen-paper or online*	• Quizlike prompts involving code snippets that require open-ended responses probing for explanations or descriptions of what a code snippet does
Showcasing | Peer & Self Assessment • *Help assess collaboration and communication* • *Can be engaging as they involve the whole-class or peer groups* • *Usually time-consuming* *Modality: physical space; video/audio*	• Explanations - these could be written or oral or audio/video recorded that accompany students' code about their programming project • Show & Tell: project presentations to share various aspects of the project
Video/Audio Self Explanation & Reflection • *Aid reflection and ipsative assessment—assessment as learning* • *Time-consuming* *Modality: pen-paper or online*	• Reflective journals to track progress on a large project • Reflective prompts that reveal learner experience—thrills, frustrations & difficulties, collaboration; other aspects of learning
Artifact-based Interviews	• Conversation with teacher about a project

Giving students an assignment to code a project of choice comes with its own set of considerations as does administering a quiz at the start or end of a class period. For example, projects of choice are undoubtedly an authentic form of assessment that is well-suited to project-based learning. Many chapters in this book advocate programming to engage students' creativity through programming projects, and rightly so—they provide students an opportunity to be motivated and engaged and express their creativity in a way a multiple-choice quiz could never do. However, they are time-consuming as a formative assessment activity and even more so to score. Furthermore, scoring is subjective. Additionally, a finished project does not reveal whether a student got the program to work through "trial and error" or from borrowing a code snippet from a partner or some other program without deep understanding. However, a well-designed multiple-choice question can very quickly reveal whether a student understands a certain concept or not.

Multiple-choice questions need not be limited to tests of vocabulary, syntax, and other low-level "knowledge" questions but rather could and should target higher levels of Bloom's taxonomy (understand, apply, analyze evaluate, and create) through code snippets that require students to read/comprehend code to answer the question.

Ideally, a teacher will balance programming assignments with more objective assessment instruments that illuminate student understanding of specific computing concepts and other computational thinking (CT) skills such as debugging, code tracing, problem decomposition, and pattern generalization. Short, high-frequency, **low-stakes** autogradable quizzes help to keep learners aligned with the content and understanding goals of the course. The classroom culture should be such that they are seen not as "tests" for grading the student but as a means to provide feedback to both the student and the teacher.

Summative Feedback

Although this chapter is focused mainly on formative feedback, summative assessments should also be used to get a sense for how well students are able to coalesce all their learning over the course of a term. Many of the types of assessment described next can also serve the purpose of summative assessment. Final open-ended projects, artifact-based interviews, student reflections, student portfolios, and tests with a mix of multiple-choice and open-response items are other instruments for summatively measuring student learning.

EXAMPLES OF FORMATIVE ASSESSMENTS

▶ A. Informal Teacher Observation and Conversations With Students

A reliable way for a teacher to ascertain what students do and do not understand is through observation while they work on an assignment. It is often easy to spot their struggle with a concept, gauge their understanding and implementation. Teachers can also see whether students are developing sound debugging strategies. Paying attention to student conversations with peers is invaluable in providing insight into their understanding and ability to pose good questions and arguments. (See **Chapter 17** on what questions you can ask and how to respond to student questions.)

As teachers observe, they may pause to have short conversations with students. Having students show their code for a certain concept or explain a problem they just solved provides excellent opportunities for feedback. The observation and conversation time may be as short as, say 3–5 minutes, to check the pulse of the students.

It's important to have a way to record observations and conversations quickly, either on paper or digitally. You may then use the data you collected to inform future instruction both for students who need additional help and for those who are ready for additional challenges.

▶ B. Entry and Exit Tickets

Time is often a scarce resource in computer science classes. Learning a concept may extend over multiple classes with a week between classes. Using quick check-ins at the beginning or end of classes can be helpful. With primary students (grades K–2), exit tickets may be as simple as choosing an emoji or a picture of faces showing emotions to indicate if they think they understood the lesson (smile, neutral, frown). For older students, an exit ticket typically includes a question that will help to identify if the student understood the content for the day and may also include their opinion of how the day went for them. For the former, ideas from Section C—Quizzes—can be used to keep the exit ticket to about 5 minutes at the end of class and are also useful for quick feedback. Google Forms or assessment platforms (such as Edfinity.com) are good ways to collect this information. The information collected needs to be minimal, so it is easy to sort the answers into three main categories—didn't get it, sort of got it, got it—so students needing help can get further instruction.

▶ C. Quizzes: Easy to Grade; Provide Quick Feedback

▶ Multiple-Choice Quizzes

Well-designed multiple-choice quizzes can be powerful mechanisms that provide quick feedback and can also probe student understanding. Teachers can measure different types of knowledge and understanding through multiple-choice questions: knowledge of terminology and syntax, code comprehension, conceptual understanding of how foundational constructs (like loops, conditionals, or variables) work, identifying and proposing a fix for a bug, and code comparison for accuracy and efficiency.

1. Multiple-choice questions that don't measure deep understanding but check to see if students have learned the terminology or syntax you just introduced.

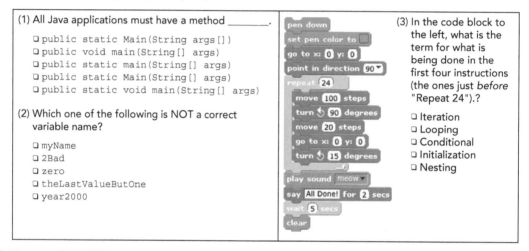

2. Which one of the following is NOT a correct variable name?

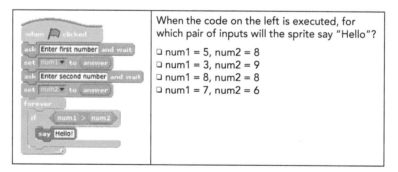

3. The following multiple-choice question revealed misconceptions about students' understanding of how variables work, and when they are (or are not) updated. In Grover's research (2014), a majority of students answered C.

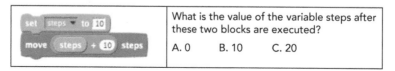

4. Multiple-choice question to locate bug and debug code.

Raul wants to make a timer that will count down from 30 to 0. Raul has written the following code using a time variable:	(1) Will Raul's code work as desired? Yes / No (2) In Raul's code, will the Repeat Until loop ever stop (i.e., will the "time=0" condition ever be satisfied?)? Yes / No (3) If you had to change *just one thing* to fix the bug, what would you change? ❑ The `Set` time block ❑ The `Repeat Until` "time=0" condition ❑ The `wait` block ❑ The `change` time by block ❑ The `stop all` block

when ⚑ clicked
set time ▾ to 30
repeat until (time = 0)
  wait 1 secs
  change time ▾ by 1
stop all ◯

▶ Innovative Autogradable Technology-Enhanced Assessments

Thanks to the affordances of technology, new types of assessment can also be autograded for quick feedback. Emergent assessment platforms such as Edfinity (edfinity.com) allow for a growing number of new assessment types beyond multiple choice or multiple answer or fixed response that make assessment more interesting but at the same time provide quick feedback to the teacher and learners. Such platforms also allow for explanations or detailed descriptions of solutions that help the learners understand why their response was incorrect (or even if it was correct) and allow for multiple attempts to a problem by the student.

1. **Parsons Problems: Rearranging Given Blocks of Code**

   A Parsons problem is where code statements or algorithm steps is given to the pupil, and they have to rearrange it into the right order. These can be used early in the learning process when students are uncomfortable starting with a blank slate to write code. In Figure 1a, students are given a Parsons puzzle of an algorithm that helps them come to grips with assigning values to variables and interacting with multiple variables. Parsons puzzles are also popular in interactive textbooks involving text-based programming used in high school and postsecondary classrooms (Figure 1b).

   Parsons problems can also be used within block-based programming languages, asking pupils to rearrange blocks of code to complete a project.

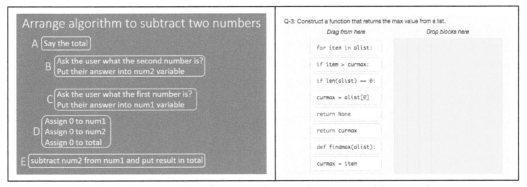

Figure 1 (a). Algorithmic Parsons problem for younger learners; b) Parsons problem in Python (source: Runestone Interactive)

2. Hotspot and Point-and-Click Items

Figures 2a and 2b show examples of problems that measure code comprehension through requiring students to click or select parts of code that answer the question.

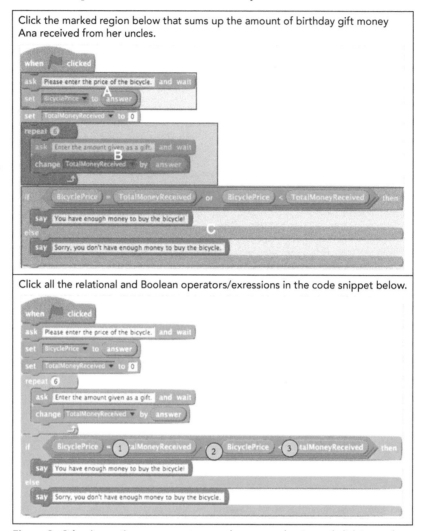

Figure 2a & b. . Innovative assessments types: hotspot and point-and-click items that measure students code comprehension

3. Unit-Test Coding Assessments

These assessment types require students to enter code snippets that are then tested and autograded (Figure 3). They also show students the correct solution.

```
Go          ...Save, Compile, Run (ctrl-enter)      Show Solution

def monkey_trouble(a_smile, b_smile):
    if (a_smile and b_smile):
        return True
    if (not a_smile and not b_smile):
        return True
    return False
```

Figure 3. Unit-test coding example

4. Quizzes With Open-Response Items

These are similar to multiple-choice quizzes but require an open response that may include explanations for their answer, as shown in Figure 4. Such items are time-consuming and subjective to score, even with a rubric.

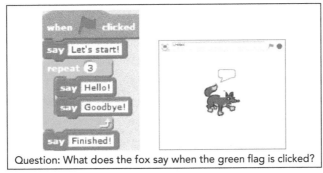

Question: What does the fox say when the green flag is clicked?

Figure 4. Example of an open-response item

▶ D. Programming Assignments and Projects

Programming assignments require actual programming, but they can come in various forms, as described in Table 1. They could be completely open ended or open projects that combine choice but with constraints, such as requiring the use of a specific construct (*"Code a game in Scratch that uses one or more variables and a* repeat until *loop"*). They could have an end goal that is specified but provide flexibility in terms of added features. Students could be given *partially coded program*s to complete or asked to *debug buggy programs*. See the fairy assessment in Alice (Figure 5) for examples of these two types. Next, we discuss ways to guide and assess student work in an open-ended project with constraints.

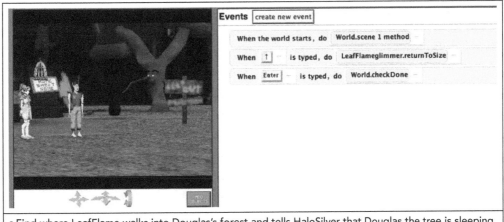

- Find where LeafFlame walks into Douglas's forest and tells HaloSilver that Douglas the tree is sleeping and won't bother them.
- Make HaloSilver's body turn to face Douglas the tree at the same time that LeafFlame walks into Douglas's forest and talks to HaloSilver.
- Make HaloSilver's turn take as long as LeafFlame is talking.
- Fix the other things as instructed by LeafFlame and HaloSilver when you run the program.

Figure 5. Fairy assessment in *Alice* requiring code completion and bug fixing

▶ Scaffolds and Assessment Measures

This is an example that Powers and colleagues designed and used in New York City schools. The goal was to use everything students had been learning to create an integrated project about a story that they enjoyed reading during the past year. Students designed the next chapter of their story with a partner to infuse their own creativity in this project. They planned on paper, chose sprites, created sequences using code blocks, and created code using events and parallelism. Students then shared their animations with teachers and parents during a project showcase. Students completed checklists (Table 2) and student reflection questions, received peer feedback (Table 3), and used a rubric to guide their performance (Table 4). Projects were shared to the Class Studio in Scratch for students to comment on and share with the community.

Table 2. Project phases and planning checklist for students

Unit 5: ELA Integration With Scratch	
Part 1: Decomposition Day (Planning)	❑ Pick a book ❑ Outline characters ❑ Choose setting ❑ Sequence of events
Scene 1: Building	❑ Choose main sprites ❑ Choose your first background ❑ Code sprites to start on your first background and first costume ❑ Code changing sprites costumes ❑ Add messaging (broadcasting and receiving messages, wait blocks)
Scene 2: Building	❑ Choose any new sprites you need in this scene ❑ Choose your second background ❑ Continue to add messaging (broadcasting and receiving messages, wait blocks)
Self-Evaluation	❑ Run your project to look for bugs! ❑ Use the hide/show blocks for any sprites that do not need to be in all scenes ❑ "Clean up" your code— trash unused blocks ❑ Debug as you work!
Peer Feedback	❑ Give 2 stars and a wish to at least one other project
Revising/Editing	❑ Use what your partner said to improve your project
Catch-Up or Scene 3 (Spicy!)	❑ Finish your project ❑ Add another scene
Showcase	❑ Present your project
Self-Reflection	❑ Respond to prompts about your project and CT

Questions for Student Reflection

1. What are you most **proud** of about **creating** your project?

2. What was the most challenging part of building your project? How did you **persevere** and overcome this challenge?

3. Did you have to **debug** any issues in your project? How did you spot the bug, and what did you do to fix it?

4. How was telling a story in **Scratch** similar to writing a story on paper? How was it different?

5. Did you like using Scratch to publish your next chapter or scene? Why or why not?

6. How were you able to use **peer feedback** to help you modify your project?

Which one of these thinking skills did you use the most in your project: **logic, evaluation, algorithms, patterns, decomposition, abstraction?** How?

Table 3. Peer Feedback Form

Scene 1:
❑ It is clear what my partner's book is.
❑ There are two main sprites (characters).
❑ The backdrop matches the setting.
❑ There is dialogue between the characters.
❑ The code runs smoothly (no bugs).

Scene 2:
❑ The backdrop changes in Scene 2.
❑ The sprites (characters) continue their dialogue.
❑ The program switches backdrops and sprite costumes without bugs.

Evaluation
❑ The sequence of events makes sense.
❑ There are no bugs when I run the program.
❑ Hide/show blocks are used for sprites that don't belong in the scenes.
❑ The code is "cleaned up"— there are no unused blocks.

Written Feedback: *Then you can add your feedback on their project page!

  Two Stars   Wish

Table 4. Student performance rubric

Project	4 Exceptional	3 Proficient	2 Developing	1 Beginning
Sprites (*ELA 3.3)	I used at least 3 sprites in my program and had multiple costume changes and detailed dialogue.	I used at least 2 sprites and had costume changes and dialogue.	I used at least 2 sprites and attempted costume changes and dialogue.	I am still working on adding sprites that change costumes and have dialogue.
Backdrops	I used more than 2 backdrops and coded them to change efficiently during the program.	I used at least 2 backdrops and coded them to change during the program.	I used 2 backdrops and attempted to code them to change during the program.	I have 1 or no backdrops and am working on coding them to change during my program.
Sequence of Events (*ELA 3.3)	I continued a story from third grade using Scratch. My story has a logical and creative sequence of events.	I continued a story from third grade using Scratch. My story has a logical sequence of events.	I attempted to continue a story from third grade and tried to create a logical sequence of events.	I am still working on creating a logical sequence of events based on a book I've read.
Time Management	I finished all of my project before the end of class time and used the extra time to make improvements.	I used project time well and met all deadlines.	Sometimes I was able to meet deadlines.	I need to find new ways to complete my tasks to meet deadlines.
Reflection	In my reflection and showcase, I clearly express my thoughts in different ways about the questions I am asked.	In my reflection and showcase, I express my thoughts about the questions I am asked.	In my reflection and showcase, I answer the questions I am asked.	With help, I answer the questions I am asked in my reflection and showcase.

▶ E. Code Reviews and Project Showcases

Programming classrooms are collaborative spaces where students work individually or in pairs or small groups to create computational artifacts that are often driven by student choice and interest. Being able to "show and tell" or share their creations to the rest of the class is a great opportunity for teachers to get a sense of not only student engagement, motivation, and creativity but also how well students collaborated and how they communicate their programming efforts to other students. Such a code review is an opportunity for students to explain the goals of their project and explain to their peers how they accomplished their goal. Students should be encouraged to step into the code to show key parts of their programs and also share what bugs they encountered and what moves fixed the code. Such an activity can be guided by checklists and prompts (Tables 2 and 3; Figure 6) to encourage students to pay attention and learn from the experience.

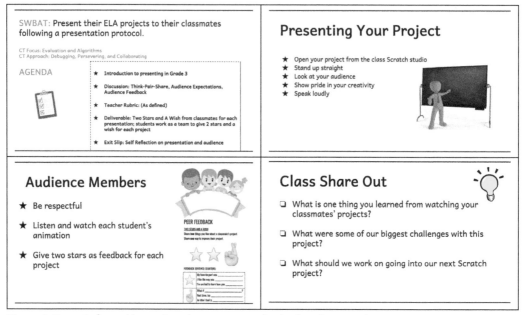

Figure 6. Prompts for making project showcases a productive learning experience

While code reviews are beneficial, they are not imperative for every programming project as they are time-consuming (especially compared to quizzes and entry/exit tickets). Although demos and code reviews could assume the form of one-on-one reviews with teachers, there are other options that Sedgwick has successfully used.

- **Video:** Students can record a video of their programming project that includes them showing and explaining their code or a portion of their code. Students could also create tutorials for other students.

- **Code Documentation:** Students can copy their code into Google Slides or other presentation software, and then document what it does (Figure 7).

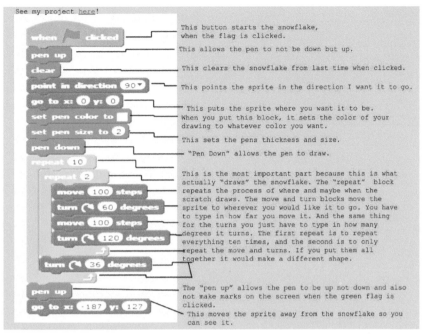

See my project here!

This button starts the snowflake, when the flag is clicked.

This allows the pen to not be down but up.

This clears the snowflake from last time when clicked.

This points the sprite in the direction I want it to go.

This puts the sprite where you want it to be. When you put this block, it sets the color of your drawing to whatever color you want.

This sets the pens thickness and size.

"Pen Down" allows the pen to draw.

This is the most important part because this is what actually "draws" the snowflake. The "repeat" block repeats the process of where and maybe when the scratch draws. The move and turn blocks move the sprite to wherever you would like it to go. You have to type in how far you move it. And the same thing for the turns you just have to type in how many degrees it turns. The first repeat is to repeat everything ten times, and the second is to only repeat the move and turns. If you put them all together it would make a different shape.

The "pen up" allows the pen to be up not down and also not make marks on the screen when the green flag is clicked.

This moves the sprite away from the snowflake so you can see it.

Figure 7. Code documentation example showing detailed comments describing the code

▶ F. Artifact-Based Interviews (ABIs)

Artifact-based interviews, first used by Brigid Barron and her colleagues in 2002, have been invaluable in eliciting student explanations by cueing student memory and perspectives using students' own projects. Teachers can use ABIs to ask students to explain the goal of the project and they got there or to justify their choices by asking questions, such as "How do you know?" "How did you decide?" and "Why do you believe that?" ABIs questions can also be part of the process of summative reflection on the entire class and experience. For example,

- How did you decide on your project?
- What does it do? How did you go about coding your project?
- What was it like working on this project? (Offer suggestions such as *fun, challenging, difficult, creative,* or *boring.*)
- Overall, how did you feel about this course?
- How does it feel to know more about computer science?
- Thinking back on the course, what did you enjoy the most? What was the hardest part?

▶ G. Peer and Self-Assessment

Students in a programming classroom should be encouraged to provide feedback to each other and also assess each other's as well as their own work. However, it is important that they be guided by well-designed rubrics to support them in the process of peer and self-assessment. Tables 2 and 3 are examples of these. Figure 8 is an example from Sedgwick's work of a rubric that can be used of self or peer-assessment for a Scratch mathematics game programming project. Rubric elements can also be tied to standards such as CSTA standards for computer science.

1 = Not met   2 = Partially met   3 = Met   4 = Exceeds expectations

Criteria	1	2	3	4	Feedback
Project has an engaging theme with sprites and backdrops that support the theme.					
Project uses a loop to ask player mathematics questions. *CSTA Standard: 1B-AP-10 Create programs that include sequences, events, loops, and conditionals*					
Project uses conditionals to check if the player answered the mathematics question correctly and notifies player if the answer is correct or not correct. *CSTA Standard: 1B-AP-10 Create programs that include sequences, events, loops, and conditionals.*					
Project uses appropriately named variables to store random numbers for the multiplicand and multiplier (if multiplication game) or the addends (if addition game) and uses the variables to ask the player mathematics questions. *CSTA Standard: 1B-AP-09 Create programs that use variables to store and modify data.*					
Project was tested and runs correctly. *CSTA Standard: 1B-AP-15 Test and debug a program or algorithm to ensure it runs as intended.*					
Project uses conditionals to check if the player answered the mathematics question correctly and notifies player if the answer is correct or not correct. *CSTA Standard: 1B-AP-10 Create programs that include sequences, events, loops, and conditionals.*					
Project uses appropriately named variables to store random numbers for the multiplicand and multiplier (if a multiplication game) or the addends (if an addition game) and uses variables to ask the player mathematics questions. *CSTA Standard: 1B-AP-09 Create programs that use variables to store and modify data.*					

Figure 8. Code documentation example showing detailed comments describing the code

▶ H. Reflection Journals in Project-Based Programming

Classrooms where learning of programming is centered on creating projects over several days or weeks (such as the one described in **Chapter 8** on project-based constructionist learning), formative feedback tools include

- A checklist to understand a student's status on a project - this allows teachers to note if progress has stalled.
- Checkpoints that allow the teacher to review projects at designated junctures.
- Design notebooks, where students record plans, document the progress of a project, and reflect on things that went well or problems that arose in making their projects. Getting students to record their progress and reflect in short (5-minute) daily entries at the end of the day (like an exit ticket) in response to prompts such as "What went well today?" "What problem(s) came up?" or "What is a tip or trick you would suggest to another student doing this project?" are useful.

Reflection questions around code are ipsative or "assessment as learning." Students can also be prompted to add summative reflections about their final project. For example

- How is this project similar to or different from previous projects?
- What new code or tools did I add to this project that I hadn't used before?
- How can I use what I learned in this class in future projects?
- What questions do I have about coding that I'd like to explore next time

READINGS AND RESEARCH

Ever since the Black and Wiliam's (1998) landmark study on the benefits of formative assessment and feedback for learning, the emphasis on the integration of assessment and instruction has grown, with the goal of seamlessly combining teaching with an ongoing analysis of student progress toward instructional goals (Heritage, 2007). Bloom's taxonomy (Figure 9) provides a useful framework to think about various forms of activities and assessments in a classroom and how to aim activities at various levels of skill and thinking. The SOLO taxonomy by Biggs and Collins has also been found to be useful in designing assessments for programming (Lister et al., 2006).

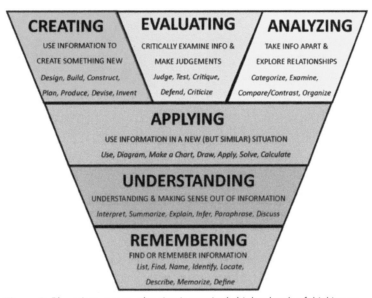

Figure 9. Bloom's taxonomy showing increasingly higher levels of thinking as you move up (Source: The Derek Bok Center for Teaching & Learning, Harvard University)

Well-designed multiple-choice assessments can be used to further learners' understanding, provide feedback, and keep the learners engaged in activities such as reading code that are as crucial a skill as writing code in building understanding of algorithmic thinking (Lister, Fidge, & Teague, 2009). Many of the multiple-choice assessment examples described in this chapter are drawn from Grover's dissertation research (Grover, 2014). These assessments aimed to help learners develop familiarity with code tracing and the ability to understand an algorithm (Lopez, Whalley, Robbins, & Lister, 2008). Some formative assessments also involved Parsons problems (Parsons & Haden, 2006; Denny, Luxton-Reilly, & Simon, 2008) created in Scratch where students were presented jumbled blocks required for a program that they were required to snap together in the correct order. In addition, they were given closed- and open-ended projects in Scratch. The latter provided students authentic means of showcasing their learning through projects that were personally meaningful. Open-ended projects can also provide several insights—in the aggregate—to the teacher on the types of projects students tend to create and what basic and advanced constructs they are comfortable using (Grover, Basu, & Schank, 2018).

You can read about artifact-based interviews in Barron et al. (2002), Grover (2017), and O'Leary (2019). O'Leary (2019) also describes how to implement ipsative assessments, or assessments as learning.

Assessment platforms such as **Edfinity** (edfinity.com), which Grover is using in her current research, provide features for autograding assessments, adding explanations (in addition to the correct solution) that students could read after submitting their answer, and providing multiple attempts for an incorrect answer. These platforms also enable the designing of innovative assessments such as Parsons problems, which are becoming increasingly popular in introductory programming settings, thanks to research about their benefits (e.g., Ericson et al., 2017).

BIBLIOGRAPHY

Barron, B., & Daring-Hammond, L. (2008). How can we teach for meaningful learning? In L. Daring-Hammond, B. Barron, P. D. Pearson, A. H. Schoenfeld, E. K. Stage, T. D. Zimmerman, G. N. Cervetti, & J. L. Tilson (Eds.), *Powerful learning: What we know about teaching for understanding.* Jossey-Bass.

Barron, B., Martin, C., Roberts, E., Osipovich, A., & Ross, M. (2002). Assisting and assessing the development of technological fluencies: Insights from a project-based approach to teaching computer science. In *Proceedings of The Fifth International Conference of the Learning Sciences* (pp. 668-669). ISLS.

Biggs, J. B., & Collis, K. F. (1982). *Evaluating the quality of learning: The SOLO taxonomy (Structure of the Observed Learning Outcome).* Academic Press.

Black, P., & Wiliam, D. (1998). *Assessment and classroom learning. Assessment in Education: Principles, Policy & Practice,* 5(1), 7—74.

Denny, P., Luxton-Reilly, A., & Simon, B. (2008, September). Evaluating a new exam question: Parsons problems. In *Proceedings of the Fourth International Workshop on Computing Education Research* (pp. 113—124). ACM.

Ericson, B. J., Margulieux, L. E., & Rick, J. (2017, November). Solving Parsons problems versus fixing and writing code. In *Proceedings of the 17th Koli Calling International Conference on Computing Education Research* (pp. 20–29).

Grover, S. (2017). Assessing algorithmic and computational thinking in K–12: Lessons from a middle school classroom. In *Emerging research, practice, and policy on computational thinking* (pp. 269–288). Springer International Publishing.

Grover. S. (2014). Foundations for advancing computational thinking: Balanced designs for deeper learning in an online computer science course for middle school students. *Stanford University.*

Grover, S., Basu, S., & Schank, P. (2018, February). What we can learn about student learning from open-ended programming projects in middle school computer science. In *Proceedings of the 49th ACM Technical Symposium on Computer Science Education* (pp. 999–1004).

Grover, S., Pea, R., & Cooper, S. (2015a). "Systems of assessments" for deeper learning of computational thinking in K–12. *Presented at the annual meeting of the American Educational Research Association,* Chicago, IL.

Heritage, M. (2007). Formative assessment: What do teachers need to know and do?. *Phi Delta Kappan,* 89(2), 140–145.

Lister, R., Simon, B., Thompson, E., Whalley, J. L., & Prasad, C. (2006). Not seeing the forest for the trees: novice programmers and the SOLO taxonomy. *ACM SIGCSE Bulletin, 38*(3), 118-122.

Lopez, M., Whalley, J., Robbins, P., & Lister, R. (2008). Relationships between reading, tracing and writing skills in introductory programming. In *Proceedings of the Fourth international Workshop on Computing Education Research* (pp. 101–112). ACM.

Moskal, B., Lurie, D., & Cooper, S. (2004). Evaluating the effectiveness of a new instructional approach. *ACM SIGCSE Bulletin, 36*(1), 75–79.

O'Leary, J. (2019). Introduction to ipsative assessment. Retrieved from https://jaredoleary.com/presentations/introduction-to-ipsative-assessment.

Parsons, D., & Haden, P. (2006). Parson's programming puzzles: A fun and effective learning tool for first programming courses. In *Proceedings of the 8th Australasian Conference on Computing Education* (Vol. 52, pp. 157–163). Australian Computer Society.

Werner, L., Denner, J., Campe, S., & Kawamoto, D. C. (2012). The fairy performance assessment: Measuring computational thinking in middle school. In *Proceedings of the 43rd ACM Technical Symposium on Computer Science Education (SIGCSE '12)* (pp. 215–220). ACM.

Guided Exploration Through Unplugged Activities

Paul Curzon & Shuchi Grover

WHAT IS GUIDED EXPLORATION?

The tendency in introductory programming classrooms today is often to have students jump into coding right away thanks to the "low floor" feature of block-based environments like Scratch, Snap!, and others, which make it possible to create simple working programs quite literally in a snap! Exploration and discovery learning have been shown to offer many benefits, such as affording students more agency in the learning process and stimulating metacognitive activities, such as hypothesis testing. However, researchers have also noted limitations of unstructured exploration or discovery learning in several contexts. This includes and especially applies to introductory programming. For example, if learners are given too much freedom, they may fail to encounter programming concepts that they must grasp and understand. For this reason, it is important to supplement exploratory learning with guidance that helps focus learners' cognitive and behavioral activities in productive directions. Additionally, even though guided exploration typically adds structure and sequence to the activity, in the spirit of "exploration," errors are framed as a positive step in the process of building an understanding of the ideas in question—they are encouraged and used as a stepping-stone to better understanding.

One approach to guided exploration of programming concepts is to use "unplugged" activities—away from the computer and programming environments. Such unplugged and non-programming activities have a rich history in helping learners engage with programming concepts. They provide a powerful way to gain a deep understanding of the concepts being explored. They make intangible, invisible programming semantics visible and manipulatable and give ways for students to ask questions about the things they do not understand, even before they have acquired the technical language to do so.

> Tell me and I forget. Teach me and I remember. Involve me and I learn.
> – Benjamin Franklin

WHY GUIDED EXPLORATION?

Decades of research have documented novice learners' difficulties in learning to program. At a broad level, learning to program involves acquiring syntactic, conceptual (or semantic), and strategic (or pragmatic) knowledge.

- **Syntactic knowledge** refers to knowledge of the programming language or environment and its syntax: the symbols and grammar needed to express a particular computational idea in a particular language. It is concerned with keywords, brackets, semicolons, and the like and how they legally combine to make a valid program.

- **Conceptual knowledge** refers to an understanding of concepts (such as loops, variables, expressions, and conditionals). It also includes the principles of programming that require novices to develop proper mental models of how a program executes, including its control flow.
- **Strategic knowledge** refers to knowing how to use syntactic and conceptual knowledge to generate, interpret, and debug programs.

Some of the most significant problems with learning to program pertain to conceptual knowledge and result from weak conceptual understanding of programs and programming. Unguided learning can introduce this knowledge but, given their complexity, can do so in a patchy and shallow way, with the student having no way to recognize the critical things they do not know.

Learners today typically enter programming through block-based languages. These make it easier to create executable code than do text-based coding environments because block-fitting allows for a more graphical and iconic, rather than lexical and symbolic, treatment of syntactical requirements. This method reduces the cognitive overhead of syntax and the frequency of syntax errors. However, understanding conceptual aspects of programming—whether block- or text-based—remains a complex activity that novices find difficult. Learners' difficulties are often attributed to weak or incorrect mental models that result in poor understanding and misconceptions of foundational computer science (CS) concepts. For example, an assignment could work in many different ways (and in different languages and contexts): From attaching a label to a value to aliasing through references, they could also work right to left or left to right, be like mathematical equality, and so on. If the student comes to believe the wrong model for the language through early examples or previous understanding of symbols like "=" in mathematics, then they can think they understand but suddenly find nothing is as it seems and become lost, never to recover. These issues have been discussed extensively in **Chapter 14, Naïve Conceptions of Novice Programmers**. Waite and Grover share strategies in **Chapter 23, Worked Examples and Other Scaffolding Strategies** for scaffolding the technical learning while working with actual programs and programming in programming languages and environments. Here we focus on the use of unplugged and related guided methods to help students quickly form the right mental models from the outset and in a way that complements exploratory learning.

▶ Why Use Unplugged Approaches for Guided Exploration?

Falling into the trap of focusing programming learning activity on technical language and meanings is easy—programming is, after all, a technical skill based on formal languages. Scaffolding students to understand the underlying concepts thoroughly is equally, if not more, important. To do this effectively, and in the constructivist tradition, we need to link the abstract ideas to concrete everyday context and language the student is already familiar with. Karl Maton's *Legitimation Code Theory*, which is being used widely to shape knowledge-building research and practice in education, sociology and linguistics, shows why this is important and offers a framework of how to do it well. In particular, the theory, and especially its dimension of semantics (in the general rather than computer science sense), stresses the importance of considering what are called *semantic density* and *semantic gravity*.

Semantic density is concerned with the complexity of meaning within the language used in explanations and activities: how technical is the language used? A proficient programmer can talk (and code) using technical language in precise and accurate ways. For a novice, using the technical language is difficult—this is what they are aiming to learn. *Semantic gravity* is concerned with the use of linguistic abstraction and context: how concrete are the explanations and activities in the sense of being linked to the student's existing knowledge and experience? For a proficient programmer, for example, the level of abstraction they can cope with when learning new languages is high. For a novice, however, the language and experiences must be embedded in the everyday knowledge they have outside of programming.

Figure 1 shows semantic density and semantic gravity as two axes of a plane with four quadrants. If we teach wholly in the top-right quadrant of Figure 1, which is natural for novice teachers, then learners new to programming can struggle to learn concepts deeply. Often the pedagogy espoused by creators of easy-to-use block-based programming languages lives in this region, and pure exploratory learning takes place there. In contrast, the bottom-left quadrant involves using everyday language and everyday concepts. It explains concepts using metaphors, analogies, and everyday examples. If we teach totally in this quadrant, without a link to the technical abstract concepts, the students understand everything presented but learn little of the subject matter that is the real focus. They will understand everything we say about recipes, say, but learn nothing about programs in the process.

Good teaching involves taking students on a journey back and forth between these two quadrants.

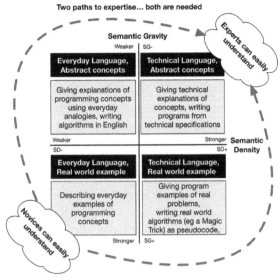

Figure 1. Quadrants based on semantic gravity and density showing potential routes to learning. (Adapted from Maton (2013) to apply to programming).

Examples in this chapter demonstrate how to scaffold students from the bottom-left of possessing only nontechnical language and understanding only everyday language to one where they have mastery of both technical language and concepts: the syntax and semantics of the language and the surrounding terminology. Students will learn nothing of the actual programming concepts if we work in the everyday quadrant alone. Therefore, we need to create a bridge from the everyday things to the technical language and concepts in the programming environment explicitly. The diagram suggests two different ways to do this, via real-world examples but using technical language, and via abstract concepts but using everyday language. Both ways are needed for effective mastery of concepts.

Effective learning is about taking students from the bottom left to top right of the diagram in what Maton called a semantic wave. Wide-ranging experience with Legitimation Code Theory in other disciplines suggests that following this wave pattern, as in Figure 2, is a strong way to structure learning sessions. Here, we start in the top-right

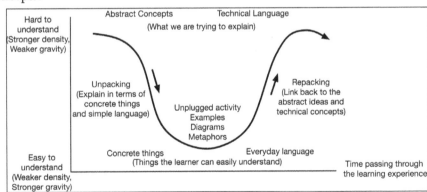

Figure 2. Traversing a semantic wave (adapted from Maton [2013])

quadrant introducing the concepts that are the learning outcomes for the session to make clear what it is that we are learning. This may be done by just introducing the learning outcomes or in a more staged way. However, we then use both everyday examples and non-technical language to explain those concepts (descending the semantic wave). Finally, we explicitly link those examples back to the technical, abstract things we really want the learners to understand. This is likely best done gradually, repacking the concepts a step at a time and following yet more smaller semantic waves. It is also best if the students are actively doing the repacking, rather than the teacher. with students just passive observers.

Applying this theory to programming suggests that to give deep conceptual understanding linked to terminology, we need to focus not only on technical language and meanings—in the way code reading, tracing, and coding activities do—if we are to help novices to program (as explained in **Chapters 14 and 23**) but also on activities that make links from everyday experience and in everyday language. Being closer to existing student experience, these activities are a sensible place to start and then work toward building the more technical language on top of the concepts highlighted (and traversing the quadrant the other way). You can link programming concepts to everyday experience in various ways, including using metaphors, analogies and similes, physical (unplugged) activities, writing activities, and storytelling.

EXAMPLES OF GUIDED EXPLORATION WITH UNPLUGGED ACTIVITIES

In this section, we describe generic ideas such as storytelling, role-play, puzzles, and use of metaphors and also include descriptions of some specific unplugged activities that can be used to introduce topics such as variables, conditionals, logical operators, and expressions.

▶ Role-Play Activities

One way to follow a semantic wave is to use unplugged activities that role-play the computation as a program executes. For example, deeply understanding how sequences of assignments work is a vital early step in learning to program. A simple metaphor of variables as boxes is fine as a first step but it can lead to misconceptions because it is too simplistic and conjures incorrect mental models. Instead, a more accurate metaphor developed by Curzon's research group in the UK is the "*Box variable*" activity. Here, variables are special storage boxes with integral copiers and shredders. This setup allows one to avoid or overturn common misconceptions such as that the data are moved rather than copied and that variables can hold multiple values when in fact they hold single values. When the box is accessed, the photocopier passes out a copy of what is stored. When something new is assigned to the box, the shredder automatically shreds what was there before.

This activity provides many hooks to repack directly to the parts of the technical meaning of how assignment works. Rather than just explaining this metaphor, it can be done with more power as an unplugged demonstration or physical role-play with students acting as the variables while holding boxes. A program such as simple swap code can be used as the computation to execute to ensure all students do have a correct mental model before they do hands-on programming or after exploratory learning with existing programs.

This kind of role-play demonstration of computation is powerful because it allows students to easily explore the concepts and ask questions at the bottom of the semantic wave (e.g., by pointing at people or role-play objects and asking "what happens if she . . ." or "what is he doing?"). The key to making this work is to forge repacking links that connect what the students have seen in the everyday, physical example to what the program it simulates is doing. It is not done as an exercise in moving things between boxes but as an illustration of the program executing. This means it is important that the teacher constantly refers back to the code as they step through the activity. Doing this essentially involves traversing a whole series of minor semantic waves within the bigger one. This repacking can be taken further by having students do the role-play on other examples in groups. This could lead directly to trace exercises where boxes are used but the "boxes" are pictures— that later leads to the refinement of trace tables with columns instead of boxes. At this point, the students are traversing the quadrants via the other route, having switched to the technical language of programs, but with the examples still linked to the everyday ideas of things being copied between boxes.

To work well, it is vital that unplugged activities like this are directly related to actual code and linked to direct activities such as tracing to allow for repacking of the concepts and so rising up the semantic wave.

Role-playing activities have other advantages in addition to the way they help traverse semantic waves. They can also be very theatrical, and so memorable from one session to another, and therefore provide hooks to refer back to in future sessions. Later descents of semantic waves to explain topics building on earlier ones can refer back to the now shared and memorable experience of the activity. This acts as a foundation to build on when referring to the technical ideas and language of the earlier lesson.

▶ Memorable Stories

Stories and parables add an extra level of memorability, especially if they use storytelling techniques such as having a human dimension, using twists, and so on. They strengthen the everyday context. For example, a story we use to teach divide-and-conquer approaches to programming—specifically, search algorithms—concerns how to help someone who is suffering from locked-in syndrome to communicate. They are totally paralyzed except perhaps for blinking, so cannot speak, but their intelligence is unaffected. A detailed description of this activity can be found in Curzon and McOwan's book *The Power of Computational Thinking*. The story of Jean-Dominique Bauby focuses on how he wrote his autobiography with locked-in syndrome. To write the book, his helper talked through the alphabet and then he blinked at the next letter. This is *linear search*. Having explained this, in the session, a divide-and-conquer algorithm of having the alphabet is then explored, showing how it could be done with far fewer letters spoken (five per letter communicated at worst). After the class agreed this would be a big improvement, however, there is a twist in the story. The new algorithm is fewer letters spoken by the helper but five times more blinks for Bauby. If blinking is hard, we've made communicating harder for him. We should have found out first. The storytelling structure also contains within it a short, unplugged role-play activity and a game (see the next section). It follows a series of semantic waves throughout the storytelling and is a good illustration of how to combine these approaches to make storytelling participative and active.

▶ Games and Puzzles

▶ 20 Questions for Divide and Conquer and Binary Search

Games and puzzles can be used effectively to provide everyday context. For example, to explore why divide and conquer is so much better than straightforward algorithms as part of the above locked-in syndrome story, we play a game of 20 questions. During the game, the students think about what makes a good or bad question. We are here using the game as an everyday context and using everyday language to describe it. Following a semantic wave, we then explicitly link the elements of the game back to a programming context (binary search of an array).

▶ Simon Says and a Dice Game for Conditionals and Expressions

In the game *Simon Says*, one player takes the role of Simon, or the leader who gives commands to other players. Players must follow the leader's commands if they are prefaced with the phrase "Simon says." The point of the game is to think quickly and to distinguish between real and fake commands. In the classroom version of the game, the rules can be modified to help students understand how to enact conditional statements and/or evaluate Boolean expressions. The leader could be a student or the teacher.

Here is one example enactment of the game—students play *Simon Says* as a whole-class activity that begins with all students standing up. The teacher then calls out statements. If the answer is false for a student, they have to sit down. Here are some examples: "I am wearing sneakers" (students NOT wearing sneakers sit down). The teacher continues until all students are seated. The activity then progresses to students taking action based on evaluating an explicit IF statement (e.g., "If I am wearing sneakers, I raise my right hand")

and finally based on an IF-ELSE statement (e.g., "If I am wearing any red, then I stand on one leg, ELSE I raise my right hand"). An extension of the activity involves adding Boolean operators to the condition being evaluated and having students sitting down if the expression evaluates to true or false. For example, "If I'm a girl AND wearing red" or "If I'm a girl OR wearing red" I sit down. Students and/or the teacher can act as a referee to flag students who make errors during the game.

Dice Game

Another fun game that can follow *Simon Says* involves pairs of students playing a dice game in pairs that requires students to evaluate arithmetic and relational expressions and conditionals. Players roll the die and Player 1 or 2 gets a point based on the outcome of evaluating an expression involving written arithmetic and relational operators, such as *IF Dice1 + Dice2 < 12, THEN Player 1 gets a point.* (See **Chapter 15, Operators and Expressions,** for details on this activity.)

▶ Written or Verbal Explanations

Writing in plain English (or other language of instruction) about the concepts both using programming examples and in terms of everyday things is another kind of activity that helps. Note this is not about giving copied or rote-learned technical definitions or just writing technical definitions in one's own words. It is about giving clear explanations in one's own words that others could read and understand. Such explanations are likely to follow semantic waves themselves, drawing on examples to illustrate the concepts, for example.

If students are to traverse semantic waves that take them around both sides of the quadrant diagram, then writing about programming concepts in this way is an important activity. It essentially involves answering "Please explain" questions. Writing is a powerful way to learn as long as it is not regurgitating rote-learned facts and does traverse a semantic wave. By contrast, answering "Please define" questions operates wholly at the top right of the diagram: it is writing about technical concepts with technical language in a technical context. To traverse from the bottom left, students need to give explanations in their own words, and ideally use their own examples, that link the technical concepts to everyday equivalents as well as programming ones. An example would be to write about how a counter-controlled loop is like counting on your fingers to keep track of how many times you have done something. This is all in the everyday world; it is only by linking this directly to an actual fragment of code, such as a specific for a loop, that the explanation repacks the concept and traverses up the wave.

▶ Story Variables

Story Variables is an example of an activity (developed by Grover's research group in the United States) in which we can help students understand the core ideas and tenets related to a concept—such as variables—through the use of everyday examples that elicit students' ideas, in their own words, about the concept.

Using *Story Variables*, students work collaboratively in pairs to find commonality across a series of short "stories" containing *quantities* that vary (Figure 3a, b, and c). Examples of such stories are (see Figure 3a):

- *"Excuse me—last week I bought one of these pens here for $1.50. Are you really telling me they now cost $3?"*

- *"I watched the basketball game last night. At halftime we were tied, but in the end, they beat us 94–90."*

Through discussions, students come up with a definition of *variable*, practice identifying and naming variables meaningfully, and analyze a variable's changing values to determine its specific types and expected ranges. Students then work in pairs to identify their own real-world short stories involving such changing variables.

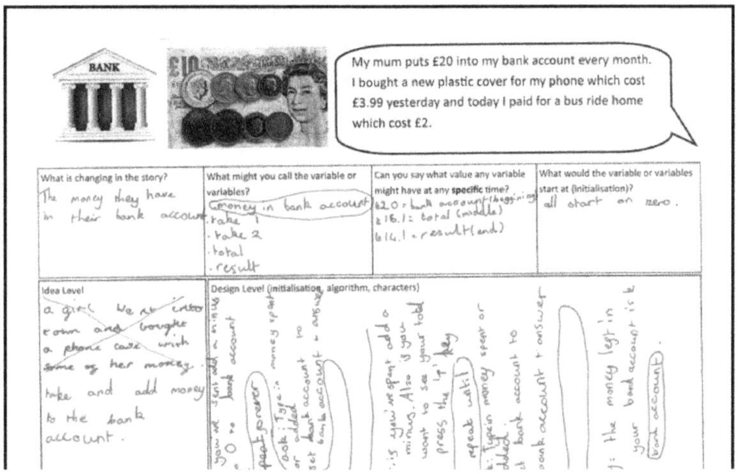

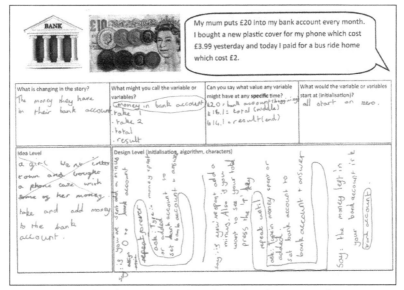

Figure 3a. Short everyday narratives in the *Story Variables* activity

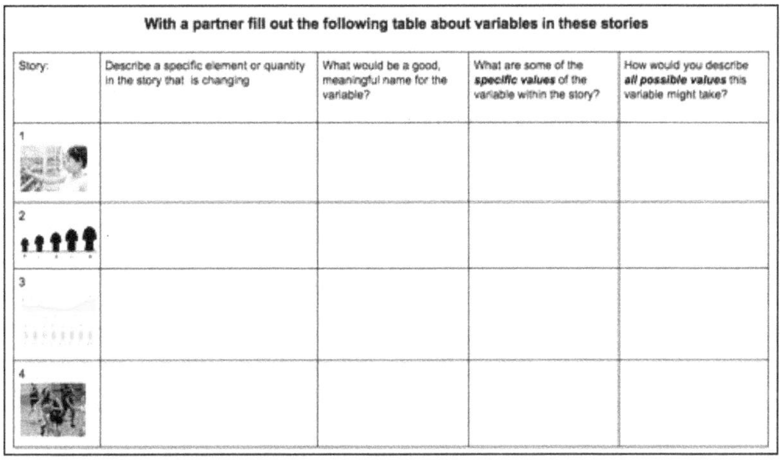

With a partner fill out the following table about variables in these stories				
Story:	Describe a specific element or quantity in the story that is changing	What would be a good, meaningful name for the variable?	What are some of the **specific values** of the variable within the story?	How would you describe **all possible values** this variable might take?
1				
2				
3				
4				

Figure 3b. Identifying variables, meaningful naming, and values in the *Story Variables* activity (Image source: Grover et al., 2019)

Figure 3c. Examples of primary school pupils' work in the UK using the *Story Variables* activity (Image source: Philip Bagge)

As a final activity, teachers can use video clips on YouTube of a popular video game (like *Pac-Man* or *Mario Kart*). Table 1 suggests candidate video games and links that can be used. Watch the video while students take notes on the variables they notice. Hold a group discussion as students mention the variables they spotted, and push kids to suggest items that they weren't certain are variables. Pick one or two and decide, as a class, what a good name is for the variable (e.g., score), what the possible values are for the variable (e.g., any number), what values we saw (e.g., 100 points), and, where appropriate, logical ranges and constraints on such values for each.

Table 1. Video games suggestions for the final *Story Variables* activity

Complexity	Game Title	Example Variables	Suggested Link
Very Low	*Tetris*	Position, Type of Piece, Orientation, Score	https://www.youtube.com/watch?v=AQkAzwaBZV0
Very Low	*Pac-Man*	Score, Level, Power Mode, Position, Orientation,	https://www.youtube.com/watch?v=Sg2ONBSbvb0
Low	*Super Mario*	Lives, Level, Position, Coins, Little/Big/Fire Flower Mario	https://www.youtube.com/watch?v=BaE733PnoQw
Complex	*Clash of Clans*	Level, Elixir, Gold, Army Members,	https://www.youtube.com/watch?v=AkWQwG0hkX0
Very Complex	*Minecraft*	Food, Hearts, Stone, Wood (many different other things)	https://www.youtube.com/watch?v=UJGH8Tbs9P4

BRIDGING TO ACTIVITIES IN PROGRAMMING

An important part of the unplugged to programming trajectory is to make explicit bridges between the unplugged contexts and the technical programming contexts. A range of ways to do this are available, but trace and other code-reading activities (as described in **Chapters 14 and 23**) are a good way to do this bridging, rather than transitioning directly to programming itself. The techniques described combined with formal trace activities can, in particular, be a powerful way to help students over boundary concepts—such as the barrier many hit of forming an incorrect mental model of assignment—or in understanding how to use logical connectives.

However, in all situations, it is vitally important that the students repack the ideas, linking them back up to technical language and examples, that is, actual programs. Ideally, as in the *Box Variables* activity described above, this linking is integrated directly into the activity, although this not always practical or appropriate. For example, when telling the *Searching to Speak* story, the aim is explicitly to demonstrate the concepts in a rich, nonprogramming context. To lead to deep understanding in the programming context, this story needs to be followed by explicit links back to programming. One way is to look at programs that do both a linear search and a divide-and-conquer search of an array, and explicitly link what they do back to what is done in the story. In the story the students act out searching for the letter the other person is thinking of by following a linear search algorithm. This gives an opportunity, in the linking phase, to trace programs using equivalent examples. Similarly, some of the *Story Variables* examples can form the basis of actual programs, like a basketball game program in a visual block-based programming environment or a simplified version of a game like Tetris (See Figure 4) that involves navigating a creature's motion around the screen to capture (collide with) good energy sources while avoiding dangers (static or in random motion).

> *It is important to explicitly make the connection to the unplugged variables activity to help the learners understand what variables to create and how and when they are updated.*

> You are programming a maze game.
> - The screen shows a cat, maze walls, and gold coins.
> - You make a cat move around the screen trying to find gold coins.
> - The maze walls and coins stay in the same location every time you play the game.
> - You start with a score of 0.
> - You have five lives at the start.
> - If the cat touches a gold coin
>   - You gain a life, and
>   - Your score increases by 100.
> - If the cat touches a wall
>   - You lose a life, and
>   - Your score decreases by 100.
>
> The game ends when you reach a score of 500 or have no lives left.
>
> If your score is 500 when the game ends, you win. If your score is less than 500 when the game ends, you lose.
>
> Describe the variables that are needed to program this game.
> - What would you name the variables?
> - Describe the purpose of the variables.
> - What is the starting value of the variables?
> - How and when do the variable values get updated?

Figure 4. Example exercise linking variables to the programming concept

> By being memorable, unplugged activities form very powerful hooks to link to in later learning. You can use them when explaining programming concepts and looking at programming examples later, in the world of technical language and abstract concepts. By mentioning the story or activity, you bring back memories of the experience which allows you to traverse a semantic wave.

This is especially important for programming because programming relies on whole invented languages embedded with very precise meaning. If we set student activities only at the level of technical programming language syntax and semantics, then students will be working consistently high on the semantic profile—essentially flatlining the semantic profile. Wide-ranging research in other disciplines suggests this kind of profile gives a poor learning experience, even in less abstract and technical contexts than programming. By guiding students to understand the concepts deeply by traversing semantic waves, we help them gain mastery of both the technical language and the underlying concepts, so that they use words in ways packed with rich meaning for them.

THINGS TO WATCH OUT FOR!

The theory discussed suggests a range of things to both avoid and aim for when designing learning experiences.

DON'Ts
- DO NOT provide flatlined learning experiences. Operating completely in the world of technical language and abstract concepts, as in the top-right quadrant of Figure 1 (flatlining high on the semantic profile graph), leads to poor learning experiences, because everything is incomprehensible jargon to a novice. Similarly, providing experiences that use everyday examples but do not link the activity directly to programming concepts, as in the bottom-left quadrant of Figure 1 (flatlining low on the semantic profile graph), is also unhelpful to students. The learner is learning nothing new and nothing of the technical subject.

- DO NOT provide learning experiences that only descend the semantic wave, unpacking terminology and concepts, and move on to a new topic before students have had the chance to repack those ideas back into technical contexts.
- DO NOT teach programming only in front of computers. The best place to understand concepts is often in the real world.

DOs

- DO use metaphors, analogies, and unplugged activities regularly as part of teaching programming to ensure students gain a deep understanding.
- DO watch out for the limitations of metaphors, and make clear where the metaphor ends. Taking a metaphor too far can lead to misunderstanding (as with using a simple box metaphor for variables). As Abelson, Ledeen, and Lewis state in their 2008 classic, *Blown to Bits*, "Getting the right metaphor is important, but so is knowing the limitations of our metaphors. An imperfect metaphor can mislead as much as an apt metaphor can illuminate (p. 4)."
- DO, however, ensure the activities and explanations explicitly make links back to the technical programming versions of the concepts.
- DO design learning activities in ways that traverse the quadrant of Figure 1 between bottom left and top right, following both routes, not just one or the other.
- DO ensure that activities, lesson plans, and activities follow a semantic wave structure, moving from technical, abstract concepts to concrete, everyday ones and back again, ensuring students both unpack and repack the concepts.
- DO combine computational role-play activities with more formal pencil-and-paper trace activities of actual code.

Small details of the design of a learning experience can make a big difference to the effectiveness. Reflecting on what does and does not matter in a lesson plan can make all the difference.

RESEARCH AND READINGS

Discovery learning does not fare too well for deeper understanding of conceptual topics. This has been repeatedly borne out in several research studies in various contexts and presented in seminal reading such as Kirschner, Sweller, and Clark, (2006) and Mayer (2004). Extensive studies on the cognitive demands of learning programming were conducted by Roy Pea and Midian Kurland in the 1980s around the use of Logo and BASIC in elementary and high school classrooms (such as Pea & Kurland, 1984). Their papers, in addition to an anthology of research papers from extensive research in the 1980s that were published in Soloway and Spohrer's 1988 book, *Studying the Novice Programmer* (now in its second edition, released in 2013), remain deeply influential and relevant today, even though the context of learning introductory programming has changed with the advent of "low floor" block-based programming environments that offer an easier entry point into programming.

The term "unplugged computing" derives from the work of Tim Bell and colleagues at the University of Canterbury, New Zealand, and their highly influential **CS Unplugged** project (csunplugged.org) where they have provided an extensive range of high-quality unplugged activities (Bell et al., 2009; Bell & Lodi, 2019). Initially it was intended as a way to inspire primary-age children about the subject in general, but as a result of their work, Unplugged Computing became an area of CS education in its own right, and has become an important pedagogical approach. Their activities are now available in various languages and are used worldwide.

Rigorous research on the effectiveness of unplugged computing and of how to design effective activities is very limited, however. What studies have been conducted have also produced mixed results. For example, a survey of teachers in the UK suggested teachers themselves believed unplugged approaches are one of the most successful ways to teach the subject (Sentance & Csizmadia, 2016). Yadav and colleagues in the United States have also found that teachers find a certain degree of comfort in starting off their teaching of CS and programming through unplugged activities. However, several studies have questioned whether unplugged activities are actually effective (Feaster, Segars, Wahba, & Hallstrom, 2011; Taub, Armoni, & Ben-Ari, 2012; Thies & Vahrenhold, 2012, 2016). The need to adapt lesson plans so they are appropriate for a specific context is highlighted. We hypothesize, however, that the mixed results may in part be due to looking at unplugged activities in isolation. As described earlier, to be effective, we argue, there must be bridging activities to the technical contexts. These bridging activities certainly do need to be appropriate to the classroom context. Much more research is needed in this area, however.

Curzon has explored the integration of unplugged techniques into the teaching of introductory programming to undergraduates over many years. Out of this work, Curzon and McOwan (2008) have developed a wide range of unplugged activities specifically for K–12 teaching (made available through http://teachinglondoncomputing. org). These range across games, puzzles, role-playing, storytelling, and especially pioneering using magic tricks to introduce a wide range of computing concepts (Curzon & McOwan, 2008, 2013). Inventing a magic trick involves developing a precise algorithm with a guaranteed magical effect. Tricks are therefore very engaging ways to introduce a wide range of computing concepts including programming ones. A wide range of magic-based resources can be found at teachinglondoncomputing.org/magic/.

Grover worked with her (former) research team at SRI International to design and test a range of unplugged as well as non-programming digital activities (games and microworlds) aimed at grade-six, -seven, and -eight classrooms that target concepts that have been shown to be difficult for novice learners of programming, such as variables, expressions, loops, and abstraction (VELA). The *Simon Says*, *Story Variables*, *Dice Game*, and Maze programming activities in this chapter have been drawn from the VELA research project funded by the U.S. National Science Foundation. The digital non-programming VELA activities suite can be found at csforall.sri.com.

The theory of semantic waves (Maton, 2013) has been applied across many disciplines that show in practice it is a strong and generally applicable theory (Maton, 2014; Maton, Hood & Shay, 2016). The theory provides a concrete way to analyze and improve lesson plans, which is potentially of great use in unplugged teaching contexts. To date, however, little research in the specific area of computer science education has been carried out generally, never mind unplugged computing. Curzon et al. (2018) suggested it as a way to explain why unplugged activities work (and why sometimes they do not) and as a framework when designing such activities. Waite et al. (2019) take a first step in explicitly applying it as an analysis tool to explore the effectiveness of unplugged activities. They analyzed the popular and successful Barefoot Computing (www.barefootcomputing.org) unplugged activity, *Crazy Characters*, that is widely used in the UK. This analysis showed that it does in fact follow a semantic wave structure, which could explain part of its success.

BIBLIOGRAPHY

Abelson, H., Ledeen, K., & Lewis, H. (2008). *Blown to bits: Your life, liberty, and happiness after the digital explosion.* Addison-Wesley Professional.

Bell, T., Alexander, J., Freeman, I., & Grimley, M. (2009). Computer science unplugged: School students doing real computing without computers. *The New Zealand Journal of Applied Computing and Information Technology*, 13(1), 20–29.

Bell, T., & Lodi, M. (2019). Constructing computational thinking without using computers. *Constructivist Foundations*, 14, 3. https://constructivist.info/14/3

Curzon, P., & McOwan, P. W. (2017). *The power of computational thinking*. World Scientific. Chapter 1.

Curzon, P., & McOwan, P. W. (2008). Engaging with computer science through magic shows. *ACM SIGCSE Bulletin*, 40(3), 179–183.

Curzon, P., & McOwan, P. W. (2013). Teaching formal methods using magic tricks. *Fun with Formal Methods*, a workshop at the 25th International Conference on Computer Aided Verification. St. Petersburg, Russia.

Curzon, P., McOwan P. W., Donohue, J., Wright, S., & Marsh, D. W. (2018). Teaching computer science concepts. In S. Sentance, E. Barendsen, and C. Schulte (Eds.), *Computer science education: Perspectives on teaching and learning in school* (pp. 91–108). Bloomsbury Publishing.

Feaster, Y., Segars, L., Wahba, S. K., & Hallstrom, J. O. (2011). Teaching CS unplugged in the high school (with limited success). *Proceedings of the 16th Annual Joint Conference on Innovation and 60 Technology in Computer Science Education, ITiCSE '11*. Darmstadt, Germany: ACM, 248–252. doi:10.1145/1999747.1999817

Grover, S., Jackiw, N., & Lundh, P. (2019). Concepts before coding: Non-programming interactives to advance learning of introductory programming concepts in middle school. *Computer Science Education, 29*(2–3), 106–135.

Kirschner, P. A., Sweller, J., & Clark, R. E. (2006). Why minimal guidance during instruction does not work: An analysis of the failure of constructivist, discovery, problem-based, experiential, and inquiry-based teaching. *Educational Psychologist, 41*(2), 75–86.

Maton, K. (2013). Making semantic waves: a key to cumulative knowledge-building. *Linguistics and Education, 24*, 8–22.

Maton, K. (2014). *Knowledge and knowers: Towards a realist sociology of education*. Routledge.

Maton, K., Hood, S., & Shay. S. (2016). *Knowledge-building: Educational studies in legitimation code theory*. Routledge.

Mayer, R. E. (2004). Should there be a three-strikes rule against pure discovery learning? *American Psychologist, 59*(1), 14.

Pea, R. D., & Kurland, D. M. (1984). On the cognitive effects of learning computer programming. *New Ideas in Psychology, 2*(2), 137–168.

Sentance, S., & Csizmadia, A. (2016). Computing in the curriculum: Challenges and strategies from a teacher's perspective. *Education and Information Technologies*, 1–27.

E. Soloway, E. & Spohrer, J. C. (1988). *Studying the novice programmer*. Lawrence Erlbaum.

Taub, R., Armoni, M., & Ben-Ari, M. (2012). CS unplugged and middle-school students' views, attitudes, and intentions regarding CS. *ACM Transactions on Computing Education (TOCE), 12*(2), 8.

Thies, R., & Vahrenhold, J. (2012). Reflections on outreach programs in CS classes: Learning objectives for unplugged activities. *Proceedings of the 43rd ACM Technical Symposium on Computer Science Education*, ACM, 487–492.

Thies, R., & Vahrenhold, J. (2016). Back to school: Computer science unplugged in the wild. *Proceedings of the 2016 ACM Conference on Innovation and Technology in Computer Science Education*. ACM, 118–123.

Waite, J., Maton, K., Curzon, P., & Tuttiett. L. (2019). Unplugged computing and semantic waves: Analysing crazy characters. In *UK & Ireland Computing Education Research Conference (UKICER)*, 2019, Canterbury, United Kingdom. ACM. DOI: 10.1145/3351287.3351291

Hard Fun With Hands-On Constructionist Project-Based Learning

Deborah A. Fields and Yasmin B. Kafai

INTRODUCTION

All sorts of things can happen when you're open to new ideas and playing around with things.
– Stephanie Kwolek

> "[Hard fun] is expressed in many different ways, all of which all boil down to the conclusion that everyone likes hard, challenging things to do. But they have to be the right things matched to the individual and to the culture of the times. . . . [T]hey must connect with the kids and also with the areas of knowledge, skills and (don't let us forget) ethic adults will need for the future world." *(Papert, 2002)*

"Hard fun" is one of the key phrases associated with Constructionism, a learning philosophy developed by Seymour Papert in the 1980s with faculty and students at MIT. Behind this seemingly contradictory phrase is the idea that learners actually enjoy or have "fun" when making complex or "hard" things. In the process, they can develop deep understanding about subject matters and about themselves as learners. Papert (1980) viewed learning as the process of creating artifacts (digital or physical) of personal and social relevance and, by doing so, connecting old and new knowledge as well as interacting with others. Although this description of learning is not necessarily concerned with computers, Papert also points to special affordances of computers for learning: when students develop programs, they make visible their thinking to others—students and teachers alike—which provide opportunities for conversation, critique, and reflection. These *social* dimensions of learning should not be forgotten because all too often we think about programming as a solitary activity, when it is in fact an inherently social process. Providing an audience for learning artifacts is critical and can be accomplished in various ways through collaborative projects, peer critiques, or sharing projects in an online community.

But hard fun also points to a *personal* dimension of learning, that of interest and enjoyment. When we ask students to program, their projects should connect with their personal interests, whether those projects are about making a flower on a computer screen or creating music, movies, video games, wearable fashion, and more. Today the world is full of digital artifacts that provide many students with a firsthand experience of playing a video game, listening to music online, or seeing animations on the screen. From a constructionist perspective, these personal experiences and interests should be leveraged—and not ignored—in learning when we ask students to make or program games, music, or animations.

Finally, we should not ignore the *tangible* dimensions of learning. Papert saw great promise when learners can connect objects on the screen to their own bodies and those in the physical world. A concrete example is when a learner can program movements for an object on the screen but then also execute the steps themselves to verify the program.

A particular benefit of making these tangible connections between the digital and physical is that they make the workings of interactions more transparent and understandable because all too often today's digital devices are hiding all their inner workings in shiny cases.

> Key in this constructionist view of learning is that the artifacts of the mind have to move into the public world where they can be examined, shared, valued, and enjoyed by others.

In this chapter, we examine the personal, social, and tangible dimensions of hands-on computing with two construction kits: one is the programming platform and community Scratch, and the other is a construction kit for physical computing with electronic textiles. We also propose six principles with concrete examples for applying constructionism in classroom activities and teaching interactions. Although we root our examples in Scratch and electronic textiles, the principles could be applied to develop any number of "hard fun" constructionist activities.

HANDS-ON PROJECT-BASED LEARNING WITH SCRATCH AND ELECTRONIC TEXTILES

Scratch (https://scratch.mit.edu), one of the most popular online programming tools and communities for young programmers, is a media-rich programming language that allows youth to design, share, and remix software programs in the form of games, stories, and animations and also a vibrant online community with now over 30 million projects and growing. There is also an online ScratchEd teacher community in which teachers share ideas for programming activities and lesson plans for all grade levels and subject matters. The millions of projects created and shared online by members from around the world illustrate the critical function that personal and social dimensions play for entering and engaging with programming.

Our other example is a physical computing construction kit for making electronic textiles (hereafter, e-textiles). E-textiles are hybrid designs, using conductive thread to sew LEDs, sewable microcontrollers (e.g., BBC Micro:bit, LilyPad Arduino, Adafruit Circuit Playground), sensors, and other actuators into fabric or similarly soft media. (See **Chapter 24** on physical computing for more ideas.) A unit called Stitching the Loop uses e-textiles within the Exploring Computer Science curriculum, a yearlong introductory course for high school students in the United States. Here students work over 10–12 weeks on four open-ended projects (see Figure 1) with creative constraints that help them learn challenging concepts in computing, electronics, and crafting three-dimensional designs while also supporting personal expression and creativity.

Below we describe six pedagogical principles for practically applying constructionism in personally relevant ways that engage deep learning, with multiple concrete examples to provide illustrations for how this can be achieved in the classroom.

▶ Principle 1: Promoting Creativity Within Constraints

As Miles Berry in **Chapter 3**, **Creative Coding**, also suggests, one challenge in applying constructionism to classrooms is supporting creativity and student interest while helping everyone learn core computing concepts and practices at the same time. One pedagogical principle we can apply to this challenge comes from the arts: the idea of *creativity within constraints*. This involves thoughtfully developing a project that elicits or requires the use of certain concepts and ideas while also allowing for a great deal of student creativity. Everyone learns common concepts and skills while also expressing themselves individually. To go about developing projects that support creativity within constraints, first think about what skills students need to learn. Then develop a project where those skills are essential to completing the project.

As an example, parallelism and event-driven programming are two key concepts that novice students can learn. In Scratch, parallelism can be accomplished by making two objects (or sprites) start actions concurrently (e.g., using the green flag to initiate activities of multiple sprites). Similarly, event-driven programming can be accomplished by using the green flag but also by using "broadcast" and "broadcast received" commands, which allow sprites to initiate an event in another sprite (or even itself). One educational project we came up with to help students learn these concepts is making a story with at least two characters and a scene change in Scratch. Coordinating multiple characters to start at the same time promotes use of the green flag to initiate the story. The scene change requires that students begin a second event, for instance, by changing the background and then causing a character to appear. Coordinating multiple characters and a background lends itself to using events and parallelism as intrinsically easier ways than extended sequencing or timing, leading students to use these concepts to accomplish their stories. Yet within this constrained challenge, students have room to make a myriad of stories with whatever characters and ideas are important to them. We have seen stories about sharks eating divers, a pony on a self-discovery journey, or two people playing video games. This is just one example of a project with creative constraints: we have also used music videos (to promote variable use with the Scratch "timer" variable), a multilevel video game (to promote conditional use and data as variables), and, as we share below, a series of projects.

▶ Principle 2: Growing Complexity in a Series of Projects

Another task that we face as educators is to help students deepen their skills in a domain. To promote deeper skills, we create a *series of projects*, allowing students to build on prior skills in new creative projects. This takes the burden off of one project to meet all the concepts and skills that we hope students develop, and also lowers the stakes for success in a single project. Examples of curricula that introduce basic Scratch programming through a series of projects include the Creative Computing Guide and Google CS First.

As another example, our e-textiles high school curriculum is organized around a series of four increasingly complex projects that introduce students to core concepts of circuitry, Arduino computing, and crafting with different types of materials. The projects include 1) a paper card to introduce simple circuitry; 2) a wristband with lights in parallel and a switch to close it; 3) a classroom mural where pairs of students making pieces with four lights and two switches to create four coded lighting effects. The final project (4) is colloquially termed the "human sensor project" because it incorporates two aluminum foil patches that, when both are squeezed by a person, conduct electricity based on the intensity of the squeeze. Students must code at least four lighting patterns triggered by differing levels of squeezes. As students progress through the projects, they build on their knowledge and skills from one to the next. Each project increases in time (from 1–2 hours to 2–3 weeks), adds new computing concepts (from simple sequences to sensor-based conditionals), and introduces students to new techniques of sewing, debugging, and iteration. No project is a single point of failure: a student may struggle (even fail!) with one and still progress in the next. *Think of the skills, concepts, practices, and mindsets students need to learn and create a series of projects with those in mind. Revise your project series as needed once you have a chance to apply it in the classroom.*

Figure 1. Series of student projects in the e-textiles curriculum (pictures taken by students and used with permission): paper circuit card (upper left), wristband (upper right), mural (lower left—night sky class theme), human sensor project (lower right—mustache pillow)

▶ Principle 3: Starting With Aesthetics First

Even allowing for creativity within constraints, students sometimes get caught up in the requirements of a project, putting personal relevance on a lower priority to perceived essentials. To balance this tendency, we offer the principle of "*aesthetics first*," foregrounding students' rough ideas for how a project should look and act before getting into the nitty-gritty of how to actually accomplish it.

In any project, we can emphasize "aesthetics first" through a personal design or sketch at the beginning of every project: how should it act or what should it look like? With a Scratch story this might be a storyboard sketch. In an e-textiles project this might involve a rough drawing. In early studies with e-textiles, we learned the hard way that starting with instruction (i.e., ways to design circuits or how to code lights) instead of personal design resulted in poor engagement on the part of students. In fact, students cared so little about their light-up projects that they handed them back at the end of class! In contrast, having students sketch out what they want their projects to look like encourages **personal ownership** from the beginning and sets students up to persevere through challenges, even if those sketches are technically or practically infeasible (i.e., your name in bling LEDs or a 20-scene Scratch story). In the process of making their projects, students revise their diagram multiple times, but their interests remain a top priority.

> In actuality, we have found that the most difficult learning—the "hardest fun"—happens when students make aesthetically driven decisions to fix or improve their projects. Students create unique challenges because of their custom designs. Further, because they are unique and personal, students are often willing to persevere, seek additional help, and go the extra mile to accomplish their vision.

This individualization also means that students can share knowledge and help each other without directly copying another person, because direct copying is nearly impossible when students foreground their own personal aesthetic visions of their projects.

▶ Principle 4: Celebrating Mistakes

A related challenge is supporting students in valuing the *process* of making projects, not just the final product. After all, learning by making mistakes, revising or debugging projects, and finding solutions is one of the most rewarding aspects of a constructionist learning process. To this challenge we offer the principle of "*celebrating mistakes*" as a core part of classroom practice.

We have witnessed at least three ways that teachers highlight mistakes, errors, and revisions and make them into a legitimate part of creating projects. First, teachers can show one of their own unfinished Scratch (or other computing) projects and ask the class how they might improve and fix it. This is an excellent model for starting peer-critique sessions where students can ask for help and solicit ideas and feedback. Second, teachers can also highlight their own iterative practices of creation, including their mistakes, errors, and less-than-perfect projects in front of the classroom. Why not share a project and recount a time when something went wrong? We saw one teacher show her class a sewn e-textile project where her sewing was poor quality on one side and excellent quality on the other side. Students were able to point out which side was better, and she coached them not to be haphazard like she was. Third, teachers can celebrate student mistakes and make them into classroom learning opportunities. One teacher we know created a classroom tradition of noticing a student's mistake and then saying loudly, "This is my favorite mistake of the day!" This gave him the opportunity to show the mistake to the class and for help in identifying what was wrong and why. These methods make students' mistakes into a form of shared classroom knowledge, foregrounding students as experts in the classroom, a key practice of equity-based and constructionist teaching principles that situates knowledge in the hands of learners and not just teachers.

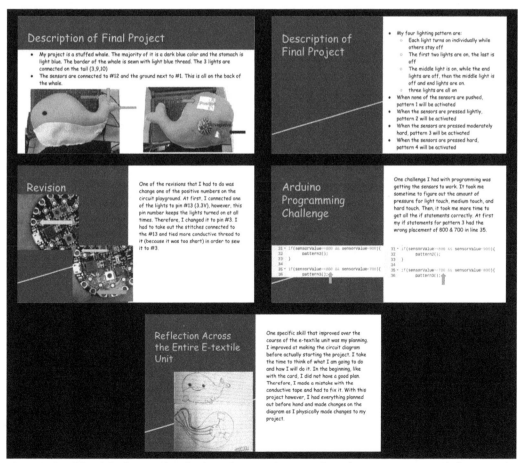

Figure 2. Portfolio slides by a student finishing the e-textiles curriculum: description, revision, challenge, and reflection (Note the arrows, figure titles, and textual descriptions used to annotate evidence.)

▶ Principle 5: Keeping Track of Progress

A major difficulty in constructionist learning environments is supporting students at different stages of their projects. Students move at different paces, some putting more effort in certain parts of their projects, some speeding through the essentials, some learning certain concepts more easily than others. In response, we must find means of "*keeping track*" of students' progress and helping them in the moment.

Teachers we have worked with have developed several means of keeping track of and supporting students on a regular basis. One tool that some teachers have used is a *checklist* where they note at the end of every class period where each student is on a project. This allows them to note who might be stuck and helps them check in with each student. Another way to keep track of students is to have certain *checkpoints* that require teacher approval. For instance, in every e-textile project we require students to get teacher approval of a circuit diagram or project plan before they move on to sew/construct it. This ensures that at least students have a viable plan, and if they don't, the teacher can provide ideas for revisions. A particularly useful tool for tracking student progress is *design notebooks*, where students record plans, document the progress of a project, and reflect on things that went well or problems that arose in making their projects. In constructionist-based classes, we encourage students to record their progress and reflect in short (5 minutes) daily entries in response to prompts such as "What went well today?" "What problem(s) came up?" or "What is a tip or trick you would suggest to another student doing this project?" One teacher we worked with made design notebooks a daily "exit ticket" and had students hold up their notebooks for her to read and star as they left. This gave her daily knowledge on where students were in their design process and what kind of help they might need. One could also use design notebook entries to start class or evaluate student progress.

▶ Principle 6: Reflecting as Computational Communication

One requirement for teachers is to assess student learning, presenting a thorny problem in constructionist learning spaces where tests and surveys are not the most authentic ways to measure what students have learned from making computational projects. Instead, we propose *reflective portfolios* as cumulative artifacts to accompany students' projects and facilitate assessment. Reflective portfolios can promote metacognition, make visible students' learning processes, and also serve as vehicles for practicing *computational communication*.

One portfolio template we use includes three parts: 1) describe your project, 2) reflect on two changes you made or problems you encountered (and how you dealt with them), and 3) consider what you have learned throughout the course of making the project. In each area students must provide accompanying evidence for what they are saying. For instance, in the project descriptions students can provide pictures of how their project works or screenshots of code. In the section on revisions and problems, students can show before and after pictures or point to sections of code that they improved. In the final reflection on learning, students can explain how a skill like coding has improved or how they have developed in a more abstract area like planning or perseverance. All of this supports our ability to assess not only student learning but also students' metacognition about their process of making a project.

Through creating portfolios, students can also learn to better communicate computational ideas. Yet without coaching, students often write generic statements and fail to annotate evidence, leaving pictures or code with no explanations and sometimes no relation to their descriptions. One way to help students improve their computational communication is to have a class discussion showing examples of prior student work. This could include examples of varying qualities of textual communication ("Can you understand what their project is and what it does?") and annotation ("What is this picture showing? What would help to know why the author put it there?"). It also helps to present clear expectations of what counts as "good" in both writing and annotating evidence, for instance, through a detailed rubric. Beyond the important learning benefits of portfolios, engaging students in the professional practice of communicating what they have made, why, and how helps students to author their own identities as developing programmers and creators.

FINAL THOUGHTS

Success stories of the Scratch platform and community and the maker movement have demonstrated that millions of kids can be interested in programming and in making electronics in classrooms, afterschool, and online spaces. Learning through making can be "hard fun" with high rewards but only when the object being made is a challenge to the creator and when the creators are socially and educationally supported throughout the making process. Teachers' roles in nurturing students' **learning while making** is challenging work that is often hidden. Instead of taking an upfront role to deliver knowledge, we as educators take on more subtle but no less important roles as designers and facilitators: creating assignments that promote creativity with constraints; deepening students' knowledge through multiple projects; supporting foreground aesthetics to promote student investment; celebrating mistakes through carefully curated classroom practices; tracking students at different paces; and designing reflective instruments to assess learning and promote metacognition and computational communication. This is background work that enables "hard fun," connecting students to knowledge, skills, interests, and each other.

RESEARCH AND READINGS

We have conducted extensive research on constructionism (Papert, 1980) in software and physical computing environments over the years, along with colleagues at other universities. This chapter draws on our own research (e.g., Kafai, 2006; Kafai, Fields, & Searle, 2014) as well as other scholarly research on constructionism, electronic textiles, Scratch, and learning environments that support them (see the papers in the Bibliography by Fields, Kafai, and Giang [2017]).

For more details on the electronic textiles curriculum we created, see https://exploringcs.org/e-textiles; for more on supporting constructionist DIY activities online, see http://tinyurl.com/kidsdiymedia. The references below have additional details on supporting aesthetics (Kafai & Fields, 2018), portfolios (Lui, Fields, & Kafai, 2019; Shaw, Fields, & Kafai, 2019); and expert teaching practices in classrooms (Fields, Kafai, Nakajima, Goode, & Margolis, 2018).

The Scratch Creative Computing Guide can be found at http://scratched.gse.harvard.edu/guide/), and Google's CS First project-based curriculum at https://csfirst.withgoogle.com/.

BIBLIOGRAPHY

Fields, D. A., Kafai, Y.B., Nakajima, T.M., Goode, J., & Margolis, J. (2018). Putting making into high school computer science classrooms: Promoting equity in teaching and learning with electronic textiles in *Exploring Computer Science. Equity, Excellence, and Education, 51*(1), 21–35.

Fields, D. A., Kafai, Y. B., & Giang, M. T. (2017). Fields, D. A., Kafai, Y. B., & Giang, M. T. (2017). Youth computational participation in the wild: Understanding experience and equity in participating and programming in the online scratch community. ACM *Transactions of Computing Education, 17*(3), 1-22.

Grimes, S. M., Fields, D. A., & Roger, S. (2019). *Best practices for designing connected, digital DIY media platforms for kids. The Kids Do-It-Yourself Media Partnership*. Available at http://tinyurl.com/kidsdiymedia.

Kafai, Y. B. (2006). Constructionism. In R. K. Sawyer (Ed.), *The Cambridge handbook of the learning sciences* (pp. 35–46). Cambridge University Press.

Kafai, Y. B., & Fields, D. A. (2018). Some reflections on designing constructionist activities for classrooms. In V. Dagiene & E. Jastuė, Constructionism 2018: *Constructionism, computational thinking and educational innovation: Conference proceedings*, Vilnius, Lithuania, pp. 606–612. Available at http://www.constructionism2018.fsf.vu.lt/proceedings.

Kafai, Y. B. Fields, D. A., & Searle, K. A. (2014). Electronic textiles as disruptive designs in schools: Supporting and challenging maker activities for learning. *Harvard Educational Review, 84*(4), 532–556.

Lui, D. A., Fields, D. A., Kafai, Y. B. (2019). Student maker portfolios: Promoting computational communication and reflection in crafting e-textiles. In *Proceedings of 8th Annual Conference on Creativity and Fabrication in Education (Fablearn '19)*. ACM, 10–17.

Papert, S. (2002). Hard fun. *Bangor Daily News*. Available at: http://www.papert.org/articles/HardFun.html.

Papert, S. (1980). *Mindstorms: Children, computers, and powerful ideas*. Basic Books, Inc.

Shaw, M., Fields, D. A., & Kafai, Y. B. (2019). Crafting identities: Portfolios as meta-artifacts for narrating selves in portfolios in an e-textiles class. *International Journal of Multicultural Education, 21*(1), 22–41.

Integrating Programming Into Other Subjects

Shuchi Grover & Aman Yadav

INTRODUCTION

The goal of teaching programming in K–12 school years is to introduce learners to a fundamental skill for the times we live in. AlgoRithms are touted to be the "**fourth R**" alongside Reading, wRiting, and aRithmetic. However, a computer science classroom is not the only space to learn coding. Many subjects offer students engaging ways to learn programming in the context of those disciplines. In fact, some believe that teaching programming within a science or a social studies class enhances the learning experience because of the concrete contexts in which it can be demonstrated. Furthermore, problem solving along with coding offers the opportunity to develop a key 21st-century skill, **computational thinking (CT)**—a composite set of thinking and problem-solving skills closely related to, and learned through, coding. This chapter discusses techniques for integrating CT and coding in lessons, and presents vignettes from elementary and secondary classrooms that teachers can draw inspiration from, to bring CS to their students.

> *My basic idea is that programming is the most powerful medium of developing the sophisticated and rigorous thinking needed for mathematics, for grammar, for physics, for statistics, for all the hard subjects…*
> – Seymour Papert

WHY INTEGRATE PROGRAMMING IN OTHER SUBJECTS?

Seymour Papert's pioneering work on using programming in mathematics classrooms in the 1980s laid the foundation for integrating programming into other subjects. Just as meaningful and authentic use of technology tools help enrich learning in the classroom, coding enriches the learning of the host domain. But the benefits of integrating coding in other subjects are bidirectional—integration also helps students learn computing "in context." This is especially true of STEM subjects.

> *Computing and STEM share a deeply symbiotic relationship, and as such, mathematics and science classrooms provide perhaps the most intuitive and easy non-CS contexts for integrating computing. . . . STEM contexts can enrich computational learning while also providing valuable opportunities to embed coding and CT in established and accessible (as well as required) STEM courses.*—Grover and Pea (2018).

Although there has been much focus on teachers' understanding of computational thinking and programming constructs as well as their attitude toward computational thinking ideas, Yadav and colleagues have concluded through their research that CT can also change teachers' disciplinary teaching practice. Foregrounding CT provides teachers with tools and practices they can use to deepen disciplinary learning by providing students with an opportunity to engage in "thinking skills" that are not always explicitly focused on, especially at the elementary level. For example, in the mathematics example discussed later in this chapter, as teachers ask students to draw a triangle in Scratch, they are drawn into thinking about interior and exterior angles. This is because rotating the Scratch sprite requires the use of the exterior angle, even though one might intuitively use the interior angle. It provides an opportunity for the students to dive deeper into geometrical ideas that might not otherwise come up without the use of the Scratch tool. In addition, a key goal, especially in science and mathematics classrooms, is to help students learn how to generalize and think about scientific phenomena and mathematical concepts abstractly. Programming can be used to push students to build the mental models for generalization—or *concretize abstraction*, if that makes sense! As with students, non CS-teachers also appreciate ideas and concepts more deeply when they integrate programming into their subjects.

IDEAS FOR INTEGRATING PROGRAMMING INTO SUBJECTS ACROSS PRIMARY AND SECONDARY GRADES

Programming can be integrated into almost all school subjects to help students learning coding in context or apply their previously learned coding skills to enrich learning in another subject. The following sections provide more detailed examples situated in the context of elementary (or primary) as well as secondary classrooms for integrating programming in mathematics, language arts, science, social studies, and music. Several freely available curricula focus on the integration of coding and learning of other disciplinary content (some of which we have drawn from in the following examples). Worth mentioning here are Project GUTS, Bootstrap, Northwestern University's CT-STEM, Vanderbilt University's C2STEM (c2stem.org), STEMcoding, and Georgia Tech's Media Computation (or "MediaComp"). While most of these curricula integrate coding and STEM subjects, MediaComp is a widely used introductory programming curriculum created by Mark Guzdial that integrates coding with manipulation of images and music. Also see **Chapter 24** on physical computing for additional examples on how to integrate physical computing (using devices such as BBC Micro:bit, Raspberry Pi, and Lilypad Arduino) into subjects such as science and geography.

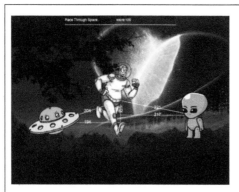

The **Bootstrap family** of evidence-based curricular modules are designed to integrate computing into mainstream subjects like algebra, physics, history, data science, and more, while directly supporting the content and pedagogical needs of teachers in those subjects via tools, content, and pedagogy. In contrast to other CS-focused initiatives, Bootstrap students use a programming tool that follows the behavior of mathematics, with error messages and a programming environment that's designed from the ground up for the classroom. That means teachers can teach, debug, and explain programs using the mathematics they already know, and students see mathematical concepts reinforced with every program they write. The content of each Bootstrap module is focused on the needs of the host subject—physics students can program models to explain observed phenomena; mathematics students can apply order of operations, coordinate planes, function composition, and linear, quadratic, and exponential functions to create movement, graphics, and interactivity; and history students can explore how shifts in population or economic data connect to the narratives in the textbook. Every Bootstrap subject module is designed with careful feedback from subject-area teachers, so that educators can leverage the pedagogy and best practices they already know.

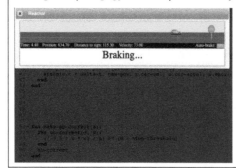
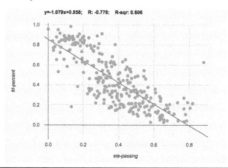

The preceding box provides a glimpse of the Bootstrap family of curriculum materials (developed by Shriram Krishnamurthi, Kathi Fisler, and Emmanuel Schanzer of Brown University) that has successfully integrated functional programming into learning in STEM as well as non-STEM subjects.

▶ Integration With Mathematics

Coding and mathematics share a deep conceptual connection. Computer science grew out of mathematics and most early computer scientists were indeed mathematicians and logicians. In fact, the term *algorithm* comes from Al-Khwarizmi, the Persian mathematician who wrote about the idea in his book *On the Calculation With Hindu Numerals*. Many fundamental ideas of computer science have their roots in discrete mathematics. Graphs, trees, and arrays are data structures that are implemented and manipulated as matrices in programs. Boolean logic has its roots in mathematical logic. Many of the popular block-based programming languages for children like Scratch, Snap*!*, and App Inventor have their roots in Logo—a language designed with the goal of teaching mathematics through "turtle geometry." Turtle geometry affords *embodied learning* where students can understand (and reason about) the turtle's motion by imagining what they would do if they were the turtle. (Seymour Papert called this "body syntonic" reasoning).

Example 1. Drawing cool geometric shapes. At the elementary level, teachers can implement programming within the context of mathematics using the Scratch programming environment. Taking a leaf out of Papert's book, students can learn by writing a Scratch program "to draw shapes having specified attributes, such as a given number of angles or a given number of equal faces." First, students learn to program by simply drawing a predetermined polygon (triangle, rectangle, etc.), during which they would need to consider interior and exterior angles for the sprite to move. To accommodate more advanced learners, the teacher could ask the students to draw any polygon based on an input from a user on the number of sides of the polygon (Figure 1a). This simple polygon-drawing idea can then be extended to draw really cool shapes using nested loops and changing pen color and size (Figure 1b). These examples can also be used with older students when they migrate to text programming, using Python's turtle geometry library. (Also see **Chapter 3, Creative Coding**.)

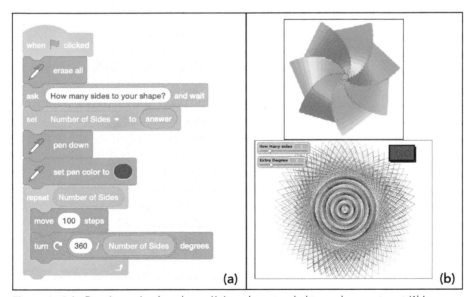

Figure 1a & b. Drawing a simple polygon (1a) can be extended to cool geometry art (1b)

At the secondary school level, we can move to a more complex integration of programming by having students model algebraic problems, code algorithmic solutions, or more deeply engage with concepts. Teachers could still use block-based environments like Scratch or Snap! for coding complex programs (for example, see **Chapter 18, Repetition and Recursion** to see how to use Snap! to code a recursion solution to the classic coin change problem). Example 2 shows how Scratch can be used to demonstrate probability and the convergence of random variables in probability. Example 3 shows how to code the algorithm to test for proportionality in Python. Example 4, shared by high school mathematics and CS teacher Dawn DuPriest, shows how to integrate physical computing using the Micro:bit accelerometer and Python's mathematics library in a trigonometry classroom to calculate the height of a distant object like a tree or building.

Example 2: Understanding the convergence of random variables in probability using a coin toss or a six-sided die and the random-number generator (Figure 2).

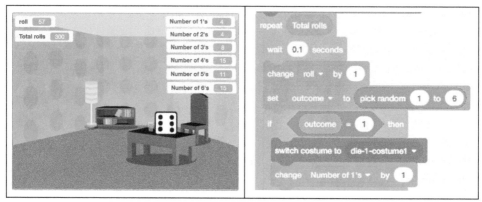

Figure 2. Scratch program demonstrating the convergence of probability of in a die roll (to 1/6)

Example 3. Coding an algorithmic solution in Python for checking proportionality—

```
print "a/b = c/d"
a = input("what is a? ")
b = input("what is b? ")
c = input("what is c? ")
d = input("what is d? ")

cross1 = float(b) * float(c)
cross2 = float(a) * float(d)

if cross1 == cross2:
  print a, "/", b, " is proportional to ", c, "/", d

else:
  print a, "/", b, " is not proportional to ", c, "/", d
```

Example 4

High school mathematics teacher Dawn DuPriest shared a wonderful example that brings together trigonometry and physics with physical computing (https://codinginmathclass.wordpress.com/2019/01/18/trig-and-physics-and-microbits/). As part of a trigonometry unit, they used Python (and its extensive mathematics library) with the Micro:bit accelerometer to calculate tilt to figure out the height of an object. She first created a viewfinder by attaching the Micro:bit to a cardboard tube. The tube could be used to sight the top of a tree or building (Figure 3a). Figure 3b shows a simple program to fetch the accelerometer readings (on pushing the A button).

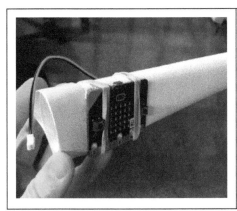

```
from microbit import
import math
while True:
        if button_a.is_pressed():
                x=accelerometer.get_x()
                display.scroll("x:")
                display.scroll(x)
                y=accelerometer.get_y()
                display.scroll("y:")
                display.scroll(y)
                z=accelerometer.get_z()
                display.scroll("z:")
                display.scroll(z)
```

Figure 3a & b. A micro:bit viewfinder (3a) and Python code to fetch accelerometer readings (3b)

They found that if the tube was held level, the x reading was close to 0, the y reading was close to a maximum of 1024, and the z was close to 0. If they held the tube pointing straight up (90 degrees), x was –1024, y was close to 0, and z remained close to 0. Therefore, as they tilted the Micro:bit, the x accelerometer goes from 0 to -1024 while the y accelerometer mirrors it and goes from 1024 to 0.

To convert accelerometer readings into an angle of inclination (in radians), they used this formula (found on the internet):

$$\theta = \sin^{-1}\left(\frac{A_{X,OUT}[g]}{1\,g}\right)$$

They applied concepts of the inclined plane to help students understand the x and y components of g (gravitational acceleration [Figure 4a]). The Python script (edited from 1b) as shown in Figure 4b calculates the angle and uses the distance from the object to calculate the height using tan(theta) = height/distance.

```
from microbit import
import math

while True:
        if button_a.is_pressed():
                x=accelerometer.get_x()
                angle=math.asin(x/1024)
                deg=math.degrees(angle)

                display.scroll(deg)
```

Figure 4a & b. (a) Concepts of the inclined plane to help students understand the x and y components of g (gravitational acceleration); (b) Python code snippet to convert the x-value to degrees

▶ Integration With Science

Science offers several opportunities for integrating block-based programming. Ecosystems, natural phenomena, and climate science present excellent situations for teachers to make science more engaging through coding. Coding also provides a great tool for teaching modeling in the science classroom in elementary, middle, and high school. The following examples provide a sense for the exciting learning possibilities when it comes to coding in science classrooms.

Example 1: Stories and games in block-based programming environments.

Young learners can describe parts of a plant or human body, or membership in the plant or animal kingdom, in interesting ways. Upper elementary and middle school students can create simple games (e.g., demonstrating the relationship between ocean temperatures and icebergs) or stories or interactive programs that describe phenomena like plant respiration or photosynthesis. Life cycles of physical phenomena and living organisms provide an excellent context for practicing algorithmic sequences.

Example 2: The STEMCoding Project, founded by The Ohio State University physicist Chris Oban, has

created several video-based lessons on YouTube (https://www.youtube.com/c/STEMcoding) for helping teachers integrate coding (in JavaScript, Processing, and p5.js) into mathematics and science classrooms. One of the first activities in the STEMcoding Project involves modifying a basic JavaScript program, shown in Figure 5, in which pressing arrow keys on the keyboard causes a circle to move at a constant velocity. Initially, the circle moves only to the right, and the student has to modify the code to allow it to move in other directions like a simple video game. Later the student adds code to draw dots at equal intervals of time as a "motion map." To enrich the learning (and align with U.S. physics and physical science standards), the activity includes velocity vs. time plots in which the velocity vector is shown. The activity organically raises discussion and inquiry about the way that real objects move because the motion starts immediately when keys are pressed and stops when keys are let go, which leads into a follow-up activity on acceleration.

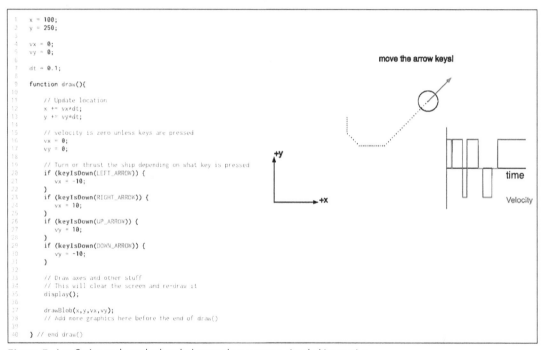

Figure 5. JavaScript code and related plots to demonstrate simple kinematics

Example 3: Agent-based modeling (ABM) in middle school and high school.

According to Uri Wilensky, creator of the NetLogo agent-based modeling environment and a leading researcher in the field of combining STEM learning and the coding of agent-based models, "ABM is a form of computational modeling in which individual entities in a computer simulation (the agents) are given rules defining their behavior. The collective interactions of a multitude of agents, each concurrently acting out its behavioral rules, can reveal complex, emergent patterns. The 'game' of ABM is to try to generate known phenomena by defining a set of agents and rules for their behavior, or to explore the possible phenomena that can be generated with such a set by varying conditions or parameters." He further suggests that this kind of integration helps build computational literacy among students—an idea first articulated by Andrea diSessa. Such integration "increases access to computing for all students in all schools; it enhances students' motivation for and depth of understanding of scientific principles by using computing in powerful ways; it brings science education in line with authentic scientific practice and the needs of 21st-century science; and it provides students with experiences of computers beyond searching and sorting, demonstrating the power of computation to help them make sense of their world." As students work with NetLogo, they can articulate their own provisional thinking in an executable form. Running their models reveals the implications of their ideas, provokes new conjectures, and drives "debugging" cycles of modeling, execution, and refinement. This iterative process is a motivating and intellectually exciting activity, driven by interactive feedback and dynamic visualizations. Working with NetLogo, kids can explore existing models by changing initial conditions and sweeping the parameter space of key variables. They may also explore "what if" questions by modifying behavioral rules to an existing model or creating new models. Browse the NetLogo website for a library of models created aimed at middle and high school topics like population biology/ecology, physics and chemistry, and earth sciences.

Project GUTS is a curriculum similarly aimed at understanding science through exploring and creating agent-based models and then using those models to run simulated experiments. The curriculum uses the use-modify-create pedagogy (see **Chapter 23**) in StarLogo Nova, a freely block-based programming language available at (https://www.slnova.org/), to allow students to progress from being able to read and interpret the code to rearranging and adapting the sequences of blocks. As students continue to develop their proficiency and understanding of the algorithms, they eventually move to choosing and sequencing the blocks to form new algorithms themselves. The curriculum includes focuses on various topics in middle school science including earth science, life science, and physical science. Figure 6 a and b shows the StarLogo simulation interface and the block-coding environment for a model of the chemical reaction between silver nitrate and copper.

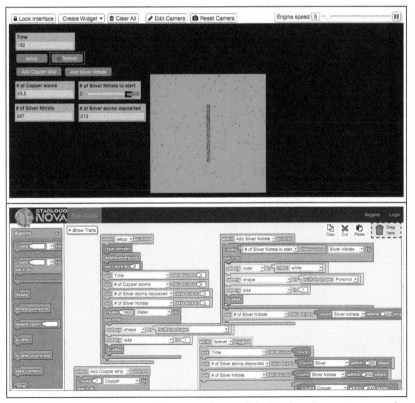

Figure 6 a & b. A StarLogo simulation interface and the block-coding environment for a model of the chemical reaction between silver nitrate and copper

▶ Integration With Language Arts

Storytelling and creating stories are great contexts for integrating coding and algorithmic thinking into the language arts classroom while allowing students to express their creativity—not only in terms of creating a narrative but also in combining them with special effects and media. Storytelling Alice was a version of Alice (https://www.alice.org/get-alice/storytelling-alice/) that was geared specifically at teaching children programming through the creation of stories. More recently ScratchJr and Scratch have been ideal platforms for creative computing and creative storytelling through programming.

Example 1. *Knock-knock joke* is a popular example that can be coded in Scratch. Students must code two sprites alternating saying each line of the joke.

> Sprite 1 says first line of joke. (*"Knock, knock."*)
>
> Sprite 2 responds. (*"Who's there?"*)
>
> Sprite 1 says second line of joke. (*<some text>*)
>
> Sprite 2 responds.(*<some text> who?*)
>
> Sprite 1 finishes joke.(<some text concatenated with a funny ending>).

Students may work in pairs to first tell a knock-knock joke to each other before they start programming. This program requires coordinating the speech of the two sprites through message passing (using the `broadcast` and `message received` blocks) or through using `wait` blocks. The latter option requires testing wait times to get the timing of the joke.

Example 2. Interactive stories. *Choose your own adventure* has been a popular programming task for programmers of all ages. Here, students code stories that ask the user for input and then take different sequences of action (using conditionals) based on the input. *Choose your own adventure* stories are excellent opportunities to teach students how to create flowcharts to plan different courses of action. Check out Jeff Atwood's blog for his adventures with programming *choose your own adventure* programs (https://blog. codinghorror.com/choosing-your-own-adventure/).

Example 3. Social network analysis of stories. Another example of integrating coding into a high school language arts classroom was shared in Grover's Edsurge blog post, *Helping Students See Hamlet and Harry Potter in a New Light With Computational Thinking*. The example integrates the idea of social network analysis with literary analysis and demonstrates how to integrate graphs (closed networks with nodes and edges) into mathematical abstractions—adjacency matrices— that can be coded as 2-dimensional arrays or data structures. Doing so provides interesting insights into literary narratives and the relationships of the characters (Figure 7a, b, and c). The example draws on the **computational literary analysis** of Shakespeare's Hamlet by Stanford professor Franco Moretti.

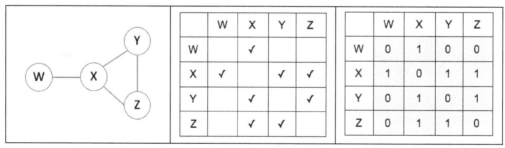

Figure 7a, b, & c. A graph representation of a story (a) converted to adjacency matrix (b & c)

	W	X	Y	Z
W		✓		
X	✓		✓	✓
Y		✓		✓
Z		✓	✓	

	W	X	Y	Z
W	0	1	0	0
X	1	0	1	1
Y	0	1	0	1
Z	0	1	1	0

▶ Integration With Social Studies

Imagine being able to code programs (stories or games) about primary school social studies topics like my world, my town, my community, my school, or geography games? The possibilities are exciting and limitless! In addition to stories, apps, quizzes, and games about historical or contemporary events, here are a few specific examples of how coding can be incorporated into social studies.

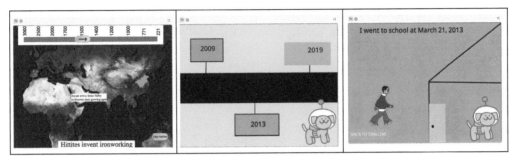

Figure 8. Programming historical and personal timelines.

Example 1: Interactive time lines in block-based programming languages. Scratch, Snap!, and Alice are great tools for coding interactive time lines that depict historical events or discoveries over time (Figure 8a) or even students' own life stories (Figure 8b and c).

Example 2: Studying migration patterns. In the E-STITCH curriculum designed by Colby Tofel-Grehl and Kristin Searle along with colleagues at Utah State University, teachers use coding with the LilyPad Arduino to engage middle school students while reading books that share stories of migration, enslavement, and forced relocations of indigenous populations in the United States. From their readings of these books, students then design, construct, and code time lines that showcase the widely varied stories of American migration, immigration, and enslavement. For example, while reading *A Place Where Sunflowers Grow* by Amy Tai, students construct computational circuits that explore the key aspects of this story about the Japanese internment that occurred during World War II (Figure 9a). This project is followed by one in which students construct quilt squares, modeled after those used by abolitionists to guide escaped slaves along the Underground Railroad (Figure 9b). Students then collaborate to code their connected quilt squares and create a collaborative class display that showcases these stories. In the final project, students design a "meaningful moment quilt square" that showcases an important moment from their own migration or life story. The students use computational thinking and coding skills to develop paper circuit and e-textile projects that merge their reading of primary historical sources and family histories with the building of computational circuits that visually and physically model the migratory events that have shaped U.S. history and that of the individuals who inhabit it.

Example 3: Python scripts for studying criminal justice. Web scraping, or the act of gathering data from a website, can be easily accomplished using Python scripts. Several websites guide users to write Python scripts to do this, including one that provides a tutorial on how to accomplish this in as little as 4 minutes! These sites typically use the Python packages Requests and Beautiful Soup. Using such scripts to analyze social issues can be a powerful way of integrating programming in a high school social studies classroom. One such example shared in a Harvard Kennedy School newsletter demonstrates how a Python script written to scrape the Polk County (Iowa) Prison Inmate Listing site can extract a list of inmates and for each inmate extract data like race and city of residence (see Figure 10). Having such data at hand can lead to new insights and new ways of examining topics such as the criminal justice system. Data, as the authors rightly claim, can tell a story. The entire code can be found here on this GitHub site: https://gist.github.com/phillipsm/404780e419c49a5b62a8.

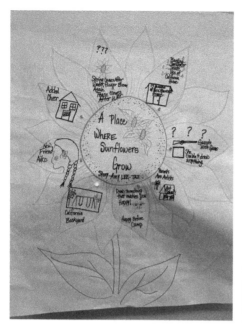 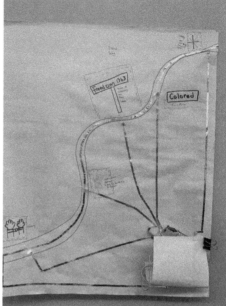

Figure 9a & b. Integrating physical computing & CT in social studies classrooms
(source: https://chaoslearninglab.weebly.com)

```python
1    url_to_scrape = 'http://apps2.polkcountyiowa.gov/inmatesontheweb/'
2
3    r = requests.get(url_to_scrape)
4
5    soup = BeautifulSoup(r.text)
6
7    inmates_links = []
8
9    for table_row in soup.select(".inmatesList tr"):
10           table_cells = table_row.findAll('td')
11
12           if len(table_cells) > 0:
13                   relative_link_to_inmate_details = table_cells[0].find('a')['href']
14                   absolute_link_to_inmate_details = url_to_scrape + relative_link_to
15                   inmates_links.append(absolute_link_to_inmate_details)
```

Figure10. Web scraping public websites with Python to examine social justice topics

▶ Integration With Music

Media Computation, an introductory programming curriculum designed at Georgia Tech by Mark Guzdial, has been used at the high school and college level to introduce students to concepts of programming in the context of working with images and sound. Coding can be integrated in music and arts classrooms in elementary and middle school as well, thanks to specific sound-related features and libraries provided in popular block-based and text-based programming languages. According to Jared O'Leary, an enthusiastic proponent of the integration of music and coding, one needs and builds an understanding of both music and code when engaging in music- and sound-related coding projects. Three brief examples of how music and coding can be integrated to engage students in both subjects follow.

Example 1: "Hot Cross Buns" in block-based and text programming

In this example shared by Jared O'Leary, PhD, students learn to code to play "Hot Cross Buns." Figure 11(a) shows the sequence of Scratch blocks (on the left) that causes a MIDI clarinet to play "Hot Cross Buns" at 120 beats per minute when a user clicks the green flag to run the program. Figure 11(b) also plays "Hot Cross Buns"; however, the individual blocks in the sequence of code on the left are "functions" that play the phrases on the right with the corresponding name. Functions make it easier not only to reuse chunks of code but also to understand what each chunk of code in a sequence is doing. Figure 11(c) shows sample code for creating the melody for "Hot Cross Buns" with Sonic Pi (http://sonic-pi.net/). The "release" determines how long an individual note will play for, whereas "sleep" determines how long the computer will wait until executing the next line of code.

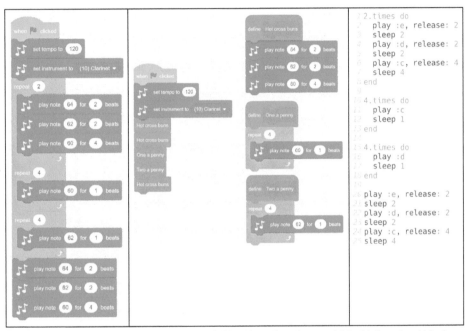

Figure 11a, b, & c. Hot Cross Buns in Scratch (a) without functions and (b) with functional blocks and (c) in Sonic-pi (O'Leary, 2020)

Example 2: Create your own notes, music, and special effects in Snap!

Snap! creator Jens Mönig (also coauthor of Chapter 13 in this book) demonstrates some cool examples of music creation that can be accomplished in Snap!.

Because the samples in a sound are just numbers between −1 and 1, we can generate our own noise by simply adding random numbers within these bounds to a list. It sounds like . . . white noise (Fig 12a)! You can repeat such a list with random numbers ("noise") over and over until you get a complex tone with a discernible frequency (Fig 12b). Then simply changing the size of the noise—the number of random elements—changes the frequency of the complex tone. For example, halving the size of the noise repeats it twice as fast, and—sure enough—we hear that as an octave above our first experiment. You now have a way to generate your own notes and music! For example, you can play arbitrary frequencies from random seeds (Fig 12c).

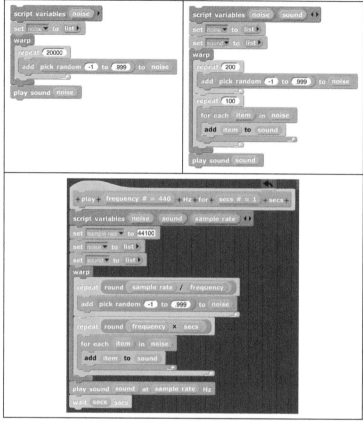

Figure 12 a, b, c. Creating your own notes in Snap! by using random numbers

You may also create your own echo/reverberation effect by averaging each sample in a sound with an earlier one (Fig 13a). The "echo effect" block in Figure 13b parameterizes the delay in relation to the sample rate and volume decay.

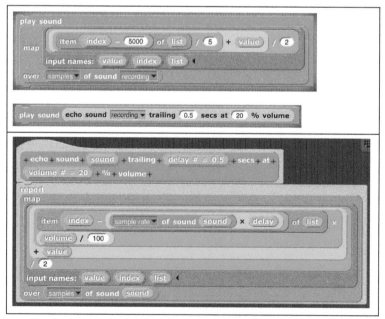

Figure 13a, b. Creating your own echo/reverberation effect in Snap!

Example 3: Generating aleatoric (or chance) music

In this example, also shared by Jared O'Leary, PhD, random-number generators are used to create aleatoric music, in which some element of the composition is left to chance. Figure 14 shows an example of using randomization to create an aleatoric hi-hat sound. The code if one_in( ) will execute code only if the number is randomly selected out of the numbers in the parentheses, so if one_in(2) has a 50% chance of running. The code rrand(,) will select a random number within a range from the first number to the second number; rrand(0.2, 0.7) will randomly select a number between 0.2 and 0.7.

```
live_loop :hhat do
  hh_amp = (ring 0.4, 0)
  hh_arr = [(ring 20, 18), (ring 10, 12, 20, 12), (ring 5, 12), (ring 1, 8)]
  hh_r = (ring 2, 4)

  if one_in(2)
    sample :drum_splash_hard, amp: rrand(0.2, 0.7), rate: rrand(0.999, 1.001) if one_in(2)
  else
    sample :drum_splash_soft, amp: rrand(0.2, 0.7), rate: rrand(0.999, 1.001) if one_in(2)
  end

  32.times do
    if one_in(2) && count > 1
      2.times do
        hh_unquant = rrand(0, master_unquant)
        sleep hh_unquant / 2
        sample :drum_cymbal_closed, amp: (rrand(0.15, 0.4) + hh_amp.tick), rate: rrand(0.999, 1.001) unless one_in(hh_arr[count - 1].tick)
        sleep t - (hh_unquant / 2)

        sleep hh_unquant / 2
        sample :drum_cymbal_closed, amp: (rrand(0.15, 0.4) + hh_amp.tick), rate: rrand(0.999, 1.001) if one_in(hh_arr[count - 1].tick) && count > 1
        sleep t - (hh_unquant / 2)
      end
    else
      hh_unquant = rrand(0, master_unquant)
      sleep hh_unquant / 2
      sample :drum_cymbal_closed, amp: (rrand(0.15, 0.4) + hh_amp.tick), rate: rrand(0.999, 1.001) if one_in(4) || count == 1
      sleep s - (hh_unquant / 2)

      hh_unquant = rrand(0, master_unquant)
      sleep hh_unquant / 2
      sample :drum_cymbal_closed, amp: (rrand(0.15, 0.4) + hh_amp.tick), rate: rrand(0.999, 1.001) if one_in(4) && count != 1
      sleep s - (hh_unquant / 2)
    end
  end
end
```

Figure 14. Using randomization to create an aleatoric hi-hat sound

GENERAL CONCERNS RELATED TO INTEGRATION

Teacher familiarity with coding. Although integrating programming into subject areas exposes students to computational ideas and tools, and also explores disciplinary ideas in depth, there are several challenges to integration. Primary among these is developing sufficient knowledge of programming for teachers to integrate it into their subject areas. Given that teacher preparation programs do not have the time for teachers to learn even basic programming concepts during their preservice teacher training, the majority of teachers are not familiar with programming and related tools. As such, expecting subject teachers to take on additional burden of learning to program and develop activities that integrate programming to meet disciplinary learning objects without appropriate support may be unreasonable. To support integrating programming into subjects, we need to not only develop teachers' competencies in programming but also scaffold their learning throughout the school year. In addition, a subject teacher could be encouraged to collaborate with the CS teacher or technology specialist in the school who teaches CS or coding. In addition, the progression developed by Grover (Figure 15) has been found to be useful to help teachers and students move gently from simple integration (with simple coding and unplugged activities) to more complex integration of programming into subjects.

Additionally, policy-makers and administrative bodies could also incentivize teachers to learn programming to help support their content area objectives. Schools should also consider supporting technology coaches to develop capacity to support teachers to integrate programming.

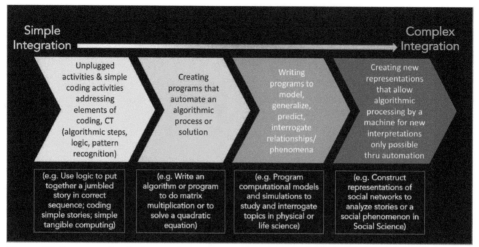

Figure 15. A progression for integrating coding and CT into the curriculum (Grover 2018)

Students' prior knowledge of coding. Lack of prior knowledge of coding among students creates a challenge for teachers, and results in an additional burden of teaching students the fundamentals of coding in addition to topics and learning objectives of the host subject. If possible, teachers should try to carve a few days out of the term to make students familiar with the fundamental concepts of coding and the features of the coding environment. Short of this, students may struggle with an inordinately high cognitive load if they have to understand programming alongside learning concepts of the subject. Synergistic learning of both programming and the subject is possible as shown in the aforementioned examples of Bootstrap and agent-based modeling. Ease of use of the programming tool is thus a key factor in determining which programming environment and activity a teacher chooses to integrate programming.

Testing and assessment. In addition to teacher preparation, policy goals often focus on a core set of subjects and knowledge that students need to learn and be measured in—usually subjects such as math, science, and literacy. Given the heavy focus on meeting test-preparation requirements, schools and teachers are under pressure and often see adding programming as side-tracking from their core learning goals. Policy-makers and boards of education should reconsider their testing instruments. Prioritizing 21st-century learning requires a multipronged approach that shifts away from testing of knowledge to focus more on deeper understanding, application, and also the creative aspects associated with integrating computing. Large assessment organizations such as PISA (OECD's Programme for International Student Assessment) have begun to integrate measurement of computational thinking in subjects such as mathematics (http://www.oecd.org/pisa/pisaproducts/pisa-2021-mathematics-framework-draft.pdf).

Last, assessing and measuring student learning in integrated settings is a challenge for the teacher as well. What should the summative assessment (or final exam) measure? Should they measure learning of coding in addition to learning of the school subject? Should they measure these separately or through some form of integrated learning? It would not be unwise to assume that some teachers would want students to be prepared for a traditional final exam that does not involve programming. In such cases, teachers could plan to integrate coding in a unit as a "review" of the topic. Or they could just teach the topic in a rich, integrated lesson that bears the potential to result in deeper understanding in the host domain, and demonstrates—through students' exam results—that it is indeed the case!

School infrastructure and access to computers. Given the resources required to teach programming, it is important to bear in mind that many schools do not even have adequate basic infrastructure, such as computers. Although an unplugged approach to computational thinking might serve as an on ramp for teachers to bring CT into their classroom, it creates an inequitable system where certain groups do not get access to the real power of computing by engaging in programming. Therefore, it is important for policy-makers to allocate funds to allow school to get adequate resources needed to teach and integrate programming.

ACKNOWLEDGMENTS

Our gratitude to Colby Tofel-Grehl, Emmanuel Schanzer, Jared O'Leary, Dawn DuPriest, Irene Lee, and Jens Mönig for sharing examples from their work for this chapter.

RESEARCH AND READINGS

Much of the pioneering work on the integration of coding and mathematics was done at the MIT Media Lab in the 1970s to 1990s. The writings of Seymour Papert, Andrea diSessa, Hal Abelson, and Uri Wilensky yield deep insight into their profoundly innovative thinking about computing as a medium and literacy. Their work influenced the development of tools such as Logo, StarLogo, Netlogo, and Boxer—many of which we use even today. Their work and writings are the foundation for constructionism as a pedagogy (which has evolved since then to be more mindful of classroom realities and the learning process). In recent years, the renewed focus of CS and coding in K–12 and the integration of CT into the disciples has breathed new life into that earlier work. New pedagogies and curricular ideas drawn from more recent research in the learning sciences are being employed to bring teachers on board and prepare them for the oftentimes challenging task of integration. Grover and Yadav, along with many others, have conducted extensive research on pedagogies and curricula for STEM and computing integration. Research on the use of popular curricular resources mentioned in this chapter, including CT-STEM, Project GUTS, Bootstrap, STEMcoding, and Media Computation, are also worth checking out.

BIBLIOGRAPHY

Abelson, H., & DiSessa, A. A. (1986). *Turtle geometry: The computer as a medium for exploring mathematics*. MIT Press.

DiSessa, A. A. (2001). *Changing minds: Computers, learning, and literacy*. MIT Press.

Grover, S. (March, 2018). The 5th "C" of 21st century skills? Try computational thinking. *edSurge*. Retrieved from https://www.edsurge.com/news/2018-02-25-the-5th-c-of-21st-century-skills-try-computational-thinking-not-coding.

Grover, S. (November, 2018). Helping students see Hamlet and Harry Potter in a new light with computational thinking. *edSurge*. Retrieved from https://www.edsurge.com/news/2019-12-19-how-an-unplugged-approach-to-computational-thinking-can-move-schools-to-computer-science.

Grover, S. (November, 2018). A tale of two CTs (and a revised timeline for computational thinking). *Communications of the ACM*. Retrieved from https://cacm.acm.org/blogs/blog-cacm/232488-a-tale-of-two-cts-and-a-revised-timeline-for-computational-thinking/fulltext.

Grover, S., & Pea, R. (2018). Computational Thinking: A competency whose time has come. In S. Sentance, E. Barendsen, & S. Carsten (Eds.), *Computer science education: Perspectives on teaching and learning in school* (pp. 19–38). Bloomsbury.

Lee, I., Martin, F., & Apone, K. (2014). Integrating computational thinking across the K–8 curriculum. *ACM Inroads, 5*(4), 64–71.

Papert, S. (1980). *Mindstorms*. Basic Books, 607.

Ridgway, R. (2018). Project GUTS. *Science Scope, 42*(3), 28–33.

Schanzer, E., Fisler, K., Krishnamurthi, S., & Felleisen, M. (2015, February). Transferring skills at solving word problems from computing to algebra through Bootstrap. In *Proceedings of the 46th ACM Technical symposium on computer science education* (pp. 616–621).

Wilensky, U., Brady, C. E., & Horn, M. S. (2014). Fostering computational literacy in science classrooms. *Communications of the ACM, 57*(8), 24–28.

Yadav, A., & Berges, M. (2019). Computer science pedagogical content knowledge: Characterizing teacher performance. *ACM Transactions on Computing Education, 19*(3). DOI: 10.1145/3303770

Yadav A., Krist, C., Good. J., & Caeli. E. (2018). Computational thinking in elementary classrooms: Measuring teacher understanding of computational ideas for teaching science. *Computer Science Education.* DOI: 10.1080/08993408.2018.1560550

Yadav A., & Cooper, S. (2017). Fostering creativity through computing. *Communications of the ACM, 60* (2), 31–33. DOI: 10.1145/3029595

Yadav, A., Mayfield, C., Zhou, N., Hambrusch, S., & Korb, J. T. (2014). Computational thinking in elementary and secondary teacher education. *ACM Transactions on Computing Education, 14*(1), 1–16.

Yadav, A., Oliver, A., & Zamansky, M. (2019). How an unplugged approach to computational thinking can move schools to computer science. *edSurge.* Retrieved from https://www.edsurge.com/news/2019-12-19-how-an-unplugged-approach-to-computational-thinking-can-move-schools-to-computer-science

JavaScript, Python, Scratch, or Something Else? Navigating the Bustling World of Introductory Programming Languages

CHAPTER
10

David Weintrop and Shuchi Grover

> *The tools we use have a profound and devious influence on our thinking habits, and therefore on our thinking abilities.*
> – Edsger Dijkstra

INTRODUCTION

Choosing a programming language (or environment[1]) to use for instruction is an early and consequential decision for computer science educators. Helping equip educators to navigate this bustling world of programming languages with the knowledge to make an informed decision as to which technologies to use, what dimensions to consider in evaluating a potential resource, and how to incorporate it into their classroom to best fit the needs of their learners can be invaluable, especially for those new to the field of computer science. As such, the primary audience for this chapter is those who identify themselves as computer science (or computing) educators in schools. This includes classroom teachers as well as those who participate in out-of-school computing programs and parents who want to know more about ways to get kids interested in the world of computing. Beyond that, we hope this chapter may serve as a useful resource for technology and curriculum designers as a way to help think through the various decisions one encounters in the design and implementation of learning technologies and materials.

To achieve the goal of helping educators make informed decisions around computing languages and environments, this chapter is broken into two main sections. First, we introduce key dimensions to consider in evaluating introductory tools. Second, we provide a review of a number of popular introductory programming languages. We chose the languages reviewed both for their widespread use but also because they provide a sense of the breadth of technologies available for introducing learners to computing. In constructing the chapter with this structure, we hope to provide useful and actionable knowledge for making informed choices both from the set of technologies currently available today but also from the next generation of technologies for introducing learners to computing, whatever that may look like. Although language choice is important, it is the deeper ideas of algorithmic thinking and developing the habits of programming that endure even as programming languages change and evolve. The concluding section in this chapter touches briefly on these ideas of transfer of learning that transcend programming languages.

---

[1] Although technically programming languages and programming environments can be thought of as distinct, the distinction might be counterproductive for this book because many novice tools are both (e.g., Scratch). As such, we use the terms interchangeably.

DIMENSIONS FOR EVALUATING NOVICE PROGRAMMING ENVIRONMENTS

The goal of this opening section is to present a series of dimensions to consider when deciding what language to use. It is important to note that these dimensions are not necessarily mutually exclusive but capture distinct aspects of the language. Further, the relative importance of various characteristics is strongly influenced by the learning environment and the goals laid out for the learning experience. The next section introduces several noteworthy introductory languages and discusses each of them through the lens of these dimensions to make the ideas of this section more concrete.

▶ Low Floor

"Low floor" (along with "high ceiling") is a design philosophy that Seymour Papert advocated when he designed Logo. It refers to the ease with which even a young child—or any novice learner of programming—can get started with creating working programs and animations. In the early days of personal computing, applications like HyperCard embodied this philosophy. In the past two decades, block-based languages like Alice, AgentSheets, Scratch, Snap!, and App Inventor have considerably lowered the barrier to creating interactive programs and creative animations, stories, and games. Researchers studying block-based languages contend that

- Learning a programming vocabulary is difficult. Blocks simplify this problem because picking a block from a palette is far easier than remembering a word: Blocks rely on recognition instead of recall.

- Text-based code is difficult to use because it presents a high cognitive load for new programmers. Blocks reduce the cognitive load by chunking code into a smaller number of meaningful elements.

- Assembling code is error prone. Blocks help users assemble code without basic errors by providing con-strained direct manipulation of structure (e.g., two incompatible concepts do not have connecting parts).

▶ High Ceiling and Expressive Power

A second dimension that is important to consider is what can be accomplished with a given programming language. Can a learner use it to accomplish meaningful tasks that may have real-world impact or is it best used as an introductory tool, and once learners want to write nontrivial programs, they will need to move on to something else? In other words, how far one can go with a given language is important to consider. An environment is considered to be "high ceiling" if it can be used to accomplish significant outcomes. Aspects that impact a language's ceiling include the features of the language (e.g., can you define functions, does it support parallelism, etc.). Logo was one of the first languages to embody a *high ceiling* with *low floor* (see Figure 6). A second dimension to consider is the environment in which it runs and if/how it can connect with resources beyond the environment. For example, Scratch programs all run inside the Scratch environment, which is based around sprites moving on a stage, whereas environments like Snap! and Pencil Code support this type of programming (moving a sprite on a stage) while also giving the user direct access to HTML and JavaScript features allowing programs to be shared beyond the specific environment. Another example of this can be seen with App Inventor, where there are numerous examples of young learners writing apps that end up being used by thousands of users and having a meaningful impact on the world.

Though this dimension of "high ceiling" is at times thought to be in tension with an environment being "low threshold," that need not be the case. A good example can be seen with the NetLogo programming environment, which is used for modeling in science classrooms but also cutting-edge scientific research, running on supercomputing clusters and involving millions of agents.

One final note to mention when discussing the notion of "high ceiling": Programming modality (e.g., block-based vs. text-based) is not the same as expressive power. In other words, just because a tool is text-based, it is not inherently more powerful than a block-based language. For example, learners of Java, JavaScript, and Python can practice their skills in the interfaces of the block-based versions of Java, JavaScript, and Python.

▶ Wide Walls and Diversity of Artifacts

One feature of the blossoming of introductory programming tools is an expansion of the types of programs that can be created. Whereas learners were once constrained to text-only programs or very basic drawing packages, modern introductory tools integrate visual, audio, and even physical components to support a range of types of programs and forms of engagement. Captured under the term "wide walls," the idea is that an environment should support many different types of projects so people with many different interests and preferences can all become engaged. When considering a potential programming language, it is important to consider the universe of possible programs and computational artifacts learners can create. An important aspect of wide walls is allowing learners to incorporate aspects of themselves, their values, their ideas, and their communities into the programs they write. In doing so, it provides a way to support learners from diverse cultural backgrounds and welcome all students into the field of computing.

A second noteworthy aspect of wide walls is the consideration of the platforms on which a program can run and the settings/contexts that it enables. For example, the App Inventor environment is designed specifically to allow novices to program applications for smartphones. This includes making it possible for programming beginners to write programs that take advantage of the capabilities and sensors built into the phone such as speakers, microphones, GPS, and accelerometers. This opens up a whole new suite of ways for novices to allow their users to interact with their programs. Further, because the applications run on the smartphone directly, users can take their programs with them, further expanding the notion of wide walls because the programs are no longer constrained to computer labs or contexts where a user needs to be in front of a laptop.

▶ Social Dimensions

When deciding what programming language to use, it is also important to consider if and how the environment supports the social dimensions of programming. Can learners share their finished programs with others? What about their code? Are there opportunities for them to participate in a larger community based on the programming environment? Are there venues for them to ask for or give feedback on programs written using this environment? Are there examples available for a learner to explore and learn from?

One growing trend in making programming more social is the creation of curated websites and online communities for learners to share, comment on, and "remix" programs. In creating online spaces to view and run others' programs, new ways to participate in coding communities become possible such as commenting on or extending programs written by others before creating programs of your own. Likewise, these online spaces create opportunities for communities to form and peer-to-peer communication and collaboration. These online collections also serve as a way for novices to learn about the capabilities of the platform and get ideas for projects. A growing body of research is showing how these social dimensions of introductory programming platforms can be a powerful way to welcome novices into the field of computing, especially among learners who otherwise might not choose to participate.

▶ Access to Curricula and Community/Professional Development Support

Teachers may also choose languages based on the level of support they get through available curricula that can be readily used and active communities of teachers that can provide support and resources. Some introductory programming environments have companion textbooks authored by the same team that created the environment (e.g., Alice) whereas other environments have spawned numerous companion textbooks, activities guides, or workbooks of various forms. A growing number of online courses and course syllabi are freely available that are aligned to specific programming environments (e.g., the Beauty and Joy of Computing uses Snap!). The physical computing space also has rich online supports, including websites that curate how-to guides to help novices get up and running.

▶ Preparation for Future Learning and Transition to Professional Languages

A final consideration for choosing a programming language is the end goal for the learners and the degree to which the introductory language prepares them for future computer science learning. If the goal is to prepare learners to take more advanced computer science classes, then it is important to choose a language that supports the transition to professional programming languages. A number of such tools exist and are discussed in further detail later in this chapter in the section titled Blending and Bridging Block-Based and Text-Based Approaches. In contrast, if the goal of the course is to welcome learners to the field of computer science and increase interest and awareness of the field, then the notion of "future learning" takes a different form. In these types of courses, the priority is engagement and interest building, and thus preparation for future learning takes the form of developing an identity as a person who can program and wants to pursue computing. As such, showing how an activity like programming a Bee-Bot or constructing a program-controlled Lego structure connects to programming environments with a higher ceiling becomes the focus of instruction (at least with respect to considering future learning).

PROGRAMMING LANGUAGES FOR NOVICES

Having discussed important dimensions on which to evaluate introductory programming tools, this section reviews some of the more widely used introductory programming languages. It is intended to serve as a survey of the current landscape, highlighting both popular languages as well as popular types of programming environments. For each type of language or environment, we briefly discuss its defining characteristics and then introduce significant languages within that category, reviewing unique characteristics of each. In some cases subsections are devoted to particularly noteworthy languages; in other cases, the language is mentioned only as part of the high-level description with references provided for further reading. This section is broken up into five categories based on either the nature of the programming language itself or the context in which programming is situated. It is important to note that these categories are not necessarily mutually exclusive, but we believe this high-level structure is a useful categorization for making sense of the current landscape. Further readings about the languages are provided at the conclusion of this chapter.

▶ Block-Based Languages

Although not a recent innovation, block-based programming languages (Figure 1) have become widespread in the last two decades for introducing novices to the practice of programming and the field of computer science more broadly. Led by the popularity of tools like Scratch, Alice, Snap!, and App Inventor and the ease of creation of new block-based microworlds thanks to libraries like Google's Blockly (a JavaScript library for building visual programming editors), block-based programming has become a common way to make introductory environments "low floor." Block-based programming languages use a *programming-command-as-puzzle-piece* metaphor to provide visual cues as to how and where a command can be used. Authoring programs take the form of dragging and dropping commands together. If two commands cannot fit together to form a valid statement, the environment prevents them from snapping together, thus preventing syntax errors and making it easier for novices to author functioning programs from day one. A growing body of research is uncovering the benefits to using block-based languages in introductory programming contexts. In recent years, more powerful environments like GP considerably raise the ceiling on what can be accomplished in block-based programming. We describe four of the most popular block-based environments here.

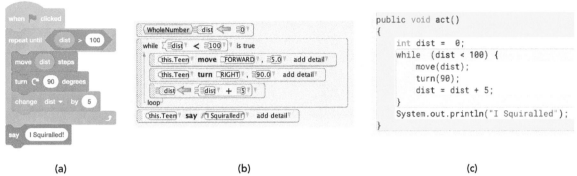

| (a) | (b) | (c) |

Figure 1a, b, and c. The same program written in two block-based languages: Scratch (a) and Alice (b) and one-text based language Java rendered in Greenfoot (c).

▶ Scratch

Scratch is a visual block-based programming language used extensively in and out of classrooms to introduce young learners (usually between the ages of 10–17) to programming. Scratch builds on the "turtle geometry" paradigm of earlier languages (like Logo) from MIT Media Lab, but the turtle has been replaced by the Scratch cat on a 2-dimensional canvas. Programs can have any number of objects (or sprites), each of which can have scripts controlling them. Scratch focuses on programming as a vehicle for self-expression and urges children to design, share, and "remix" projects in the form of games, stories, and animations. Scratch is available in many languages and also allows for extensions with physical computing through Makey Makey, Micro:bit, LEGO Education WeDo, and LEGO MINDSTORMS (see Figure 2).

Another noteworthy feature of Scratch is its online community. From its inception, Scratch emphasized the social dimensions of programming by supporting an online community that allows students to easily share, like, and remix projects. When a learner writes a program in Scratch, if they want to, they can easily share it with the larger Scratch community. In doing so, it becomes possible for others to run their program, look at the code that is controlling it, and even make a copy of it for themselves to modify it (called remixing). There is also a ScratchEd community in which teachers share ideas for programming activities and lesson plans for all grade levels and subject matters. All these features contribute to Scratch's immense popularity worldwide.

Figure 2. The Scratch interface (left) and a set of extensions to the Scratch blocks library (right)

▶ Alice

Alice (created at Carnegie Mellon University) is one of the first block-based programming environments that emerged in the mid-1990s seeking to make it easy for novice learners to create animations, interactive stories, or games in 3-D using the object-oriented programming paradigm. Alice programs focus on introducing entities into the 3-D landscape that can then be programmatically controlled, making it easy to customize their appearances and movements in the world (Figure 3). Additionally, the Alice Project also provides supplemental tools and materials, such as its Bridge to Java, to make it easy for (older) students to transition from block-based to text-based programming. The creators of Alice have authored numerous textbooks, which provide a de facto curriculum that teachers can follow in an introductory programming classroom (mostly in secondary school). Features like undo/redo, disabling portions of code while testing, the ability to step through coding, and testing/debugging easy in Alice. Like Scratch, Alice is also available in several languages and supports an online community that showcases "featured projects" and serves as a source of support to teachers and users of Alice. Oracle Corporation provides training materials for Alice.

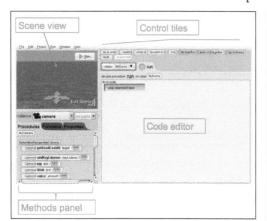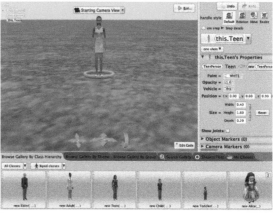

Figure 3. The Alice programming environment (left) and scene editor (right)

▶ Snap!

Snap! (developed at University of California, Berkeley) was inspired by Scratch and shares many of its defining features, like the user interface with the Stage, Scripting Area, and Blocks Palette and the ability to run live, parallel blocks of code. The goal of the creators of Snap! was to add additional capabilities to block-based languages to raise the ceiling, so to speak, and make them computationally powerful. Snap! includes several powerful language features not available in Scratch, including first-class functions and more sophisticated support for functions and collections. Snap! Extensions such as NetsBlox, provide support for message passing, networked applications and pulling external data sources into a program (through remote procedure calls). Like Alice, Snap! also allows for users to step through code. Snap! is the language used in the popular Beauty and Joy of Computing (BJC) curriculum, which has been successfully taught at the high school and college levels. See Figure 4.

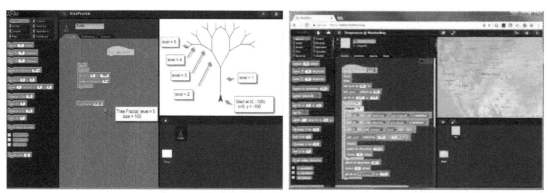

Figure 4. The Snap! programming environment, showing how to author recursive programs (left) and connect to data sources via NetsBlox (right)

MIT App Inventor (or simply, App Inventor) is a visual block-based programming environment that allows everyone—even children—to build fully functional apps for smartphones and tablets. The goal of App Inventor is to provide a blocks-based tool that facilitates the creation of complex, high-impact mobile apps in significantly less time than in traditional programming environments. App Inventor uses an event-based programming model where user-initiated actions (such as button clicks, swipes, and shakes) initiate scripts, thanks to App Inventor's focus on mobile application development. Additionally, App Inventor apps can invoke other applications and give the programmer access to other functions of a phone like the camera, SMS texting, and sensors for location, sound, and video. App Inventor also has features for data persistence on a web database and allows data to be imported from different sources such as social media. Programs written in App Inventor can easily be downloaded onto phones so they can be run on the devices they are created for. See Figure 5.

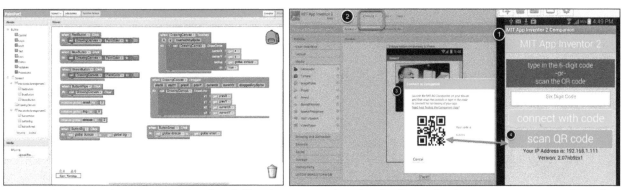

Figure 5. App Inventor's programming interface (left) and one approach to downloading an App Inventor app onto your phone via QR code

▶ Text-Based Languages

Until recently, all programming languages were text-based. Unlike block-based languages that include visual cues for how to assemble programs and support a drag-and-drop approach, text-based languages require you to write programs by typing commands out character by character. The vast majority of advanced computer science coursework and nearly all professional programming tasks use text-based languages. These languages include Java, C++, Python, Scheme, and JavaScript, among many others, which are "high ceiling" in that they make all capabilities of computing accessible to the programmer. Given the history and prevalence of text-based languages, several text-based programming languages are also explicitly designed for introducing programming to novices. This includes early languages like Logo and BASIC that were popular among both K–12 and undergraduate settings in the 1980s. More recently, languages (and environments) like Greenfoot and p5.js (a JavaScript library) are being successfully used to introduce learners to object-oriented programming in Java and web programming in JavaScript, respectively. In a similar vein, Pyret introduces learners to functional programming in a Python-like language. One commonly made argument for the use of text-based programming languages in introductory contexts is to prepare learners for more advanced programming activities where text-based languages are far more prevalent.

▶ Introductory Text-Based Languages

As early as the 1970s, people started working on the challenge of how to make programming more accessible to learners. This work began with Papert and his research group around the creation of Logo, a *low-floor*, *high-ceiling* programming language designed explicitly for children. See Figure 6 for an example of generating beautiful fractal images using a recursive procedure in Logo. The Logo programming language allowed learners to control a physical, and then later virtual, object called a "turtle" that would carry out the user's instructions. Through controlling the turtle, novices could write programs to draw pictures and create sophisticated geometric shapes. At the same time, Logo could also be used for other basic text-related activities, such as language manipulation. Logo was influential in shaping many of the languages (both text-based and graphical) discussed in this chapter. Along with languages designed for younger learners, a number of text-based languages are designed for learners of all ages. These languages often have simpler syntax and/or include a smaller set of primitives to make it easier to learn. Early examples of such languages include BASIC and Pascal. In addition, new text-based languages such as Quorum (see Figure 7) that are screen-reader-friendly (unlike block-based programming environments) are designed to be accessible by the visually impaired for learning introductory programming. The syntax of Quorum is simple and easy to use for all learners, not only the visually impaired. For example, the expression of iteration and conditionals is shown in Figure 6. The indentation is only for visual effect and not a syntactical requirement as in Python.

```
; Recursive procedure
to DrawFractalLine :level :length
 ifelse :level < 1 [
 forward :length] [
 DrawFractalLine (sum -1 :level) (quotient :length 3.00)
 left 60
 DrawFractalLine (sum -1 :level) (quotient :length 3.00)
 right 120
 DrawFractalLine (sum -1 :level) (quotient :length 3.00)
 left 60
 DrawFractalLine (sum -1 :level) (quotient :length 3.00)
 ]
end
; procedure to clear screen and position turtle
to SetupTurtle
 cg setpensize 1 setpos [-160 -10] right 60 clean pd
end
; setup turtle then draw Koch's snowflake(5)
SetupTurtle
repeat 3 [DrawFractalLine 5 330 right 120]
```

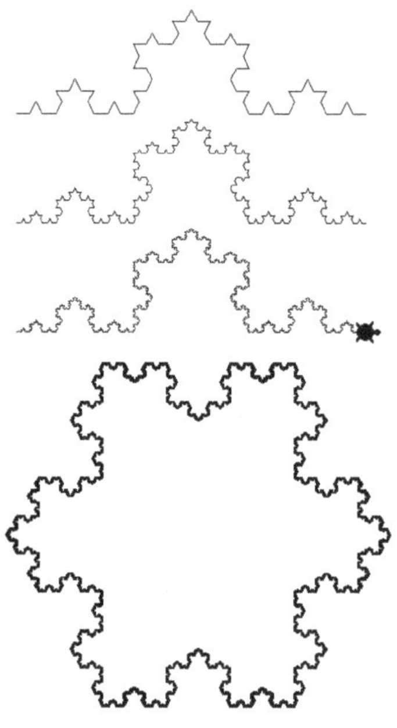

Figure 6. Logo's high-ceiling and low-floor exemplified in the drawing of Koch's Snowflake using recursion

```
1. Iteration
        repeat 10 times
                output "hello world"
        end
2. Conditional
        n = 10
        if n > 5
                output n
        else
                output "not large enough"
        end
```

Figure 7. The Quorum programming language.

▶ Professional Text-Based Languages

Along with introductory text-based languages, a small set of professional languages are commonly used for computer science instruction. Over the last decade, C++, Java, and Python, stand out as the most commonly used general-purpose programming languages used in educational contexts. They support many foundational concepts of computer science (e.g., native data structures, a variety of data types and control structures) while also being in widespread use in industry. Part of the logic behind using languages like these is that they can serve as a means to learn the foundations of computer science such that should learners need to go on to learn another language, they will be well equipped to do so. Recently, there has been a growth in using programming languages native to the web in introductory contexts, chief among them being JavaScript. The main strength of this approach is the ubiquity of web browsers and the ability to use the web itself as a context for learning to program. A second text-based language gaining popularity is Processing, which is a language designed for beginners that includes a graphics library, so learners are authoring interactive visual programs from day one. Also worth mention is **p5.js**— a Processing library for JavaScript that brings visual, interactivity to web programming learning contexts. Another feature of learning to program with professional tools is the large universe of development tools and libraries that accompany them. For example, thousands of Java and Python libraries exist that can be incorporated into introductory computing courses to easily extend the basics of the language to support anything from database queries to video game graphics libraries to advanced statistical modeling tools.

▶ Blending and Bridging Block-Based and Text-Based Approaches

Although the prior two sections categorize programming languages as either block-based or text-based, this division is not entirely accurate. A growing number of dual-modality languages have both block-based and text-based interfaces, allowing learners to move back and forth between the two. The idea with this approach is to allow learners themselves to decide what type of programming interface they want to see. This approach can be seen in Pencil Code and Code.org's AppLab.

Along with dual-modality environments, a number of hybrid programming environments blend features of block-based and text-based languages. For example, it is possible to have a text-based language that also presents users with a blocks palette of available commands that allows them to add commands to their program via drag and drop. Another noteworthy hybrid language is the frame-based editing approach supported by Greenfoot 3. Like block-based environments, frame-based editors make the unit of operation a valid command (e.g., a block) rather than individual characters, thus preventing syntax errors by making sure you can add commands only in valid places. At the same time, frame-based editing is keyboard-driven like conventional text-based languages.

Lastly, some block-based programming environments provide a "bridge" to text-based programming languages/environments. Alice 3, for example, allows learners to convert their Alice program into a working Java program. The idea for such "bridging" is to help students who have learned coding in the visual block-based environment to transition to text-based coding. Besides the educational benefits, such tools allow for hybrid development whereby the visual blocks language can be used to create a portion of the app and Java is used to add functionality that is difficult to develop in the block-based language.

▶ Physical Computing

Physical, or tangible, computing describes objects that bring the foundations of computing out from behind the screen and places them in the palms of learners. These often take the form of microcontrollers that have small onboard chips and allow learners to attach various sensors and motors to interact with the physical world. Physical computing is a popular and creative context in which to teach students programming. According to Sentance and Childs, who authored **Chapter 24** in this book, physical computing "intersects a range of activities often associated with design technology, electronics, robotics, and computer science." Hardware devices that are currently popular for teaching programming in the context of physical computing include devices such as BBC Micro:bit, Raspberry Pi, LilyPad Arduino (for e-textiles, as described in **Chapter 8** by Fields and Kafai), LEGO products such as WeDo and MINDSTORMS, Makey Makey, PicoBoard, and many more. In addition, many programmable robots are aimed at younger learners, including Sphero, Dash and Dot, Ozobot, Kibo, Bee-Bot, and Cubetto. For more on how to teach introductory programming in the context of physical computing, refer to **Chapter 24, X-ing Boundaries With Physical Computing**.

▶ Preliterate and Symbolic Languages

Recent design innovations have resulted in programming environments that cater to increasingly younger learners. One such approach for introducing young learners to programming is through the use of symbols and icons for children who may not have yet learned to read. Popular among such programming environments are ScratchJr, Kodable, Hopscotch, and Lightbot Jr. Many of these environments support a touchscreen interface and can be used on hand-held devices. It has been shown that children as young as 5 can learn the logic and foundational ideas of programming. Though true of children of all ages, but for the very young learners especially, programming should be about a new medium for creativity and expression and teaching life skills such as making and correcting mistakes and persistence through the process of problem-solving.

BEYOND PROGRAMMING LANGUAGES—TRANSFER AND DEEPER LEARNING

Regardless of the language used to introduce learners to programming, teachers must view introductory programming languages as vehicles for building an understanding of the deeper ideas and concepts that underlie all programming. It is important to remember that the languages popular as of this writing may not exist some years from now, but the deeper ideas of coding and programming will endure.

Yes, programming experiences are shaped by the language or environment that is used. However, regardless of the language, introductory programming experiences should be designed to ensure learners understand the fundamental structures of programs—that programs are essentially codified algorithms comprising sequences of commands, of concepts such as repetition (that can be enacted through looping constructs or recursion) and selection (enacted through conditional or "switch" statements), and of appropriate data structures. Programming is a vehicle for students to understand computational problem-solving and computational thinking, which include aspects such as problem decomposition, modularity (functions), data representation and manipulation through the use of appropriate data structures, iterative refinement, and testing and debugging.

Strategies for scaffolding learner engagement with conceptual foundations are described in the chapters on pedagogic scaffolds (**Chapter 23, Worked Examples and Scaffolding Strategies**) and guided exploration (**Chapter 7, Guided Exploration With Unplugged Activities**). Other strategies to mediate for transfer to future (including text-based) programming contexts include "expansive framing" of programming contexts and the use of analogous representations (or multiple representations of computational solutions).

Expansive framing (studied by late researcher, Randi Engle, at University of California, Berkeley) is a powerful, socially framed, context-based transfer technique that can be promoted by creating an *expectation for future transfer* in which students see that what they are learning will maintain relevance over time (and in our case, across programming environments). Expansive framing of programming—the role coding plays and will continue to play (no matter what career students choose)—serves the twin purposes of improving students' perceptions of computing (as part of deeper learning) as well as generating interest and excitement and, thus, motivating the learning, priming, or preparing students for future use (transfer) of what they were learning in future contexts and settings.

In addition to demonstrating the promise of expansive framing, Grover's work has shown that *analogous representations* of algorithmic solutions help learners *see* computational constructs in forms beyond the shackles of a specific syntactical structure—that guiding students to *draw analogies between different formalisms* can foster deep and abstract understanding of fundamental concepts of CT. These formalisms could include pseudocode versions of the algorithmic solution (see Figure 8).

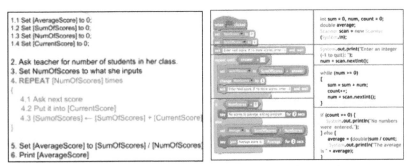

Figure 8. Pseudocode, Scratch and Java code representing solutions of a program that calculates the average demonstrating deeper structural similarities in code beyond syntax

WHAT THIS CHAPTER HAS NOT DEALT WITH

This chapter shares many important ideas on the bustling world of programming languages that are relevant to teaching introductory programming in primary and secondary school education. We have attempted to cover this vast world by focusing on languages and environments that are being, and have been, extensively used in introductory programming settings, especially for school-aged children. That said, we have not dealt with a few aspects of introductory programming languages that some teachers may want to delve deeper into.

The first is **functional programming**—a way of programming that is not extensively taught or used in introductory programming in schools but has been known to have benefits. Functional programming is a programming paradigm—a style of building the structure and elements of computer programs—that treats computation as the evaluation of mathematical functions and avoids changing state and mutable data. Because many misconceptions of novice programmers are tied to state and the notional machine related to imperative programming, proponents of functional programming believe that programming could be more easily taught and learned if learners were taught in languages that did not require dealing with these troublesome aspects. Lisp, Scheme, Haskell, Racket, Scala, Clojure, and Wolfram are well-known functional programming languages. Scheme, Racket, and Pyret are popular in some K–12 introductory programming settings, specifically with learners in mind. The popular Bootstrap curriculum that integrates learning of algebra, data science, and physics with programming uses Racket and Pyret. For more on teaching and learning functional programs, we recommend checking out *How to Design Programs*, an introductory programming primer that focuses on design principles and good habits of programming.

A second issue is the vast (and growing) world of **domain- and task-specific programming languages**. The idea with this class of tools is that the language and environment are designed to solve one specific task or operate within a specific domain. So rather than trying to be a general-purpose language that can be used to solve a wide array of problems, the language is much more narrowly scoped. The advantage of this design is that it becomes possible to more tightly couple language features to a task, thus making it easier for novices to use. Examples of these types of domain-specific languages include statistical languages like R, mathematical languages like MATLAB, and data analysis languages, like Vega-Lite and CODAP, which are both designed to help with tasks related to statistics, data science, and analysis. Another flavor of domain-specific languages are those related to modeling and simulation. Languages like NetLogo and StarLogo Nova provide environments for 'agent-based modeling' and can be used to model complex systems and emergent phenomena. As such, they have a natural home in science classrooms (see **Chapter 9** on integrating coding in science and other subjects) but may not make sense to be the focal tools for a CS curriculum.

A final, and important, aspect of introductory computing that this chapter has not addressed is that of accessibility in **programming environments for learners with disabilities**. Many of the programming languages described in this chapter have been designed to have low thresholds and wide walls with a view to making programming more equitable and accommodating diverse learners with varied abilities. However, programming environments for the visually impaired rely on screen readers, and block-based languages are not screen-reader friendly. Languages and environments that are accessible to learners with physical disabilities have been under-developed and under-researched. This is changing, albeit slowly, with the emergence of languages like Quorum (discussed earlier this chapter) and tools like Microsoft's Code Jumper, which uses tactile "code blocks" of different shapes that can be attached together to execute a program.

RESEARCH AND READINGS

This chapter serves as an initial peek into the world of introductory programming languages and tools. As suggested throughout, there is a large, and rapidly growing, body of literature to explore to learn more about the environments and ideas discussed here. To begin, several survey papers describe the set of available environments (Duncan, Bell, & Tanimoto, 2014; Kelleher & Pausch, 2005) as well as serve as high-level reviews of what we know about teaching people programming and computer science more broadly (Robins, Rountree, & Rountree, 2003; Sentance, Barendsen, & Schulte, 2018). This chapter discusses a number of block-based programming tools which have been the focus of much research. A number of papers give a good sense of what we know about block-based programming (Bau et al., 2017; Franklin et al., 2017; Grover & Basu, 2017; Grover et al., 2018; Weintrop, 2019). For details on the philosophy and design of introductory block-based programming environments, it helps to refer to publications by the creators describing the tool, e.g., Cooper, Dann, & Pausch (2000) for Alice; Maloney et al. (2004) for Scratch; Harvey & Mönig (2010) for Snap! (formerly BYOB) and Broll et al. (2016) for its NetsBlox extension; Kölling (2010) for Greenfoot; Wolber, Abelson, Spertus, & Looney (2011) for App Inventor; Bau & Bau (2014) for Pencilcode; and Fraser (2015) for Blockly.

The chapter also touched on research related to environments that span and blend block-based and text-based approaches (Kölling, Brown, & Altadmri, 2017; Matsuzawa et al., 2015; Weintrop & Holbert, 2017; Weintrop & Wilensky, 2017) as well as research focused on the transition from block-based to text-based tools (Armoni, Meerbaum-Salant, & Ben-Ari, 2015; Dann et al., 2012; Grover, Pea, & Cooper, 2014, 2015; Weintrop & Wilensky, 2019). There is also a large body of work on social aspects of learning to program and efforts to make programming more equitable and inviting (Goode, Chapman, & Margolis, 2012; Kafai et al., 2014; Kelleher, Pausch, & Kiesler, 2007; Maloney et al., 2008; Resnick et al., 2009; Ryoo et al., 2013; Wolber 2011) that we encourage the reader to also explore.

BIBLIOGRAPHY

Armoni, M., Meerbaum-Salant, O., & Ben-Ari, M. (2015). From Scratch to "real" programming. *ACM Transactions on Computing Education (TOCE), 14*(4), 1-15.

Bau, D., & Bau, D. A. (2014). A preview of Pencil Code: A tool for developing mastery of programming. In *Proceedings of the 2nd Workshop on Programming for Mobile & Touch* (pp. 21-24).

Bau, D., Gray, J., Kelleher, C., Sheldon, J., & Turbak, F. (2017). Learnable programming: Blocks and beyond. *Communications of the ACM, 60*(6), 72–80.

Broll, B., Völgyesi, P., Sallai, J., & Lédeczi, A. (2016). NetsBlox: A visual language and web-based environment for teaching distributed programming. *NetsBlox.org*

Cooper, S., Dann, W., & Pausch, R. (2000). Alice: a 3-D tool for introductory programming concepts. In *Journal of Computing Sciences in Colleges, 15*(5), pp. 107-116. Consortium for Computing Sciences in Colleges.

Dann, W., Cosgrove, D., Slater, D., Culyba, D., & Cooper, S. (2012, February). Mediated transfer: Alice 3 to Java. In *Proceedings of the 43rd ACM Technical Symposium on Computer Science Education* (pp. 141–146).

Duncan, C., Bell, T., & Tanimoto, S. (2014). Should your 8-year-old learn coding? *Proceedings of the 9th Workshop in Primary and Secondary Computing Education*, 60–69.

Franklin, D., Skifstad, G., Rolock, R., Mehrotra, I., Ding, V., Hansen, A., … Harlow, D. (2017). Using upper-elementary student performance to understand conceptual sequencing in a blocks-based curriculum. *Proceedings of the 2017 ACM SIGCSE Technical Symposium on Computer Science Education*, 231–236.

Fraser, N. (2015). Ten things we've learned from Blockly. In *2015 IEEE Blocks and Beyond Workshop (Blocks and Beyond)* (pp. 49-50). IEEE.

Goode, J., Chapman, G., & Margolis, J. (2012). Beyond curriculum: The exploring computer science program. *ACM Inroads, 3*(2), 47–53.

Grover, S., & Basu, S. (2017). Measuring student learning in introductory block-based programming: Examining misconceptions of loops, variables, and Boolean logic. *Proceedings of the 2017 ACM SIGCSE Technical Symposium on Computer Science Education*, 267–272.

Grover, S., Pea, R., & Cooper, S. (2014). Expansive framing and preparation for future learning in middle-school computer science. In *Proceedings of ICLS, 2014*. Boulder, CO: International Society of the Learning Sciences.

Grover, S., Pea, R., & Cooper, S. (2015). Designing for deeper learning in a blended computer science course for middle school students. *Computer Science Education, 25*(2), 199–237.

Grover, S., Basu, S., & Schank, P. (2018). What we can learn about student learning from open-ended programming projects in middle school computer science. In *Proceedings of the 49th ACM Technical Symposium on Computer Science Education* (pp. 999-1004).

Kafai, Y. B., Lee, E., Searle, K., Fields, D., Kaplan, E., & Lui, D. (2014). A crafts-oriented approach to computing in high school: Introducing computational concepts, practices, and perspectives with electronic textiles. *Transactions on Computing Education, 14*(1), 1–1:20.

Kelleher, C., & Pausch, R. (2005). Lowering the barriers to programming: A taxonomy of programming environments and languages for novice programmers. *ACM Computing Surveys, 37*(2), 83–137.

Kelleher, C., Pausch, R., & Kiesler, S. (2007). Storytelling Alice motivates middle school girls to learn computer programming. *Proceedings of the SIGCHI Conference on Human Factors in Computing Systems*, 1455–1464.

Kölling, M. (2010). The Greenfoot programming environment. *ACM Transactions on Computing Education (TOCE), 10*(4), 1-21.

Kölling, M., Brown, N. C. C., & Altadmri, A. (2017). Frame-based editing. *Journal of Visual Languages and Sentient Systems, 3*, 40–67.

Maloney, J., Burd, L., Kafai, Y., Rusk, N., Silverman, B., & Resnick, M. (2004). Scratch: a sneak preview. In *Proceedings. Second International Conference on Creating, Connecting and Collaborating through Computing, 2004.* (pp. 104-109). IEEE.

Maloney, J. H., Peppler, K., Kafai, Y., Resnick, M., & Rusk, N. (2008). Programming by choice: Urban youth learning programming with Scratch. *ACM SIGCSE Bulletin, 40*(1), 367–371.

Matsuzawa, Y., Ohata, T., Sugiura, M., & Sakai, S. (2015). Language migration in non-CS introductory programming through mutual language translation environment. *Proceedings of the 46th ACM Technical Symposium on Computer Science Education*, 185–190.

Resnick, M., Silverman, B., Kafai, Y., Maloney, J., Monroy-Hernández, A., Rusk, N., … Silver, J. (2009). Scratch: Programming for all. *Communications of the ACM, 52*(11), 60.

Robins, A., Rountree, J., & Rountree, N. (2003). Learning and teaching programming: A review and discussion. *Computer Science Education, 13*(2), 137–172.

Ryoo, J. J., Margolis, J., Lee, C. H., Sandoval, C. D., & Goode, J. (2013). Democratizing computer science knowledge: Transforming the face of computer science through public high school education. *Learning, Media and Technology, 38*(2), 161–181.

Sentance, S., Barendsen, E., & Schulte, C. (2018). *Computer science education: Perspectives on teaching and learning in school.* Bloomsbury Publishing.

Weintrop, D. (2019). Block-based programming in computer science education. *Communications of the ACM, 62*(8), 22–25.

Weintrop, D., & Holbert, N. (2017). From blocks to text and back: Programming patterns in a dual-modality environment. *Proceedings of the 2017 ACM SIGCSE Technical Symposium on Computer Science Education*, 633–638.

Weintrop, D., & Wilensky, U. (2017). Between a block and a typeface: Designing and evaluating hybrid programming environments. *Proceedings of the 2017 Conference on Interaction Design and Children*, 183–192.

Weintrop, D., & Wilensky, U. (2019). Transitioning from introductory block-based and text-based environments to professional programming languages in high school computer science classrooms. *Computers & Education, 142*, 103646.

Wolber, D. (2011). App inventor and real-world motivation. In *Proceedings of the 42nd ACM Technical Symposium on Computer Science Education* (pp. 601–606).

Wolber, D., Abelson, H., Spertus, E., & Looney, L. (2011). *App Inventor.* O'Reilly Media, Inc.

Knowledge, Skills, Attitudes, and Beliefs: Learning Goals for Introductory Programming

Rebecca Vivian, Shuchi Grover & Katrina Falkner

> *Educating the mind without educating the heart is no education at all*
> – Aristotle

INTRODUCTION

Learning computer programming can be a nuanced experience. It can empower learners as much as it can challenge their self-beliefs and their perceptions of computing. A key goal of 21st century education is to help learners build not just knowledge about new concepts, skills, and practices but also ways of thinking, interests and identities, and beliefs and skills to succeed in this connected, technology-infused world. This is true of teaching computing as well.

This chapter outlines key knowledge and skills as well as positive attitudes, beliefs, and mindsets related to learning programming. We also unpack practical learning and teaching strategies. The overarching goal is to build teacher capacity and confidence that can support students in flourishing as confident learners with increased interest and agency in the learning process. Ensuring students have the necessary problem-solving and self-regulatory learning skills to design, build, and test programming solutions supports the development of resilient learners who also recognize that taking risks is a necessary part of the programming process. Pedagogies for the primary and secondary years must also appropriately scaffold the learning of key computational thinking concepts and programming skills, and development of positive mindsets toward computing and programming.

We use the deeper learning framework (Figure 1) to frame three domains of competence and development that we must attend to in any programming classroom.

- *Cognitive domain*—domain-specific knowledge and skills, as well as thinking, reasoning, and problem-solving skills

- *Interpersonal domain*—collaboration and communication and expressing information to others and working together

- *Intrapersonal domain*—beliefs, mindsets, and attitudes

Several of the skills related to these three domains are discussed in other chapters in this book. Many

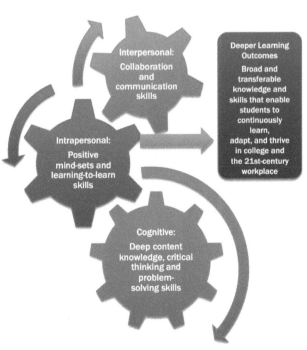

Figure 1. Deeper learning calls for attending to cognitive, interpersonal, and intrapersonal skills to prepare K-12 students for college and beyond.

of the cognitive skills (including programming concepts and practices) are covered by the bulk of the chapters in this book. Likewise, interpersonal skills including collaboration through pair programming are also addressed in dedicated chapters. As such, this chapter provides more detail on related domains and elements not addressed elsewhere in the book.

COGNITIVE SKILLS: PROGRAMMING CONCEPTS AND PRACTICES

Cognitive skills required for programming include a combination of the knowledge of programming concepts and practices involved as well as thinking skills and practices that underpin programming. Several chapters of this book cover these key concepts and practices. This aspect of programming involves the enactment of content knowledge, critical thinking, and problem-solving skills.

▶ Programming Knowledge and Practices—Syntax and Semantics

Knowledge and skills specific to programming and programming languages are required for designing programming solutions. In much the same manner as English has rules and conventions for writing, effective coding mandates unique rules and conventions as well. These rules fall into two key categories— semantics and syntax.

Semantics is concerned with the meaning of the code: what fragments of code mean and do within a program and how they are interpreted. *Syntax* is a set of rules for writing code and the structure of the programming language, similar to grammar for English. Correct syntax is permitted phrases of code—validated sequences of symbols and instructions used in a program, such as opening and closing brackets—similar to the use of capital letters and full stops in everyday writing.

Text-based programming environments require students to be more mindful about the syntax in their code. An error (or "bug") can easily occur from simply a missing semicolon or bracket. Block-based programming environments remove the nuances and nuisances of syntax and associated errors, allowing young students or novices to focus on the semantics of their program by combining blocks that represent code constructs with fixed syntax. Newer environments such as Pencil Code that allow students to transition from block-based to text-based programming can be used to provide an on-ramp to learning that syntax, rules, and conventions of writing code (Figure 2). **Chapter 10** discusses in detail the features of various introductory programming environments along several key dimensions.

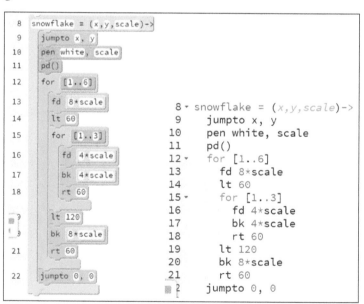

Figure 2. Example block-based and text-based programming in Pencil Code

Conventions are generally accepted usage or practice but are not enforced. In programming, conventions can include the naming of variables that are sensible, chunking of code for readability and the use of commenting to describe code fragments to other users. These good *habits of programming* are the focus of **Chapter 25**.

> Teaching students about programming rules and conventions from the outset can help them strive for effective and elegant code that is easy to read, and error-free. Teaching students how to read and interpret the meaning of code can aid code literacy—a skill that is important for programming. *Code reading and writing go hand-in-hand.*

THINKING SKILLS AND PRACTICES OF PROGRAMMING

Computational thinking, systems thinking, and design thinking are fundamental thinking and problem-solving skills that we aim for students to develop through their learning of programming. Together they form a set of skills that are considered valuable in all citizens today and in the future. As students undertake programming activities, they are likely engaging in elements of these thinking skills and processes. To support students in their success, we can explicitly integrate the teaching of these skills into our programming lessons to improve learning. Taking the time to build students' capacity in these various ways of thinking before, during, and after learning activities can build students' capacity to successfully design, implement, and evaluate solutions.

In this section, we introduce these ways of thinking and provide practical examples of classroom activities that can be integrated into units of teaching and programming activities to enhance and improve student skills.

▶ Computational Thinking

Computational thinking describes the processes and strategies we use when thinking about how a computer can help us to solve complex problems and create systems. As computing increasingly plays a role across many different industries today, developing students' ways of thinking in terms of how to harness computing and how to design computational solutions is important. Even if students go into fields other than computing, computational thinking can help students create solutions, speak the language, and understand how to work with technologists in their chosen profession.

Although the key constructs of computational thinking vary in the literature, they typically involve the elements shown in Table 1. Several chapters in this book deal with elements of computational thinking in the context of programming. We touch upon three of them.

Table 1. A breakdown of the elements of computational thinking (CT)

Element of CT	Description	Activity Examples
Logical reasoning	Analyzing a program to predict the behavior or output	Reading/tracing code and making a prediction of the output
Algorithmic thinking	Creating step-by-step instructions and rules for solving problems	Describing or planning code needed (e.g., using flowcharts, pseudocode, or sequencing cards)
Abstraction	Removing unnecessary detail and identifying general principles	Being able to identify a chunk of code where functions can be used
Pattern recognition	Observing and finding similarities and patterns in data	Identifying repetitive code and determining where loops can be used; analyzing data and describing patterns in data
Decomposition	Breaking down data, processes, or problems into smaller, more manageable parts	Brainstorming project roles and tasks (e.g., programmer, project manager, marketing) and all the parts of a project to be completed
Evaluation	Making judgments about solutions	Critically evaluating programming projects or testing projects with users for feedback

▶ Decomposition

Decomposition is a skill that individuals can use to solve small or complex problems. Breaking down a programming project into more manageable parts during the design phase can help students to more easily determine the elements that make up their program and how they can go about designing their project. It also helps develop modular solutions. Decomposition complements algorithmic design because it helps students consider what pieces of code they need (the steps) to bring their digital solution to life. This process is similar to cooking, where we need to break down a recipe to determine what we need and the logical steps that will result in a desired outcome.

Not all programming activities involve elaborate project design. It could be that students are provided with a simple programming challenge or assignment. For example, students could be tasked to move a robot from one end of a grid to another while avoiding obstacles or to solve a programming problem. In these cases, it is important that students have an understanding of the problem space. To support their ability to solve the problem, students can still consider the elements of what is being asked in the problem description or activity brief, drawing on prior knowledge and actions required to solve the problem. See **Chapter 13, Modularity with Methods and Functions** as well as **Chapter 2, Before You Program, Plan!**, for more ideas related to decomposition.

▶ Algorithmic Thinking

Algorithmic thinking helps an individual think about the specific logical sequence of steps required to solve a problem and create step-by-step instructions and rules. In the process of planning the solution (see **Chapter 2, Before You Program, Plan!**), students need to establish the correct sequence of steps needed to achieve their goals and subgoals, including breaking down the problem using decomposition. Algorithms are the instructions—or the recipe—for what the computer is to follow. Students draw on skills in logical reasoning, abstraction, and pattern recognition to design effective algorithms. While decomposition often provides high-level plans for building solutions, algorithmic thinking scaffolds can help students design and manage more specific steps that a computer can implement.

As detailed in **Chapters 1 and 2**, algorithm development can be scaffolded in a number of ways in the classroom (Figure 3). For example, with block-based programming, students can work by placing symbolic instruction cards in sequence or designing their code using pseudocode or flowcharts to represent the steps as well as input and output of a program. Pseudocode and flowcharts allow programmers to break down a high-level design into smaller, individual events indicated using processes, inputs, loops, flow, outputs, and start/end.

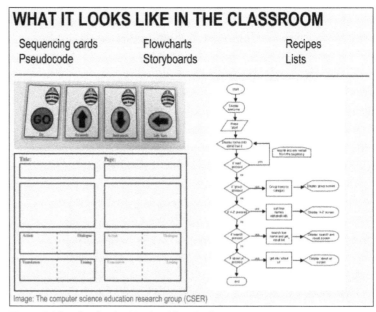

Figure 3. Ideas for developing algorithms in class. (Image source: The Computer Science Education Research (CSER) group, University of Adelaide)

▶ Testing and Debugging

Just as students are taught editing and proofreading practices in English, students need to be taught good testing and debugging practices in programming. *Testing* is the deliberate act of checking the correctness of code within a program. *Debugging* is an iterative activity in which one tests code correctness and makes corrections to the code. Some programming environments have feedback mechanisms to alert users when an error occurs in their code; however, it still requires self-regulation, critical thinking, and problem-solving skills to review, identify, and fix errors in the code. It is, however, important to help students realize that errors in code are part and parcel of programming. Everyone—from novice to expert programmers—needs to engage in testing and debugging.

> Normalizing the occurrence of bugs and frequency of testing in programming can help students see these as opportunities to improve programs and learn rather than as setbacks.

▶ Strategies for Debugging

Starting with good design principles and processes will help students understand the workings of their code and find bugs more easily. Students should test their code regularly so that they can identify any early errors. Testing code should not be something that occurs at the end of a project but rather it should be integrated into the process of coding. This process of iterative refinement is of key importance in programming.

One strategy that students can adopt to find errors in their code is tracing, which involves reading and talking through code step-by-step. Students should be looking for small errors, such as syntax mistakes like a missing bracket or comma, or for more structural issues such as a missing variable or incomplete algorithm.

Another strategy that can be useful in the classroom is peer review, in which students seek the help of their peers or swap code. This is where good *habits of programming* (as previously mentioned in syntax and semantics) helps another person more easily understand your code and hopefully find errors.

For more on helping students build these skills, see **Chapter 20, Testing and Debugging**.

▶ Systems Thinking

Systems thinking involves taking a holistic approach to solving problems, in which one identifies and examines the components of a system to understand how they interact and relate with one another and influence the functioning of an entire system. Examples of familiar systems include the water cycle, waste disposal, or a school system. Computers are digital systems made up of hardware and software that humans interact with. At a high level, students can think about the holistic design of their overall programs, including all of the hardware components (input and output devices), user interaction, and how the code works to make inputs and outputs occur (Figure 4). An example of this in practice is taking a systems approach to the design and evaluation of a Makey Makey or any other project involving physical components, such as in tangible/physical computing. Systems thinking is also especially relevant when students are dealing with coding in the context of science or ecology.

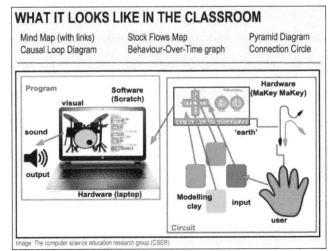

WHAT IT LOOKS LIKE IN THE CLASSROOM

| Mind Map (with links) | Stock Flows Map | Pyramid Diagram |
| Causal Loop Diagram | Behaviour-Over-Time graph | Connection Circle |

Image: The computer science education research group (CSER)

Figure 4. Ideas for developing algorithms in class. (Image source: The Computer Science Education Research (CSER) group, University of Adelaide)

▶ Design Thinking

Design thinking is a process that promotes thinking, consideration of multiple alternative solutions to problems, and rapid iterative cycles toward a desired solution. This thinking approach focuses on the audience or the user for which the solution is designed. Table 2 outlines four stages that can guide design thinking along with activities associated with each stage.

Table 2. Four stages to guide design thinking

Design Thinking Phase	Description	Activity Examples
Empathize/ Immersion	Involves really understanding the context of the problem and the experience of the stakeholders involved.	Pre-project research to inform ideas, such as observation and interaction, surveying, or interviewing people about their experiences and needs and collecting artifacts.
Define/ Synthesize	Processing and synthesis of findings from empathy work to form a stakeholder point of view that is used to address solution designs.	Creation of mindmaps or sketches, including relationships and connected ideas, based on research findings from the empathy phase.
Ideate	Exploration of multiple possible solutions through generating a large quantity of multiple possible solutions.	Reflecting on the question, problem, or goal, students rapidly brainstorm as many possible solutions they can think of within a certain time frame (e.g., 15 minutes). Students select three to explore further.
Prototype and Test	Transformation of ideas into a physical form and early testing of solutions with peers or stakeholders to inform redesign or adaption.	Useful tools for this phase are paper proto-typing, drawings, and "mock" products created with crafts or recyclables. Students gather feedback via observations and user testing to refine prototypes and ideas.

An important aspect of programming projects involves considering user interaction design. Students can design early prototypes of their solutions that demonstrate how users interact, navigate, and use their program (Figure 5). For example, in the case of designing an app for a smartphone, a student can develop a paper prototype of the screen view and model how a user will click and enter input and navigate around the app. Humans may not always use the program as intended, so it is essential that students incorporate a feedback loop into the design of their projects.

When designing solutions, students are also required to think about the human and ethical factors of their design and how to mitigate biases through the use of data and design factors in their solutions.

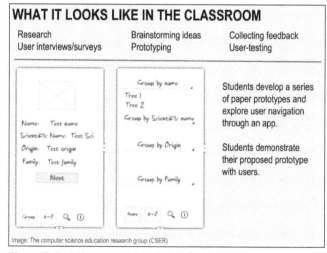

Figure 5. Activities promoting design thinking (Image source: The Computer Science Education Research (CSER) group, University of Adelaide)

INTRAPERSONAL SKILLS: MINDSETS AND BELIEFS

Learning to program is not always easy, and at times it can feel frustrating for learners when they do not know why their program is not working. Rather than relying on the teacher to solve the problem or for the student to give up feeling defeated, the goal of programming classrooms should be to empower students to have control over their learning by building resilience and autonomy in their ability to tackle any problem they encounter through the use of a variety of problem-solving strategies. A number of non-cognitive factors, such as self-efficacy, motivation, study habits, mindsets, and other interpersonal skills, affect student learning in general, and programming, in particular. Understanding what these factors are, how they come into play in the classroom, and strategies to support students in personal growth and success can help to improve their learning outcomes in programming.

We can prepare students with a set of strategies and techniques in their mental toolbox that they can use to overcome challenges, to create solutions, and to successfully find and fix errors in their code. This not only helps students develop problem-solving skills but also takes the pressure off teachers, so that they can dedicate precious class time to closely observing, questioning, and providing feedback to students during learning activities. See **Chapter 6** on formative feedback, **Chapter 8** on supporting project-based learning, and **Chapter 17** on questions and inquiry for more on useful pedagogical moves during the learning process.

▶ Persistence and Growth Mindset

Persistence is a disposition that we can help students develop, especially in programming classrooms where debugging is an integral part of the process of getting programs to work as desired. Programming involves creating solutions, but solutions will not always be perfectly executed start to finish. A classroom is a safe space to explore testing and debugging and the idea of productive failure by encouraging students to tinker, play, and experiment with ideas, strategies, and processes.

Programmers do not always have the solutions to problems and will often have to find examples of programs others have written (e.g., on GitHub). Teachers can also model that we do not always have the answer to every aspect of the programming problem and the processes students can productively use to reach desired programming solutions. Teachers can foster a classroom culture that acknowledges that bugs in code are a part of the process and that finding and solving bugs can be an exciting challenge. Bugs can be celebrated (on a "buggy wall" or "hall of failures" or your phrase of choice) and be the focus of classroom discussions as students share the various bugs they encountered in their work. Teachers can demonstrate bugs in their own live coding, thus modeling that there are bugs in *everyone's* code, share when they are unsure how to do something, and model the problem-solving strategies through thinking aloud. Common programming challenges provide an opportunity to work together with students to come up with a solution. (Also see **Chapters 8, 20,** and **26** on creating a classroom culture that celebrates mistakes as part of learning).

In the primary classroom, teachers could introduce stories with characters encountering failure, mistakes, or challenges and discuss this as a learning opportunity, linked to their experience in programming. In the secondary classroom, teachers could introduce role models (older students or technology professionals) who can talk through their experiences of failure and how they overcome challenges. Code is almost never perfect the first time, and helping students see that even role models make mistakes and encounter challenges is a positive learning experience.

The following ideas provide additional suggestions for supporting persistence:

- Remixing or extending others' projects and finding "bugs" in existing projects
- Explicitly teaching or highlighting common bugs and modeling problem-solving processes
- Developing a class "how-to" guide with strategies for reviewing code and resolving bugs
- Using pair programming, "ask three before me," or a similar system to promote peer collaboration in resolving bugs
- Providing students with resources/sites to support their programming activities
- Involving students in assessment processes to teach programming evaluation and feedback throughout programming projects
- Providing constructive feedback and teaching how students to receive feedback to improve projects

KNOWLEDGE, SKILLS, ATTITUDES, AND BELIEFS

▶ Inclusivity

A number of implicit factors can play a role in the impression students have about computer science as a discipline and their sense of belonging and affect their attitudes, self-efficacy, and motivation. As educators, we can shape these to some extent in terms of designing environments that are inclusive and selecting learning materials and activities that engage and inspire diverse learners.

Diversity is concerned with the dimensions of race, ethnicity, gender, sexual orientation, socioeconomic status, age, physical abilities, and so on. *Equity*, on the other hand, is concerned with the idea that everyone receives fair treatment and people have equal access to opportunities. Both of these features are important to consider in the design of programming activities, learning environments, and opportunities.

It is also important to provide an inclusive experience that nurtures the individual identities of all students and establishes the notion that programming is for everyone. *Identity* is a factor relating to how someone sees themselves. Often in programming, certain underrepresented groups can feel isolated or like they do not belong. *Self-efficacy* is concerned with an individual's beliefs about their capabilities to perform certain tasks and is a factor that can hinder or help students in their programming success. When students attribute success or failure in programming to external or fixed factors (such as a test being hard or not being naturally good at programming), it can be detrimental to their self-efficacy and motivation. We can help students realize their potential by acknowledging that, as with any other learning area, programming success comes from hard work and practice. Helping students to attribute success or failure to intrinsic and changeable factors, such as effort and practice, can build their self-efficacy, motivation, and resilience in programming.

▶ Designing an inclusive learning environment

The *learning environment* can play a role in how students feel to be in that space as well as the message we send about programming. Teachers can adopt a number of strategies that work toward an inclusive and safe space for all, devoid of the stereotypical "programming" culture. Regardless of the physical space where you teach students (a computer lab or your own classroom or somewhere else), we can always consider what image we would like to communicate about computer science and how students feel welcomed in that space.

As an example, at Harvey Mudd College, the computer science department invited students to redesign their labs to feature neutral imagery, for example, hot-air balloons among clouds and forest walls, that not linked to any stereotype of computing (Figure 6).

> Have a look around your space: What message does it send about computer science, the types of activities that people do as computer scientists, the tools they use, and the people who belong in that space or discipline?

The *teaching and learning materials* that we use can also significantly affect how students perceive computer science. For example, if we teach programming only through the creation of games, students may associate programming with gaming and not realize the broader applications of programming to data analysis, app creation, websites, animation, simulations, and the broader industries such as health sciences, economics, fashion, music, and so much more. One way for students to realize the potential is to showcase many examples of real-world applications and to include a variety of programming activities within the classroom. (As an example, the **CS Rocks!** playlist of YouTube videos is a favorite with tween and teen students: http://bit.ly/CS-rocks).

Figure 6. Designing gender neutral learning environments (Image source: The Computer Science Education Research (CSER) group, University of Adelaide)

Research analyzing the representation, imagery, and language used in common computer science materials has found that learning materials can promote gender inequality. For example, the infamous image of Lena, a centerfold model, which is widely used in teaching image processing, has been found to make female students uncomfortable. It is recommended that other gender-neutral images should be selected. The first step in eliminating issues such as gender bias or inequality in programming is awareness that issues and inequalities exist and that we can provide an inclusive and safe environment through conscious efforts to select inclusive materials and activities. The box to the right provides additional ideas from CS Teaching Tips.

Tips for reducing bias in the classroom:

1. Make your expectations explicit
2. Grade anonymously
3. Establish clear policies
4. Learn students' names
5. Acknowledge and manage your biases
6. Teach students about bias
7. Listen to students' experiences

(Source: http://csteachingtips.org/tips-for-reducing-bias)

Furthermore, another generally applicable strategy to create an inclusive environment is to provide students with choice and to engage them in creating solutions that align with their interests. Research has also found that some students, particularly girls and women, are drawn to programming activities referred to as computing for social good. Another way to engage students in programming is through activities that demonstrate they are programming for a purpose. This could be designing an application for smartphones that solves a local community issue that students care about solving. **Chapter 12** shares more ideas of this *culturally responsive approach* to teaching programming.

> Through broadening programming activities, selecting inclusive materials, building positive (growth) mindsets and identities, and providing inclusive learning environments, teachers are in a position to increase engagement and sense of belonging not only for underrepresented groups but for all students, leading to more diverse student cohorts interested in computing.

KNOWLEDGE, SKILLS, ATTITUDES, AND BELIEFS

INTERPERSONAL SKILLS: COLLABORATION AND COMMUNICATION

Providing opportunities for students to learn programming in schools is done not with the goal of producing armies of programmers or computer scientists but rather with the broader intention of preparing students to work and live productively in an increasingly technological world. Computing has had an impact on all fields today, and every industry is harnessing the power of technology to solve challenges and increase productivity. Regardless of the field a student chooses to work in, by learning to program they will have a deep understanding of how computing works and the technical terminology required to speak the language and describe solutions they need or want to create.

Programming is not only about communicating to the computer what we want it to do. A large part also involves communicating our code and programs to humans. Students need to learn the academic vocabulary of the domain so that they are able to effectively communicate their proposed ideas and work in teams to generate solutions. When creating a computer program, students need to be able to communicate what they have done so that their classroom peers or collaborators can understand it, use it, and remix it. This is achieved in a number of ways, such as by commenting on code, providing instructions, writing documentation, thinking about designing code for the user, and presenting project ideas and details to others. In this section, we introduce some ways to engage students in communication and collaboration.

▶ Collaboration and Communication

Programming is often misunderstood to be an isolated activity when in fact collaboration and communication are an extremely important part of the process of creating digital solutions. Mitchell Resnick, the creator of the Scratch programming environment, believes that learning to code can also be encouraged as a form of digital literacy for communication and self-expression. In this view, programming is a powerful tool that enables students to communicate their ideas, knowledge, and solutions in the form of an app, artwork, a game, an animation, or some other digital artifact.

Students can work autonomously, but having them work together or in teams can promote collaboration skills and processes around a programming project. When working with each other, students are encouraged to explain, justify, and discuss programming, which can develop their communication skills and use of technical vocabulary. In speaking the vocabulary of programming as part of the group, students also build their identity as a programmer. (Also see **Chapter 16, Peer Collaboration and Pair Programming**).

Encourage students, working with others or individually, to integrate planning and project reflection into the life cycle of their programming project and to document their thinking, algorithms, design ideas, and evaluations from start to finish.

▶ Good Code Practices With Other Coders in Mind

As mentioned previously, similar to the rules and conventions involved in writing good texts, students also need to learn about writing quality code. Clearly written and efficient code can significantly help team members collaborating on projects as well as others who want to build and extend on existing code. Imagine trying to follow a recipe presented as an entire block of text with no clear steps. Just as we write a recipe for someone else to follow easily, we write code for someone else to follow without struggle.

Starting with good habits of programming from the early phases of design through to coding can greatly help students in communicating their projects. This can be achieved through a number of practices, such as commenting on code, using structure by chunking code, using appropriate variable naming, and producing efficient code. In a visual programming environment, structure is clearly displayed in the grouping or "chunking" of blocks and scripts on the screen and, for older students, the use of indentation and paragraphs for chunking.

Part of programming projects, particularly assessments, could involve students writing instruction guides for users and other programmers to follow. Bear in mind that the instructions are different for a user of a program and someone who wants to understand how the code and program work. In a Scratch program, for example, students could include instructions for the user on their main page or integrated in their programming project, whereas comments on how the program is designed can be part of comments.

Read more on good habits of programming in **Chapter 25, Yay, My Program Works! Beyond Working Code… Developing Good Habits of Programming**.

WHAT IT LOOKS LIKE IN THE CLASSROOM		
COMMUNICATE & COLLABORATE	COMMUNICATING PROGRAMS	PRESENTING PROJECTS
Assigned team roles	Identifying programming goals	"Pitching" projects
Project time lines		Presenting prototypes
Project management software	Producing flowcharts, pseudocode, or models	Preparing user instructions
Pair programming/ buddy systems	Commenting on code	Gathering feedback from teachers, peers, industry, community
Providing & receiving constructive feedback	Tracing code	Self-evaluation
	User-interaction considerations	

Figure 7. Designing gender neutral learning environments (Image source: The Computer Science Education Research (CSER) group, University of Adelaide)

▶ Presenting Projects

A key part of programming involves being able to communicate ideas and solutions to an audience or end user. Programmers have to build their skill of being able to abstract and explain their solutions to others in a simple way without unnecessary detail. Having students present their projects can develop these skills in distilling the key elements of their program and communicating their designs.

Assessment of programming projects should not simply focus on the final "product" or artifact but provide an opportunity for students to communicate their processes and solutions. One strategy is for students to produce a portfolio of work that includes all development materials. Opportunities where students can talk through their solutions and explain code can help teachers assess their knowledge and skills of programming, check their understanding, as well as their ability to communicate their programming ideas, and provide feedback to students.

Students could present work to the teacher, the whole class, peers in other year levels, parents, or community members, such as industry representatives or people for whom they are creating projects. This facilitates an outlet and an opportunity for students to showcase their creations and also receive valuable feedback on their designs. Programming is about designing solutions for humans. Authentic opportunities for students to share and showcase their projects instills the belief that programming can be about creation for others or a form of self-expression to be shared with the world. **Chapter 6, Feedback Through Formative Check-Ins,** and **Chapter 26, Zestful Learning**, also share ideas on how to scaffold project presentations, and foster communication and collaboration in a programming classroom

KNOWLEDGE, SKILLS, ATTITUDES, AND BELIEFS

RESEARCH AND READINGS

In 2006, Jeanette Wing brought the notion of computational thinking as a "universally applicable attitude and skill set for everyone" to the forefront of conversations, drawing increased attention and research in the field. Since then, work by Grover and Pea (2013, 2018) has also initiated exploration of computational thinking in the middle years classroom, unpacking what it means for children learning visual programming. Grover's research at Stanford (Grover, Pea, & Cooper, 2015) was guided by the deeper learning perspective as defined by Pellegrino and Hilton (2012) and included work on students' perceptions of computing. The CS Rocks! playlist on YouTube was created as part of that work, and has been used extensively since.

Vivian and Falkner's (2019) work, informing parts of this chapter, has explored ways of thinking, knowledge, and skill development in CS within K–12 classrooms, connecting to familiar teacher practices. This work has been implemented in Australia by the Computer Science Education Research (CSER) Group, through a national teacher-training program, including free online courses in which teachers contribute learning activities to a shared community that informs future CS pedagogy and resource development.

Led by Colleen Lewis, the CS Teaching Tips initiative (csteachingtips.org) provides educators with practical, evidence-based strategies for the teaching of programming at all grade levels. This work has been based on interviews with over 150 CS teachers resulting in over 1,300 tips curated into tip sheet topics covering diversity, inclusivity, pair-programming, and more.

BIBLIOGRAPHY

Brennan, K., & Resnick, M. (2012). New frameworks for studying and assessing the development of computational thinking. Annual American Educational Research Association Meeting, Vancouver, BC, Canada, 1–25. Retrieved from http://web.media.mit.edu/~kbrennan/files/Brennan_Resnick_AERA2012_CT.pdf

Brown, N. C. C., & Wilson, G. (2018). Ten quick tips for teaching programming. *PLOS Computational Biology, 14*(4). https://doi.org/10.1371/journal.pcbi.1006023

Fincher, S. A., & Robins, A. V. (Eds.). (2019). *The Cambridge handbook of computing education research*. Cambridge University Press. https://doi.org/10.1017/9781108654555

Grover, S., & Pea, R. (2013). Computational thinking in K–12: A review of the state of the field. *Educational Researcher, 42*(1), 38–43. https://doi.org/10.3102/0013189X12463051

Grover, S., Pea, R., & Cooper, S. (2015). Designing for deeper learning in a blended computer science course for middle school students. *Computer Science Education, 25*(2), 199–237.

Lewis, C. M. (2017). Twelve tips for creating a culture that supports all students in computing. *ACM Inroads, 8*(4), 17–20.

Medel, P., & Pournaghshband, V. (2017). Eliminating gender bias in computer science education materials. In *Proceedings of the 2017 ACM SIGCSE Technical Symposium on Computer Science Education—SIGCSE '17* (pp. 411–416). ACM Press. https://doi.org/10.1145/3017680.3017794

Pellegrino, J. W., & Hilton, M. L. (2012). *Education for Life and Work: Developing Transferable Knowledge and Skills in the 21st Century*. National Academies Press.

Sentance, S., Barendsen, E., & Schulte, C. (2018). *Computer science education: Perspectives on teaching and learning in school*. Bloomsbury Publishing PLC.

Teague, D., & Lister, R. (2014). Programming. In *Proceedings of the 2014 Conference on Innovation & Technology in Computer Science Education—ITiCSE '14* (pp. 285–290). ACM Press. https://doi.org/10.1145/2591708.2591712

Vivian, R., & Falkner, K. (2019). Identifying teachers' technological pedagogical content knowledge for computer science in the primary years. In *Proceedings of the 2019 ACM Conference on International Computing Education Research* (pp. 147–155). ACM. https://doi.org/10.1145/3291279.3339410

Wing, J. (2006). Computational thinking. *Communications of the ACM, 49*(3), 33–36.

Learner-Centered and Culturally Relevant Pedagogy

Tia C. Madkins, Jakita O. Thomas, Jessica Solyom,
Joanna Goode, and Frieda McAlear

INTRODUCTION: CULTURALLY RELEVANT PEDAGOGY

Underrepresented minority students (for example, Black, Latinx, Native American/ Alaskan, Hawaiian / Pacific Islander in the United States) have historically experienced racial bias and structural inequities both inside and outside of school settings. Educational inequities appear at all levels, from low funding for schools with high proportions of underrepresented students of color to diminished teacher and counselor expectations, tracking students into remedial and special needs programs, and over-referring students to school disciplinary officials. For underrepresented students of color, these practices are an extension of colonial and assimilative educational practices, have led to the development of school-perpetuated (historical) trauma, and contribute to experiencing an education environment that feels irrelevant, hostile, and unwelcoming.

Culturally relevant pedagogy (CRP) was first proposed by Ladson-Billings as well as Allen and Boykin in the 1990s. CRP is founded on the idea that learning grounded in a familiar cultural context can potentially increase equitable outcomes. This framework outlines three tenets for academic success: (1) implementing academic rigor, (2) honoring students' cultural and linguistic backgrounds, and (3) helping students to understand, recognize, and critique social inequities. This mode of teaching also emphasizes an authentically caring rapport between teacher and student and connecting curriculum to students' home cultures and everyday lived experiences.

> *What we have learned about [swimming and] computer science is that all of the seemingly cultural preferences and interests are profoundly impacted by historical legacies, structural inequities, denied learning opportunities, and belief systems that justify these inequities*
> – Jane Margolis,
> *Stuck in the Shallow End*

WHY CULTURALLY RELEVANT PEDAGOGICAL PRACTICES MATTER IN COMPUTING

One emerging area of scholarship combines the well-established research and practice of culturally relevant pedagogy with programming education to develop engaging and rigorous programming instruction for underrepresented students of color. This line of research provides a conceptual foundation for integrating culturally relevant pedagogical frameworks into programming instruction across learning contexts. In programming, principles of culturally relevant pedagogy and related approaches include: (*1*) *supporting student identity development*, (*2*) *encouraging a critique of inequities in computing*, and (*3*) *addressing sociopolitical issues*.

Two examples show how this framework can be enacted within the curriculum. In high school, the introductory Exploring Computer Science (ECS) course, designed by Jane Margolis, Joanna Goode, and Gail Chapman, incorporates culturally responsive design tools, such as those explored by Ron Eglash in his work teaching computer science topics to underrepresented groups in culturally responsive ways. ECS offers students ethnocomputing learning experiences. In her account of teaching these lessons, Gayle Nicholls-Ali, a computer science teacher, found that using these culturally relevant educational tools to teach web-based software allowed high school students to apply lessons on algorithms, computing, and how to better use search engines to "create simulations of cultural arts, such as Native American beadwork, as [they] moved from concepts to making, students were excited to finally start 'programming' their rugs, baskets, and beadwork […] with little direction from [the instructor] they deep dived into the website, problem-solved, made mistakes, and iterated."

In their work in an introductory computer science course with middle school students, Yolanda Rankin and Jakita Owensby Thomas found in their research that integrating a module that leveraged food, recipes, and cooking to expose students to algorithmic thinking as a starting, or anchoring, experience led to 100% retention of Black women undergraduate students for that course.

> Such programs suggest engaging underrepresented students of color in educational experiences that strengthen their cultural, linguistic, gender, and racial identities can provide more equitable learning outcomes in computing.

CULTURALLY RELEVANT PEDAGOGY IN PRACTICE

▶ How We Selected These Practice Examples

Next, we provide practical examples of how teachers have used culturally relevant pedagogy or culturally sustaining practices in programming classrooms in schools, summer programs, or other contexts to support student outcomes. We selected these examples because they exemplify the kinds of culturally relevant or sustaining teaching practices we believe are empowering and important for teaching and learning programming. Importantly, these examples come from our observations of classroom teaching across a variety of contexts that each aim to support students of color in making authentic and meaningful connections between programming and their lives. We desired to provide exemplary instructional examples that educators can use as a guide to support their professional learning and growth. In turn, we hope teachers' practices can positively influence student learning goals and outcomes (e.g., interest, engagement, achievement) in programming. These examples are sample methods educators can draw and build upon, but they are not prescriptive approaches simply to be replicated. We encourage educators to reflect upon and refine these practices to determine what will work well for their unique schooling contexts. Furthermore, we remind educators that engaging in this work can at times be challenging and messy. Thus, we encourage teachers to integrate these practices into their pedagogical approach with an aim to evaluate and evolve their impact over time.

We organize our ideas and guidelines for CRP in programming classrooms in three categories:

A. Connect with students' cultures/life experiences

B. Empower students to become change agents

C. Relationships with students, families, and communities

▶ Connecting With Students' Cultures/Life Experiences

Rooting computing curriculum and pedagogy in the cultural experiences and the social identities of students allows them to engage and learn about programming in meaningful ways. To integrate students' rich cultural assets, life experiences, and community knowledge as the building blocks for teaching programming, we have found the following teaching strategies to be effective:

- Engage students with programming activities that are contextualized in students' school communities (e.g., creating the best transportation route for afterschool activities in their community as a way of learning minimal spanning trees)

- Make programming accessible by connecting learning to students' personal interests, social identities, perspectives, and everyday lives (e.g., inviting a student who skateboards to help introduce a culturally situated design tool about the culture and mathematics of skateboarding)

- Draw from students' cultural assets and knowledge to use as building blocks for examining programming topics (e.g., using popular music to discuss programming paradigms such as loops and linked lists, or using family recipes to discuss how the same algorithm can be represented in different ways)

- Develop project-based assignments for students to both identify an issue of concern to their lives, family, or community and to design a technology-based solution (e.g., mapping food deserts in urban neighborhoods)

- Storytelling from one's own programming education experiences where appropriate to dispel common alternative conceptions of programming concepts and model resilience and effective problem-solving practices in programming education (e.g., storytelling to illustrate the sequence of steps taken to discover that instance variables have a default value in Java)

▶ Practice Examples: Empower Students to Become Change Agents

Further, providing students with a larger societal view on the impacts and ethics of programming is necessary not only to raise awareness but to also foster student agency to address community problems and inequities that have been created, or might be addressed, by software development. Examples of how this can be done include

- Point out the sociopolitical, not just technical, influences in programming that have led to bias and discrimination being codified in algorithms and software (e.g., face-recognition misgendering rates for people of color)

- Incorporate equity discussions about the impacts of large technology firms on diverse and historically marginalized communities (e.g., what is the impact of Twitter and other tech companies on gentrification and displacement patterns in urban cities like San Francisco?)

- Engage students in critical discussions around data, privacy, surveillance, and other issues with significant impacts on human liberties and civil rights (e.g., police searches of social media accounts)

- Develop students' communication and collaboration skills with programming activities to help students develop and present their ideas and creations to others (e.g., presenting a data science project about an issue in their community using a variety of representations or designing and gathering feedback about a video game designed to address a social issue)

- Discuss and examine the structure of the technological ecosystem to identify potential points of intervention, including the role that education leaders, policymakers, venture capitalists, corporate technology leaders, and start-up founders play in shaping the programming opportunity landscape for underrepresented students of color (e.g., creating a power map of institutions, companies, and organizations that support the entry and success of people of color in tech)

▶ Practice Examples: Relationships With Students, Families, and Communities

Fostering and maintaining relationships with students and their families is an important aspect of culturally relevant pedagogy. Parents and school communities can play a vital role in supporting and sustaining engagement and participation in programming education for underrepresented students of color.

For indigenous communities, this means that computing experiences involve curriculum that facilitates ongoing interaction and cooperation among key stakeholders, including tribal and community agencies, families, students, teachers, and school administrators, to promote self-determination for tribal nations. For American Indian communities, computer science learning can assist tribal nations in developing solutions and techno-social agents that can build on the existing infrastructure and address issues unique to their political sovereign status. Given that there are over 570 federally recognized tribes, this variety of geography, cultures, practices, knowledge and thought systems, linguistic practices, and heritage languages, as well as local history, the need for careful contextualization of culturally relevant pedagogies for Native American students and schools is essential.

For educators to engage in relationship-building with students, their families, and their communities, they can:

- Spend time getting to know students and their families outside of the (in)formal classroom setting (e.g., hosting family exposure and recruiting events for programming courses before the fall semester to promote programming curricula, out-of-school programming opportunities, and tech career pathways)

- Recognize that the experiences that students bring with them into the classroom are a form of expertise that should be tapped into and used to ground and help students integrate new content or topics (e.g., discussing students' morning routine as examples of algorithmic thinking)

- Develop project-based assignments for students to both identify an issue of concern to their life, family, or community and design a technology-based solution (e.g., students engage in designing a mobile app that addresses an issue in their neighborhoods, such as job openings for teens in their local area)

- Educators can share personal experiences related to course topics or discussions and/or their trajectories into programming/tech fields (e.g., educator shares experience of being the only woman and person of color in her undergraduate courses)

- Involve families in end-of-year course activities (e.g., invite students to present their final projects to their parents and families at an end-of-year project-demonstration day)

- For schools serving predominantly Native American students, ensuring that culturally relevant curricula and pedagogies are aligned with the goals and self-determination of the relevant tribal leadership and elders is crucial to maintaining engagement with Native American students and their families (e.g., ensuring tribal leadership and elders are provided opportunities to advise and guide computing program designers and staff about culturally relevant computing courses and pedagogical approaches)

CONCLUSION

Culturally relevant pedagogies encourage learning and professional development for teachers with intentions to increase knowledge about and for underrepresented groups, as well as foster a growth mindset among community service providers, teachers, school administrators, and other students. This chapter outlines three major tenets of culturally responsive pedagogy and culturally sustaining practices for teaching computing. More specifically, various practical teaching examples are shared that highlight how computer science and programming concepts and practices can be taught in ways that support student identity in computing, encourage a critique of inequities in computing that youth find important to address, and consider how programming contexts can be used to discuss and address sociopolitical issues in students' local communities. The practices shared earlier—from connecting with students' cultures/life experiences to empowering youth to becoming change agents to building relationships with students, families, and communities to supporting relationships with tribal leadership and communities—all speak to the ways that educators can begin to make computing courses more meaningful and powerful for *all* our youth. Through iterative and self-reflective practices such as those described in this chapter, our computer science teaching community can inspire underrepresented youth to be the creators and innovators, and not simply users, of the technology that can improve our lives and world.

ACKNOWLEDGMENTS

Our gratitude to Yolanda Rankin, Allison Scott, Kimberly Scott, Jean Ryoo, and Alexis Martin for shaping this chapter.

READINGS AND RESEARCH

Building on the foundational work on culturally responsive pedagogy by Allen and Boykin (1992) and Ladson-Billings (1995), educators such as Ron Eglash (2006 and 2013) and Kimberly Scott and her colleagues (2015) have incorporated concepts such as ethnocomputing and intersectionality into their approach to teaching programming to underrepresented students. Goode, Chapman, and Margolis (2012) and Margolis and colleagues (2012) further developed and incorporated learner-centered and inquiry-based teaching practices in the Exploring Computer Science high school curriculum in the United States. For further insight into examples of how programming course content could reflect students' cultural backgrounds and identities, see Rankin and Thomas (2016) and Nicholls-Ali (2017).

BIBLIOGRAPHY

Allen, B. A., & Boykin, A. W. (1992). African-American children and the educational process:

Alleviating cultural discontinuity through prescriptive pedagogy. *School Psychology Review*, 21, 586–596.

Eglash, R., Bennett, A., O'donnell, C., Jennings, S., & Cintorino, M. (2006). Culturally situated design tools: Ethnocomputing from field site to classroom. *American Anthropologist*, 108(2), 347–362.

Eglash, R., Gilbert, J. E., Taylor, V., & Geier, S. R. (2013). Culturally responsive computing in urban, after-school contexts: Two approaches. *Urban Education*, 48, 629–656. DOI: 10.1177/0042085913499211

Goode, J., Chapman, G., & Margolis, J. (2012). Beyond curriculum: the exploring computer science program. *ACM Inroads*, 3(2), 47–53.

Ladson-Billings, G. (1995). Toward a theory of culturally relevant pedagogy. *American Educational Research Journal*, 32, 465–491. DOI: 10.3102/00028312032003465

Margolis, J., Ryoo, J. J., Sandoval, C. D., Lee, C., Goode, J., & Chapman, G. (2012). Beyond access: Broadening participation in high school computer science. *ACM Inroads*, 3(4), 72–78.

Medin, D. L., & Bang, M. (2014). *Who's asking? Native science, western science, and science education*. MIT Press.

National Congress of American Indians (2020). http://www.ncai.org/

Nicholls-Ali, G. (2017). Baskets, beads, and rugs in computer science. Blog post on *CSForAll Teachers*. Retrieved from https://www.csforallteachers.org/blog/baskets-beads-and-rugs-computer-science.

Rankin, Y. A., & Thomas, J. O. (2016). Leveraging food to achieve 100% retention in an intro CS course. *Journal of Computing Sciences in Colleges*, 32, 127–133. Retrieved from: https://dl.acm.org/doi/abs/10.5555/3015063.3015083

Scott, K. A., Sheridan, K. M., & Clark, K. (2015). Culturally responsive computing: A theory revisited. *Learning, Media and Technology, 40*, 412–436. DOI: 10.1080/17439884.2014.924966

LEARNER-CENTERED AND CULTURALLY RELEVANT PEDAGOGY

Modularity with Methods and Functions

Mike Zamansky, Jens Mönig & JonAlf Dyrland-Weaver

> *Sometimes, the elegant implementation is just a function.*
> – John Carmack

INTRODUCTION

Functions (also called methods in object-oriented languages such as Java) are important building blocks of programs. They allow a developer to break down a program into smaller, more digestible pieces that can be easily and efficiently reused. As such, they are "subprograms" within a program. Functions are also the verbs in a programming language. They are the actions performed on data. When software developers create an app, they're often assembling it out of functions that are predefined in libraries or user-defined in the app.

In this chapter, we are going to highlight the important concepts related to functions and methods along with suggestions on how to make clear those concepts through ideas for the classroom. The substantive examples and ideas described in this chapter cover both block-based (Snap!) and text-based (Python) programming and extend to advanced topics like the use of functions in recursion. We end the chapter with a spotlight on where students struggle in learning how to use functions correctly.

▶ Why Functions?

The following are some of the key concepts relating to functions and why they are an important part of programs and learning programming:

- **Modularity**: The idea that a large program can be written as a collection of smaller, more understandable functions.

- **Readability**: Small functions are easier to understand than large chunks of code and, by using sensible names for functions, programs can become easier to read and understand.

- **Maintainability**: Small functions are easier to debug, and using functions decreases the amount of text in a program, making it easier to follow its process.

- **Abstraction**: Functions can be used to take multiple lines of code and refer to them by a single name. This type of abstraction can keep your programs simpler and easier to understand.

- **Reuse**: By creating functions, programmers can reuse the same bits of code in a large program. This process is easier to understand and maintain than when a programmer has the same code cut and pasted all over their programs. Programmers can also take functions written for one project and insert them into other programs.

> **Tip to give to students:**
> *Whenever you find yourself writing almost the same code over and over again, it's a good idea to stop and think about how you can formulate the idea in a more general way as a function.*

Some teachers like to approach programming from a "functions first" point of view, that is, teach functions as early as possible, even before simple constructs like conditional statements. Others like to teach language constructs such as **if** and **loops** first and then introduce functions. Both approaches can be successful, and the lessons outlined below can be used with either approach.

RECOGNIZING BUILT-IN FUNCTIONS IN PROGRAMMING LANGUAGES

Even though learning about functions involves creating one's own functions in programs, students must recognize that built-in constructs in programming languages are internally defined as functions.

For example, in the Scratch block-based language, the `move 10 steps` block is essentially a MOVE function that takes an input (parameter) of a number, and executing the block changes the sprite's position by the input number in its current direction. Even operators such as the arithmetic, relational, and Boolean operators are essentially functions.

In text-based languages like Python, one can try out a function by typing its name at the command prompt followed by parentheses and then pressing **Enter**. For example, running the `dir()` function answers a list of words the system knows about, and running `exit()` quits Python. *Running a function is also called "evaluating" it*.

Aside from telling Python to run a function, the trailing parentheses also serve as a container for the inputs you wish the function to evaluate, and a function name followed by parentheses is referred to as a "function call." For example, evaluating the classic statement

```
print('Hello, World!')
```

outputs "Hello, World!" in the console.

And if you assign a text to a variable

```
story = 'The quick brown fox jumps over the lazy dog.'
```

and then evaluate

```
print(story)
```

the value of the variable named `story` appears: "The quick brown fox jumps over the lazy dog."

Python functions can also return a value. For example, evaluating

```
len(story)
```

returns 44, the number of letters in the string variable, `story`.

IDEAS FOR TEACHING FUNCTIONS

▶ Block-Based Programming

Although most block-based programming environments popular for younger grades provide the capability to create functions and procedures, the idea of modularity, procedures, and functions are typically not introduced in elementary grades. The following sections share ideas in block-based and text-based environments that teachers can draw on based on their classroom context.

Defining your own function—building your own block in Scratch or Snap!—involves specifying how to call it and how it works. Calling a function can be described as coming up with a new word or name that's unique in the program and by specifying the function's inputs. Ideally, the name should be reflective of the purpose of the function. Some programming languages also require you to declare which kind of output the function generates. This information documents the function's "outside" appearance and behavior (and is called the "function header").

▶ Defining Functions (Building Your Own Blocks) in Snap!

To define how a function works, you write a program that details what happens when the function is called. Because the function body (the program inside a function definition) is just a program, it can use all the features available in the programming language, including other functions that have been imported or defined. When you define your own function, make sure that its internal program—its function body—matches its header declarations, that is, if your function promises to return a value, make sure it actually does.

Figure 1a shows the definition of a block that computes the average of two numbers and an example of how to use it. This function body's code is just a simple formula. However, you can use any feature your programming language offers inside the function definition. Figure 1b shows the possible definition of a function that determines the maximum value of two numbers using a conditional IF statement and can be used to update the high score in a game. Figure 1c demonstrates a function that locates the index of a given element in a list, which uses both a loop and a conditional IF statement

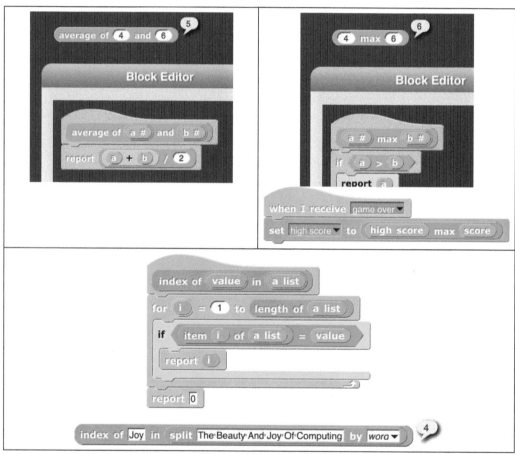

Figure 1a, b, and c. Defining and using functions (average, max, and search element in list) in Snap!

▶ Turtle Geometry and Functions for Drawing Shapes

In addition to "reporter" blocks (functions that answer a value), students can also make "command" blocks that operate on a sprite without producing a result. Here's an example of a block that moves in the shape of a triangle and how it can be used to draw a single triangle or a flower or a growing spiral (Figure 2a, b, c, and d).

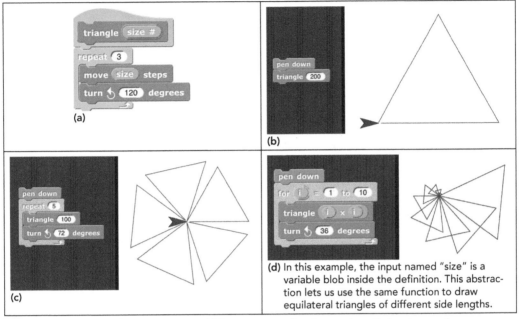

Figure 2a, b, c, and d. The many ways in which a `triangle` function can be called and re-used

Deciding which attributes of a function to generalize is a matter of taste and design. It's also fun! For example, we can abstract the TRIANGLE function into a general POLYGON function by adding another input for the number of sides. Now we can use the same function to draw any regular polygon, or the POLYGON function twice with different numbers of sides to draw a house (Figure 3a, b, and c).

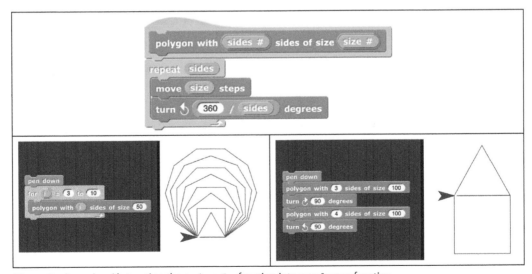

Figure 3a, b, and c. Abstracting the `triangle` function into a `polygon` function

We can also turn our "house" program into its own function that will let us draw houses of different sizes (Figure 4a, b, and c).

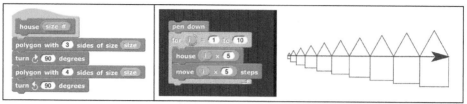

Figure 4a, b, and c. Using the `polygon` function to recreate the activity made famous in Logo by Seymour Papert in his seminal book *Mindstorms*.

▶ More Fun With Drawing Lines

Drawing with solid lines is fun, but can you also

1. Make a block that can be used instead of MOVE to draw a dashed or dotted line?

2. Make another block that instead of MOVE draws a zigzagged line?

And can you specify the size of the dashes or zigzags as an input of the block?

The solution to these two exercises can be found toward the end of this chapter. If you can spare the time, please to try solving them now before reading further.

▶ Text-Based Programming

This section first describes a three-part lesson in Python 3 that walks the teacher through key ideas of introducing modularity through functions, motivating the idea of defining functions for reuse, and motivating the need for parameters. The last section describes ideas for "language games" that provide a fun and engaging context for using and learning functions.

"Form feet and legs! Form arms and body! And, I'll form the head"—Voltron

▶ Part 1: Introducing Functions

When students write their first programs, you want them to succeed and feel accomplished quickly. To this end, it is common to provide them with a few basic commands that can be strung together without having to work with more complex programming structures. An example of such an assignment is to have your students "draw" a cat by printing ASCII characters, as follows:

```
print ("          |\---/|          ")
print ("          |  o_o  |          ")
print ("           \_ ^ _/          ")
print ("            _ _          ")
print ("         /       \          ")
print ("     0--|         |--0          ")
print ("        |         |          ")
print ("         -------          ")
print ("          |   |          ")
print ("          |   |          ")
print ("          m   m          ")
```

If you provide this as an example, your students should be able to print out their own cats in no time. You can point out a number of interesting examples and then pose a new question: "What if I wanted to print out two cats with different heads?" This query can lead the class to a discussion of breaking up the cat into different parts, namely the head, body, and legs.

It is helpful at this point to write out a template for a function. In Python, it might look like this:

```
def function_name():
        statement0
        statement1
        ...
        statementN
        return something
```

Now we have an entry point to talk about **modularity**, breaking up a problem into smaller, reuseable pieces. This leads to a discussion about functions (or methods in an object-oriented language like Java), because they allow us to reuse the same code. We can define functions for each of the three sections of the cat as follows:

```
def make_head():
  result=""
  result = result + "         |\---/|  \n"
  result = result + "         | o_o |  \n"
  result = result + "         |\_^_/|  \n"
  return result


def make_body():
  result = ""
  result = result + "            ___        \n"
  result = result + "          /     \      \n"
  result = result + "    0--|       |--0\n"
  result = result + "        |       |    \n"
  result = result + "          -------      \n"
  return result


def make_legs():
  result = ""
  result = result + "         |   |        \n"
  result = result + "         |   |        \n"
  result = result + "        m    m        \n"
  return result
```

> Notice how we develop these functions so that they build strings with the cat parts and **return** them rather than printing within the function. Students frequently have difficulty discerning when to return and when to print, and we've found it helpful to avoid printing early on in functions. We also emphasize the concept of having a function perform its designated task and then return its result Depending on the age and mathematical maturity of the students, it might be helpful to relate functions in a programming language to mathematical functions, which always have an output value. If you do this, it's important to remind your students that they are similar but not entirely the same.

If we run our program, students will notice that nothing appears to happen. Even if we call the functions, as follows:

```
make_head()
make_body()
make_legs()
```

or , closer to our desired result

```
cat = make_head()+make_body()+make_legs()
```

Only when we finally print the result do we see our cat on the screen.

```
cat = make_head() + make_body() + make_legs()
print(cat)
```

This process also reinforces the idea of keeping print statements outside your functions (except for debugging statements, but those should be held off until your students have a firm grasp of print vs, return or when the function's explicit purpose is to print).

So that students start to see the benefits of modularity, a fun class assignment is for students to design their own cat parts. Perhaps one writes

```
def make_surprised_head():
    result = ""
    result = result + "     |\   /|      \n"
    result = result + "     ||\_/||      \n"
    result = result + "     | o_o |      \n"
    result = result + "      \_O_/       \n"
    return result
```

Or

```
def make_long_body():
  result = ""
  result = result + "              --          \n"
  result = result + "           /      \       \n"
  result = result + "     0--|          |--0 \n"
  result = result + "        |          |      \n"
  result = result + "        |          |      \n"
  result = result + "        |          |      \n"
  result = result + "        |          |      \n"
  result = result + "         -------          \n"
  return result
```

Now they can create a variety of cats and, in fact, create functions to create them.

```
long_cat = make_head() + make_long_body() + make_legs()
print(long_cat)
```

As an exercise, teachers can assign the task of designing multiple cat parts and cats and share the results.

This type of approach motivates students because it is interactive and they can build something fun right away. Students directly benefit from some of the key reasons to use functions—abstraction from lines of code into functions, modularity through mixing and matching parts, and reuse by creating multiple cats.

Lessons based on this or similar examples can also be written early in an introductory class, even prior to learning conditional statements. Many teachers who subscribe to the "functions first" approach feel that when they introduce functions as early as possible, students more easily adapt to writing programs with small functions as opposed to writing programs consisting of one large monolithic main program.

▶ Part 2: Adding a Parameter

A key benefit of using functions is reuse. One form of reuse is being able to use a function over and over again in the same program. We did that when we created multiple cats. To gain more power from reuse, we can introduce more flexible functions through the use of parameters.

Note: This example requires the use of loops. If your class hasn't covered them yet, you can swap this with the next section.

Back to the previous cat drawing example, instead of a hardcoded leg function, you can develop a leg function that accepts a parameter for leg height.

```
def make_adjustable_legs(height):
    result = ""
    for i in range(height):
    result = result + "            |    |\n"
    result = result + "            m    m\n"
    return result
```

Now students can use one function to make a variety of leg heights. (Note: Update the function template to now include parameters.)

A good exercise here is to have students write a body function that first accepts a height parameter and then a height and a width parameter. More advanced students can take this concept further.

▶ Part 3: Adding Complexity—Speech Bubbles

This section can be done as a lab assignment. Students can write a function to create a speech bubble. In a language like Python, which allows you to multiply strings—that is, "Z"*5 will result in "ZZZZZ"—you can write such a function without loops: Also note that to add a backslash—\—to our string, we have to "escape" it by typing two consecutive backslashes (\\).

```
def speech_bubble(statement):
    textlength = len(statement)
    result = ""
    result = result + "      /--" + "-"*textlength + "--\\\n"
    result = result + "      |   " + " "*textlength + "   |\n"
    result = result + "      |   " + statement + "   |\n"
    result = result + "      |   " + " "*textlength + "   |\n"
    result = result + "      \\--"+'-'*textlength + "--/\n"
    result = result + "      /\n"
    result = result + "      /\n"
    return result

print(speech_bubble("Hello World!"))


        /---------------\
        |               |
        |   Hello World! |
        |               |
        \---------------/
        /
        /
    /
```

Now students can combine assorted cats and possibly other figures in a cartoon that also has a speech bubble!

```
cartoon = speech_bubble("Hi there")
cartoon = cartoon + long_cat + "\n\n"
cartoon = cartoon + speech_bubble("I'm a long cat")
cartoon = cartoon + long_cat + "\n\n"
print(cartoon)
```

▶ Languages Games With Functions

Children love playing language games. Often they invent their own "secret" slangs by substituting certain letters with others, so they can plot mischief without adults easily understanding them. In Finland and Portugal, for example, kids speak the "I language," replacing every vowel with "i." This way "Hello World" becomes "Hilli Wirld."

In Python, we can write a function that translates a text into "i-speak":

```
def ispeak(text):
    result = ''
    for letter in text:
        if letter in 'aeiou':
            result = result + 'i'
        else:
            result = result + letter
    return result
```

When we use it on our story by evaluating the following expression at the Python command prompt:

```
story = 'The quick brown fox jumps over the lazy dog.'
ispeak(story)
```

we get:

```
'Thi qiick briwn fix jimps ivir thi lizy dig.'
```

A benefit of writing a function is that we can reuse it for other purposes. By breaking up a complex program into several smaller functions, we can also modularize our code and make it easier to debug. Breaking up a program into several smaller units is also called "refactoring" it. In the case of our ispeak function, we can factor out the part that checks whether a letter is a vowel and turns it into a separate function. While we're at it, we can enhance it so it also works on capital letters.

```
def is_vowel(letter):
    return letter.lower() in 'aeiou'
```

Another idea is to allow the caller of the function to specify which letter to replace all vowels with. That way we can use the same function for the "a speak" language (also used by Finnish kids) and even make up our own ones. Here's the reformulated function.

```
def vowel_speak(text, substitute):
    result = ''
    for letter in text:
        if is_vowel(letter):
            result = result + substitute
        else:
            result = result + letter
    return result
```

Now we can write a short program that prints our story in all variants of our "vowel speak" language family.

```
for letter in 'aeiou':
    print(vowel_speak(story, letter))
```

▶ More Fun With Languages

The language games above can be extended to several others. For example

1. What happens if we invoke our `vowel_speak` function on a story, but instead of specifying a substitution letter, we pass in an empty string?

   ```
   vowel_speak(story, '')
   ```

2. Another play language is called "Uasi" (http://uasilanguage.online). It shifts every vowel over one place to the right, ("a" become "e," "u" becomes "a," and so on). Our `story` variable thus becomes: `'Thi qaock bruwn fux jamps uvir thi lezy dug.'`

3. A popular language game for online texting is "leet," or "1337," as it's sometimes written. Originally the idea was to replace every vowel with a number or a special character that looks similar to it. The letter "A" would be replaced by "4," the letter "E" by "3," and so on. The `leet` function applied to `story` it would result in

   ```
   'Th3 qu1ck br0wn f0x jumps 0v3r th3 14zy d0g.'
   ```

The solution to these exercises as well as additional language games examples can be found in the online addendum of this book. Try solving them now before consulting the solution :-)

▶ Advanced Uses of Functions

Functions are powerful because they can be applied to different inputs. With just one function, you can compute the average of any two numbers or draw a regular polygon of any size. Once you've defined a function, you can reuse it on any case it covers without having to write out the whole code every time. Functions can become super powerful when they are called inside their own definition (recursion), when they themselves become inputs to other functions, or are used within other functions. Next are brief examples of each. You can read more on how to teach recursion using Snap! or Python in **Chapter 18, Repetition and Recursion**.

▶ Functions Calling Themselves: Recursion to Draw Fractals

Remember the TRIANGLE function we defined earlier to draw an equilateral triangle of any size? If we modify the TRIANGLE function by adding just one more little section, as shown in Figure 5a, click on the script, and something absolutely amazing happens (Figure 5b)! Instead of one triangle, the function now draws a complex shape comprising a total of 364 triangles of different sizes peculiarly stacked inside each other! What you see is a kind of geometrical shape called a "fractal," because it is made up of smaller fractions that look like the whole. Fractal shapes are often found in nature, such as in trees, ferns, and erosion. This particular shape is called a Sierpinski triangle.

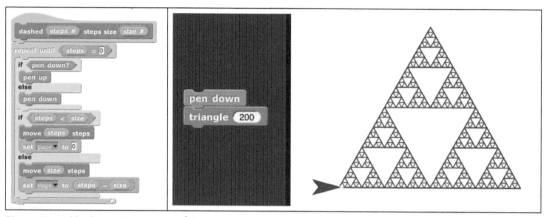

Figure 5a and b. A recursive version of the simple `triangle` function to create the mesmerizing Sierpinski triangle

▶ Using a Function Within Another Function

In the earlier examples, we drew shapes using solid lines. What if instead we wanted to draw with dashed lines (or even zigzagged ones)? Because we already know how to draw a polygon, we could make others functions just like our POLYGON function above and use new blocks named DASHED (or ZIGZAG) instead of MOVE inside its definition, as shown in Figure 6. Figure 7a and b show how this can be done by defining a "dashed polygon" function.

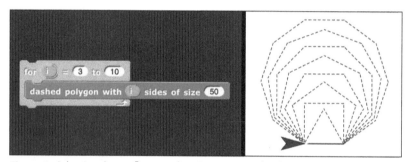

Figure 6. Adapting the `polygon` function to created polygons with dashed lines

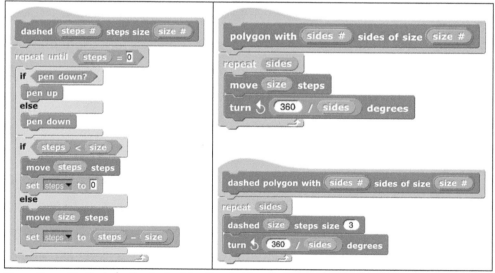

Figure 7a and b. Code for the `dashed` function that is called by the `dashed polygon` function

We can also define a function that uses the line style as a parameter and then calls the appropriate line drawing function to draw a polygon in that line style.

```
def dashed_line(len):
  stuff to draw a dashed line of length len
def zigzag_line(l):
  stuff to draw a zigzag line of length len
def polygon(line_style,sides,side_len):
  stuff to draw the polygon using line_style input to do the drawing
polygon(dashed_line,5,20) // Draw a pentagon with dashed lines
polygon(zigzag_line,6,20) // Draw a hexagon with zigzag lines
```

▶ Common Student Misconceptions and Struggles Related to Functions

Here we describe common points of confusion demonstrated by many students when they first encounter functions, and especially functions with parameters. Juha Sorva also describes students struggles related to functions (and other topics) in **Chapter 14, Naïve Conceptions of Novice Programmers**.

▶ Variable Scope

A pain point for many students involves understanding parameters.

```
def f(a):
  a = a + 1
  b = 20
  print(a)
  print(b)
  return a
a = 5
print(a)
b = f(a)
print(a)
print(b)
```

It often takes students time to understand that function f creates a new scope and that variable b in function f is different from variable b in the main program. Further, most beginner languages use "pass by value" where the parameter a in function f receives a starting value from the main program, in this case, global variable a, but a in function f is independent and different from a in the main program.

You should teach students good naming conventions, but exercises where they trace through programs such as the earlier example can help them understand these concepts as well as more advanced ones, such as pass by reference, when they come up.

▶ Print vs. Return

It is common for students to confuse the utility of print and return. This is often because most text-based languages used in introductory CS classes have environments that will print the return value of a function when called from an interpreter. Take our make_head function from earlier.

```
def make_head():
    result=""
    result = result + "    |\---/|      \n"
    result = result + "    | o_o |      \n"
    result = result + "     \_^_/       \n"
    return result
```

If you call make_head from the Python shell, the head is printed out. Now consider this version, which swaps out return for print:

```
def print_head():
    result=""
    result = result + "    |\---/|      \n"
    result = result + "    | o_o |      \n"
    result = result + "     \_^_/       \n"
    print(result)
```

It will appear to students that both functions do the same thing. One way to combat this misunderstanding is to get students comfortable with assigning variables to function values like so:

```
mh = make_head()
print(mh)
ph = print_head()
print(ph)
```

This exercise easily demonstrates the differences, but it will take time and reinforcement before students are fully comfortable with the two. It is a good practice to steer students away from printing inside functions until they are more comfortable with this distinction.

▶ Miscellaneous Issues

We've found scope and return/print to be two of the most common major pain points for beginners learning to use functions. To help with other assorted issues, including control flow and returning early from functions, we recommend teachers make liberal use of code tracing exercises as well as using debuggers to step through programs a line at a time.

Naïve Conceptions of Novice Programmers

Juha Sorva

INTRODUCTION

It's exciting to write a program that makes the computer do what you want. It's fun for students to get their hands on new commands and type or drag them into their programs.

However, in their rush to write more code and build new things, students often fail to learn foundational concepts, which eventually hampers their learning and frustrates them.

To use a programming language reliably, students need to reason about programs in terms of what the programs mean to the *system*—the programming language and its runtime environment. They need to know what the system is capable of. Just as importantly, they need to work out what the system *won't* do for them, which may not match the students' expectations or assumptions. For instance,

- In contrast to what students may assume *from human conversation*, the system won't read between the lines, automatically do "obvious" things, or avoid "unreasonable" operations.

- In contrast to what students may assume *after mathematics class*, the system won't treat assignment statements as equations and programs as groups of equations in arbitrary order.

- In contrast to what students may assume *after hearing their teacher's analogy* of "variables are like boxes," assigning to the same variable repeatedly doesn't collect multiple values in the variable.

In the jargon of computing education research, a system's relevant capabilities are known as its **notional machine**. A notional machine is not a physical computer but a *model of program execution* that can be taught to learners so that they can reason about program behavior and write programs that work. Such a model is important because there is abundant evidence that many learners struggle to trace programs accurately and commonly harbor *misconceptions* about various programming constructs. (See Figure 1 for more examples.) These misconceptions correlate with low self-efficacy for programming and cause bugs that the learners find hard to fix.

These challenges in learning are the motivation behind the pedagogical suggestions that follow. The rest of this chapter is organized as a sequence of dos and don'ts. I will first discuss how to attend to specific misconceptions in example code, and then recommend some learning activities that promote conceptual understanding and complement program-writing practice.

I'm assuming that your goal is to teach programming in an "imperative programming language" that is roughly similar to Python, Scratch, or Java; some of the details in this chapter do not apply to all programming languages. I have not separated the examples into grade levels, but the underlying principles apply to all levels.

> *On two occasions I have been asked, "Pray, Mr. Babbage, if you put into the machine wrong figures, will the right answers come out?" I am not able rightly to apprehend the kind of confusion of ideas that could provoke such a question.*
> – Charles Babbage, 1864

IDEAS AND CAUTIONS FOR ADDRESSING SPECIFIC NAÏVE CONCEPTIONS

This section describes several ideas for teachers to address novice programmers' naïve conceptions, as well as several cautions to bear in mind.

▶ IDEA 1. Target specific misconceptions with example programs.

Overcoming challenges and struggles can be a productive part of deep learning, but not all of the difficulties in learning to program are productive. If the programs that students read and write expose those pitfalls, the students are less likely to fall in. For example, students may believe that the conditionals in `while` statements are continuously checked (BCtrl1 in Figure 1). This conception is viable for some programs but not for others, as shown in Figure 2.

(Students may attribute a similar quality to `if` statements, as in BCtrl2. Several factors can contribute to these misconceptions: In everyday conversation "while" and "if" often imply continuous monitoring. The idea of the computer reacting to events is intuitive. Students know that the computer is fast and thus could conceivably check their entire program at all times.)

Program Execution in General

Gen1   The system infers the programmer's meaning from what they write, more or less like a human would.

Gen2   The system avoids "pointless" behavior and automatically takes care of "obvious" things. For example, it performs a "reasonable" default action when an `if`'s condition is not met.

Gen3   The meanings of identifiers affect what the system does. For instance, the system will ensure that a variable named `longest` will contain the longest string.

Variables and Assignment

Var1   Assignment statements are basically equations. Sequences of assignments are basically groups of equations.

Var2   A variable can have multiple values at once.

Var3   `a = b` relocates a value from b to a, emptying the source variable in the process.

Var4   `a = b` forms a link between two variables.

Var5   Assignment works differently for different data types.

Var6   A variable is only a variable if it has a single-letter name.

Var7   Any two variables with the same name are the same variable.

Booleans and Control Flow

BCtrl1   The expressions in `while` statements are continuously checked by the system: the loop exits the instant the expression becomes `false`.

BCtrl2   The expressions in `if`s are continuously checked by the system: the conditional effect triggers whenever the expression becomes `true`.

BCtrl3   Boolean expressions are used in `if`s and `while`s only. Booleans aren't values in the same sense as numbers or strings.

BCtrl4   Both branches of an `if` statement always end up being executed.

BCtrl5   Code (including subprograms) is executed in the order that it appears in the program text.

Functions, Arguments, and Return Values

Func1   Function arguments must be literals or variable names.

Func2   Argument expressions are passed in unevaluated *(lazy evaluation)*.

Func3   Parameter-passing forms links between variables in the calling code and the function.

Func4   The caller must always store the return value in a variable.

Func5   Return values automatically get stored for the caller to access.

Func6   Returning a value is similar to printing it. You do it after you've called a function.

Func7   A function must always return the value of a (local) variable.

Collections, Objects, and Classes

Obj1   Conflation of object and referring variable. E.g., `test = list(2,1,3)` makes test a part of the list object.

Obj1a   Exactly one variable (at a time) may refer to a list/object.

Obj1b   `test2 = test` renames the list/object.

Obj1c   `test2 = test` copies properties from one object into another.

Obj2   Two objects with the same state are the same object.

Obj3   A class is a collection of— or container for— objects.

Obj4   A class may have only a single member variable / method.

Obj5   Only a a single instance per class is allowed.

Figure 1: A selection of example misconceptions, loosely grouped by theme

```
number = 1
print('start')
while number < 10:          Prints 1, 5, and 9.
    print(number)           The loop terminates
    number += 4             right after number
print('stop')              reaches 13.
```

```
number = 1
print('start')                          Prints 5, 9, and 13.
while number < 10:                      The last of these happens
    number += 4                         between number
    print(number)                       reaching 13 and the
print('stop')                           last check of its value.
```

Figure 2: Running the program on the right demonstrates that while clauses aren't evaluated continuously; running the program on the left does not

As another example, students who are used to mathematics variables with single-letter names may fail to classify longer identifiers correctly, believing, for instance, that repeat (NumberOfTimes) is an entirely different language construct than other repeat commands. You can help them expand this understanding through examples that draw attention to how a variable is a variable no matter if its name is short or long.

▶ IDEA 2: Contrast the concept with what it **isn't**. Distinguish it from misconceptions. Bring it out from the contexts in which it appears.

It is easy to overlook just how many things there are to learn in some basic concepts—how many little similarities, differences, and notional-machine operations beginners need to discern—and, consequently, how much potential there is for misconceptions. For example, Figure 3—busy though it is—lists only some of what students need to learn about variables and assignment. The example code contrasts with various unproductive conceptions that students may draw upon; for instance, it demonstrates that assignment statements aren't equations.

CAUTION: Don't *focus only on what a programming concept* **is.**

(Clarifications: For simplicity, I've written of exposing students to "example code." I don't mean to imply that these programs should always be *presented* to students by a teacher or textbook. Students can be exposed to "example code" during guided experimentation in the REPL, a programming assignment designed to accentuate a particular aspect, or other guided exploration activities. That being said, minimally guided, open-ended projects *alone* are unlikely to expose students to a rich variety of examples dependably enough for efficient learning. The example code in Figures 3 and 4 is not a recipe for teaching; it illustrates the need for many examples of constructs and explains how this notional machine deals with code.)

▶ IDEA 3: Highlight individual aspects of a concept by varying it across examples while other aspects remain constant.

For instance, one aspect of variables is that they can store values of different types; you can emphasize this aspect by exposing students to examples that have the same structure but assign different types of values (Figures 3b and 3c). In addition to demonstrating variation in types, this practice underscores the fact that a single concept of variable works exactly the same way no matter if the values are integers, strings, Booleans, or something else.

Once the learners are aware of the relevant aspects, expose them to diverse, age-appropriate examples of those aspects in combination. For instance, to consolidate their understanding of variables and function calls, learners should experience examples with different expressions, types, and arguments in various combinations (perhaps like the ones in Figures 3 and 4—and many more besides).

Eventually, you can guide the learners to generalize their conceptions further. For instance, the examples in Figures 3 and 4 could help learners generalize their prior knowledge of simple expressions to expressions that are variable names, arguments, function calls, and combinations thereof. Later, the learners will generalize their understanding of variables to encompass parameters, local variables and objects' member variables.

Given their limited exposure to programs, students frequently imagine the rules of a programming language to be more restrictive than they really are; examples in Figure 1 include Func1, Func4, Func7, BCtrl3, Obj4, and Obj5.

Such partial conceptions are viable for some programs. They evolve with growing experience. Nevertheless, the imagined restrictions can be inconvenient, misleading, and frustrating for students.

CAUTION: Don't simplify so much that you encourage misconceptions.

Keeping introductory examples simple is a good idea. Watch out, though—don't inadvertently make things harder for your students. Their first encounters with a concept shouldn't give a misleadingly restricted view.

For instance, don't use only literals and variable names as arguments when you introduce function calls (Func1). Have students practice other expressions enough first so that they can use them as arguments. A REPL is great for such practice; see Figure 4.

Don't always assign a function's return value in a variable (Func4). Don't show Booleans only in `if`s and `while`s (BCtrl3). Put multiple attributes and methods in your introductory examples of objects (Obj4), create more than one instance of your example classes (Obj5), and so on.

▶ IDEA 4. Help students discern the finer **structure** within the lines or blocks. Emphasize the concepts of expression and evaluation.

The lines `result = 2 * (input + 10)`, `i = i + 1`, and `myList = list (5, 1, 2)` have different purposes: "compute a result," "increment i," and "store three numbers in `myList`." Students may think of them variously as a "result-computing assignment statement," a "counter-incrementing command," and a "command for naming lists," respectively. The lines' structural similarity may escape the students' attention: *Each evaluates an expression and assigns its value to a variable*.

Misconceptions may further distract students from that similarity. For instance, a student who is comfortable thinking that assignment statements are equations will be likely to compartmentalize `i = i + 1` as something different that exists in parallel with their (mis)conception. On the other hand, that student may gain powerful insights from learning how `i = i + 1` works and how it is fundamentally similar to `result = 2 * (input + 10)`.

*CAUTION: Don't focus on only the **purpose** of entire lines or blocks of code.*

The concepts of expression and evaluation provide a foundation for understanding several other concepts in introductory programming (see Figures 3 and 4). **Chapter 15, Operators and Expressions**, deals in depth with these foundational ideas. These key concepts enable students to reason about code in terms of its structural components while setting aside the purpose of the entire line or block of code—a crucial skill especially when debugging. Don't neglect them.

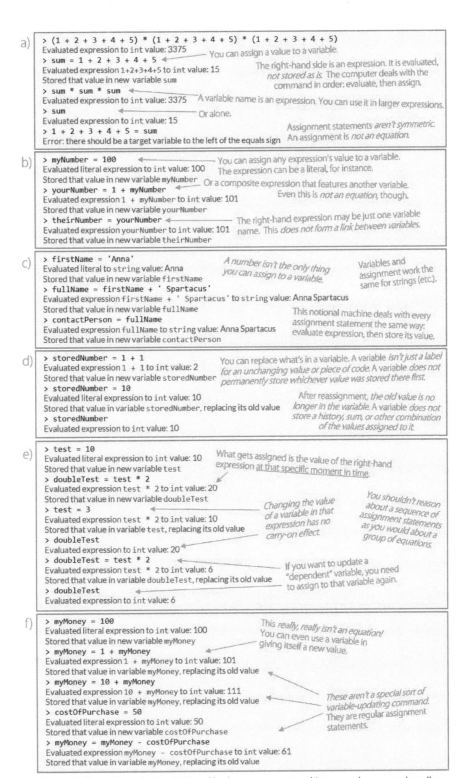

a)
```
> (1 + 2 + 3 + 4 + 5) * (1 + 2 + 3 + 4 + 5) * (1 + 2 + 3 + 4 + 5)
Evaluated expression to int value: 3375          You can assign a value to a variable.
> sum = 1 + 2 + 3 + 4 + 5                     The right-hand side is an expression. It is evaluated,
Evaluated expression 1+2+3+4+5 to int value: 15     not stored as is. The computer deals with the
Stored that value in new variable sum              command in order: evaluate, then assign.
> sum * sum * sum
Evaluated expression to int value: 3375     A variable name is an expression. You can use it in larger expressions.
> sum
Evaluated expression to int value: 15          Or alone.
> 1 + 2 + 3 + 4 + 5 = sum                       Assignment statements aren't symmetric.
Error: there should be a target variable to the left of the equals sign   An assignment is not an equation.
```

b)
```
> myNumber = 100                        You can assign any expression's value to a variable.
Evaluated literal expression to int value: 100   The expression can be a literal, for instance,
Stored that value in new variable myNumber   Or a composite expression that features another variable.
> yourNumber = 1 + myNumber             Even this is not an equation, though.
Evaluated expression 1 + myNumber to int value: 101
Stored that value in new variable yourNumber
> theirNumber = yourNumber            The right-hand expression may be just one variable
Evaluated expression yourNumber to int value: 101   name. This does not form a link between variables.
Stored that value in new variable theirNumber
```

c)
```
> firstName = 'Anna'
Evaluated literal to string value: Anna       A number isn't the only thing        Variables and
Stored that value in new variable firstName   you can assign to a variable.       assignment work the
> fullName = firstName + ' Spartacus'                                            same for strings (etc.).
Evaluated expression firstName + ' Spartacus' to string value: Anna Spartacus
Stored that value in new variable fullName
> contactPerson = fullName            This notional machine deals with every
Evaluated expression fullName to string value: Anna Spartacus   assignment statement the same way:
Stored that value in new variable contactPerson   evaluate expression, then store its value.
```

d)
```
> storedNumber = 1 + 1
Evaluated expression 1 + 1 to int value: 2       You can replace what's in a variable. A variable isn't just a label
Stored that value in new variable storedNumber   for an unchanging value or piece of code. A variable does not
> storedNumber = 10                              permanently store whichever value was stored there first.
Evaluated literal expression to int value: 10        After reassignment, the old value is no
Stored that value in variable storedNumber, replacing its old value   longer in the variable. A variable does not
> storedNumber                                        store a history, sum, or other combination
Evaluated expression to int value: 10                        of the values assigned to it.
```

e)
```
> test = 10
Evaluated literal expression to int value: 10   What gets assigned is the value of the right-hand
Stored that value in new variable test           expression at that specific moment in time.
> doubleTest = test * 2
Evaluated expression test * 2 to int value: 20                          You shouldn't reason
Stored that value in new variable doubleTest                           about a sequence of
> test = 3                            Changing the value                 assignment statements
Evaluated expression test * 2 to int value: 10   of a variable in that    as you would about a
Stored that value in variable test, replacing its old value   expression has no   group of equations.
> doubleTest                          carry-on effect.
Evaluated expression to int value: 20
> doubleTest = test * 2
Evaluated expression test * 2 to int value: 6        If you want to update a
Stored that value in variable doubleTest, replacing its old value   "dependent" variable, you need
> doubleTest                                         to assign to that variable again.
Evaluated expression to int value: 6
```

f)
```
> myMoney = 100
Evaluated literal expression to int value: 100   This really, really isn't an equation!
Stored that value in new variable myMoney        You can even use a variable in
> myMoney = 1 + myMoney                          giving itself a new value.
Evaluated expression 1 + myMoney to int value: 101
Stored that value in variable myMoney, replacing its old value
> myMoney = 10 + myMoney
Evaluated expression 10 + myMoney to int value: 111
Stored that value in variable myMoney, replacing its old value   These aren't a special sort of
> costOfPurchase = 50                                            variable-updating command.
Evaluated literal expression to int value: 50                   They are regular assignment
Stored that value in new variable costOfPurchase                statements.
> myMoney = myMoney - costOfPurchase
Evaluated expression myMoney - costOfPurchase to int value: 61
Stored that value in variable myMoney, replacing its old value
```

Figure 3: Example code in a Python-like language, entered into a verbose—and, sadly, imaginary—REPL environment that explains what the notional machine does with each input (Such explanations could also be provided by a teacher or discovered by students during a learning activity. The annotations on the right list some lessons for students to learn about variables and assignment; statements that directly contrast with documented misconceptions are italicized. These examples assume some familiarity with the concepts of expression, evaluation, value, literal, and data type.)

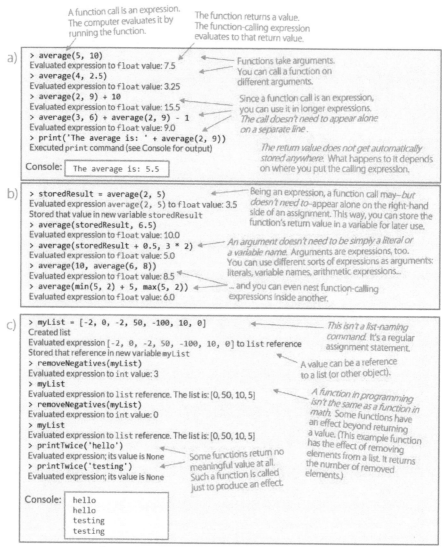

Figure 4: Some of the many lessons that students need to learn about calling functions (Statements that directly contrast with documented misconceptions are italicized. These examples build on the lessons listed in Figure 3.)

▶ IDEA 5. Watch out for language when describing programs and their elements.

Natural language is indirect and ambiguous, even when discussing computer programs. When you say "program," you may be referring to a static program text or a dynamic execution of it. "Here we pass `myVar` as an argument to `myFunc`" doesn't mean that the function literally receives the variable but the variable's value. "This line stores three numbers in `myList`" doesn't mean that `myList` is literally the name of a list but the name of a variable that stores a reference to a list.

Indirect language works when the relationship between what you say and what you mean is obvious enough; for instance, you can assume that the relationship between the name `myList`, the variable, and the list is obvious to a seasoned programmer and they won't take your utterance too literally. A novice, however, may interpret you differently: It's a common misconception to conflate lists or other objects with the variables that refer to them. (This is listed as Obj1 in Figure 1 and feeds into further misconceptions such as Obj1a–c.)

The other side of the story is that students, being used to natural language, often overlook the need to be literal: Common mistakes include attempting to use a list index where a list element was needed or an object attribute where an object reference was needed.

TIP: *Notice the nonliteral language that you and your students use about programs. Teach students to be literal when they instruct the computer.*

▶ IDEA 6: Let students practice **using** abstractions (e.g., functions, objects, classes) before they need to **define** those abstractions.

Beginner programmers have to learn many concepts that depend on each other. This burdens them with cognitive load as they attempt to reason about code and makes it likelier that they form misconceptions.

For instance, to write and understand functions, students should know something about expressions, values, arguments, parameters, variables, scope, and return values and how all those pieces work together; in that light, it's no surprise that students exhibit many misconceptions about this mesh of concepts. Some students get deeply confused about what should go inside a function and what goes outside. Students attempt to `return` something at the call site, for example, and struggle to grasp the relationship between arguments and parameters.

Fortunately, you can harness some of those challenging abstractions and mediate your students' cognitive load by letting students practice abstractions before they need to write their own.

Before students write functions (or read function definitions), for example, teach them the lessons in Figure 4. Don't use just boring functions like those in the figure; the exciting thing is that beginners can call functions that they aren't even close to being able to implement. Give them functions that do something fun or useful, and let them experience the power of computing. Give them a lot of functions; let them build fluency. Then they can proceed with confidence to the many additional lessons that they need to learn about function definitions. Also check out **Chapter 13** on functions and the **Additional Notes** section at the end of this chapter.

The same principle applies to other abstractions of sufficient complexity. Have students use objects before they define objects; have them use classes before they read or write class definitions. Some environments—most notably the BlueJ IDE for Java (www.bluej.org)—enable students to instantiate classes and interact with objects via a graphical interface. If your language has a notation for singleton objects or object literals (as, e.g., Scala or JavaScript do), you may want to use that first and introduce classes only when students are fluent with objects.

▶ IDEA 7. Use analogies but with caution

Teachers use analogy to connect what students already know to what they should learn; it's a powerful weapon. It's also a double-edged one: An analogy can give rise to misconceptions and unproductive notions of program execution.

Here's an infamous example: "A variable is like a box." Sure, there is a similarity, but a variable is also not like any old box in a lot of ways, and careless use of this analogy promotes many well- documented misconceptions, such as each variable storing all the values that have been previously assigned to it, losing its value when assigned to another, or being automatically initialized as "empty."

TIP: *Find learning opportunities not only where an analogy fits but also where it fails.*

An analogue is, by definition, not the thing itself: "Programming concept X is *like* everyday concept Y (but not quite the same as Y)." Teachers and students often focus too much on the X-is-like-Y side of the story and too little on the but-not-quite-Y side. This is dangerous, because it can lead students astray. It is also a missed opportunity: *Key insights can be found on the borders of analogies.*

> Don't simply tell your students that "variables are like boxes that store values" and leave it at that. If you employ this analogy, design an activity that will help your students appreciate how a variable is like a box and how it isn't. Maybe they'll come up with other analogies.

GENERAL APPROACHES FOR BUILDING CONCEPTUAL UNDERSTANDING

A key goal of teaching programming is to build understanding of foundational programming concepts. Such teaching strives for transfer---that is, students should be able to apply the concepts in other contexts in the future.. Transfer doesn't simply happen. As a teacher, you can support transfer from conceptual knowledge to programming skill: Build links between activities in both content and theme, and explicitly refer back to earlier activities and the lessons learned there. Conceptual practice can take any number of forms: digital or unplugged tasks, worked examples, tiny targeted code-writing tasks, multiple-choice questions, and so on. Because students don't find all useful forms of conceptual practice as much fun as writing programs, try to frame the practice so that it's motivated by—and clearly feeds back into—the students' programming projects.

> CAUTION: **Don't** expect students to transfer their conceptual knowledge to program-writing skill unless you facilitate that transfer.

This section describes specific ideas (and cautions) to help build conceptual understanding in a programming classroom. It supplements and complements the ideas presented in **Chapter 23, Worked Examples and Other Scaffolding Strategies**.

▶ IDEA 1: Make it a learning goal that students form a viable model of program execution. Design activities accordingly.

Even if you don't teach students a model of execution, they will come up with one.

Students form intuitive explanations of what programs mean. However, many of these explanations are at odds with what actually happens when the program is run, or are viable for the program at hand but don't transfer to other programs. Students' intuitive knowledge is often tacit, fragmented, and incoherent, and students apply it inconsistently. When given a program to read, many students neglect to study the code in detail, attempting instead to guess its meaning from superficial similarities to earlier examples.

> CAUTION: **Don't** expect students to intuit a viable model of execution without guidance.

Students thus need help in learning to reason about the programs that they read and write—even more so because those programs are often buggy or otherwise surprising. *Make it your goal to teach them a model of program execution.*

Treat students for the "superbug": reliance on informal conventions of human conversation to explain program behavior (Gen1–3 in Figure 1). Don't settle for lip service to the idea that the system is mechanistic, not interpretive. Design activities that help students grasp the rules of program execution.

Look beyond the obvious constructs written into program code; introduce "hidden" concepts that help learners understand what programs mean. Depending on the programming language you use and your specific goals, this could mean pointing up expression evaluation, function activations on the call stack, or references to objects, for instance, all of which exist at runtime but aren't explicitly stated in the program text.

On the other hand, teaching an execution model doesn't imply that it's necessary to teach about computer hardware or to discuss the implementation details of the system that students use. Unless it is your goal to teach that implementation in addition to basic programming, stick to concepts that help students understand program semantics.

This also doesn't mean that you must add more content to your course. Introductory courses already have the goal of teaching students to program; learning the rules of program execution is part of that but often glossed over. Any programming language you're using already involves this content, whether or not you explicitly teach it.

▶ IDEA 2: **Design code-reading activities. When introducing a construct, have students read examples of it before they use it in original code.**

To learn to write programs, students should practice writing programs. But it doesn't follow that only writing programs is the most effective and efficient way to learn that skill. Writing original code that works is predicated on being able to understand what code does; acknowledge this and help your students recognize it, too.

Give students lots of example programs; include buggy examples as well as code that works. Use the examples in different ways: Explain them to students and have students explain them to you or each other. Give students feedback on their explanations.

> *Tip: Provide varied practice with reading code. Get students to trace the execution steps of given code. Prompt students to explain given programs.*

Have students trace programs in detail, working out how the program's execution unfolds gradually: what gets assigned to variables, which expressions are evaluated and when, how parameters get passed and values returned, and so forth. In addition to those "trees," have students explain the "forest": what goal the code achieves. Prompt them to predict program output and explain why a program produces a given output. Ask students questions about programs.

Figure 5 shows a few examples of reading and tracing activities.

Even though reading code is useful, students aren't always eager to study given code carefully. Writing code gives students a sense of ownership over the program that they don't get from just reading. A hybrid of reading and writing can be a useful stepping-stone.

> *Tip: Incorporate code-reading into code-writing tasks. Have students modify or fix programs, add missing pieces of code, or combine given ones.*

For instance, you could: 1. turn a piece of code into a fill-in-the-blanks assignment (Figure 5f); 2. ask students to diagnose and fix a faulty program (Figure 5g); 3. provide a more or less ready application and have students extend its functionality; or 4. give students a partial worked-out example (i.e., step-by-step solution to a programming problem) with one or more of the final solution steps missing.

Such hybrid tasks have the additional benefit of lettings students work on larger and more interesting programs than they can create from scratch. You may wish to design the given programs so that the students need to scrutinize key sections carefully but can ignore other program components that aren't pedagogically timely.

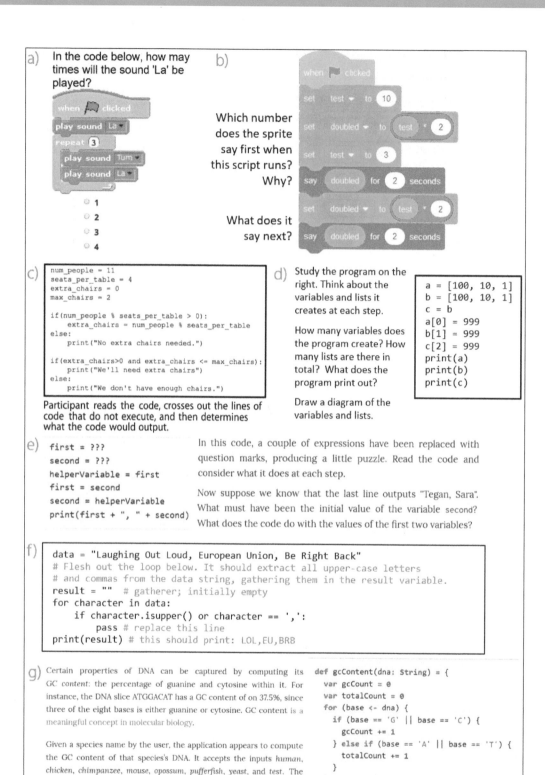

a) In the code below, how may times will the sound 'La' be played?

```
when [flag] clicked
play sound La
repeat 3
  play sound Tum
  play sound La
```

○ 1
○ 2
○ 3
○ 4

b) Which number does the sprite say first when this script runs? Why?

What does it say next?

```
when [flag] clicked
set test to 10
set doubled to test * 2
set test to 3
say doubled for 2 seconds
set doubled to test * 2
say doubled for 2 seconds
```

c)
```
num_people = 11
seats_per_table = 4
extra_chairs = 0
max_chairs = 2

if(num_people % seats_per_table > 0):
    extra_chairs = num_people % seats_per_table
else:
    print("No extra chairs needed.")

if(extra_chairs>0 and extra_chairs <= max_chairs):
    print("We'll need extra chairs")
else:
    print("We don't have enough chairs.")
```

Participant reads the code, crosses out the lines of code that do not execute, and then determines what the code would output.

d) Study the program on the right. Think about the variables and lists it creates at each step.

How many variables does the program create? How many lists are there in total? What does the program print out?

```
a = [100, 10, 1]
b = [100, 10, 1]
c = b
a[0] = 999
b[1] = 999
c[2] = 999
print(a)
print(b)
print(c)
```

Draw a diagram of the variables and lists.

e)
```
first = ???
second = ???
helperVariable = first
first = second
second = helperVariable
print(first + ", " + second)
```

In this code, a couple of expressions have been replaced with question marks, producing a little puzzle. Read the code and consider what it does at each step.

Now suppose we know that the last line outputs "Tegan, Sara". What must have been the initial value of the variable second? What does the code do with the values of the first two variables?

f)
```
data = "Laughing Out Loud, European Union, Be Right Back"
# Flesh out the loop below. It should extract all upper-case letters
# and commas from the data string, gathering them in the result variable.
result = ""  # gatherer; initially empty
for character in data:
    if character.isupper() or character == ',':
        pass # replace this line
print(result) # this should print: LOL,EU,BRB
```

g) Certain properties of DNA can be captured by computing its GC content: the percentage of guanine and cytosine within it. For instance, the DNA slice ATGGACAT has a GC content of on 37.5%, since three of the eight bases is either guanine or cytosine. GC content is a meaningful concept in molecular biology.

Given a species name by the user, the application appears to compute the GC content of that species's DNA. It accepts the inputs *human*, *chicken*, *chimpanzee*, *mouse*, *opossum*, *pufferfish*, *yeast*, and *test*. The program doesn't actually work, however; for a human, the output should be roughly 44%, not 80%. The function gcContent is incorrect. Make a small change that fixes it.

```
def gcContent(dna: String) = {
  var gcCount = 0
  var totalCount = 0
  for (base <- dna) {
    if (base == 'G' || base == 'C') {
      gcCount += 1
    } else if (base == 'A' || base == 'T') {
      totalCount += 1
    }
  }
  100.0 * gcCount / totalCount
}
```

Figure 5: Examples of short activities that involve reading and tracing code: a) a loop-prediction task in Scratch (from Grover, 2017); b) a prediction task in Scratch with code similar to Figure 3e; c) An exercise on conditionals in Python (from Xie et al., 2019); d) A task on references and object identity in Python; e) An alternative tracing activity in Python (adapted from Sorva, 2019); f) A fill-in-the-blank assignment in Python (adapted from Sorva, 2019); g) An analyze-and-fix assignment in Scala (abbreviated from Sorva, 2019)

Another hybrid activity is the so-called Parsons problem: a program-construction puzzle where the student reads given lines or blocks of code and produces a working program by rearranging them. Although somewhat artificial, Parsons problems are an efficient way to build programming skill. See Figure 6 for an example.

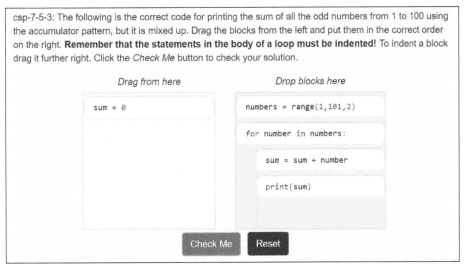

Figure 6: A program-construction puzzle, or Parsons problem, in Python (Guzdial & Ericson, 2014) (The student drags chunks of code from the left to build a program on the right. In this snapshot, the fourth line is incorrectly indented, and one line remains to be placed.)

▶ IDEA 3: Complement constructionism with a variety of activities that target conceptual understanding.

In *constructionist* teaching, students work on open-ended programming projects, building and sharing fun creations and learning along the way, which is great. Unfortunately, this popular approach often fails to teach children some of the foundational concepts that their teachers would like them to learn. In part, that is because the children are left to discover concepts on their own with limited guidance—either by design or due to a lack of resources. With older students, too, throwing them in at the deep end with minimal guidance is less efficient than one might hope.

Although constructivist tools like Scratch alleviate some issues (such as syntax), they don't solve the whole problem. It thus makes sense to blend constructivism and project-based learning with activities that deliberately guide students to conceptual understanding.

One way to do that is to practice computing content in everyday terms even before the students apply that knowledge to programming. **Chapter 7** and **Chapter 23** on guided exploration and scaffolding strategies, respectively, discuss how to guide students so that they develop more robust initial conceptions of important constructs and concepts and approaches to scaffold learning in programming. For instance, children might identify variables in written stories, games, and everyday phenomena such as the weather or sports.

▶ IDEA 4: Use visualizations and other means to make invisible and abstract concepts concrete.

People learn better from a combination of words and pictures than from words alone. Some concepts that aren't obvious in program code become more palpable if you draw them—or have your students draw or craft them. Variables, values, function calls, objects, and references are all good candidates for illustration, to name just a few. Another option is role-playing a program execution in class, with students acting as variables or functions or objects.

Find out what visualization tools are available for the programming language you use. For instance, Python Tutor generates step-by-step animations of Python code (Figure 7), and variants of it exist for several languages. Moreover, Scratch, Snap!, Alice, BlueJ, and many other programming environments come with visual debuggers, variable inspectors, and similar utilities that are potentially useful.

> **CAUTION: Don't** assume students can read visualizations without guidance or that they will appreciate visualization tools unless activities link to the tools.

However, don't expect things to be as simple as "a picture's worth a thousand words": substantial evidence shows that many students don't readily adopt visualization tools or debuggers or recognize their benefits. Reading a visualization is a skill in itself.

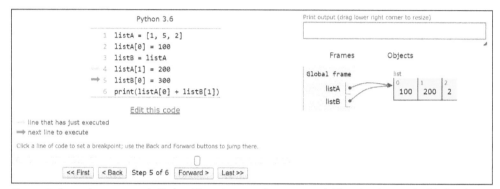

Figure 7: A running program in Python Tutor (*www.pythontutor.com*) (The visualization highlights the fact that the two variables store references, each pointing to the same list.)

Give visualizations a purpose that students can appreciate: Design activities where they support students in reading and writing programs. Use them to locate bugs and explain surprising program behavior. Guide students to explore example code and their own programs in a visualization tool. Have students predict what a step-by-step visualizer will show next. Identify conceptual lessons that are more apparent from a picture than the program text: Variables store values rather than unevaluated expressions, two variables with the same name aren't the same variable, and so on.

WORKING WITH STUDENTS

Teachers who know about common student misconceptions teach better. Books like this one provide helpful pointers, as does the research literature, but there is no substitute for interacting with your students.

Adopt learning activities and forms of assessment (such as those described in **Chapter 6, Feedback Through Formative Check-Ins**) that help you find out how your students think. Students' explanations and drawings of programs and concepts are a great source of information. Keep in mind that a student may hold multiple, apparently contradictory, ideas simultaneously and draw on whichever knowledge fragment occurs to them. A beginner may apply one conception to integer variables, another to strings, and yet another to lists, for instance; the way a beginner traces a function call may similarly vary by contextual features, such as the arguments' data types or what other code there happens to be on the same line.

The word "misconception" has a negative ring to it; one's naïve conceptions can make one feel stupid. Remember to consider what sorts of programs a student's intuitive but limited conception is viable for. Commend students on the valuable parts of their naïve conceptions and help them see that knowledge as something to be remodeled and integrated rather than eradicated.

RESEARCH AND READINGS

For a discussion of how teachers' content knowledge and knowledge of misconceptions affect student learning, see Sadler and Sonnert (2016). For beginner programmers' misconceptions, see Sorva (2012, 2018) and Qian and Lehman (2017); for recent evidence linking such misconceptions to self-efficacy and bugs, see Kallia and Sentance (2019) and Ettles et al. (2018). The "superbug" concept is from an influential article by Pea (1986). Sorva (2013) discusses research evidence for the importance of learning a model of program execution.

Lister (2016) and Xie et al. (2019) provide research perspectives to the relationship between reading and writing programs. Sentance et al. (2019) evaluate the PRIMM (Predict–Run–Investigate–Modify–Make) model of instructional design, where beginner programmers gradually progress from reading given code to writing their own. The studies of Grover and Basu (2017) and Johnson (2014) illustrate the need for structured conceptual practice when learning programming in middle school; Grover et al. (2019) evaluated conceptual learning activities that may fruitfully complement constructivism. Sorva and Seppälä (2014) discuss research-based design principles that intertwine conceptual and tracing practice with larger programming projects. For a quick overview of Parsons problems, see Ericson (2017). For evidence of their efficiency, see Ericson et al. (2017).

This chapter's advice on combinations of program examples is influenced by the more generic advice on example-based learning by Guo et al. (2012). The chapter author's online ebook on programming, which is designed for an introductory university course, incorporates many of the recommendations made in this chapter. It is freely available (Sorva, 2019).

REFERENCES

Ericson, B. J. (2017). Programming with Parsons problems. *Computing at School* (website). https://www.computingatschool.org.uk/news items/365.

Ericson, B. J., Margulieux, L. E., & Rick, J. (2017). Solving Parsons problems versus fixing and writing code. *Proceedings of the 17th Koli Calling Conference on Computing Education Research*, Koli Calling '17, pp. 20–29. ACM.

Ettles, A., Luxton-Reilly, A., & Denny, P. (2018). Common logic errors made by novice programmers. *Proceedings of the 20th Australasian Computing Education Conference*, ACE '18, pp. 83–89. ACM.

Grover, S. (2017). Assessing algorithmic and computational thinking in K–12: Lessons from a Middle School Classroom. In P. J. Rich & C. B. Hodges (eds.), *Emerging research, practice, and policy on computational thinking* (pp. 269–288). Springer.

Grover, S. & Basu, S. (2017). Measuring student learning in introductory block-based programming: Examining misconcep- tions of loops, variables, and Boolean logic. *Proceedings of the 2017 ACM SIGCSE Technical Symposium on Computer Science Education*, SIGCSE '17, pp. 267–272. ACM.

Grover, S., Jackiw, N., & Lundh, P. (2019). Concepts before coding: Non-programming interactives to advance learning of introductory programming concepts in middle school. *Computer Science Education*, 29(2–3):106–135. URL https://doi.org/10.1080/08993408.2019.1568955

Guo, J. P., Pang, M. F., Yang, L. Y., & Ding, Y. (2012). Learning from comparing multiple examples: On the dilemma of "similar" or "different." *Educational Psychology Review*, 24(2): 251–269.

Guzdial, M. & Ericson, B. (2014). *CS principles: Big ideas in programming*. Runestone Academy. URL https://runestone.academy/runestone/static/StudentCSP/index.html

Johnson, C. (2014). *"I liked it, but it made you think too much": A case study of computer game authoring in the key Stage 3 ICT Curriculum*. Doctoral dissertation, University of East Anglia, School of Education and Lifelong Learning. URL https://ueaeprints.uea.ac.uk/53381/

Kallia, M., & Sentance, S. (2019). Learning to use functions: The relationship between misconceptions and self-efficacy. *Proceedings of the 50th ACM Technical Symposium on Computer Science Education*, SIGCSE '19, pp. 752–758. ACM.

Lister, R. (2016). Toward a developmental epistemology of computer programming. *Proceedings of the 11th Workshop in Primary and Secondary Computing Education*, WiPSCE '16, pp. 5–16. ACM.

Pea, R. D. (1986). Language-independent conceptual 'bugs' in novice programming. *Journal of Educational Computing Research*, 2(1):25–36.

Qian, Y. & Lehman, J. (2017). Students' misconceptions and other difficulties in introductory programming: A literature review. *ACM Transactions on Computing Education*, 18(1):1–24.

Sadler, P. M. & Sonnert, G. (2016). Understanding misconceptions: Teaching and learning in middle school physical science. *American Educator*, pp. 26–32.

Sentance, S., Waite, J., & Kallia, M. (2019). Teaching computer programming with PRIMM: A sociocultural perspective. *Computer Science Education*, 29(2–3):136–176. URL https://doi.org/10.1080/08993408.2019.1608781

Sorva, J. (2012). Misconception catalogue. In: *Visual Program Simulation in Introductory Programming Education*, pp. 358–368. Doctoral dissertation. Department of Computer Science and Engineering, Aalto University. URL https://aaltodoc.aalto.fi/bitstream/handle/123456789/3534/isbn9789526046266.pdf

Sorva, J. (2013). Notional machines and introductory programming education. *ACM Transactions on Computing Education*, 13(2):1–31.

Sorva, J. (2018). Misconceptions and the beginner programmer. In: S. Sentance, E. Barendsen, & C. Schulte (eds.), *Computer Science Education: Perspectives on Teaching and Learning in School*, pp. 171–187. Bloomsbury. URL https://www.bloomsbury.com/uk/computer-science-education-9781350057111/

Sorva, J. (2019). Programming 1 (open-access ebook and programming course). URL https://plus.cs.aalto.fi/o1/

Sorva, J. & Seppälä, O. (2014). Research-based design of the first weeks of CS1. In: *Proceedings of the 14th Koli Calling International Conference on Computing Education Research*, Koli Calling '14, pp. 71–80. ACM. URL https://doi.org/10.1145/2674683.2674690

Xie, B., Loksa, D., Nelson, G. L., Davidson, M. J., Dong, D., Kwik, H., Tan, A. H., Hwa, L., Li, M., & Ko, A. J. (2019). A theory of instruction for introductory programming skills. *Computer Science Education*, pp. 1–49. URL https://doi.org/10.1080/08993408.2019.1565235

ADDITIONAL NOTES

To continue from Figures 3 and 4, here is a list of some lessons and misconceptions about function definitions and scope in a simple Python-like language that are relevant to ideas presented in this chapter as well as **Chapter 13, Modularity with Methods and Functions**:

- Evaluating a function-calling expression means suspending the calling code and running the function. Each time a function is called, a separate function activation happens; *a function activation and the code that defines the function are distinct concepts*. A function can call functions, thus causing further suspensions.

- Parameters are (local) variables; a function may have other local variables as well. *Local variables are inaccessible from the outside.* More specifically, *even if A calls B, that doesn't imply that B can access A's variables*. Each function activation has its own copies of local variables; these variables are temporary and *no longer exist after the function call terminates*. It is common and *perfectly acceptable for different functions to use the same names for their parameters*; the same goes for other local variables. The **values** of the argument expressions are passed into the parameters, *not the unevaluated expressions themselves.* Therefore, *you can't write a function that takes in **variables** as parameters*. It's common to use variable names as arguments, but even when you do, *no link is constructed between the argument variables and the corresponding parameter—not even if the two variables have the same name*. This also means that *you can use the same variable names in arguments and parameters, or you can use different ones*; you'll have completely separate variables either way.

- A return command terminates a function activation; upon terminating, the function returns the value of an expression (*which expression may or may not be variable name*). Returning a value sends the value to the call site; *this is not the same or even conceptually similar to printing the value*. The return value becomes the value of the calling expression.

CHAPTER
15

Operators and Expressions

Matthias Hauswirth & Shuchi Grover

It may be desirable to explain, that by the word operation, we mean any process which alters the mutual relation of two or more things, be this relation of what kind it may. This is the most general definition, and would include all subjects in the universe
– Ada Lovelace

INTRODUCTION

Most programs involve the manipulation of data. Numbers may be added, text concatenated, truth values combined, or two values simply compared with each other. The pieces of source code that perform these data manipulations are called *expressions*. Expressions may be used to compute the value to **assign** to a variable, to compute the truth value of the **condition** (true or false) that controls a loop or a conditional statement, or to compute the **arguments** needed to call a function, procedure, or method. As such, they are key programming concepts and must be highlighted as such in instruction.

Expressions consist of operators and operands. Operands denote the values, and operators denote the computation to perform on those values. **Operands** may be **literal** values directly written in the source code (such as the number 123), they may be the names of **variables** from which values are to be read, or they may be an entire expression (such as 1+2 in 3-(1+2)). **Operators** are symbols or series of symbols denoting what to do (such as + for addition, or <= for less-than-or-equal comparison). Even **function calls** (such sin(x)) can be considered operators; calling an add function is similar to using a + operator.

An expression in a programming language is a combination of one or more constants, variables, operators, and functions that the programming language interprets (according to its particular rules of precedence and of association) and computes to "return" (or produce) another value. This process (as in mathematics) is called **evaluation**. Generally speaking, an expression is any combination of operators and operands that "evaluate" to a value.

The most common operators (and expressions) are arithmetic, relational, and Boolean (or logic). **Arithmetic** operators perform arithmetic operations and usually act on numeric operands; they evaluate to a numeric value. **Relational** operators perform comparisons and evaluate to true or false (Boolean) value. **Logic** operators combine operands that themselves result in true or false. They test combinations of Boolean values. In addition are **String** operators, such as those that concatenate strings.

IDENTIFYING EXPRESSIONS IN PROGRAMS

Table 1 shows program snippets with examples of various expressions used in different ways in programs written in Java, Scheme, Python, Scratch, Snap!, and Alice. The first five examples all represent the same computation.

Table 1. Examples of program snippets containing expressions in different languages

Java

```java
class Demo {
  public static float fahrenheitToCelsius(float fahrenheit) {
    return (fahrenheit - 32) / 9 * 5;
  }
  public static double distance(double x1, double y1, double x2, double y2) {
    return Math.sqrt(Math.pow(x1 - x2, 2) + Math.pow(y1 - y2, 2));
  }
  public static void run() {
    System.out.println(fahrenheitToCelsius(80));
    System.out.println(distance(0, 0, 100, 100));
  }
}
```

Scheme

```scheme
(define (fahrenheit-to-celsius fahrenheit)
  (* (/ (- fahrenheit 32) 9) 5))
(define (distance x1 y1 x2 y2)
  (sqrt (+ (sqr (- x1 x2))
           (sqr (- y1 y2)))))
(fahrenheit-to-celsius 80)
(distance 0 0 100 100)
```

Python

```python
def fahrenheit_to_celsius(fahrenheit):
  return (fahrenheit - 32) / 9 * 5
def distance(x1, y1, x2, y2):
  return sqrt((x1 - x2) ** 2 + (y1 - y2) ** 2)

print fahrenheit_to_celsius(80)
print distance(0, 0, 100, 100)
```

Scratch

(continued on next page)

Table 1. Examples of program snippets containing expressions in different languages *(continued)*

Snap!

Alice

In the following sections, we explain the components of expressions and how to evaluate them. We then share examples of classroom activities focused on working with expressions and conclude with a section on common student mistakes related to operators and expressions.

INGREDIENTS OF AN EXPRESSION

Expressions are pieces of programs (or source code) that produce a value (we can also say that expressions can be "evaluated"). Table 2 shows examples of expressions in different programming languages. It starts with the simplest kinds of expressions and gradually shows more and more powerful ones.

Table 2. Expressions in different languages

Expression	Language	Comment
1		literal number, no operator
a	Python, JavaScript, Java, C	get variable's value, no operator
(a)	Scratch	get variable's value, no operator
- 3		negate, unary operator
1 + 2	Python, JavaScript, Java, C	add, binary operator
(1 + 2)	Scratch	add, binary operator
"Hello World!"	Python, JavaScript, Java, C	literal string, no operator
'Hello World!'	Python, JavaScript	literal string, no operator
1 - 2	Python, JavaScript, Java, C	subtract, infix notation
(1 - 2)	Scratch	subtract, infix notation
1 2 -	Forth	subtract, postfix notation
1 2 sub	PostScript	subtract, postfix notation
(- 1 2)	Scheme, Lisp, Racket	subtract, prefix notation
1 - 2 + 3	Python, JavaScript, Java, C	multiple operators
1 - (2 + 3)	Python, JavaScript, Java, C	parentheses for precedence
(1 - 2 + 3)	Scratch	nesting for precedence
true	JavaScript, Java	literal Boolean, no operator
True	Python	literal Boolean, no operator
true | false	JavaScript, Java, C	Boolean or binary operator
True or False	Python	Boolean or binary operator
"Ho" + "Ho"	Python, JavaScript, Java	string concatenation
join Hi Ho	Scratch	string concatenation (with space)

Strictly speaking, expressions are built from exactly two kinds of ingredients: **operators** and **operands**. The operators specify the computation (what to compute), whereas the operands specify the data (which values to do the computation on).

Many of the operators in expressions are familiar to anyone with fundamental mathematics skills, especially the **arithmetic** operators (+, -, *, and /) for addition, subtraction, multiplication, and division. Similarly, some **relational** operators are familiar from mathematics (such as < and > for "greater than" and "less than"), whereas other relational operators may look slightly different in programming languages than in mathematics (>= instead of ≥, or == or even === instead of =). Other operators may be less familiar, such as **Boolean logic** operators (AND or &, OR or |, and NOT or ! for the propositional logic symbols ∧, ∨, and ¬ in mathematics).

Boolean operators are logical operators foundational to computing. The three basic Boolean operators — and, or, and not — were first defined in 1854 by George Boole, an English mathematician and logician, in his book *Laws of Thought*. and and or are binary operators, whereas not is a unary operator. These operators are expressed by various symbols in different languages. Like relational operators, Boolean operators return a true or false. Truth tables (shown next) are one way to understand how these three operators work, but a simple way of describing them follows:

- and (∧): Returns true only if both operands are true (or evaluate to true, given the operands themselves are expressions) and false otherwise.

- or (∨) : Returns false only if both operands are false (or evaluate to false, given the operands themselves are expressions) and true otherwise.

- not (¬): Negates the operand. It returns true if the operand is false (or evaluates to false) and vice versa.

P	Q	$P \vee Q$
T	T	T
T	F	T
F	T	T
F	F	F

P	Q	$P \vee Q$
T	T	T
T	F	T
F	T	T
F	F	F

P	$\sim P$
T	F
F	T

Programming languages often also have operators that work with **text** (strings). For example, in languages like Java or Python, one can concatenate two strings with a +. In Scratch, this is done with the join block.

▶ Functions

Most languages provide a way to call a **function** to compute something. When in mathematics we see "sin x," in a programming language we might look at this as a call of the function sin, with the argument x. In Java or JavaScript we would write Math.sin(x) and in Python or C sin(x). Strictly speaking, from a programming language point of view, calling a function can be considered using the "function call operator," the ...(...).

Note that functions can have more than one argument. For example, the function to find the maximum of two values would need both values as an argument. In Java, this would be Math.max(3, 2).

Very importantly, a function in a program, like a function in math, has to **return** a value. Many programming languages allow the definition of "functions" that do not return values (e.g., void methods in Java, void functions in C), but those constructs are procedures, not functions. Why? Because a function can be used as an operand in an expression, such as sin(x) in sin(x) + 2. If sin(x) does not return a value, then what would the value of the left operand of the + be?

Scratch does allow programmers to define custom blocks, but it does not allow the definition of custom functions. One can define a block, and the block can take zero or more arguments, but it cannot return a value. One cannot plug a custom block as an operand into an expression. The following example would like to define a function abs(...), and use it in the expression 2 + ..., but the custom block is a procedure, thus does not return a value and cannot be plugged into an expression.

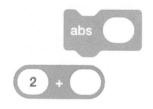

It should be noted that other block-based languages, like Snap! and Alice, do support user-created functions that return values.

▶ Other Fancy Operators

Besides the function call operator, languages that older students (in secondary school) may encounter often also provide operators to access elements of a list (e.g., *array[index]* in Java), to look up a value in a map (e.g., also *map[key]*), or to access a field of an object or data structure (e.g., *object.fieldname* in Java, JavaScript, or C).

Moreover, they may provide conditional operators, such as *condition ? thenValue : elseValue* in Java, JavaScript, or C.

Finally, the so-called short-circuit operators, such as `bool && bool` and `bool || bool` in Java, JavaScript, and C, are special versions of the Boolean logic operators `bool & bool` and `bool | bool`. The short-circuit versions take a shortcut if they can: If the left operand of `&&` evaluates to `false`, the right operand is never looked at; similarly, if the left operand of `||` evaluates to `true`, the right operand is never looked at. This may look like a simple performance optimization (avoid unnecessary work), but it also is exploited in programs like this `shouldCrash && crash()`—if `shouldCrash` is `true`, the `crash()` function is called and the system dies, but if `shouldCrash` is `false`, the `crash()` function is not called.

▶ Assignment, and Other Operators With Side Effects

Some operators do more than one thing: They perform a computation leading to a result (this is the main job of an operator, and it is what expressions are all about), but they also have a side effect. Examples of these operators are ++ and -- in C-like languages and, most importantly, the assignment operator.

In math, a = b is an equation. In programming, a = b can be seen as an assignment statement, where b is an expression and a is the name of a variable. The statement evaluates the expression and then stores the resulting value in the variable a.

However, many languages actually treat a = b as an assignment **expression**. That is, the entire expression results in a value. Thus, one could write `sin(a = b)`. What does a = b mean here? It stores the value of b into the variable a, but then also produces that value as a result. That means, the expression a = b evaluates to a value! Thus, we can write `sin(a = 3)` with the consequence that the value 3 is stored in variable a (as a side effect of evaluating the expression), and the result of the expression a = 3 (i.e., the value 3) is used as an argument for the sine function.

EXPRESSIONS AS TREES

Expressions, when written in a text-based programming language, can be quite hard to understand. Take the following Java expression as an example:

```
join( position < length( message ) ? letter( position, message ) : "?", " Yeah!" )
```

Even though this expression looks like a hard-to-understand piece of source code, this expression, like every expression, has a **clear hierarchical structure**. Understanding that hierarchical tree structure is essential for understanding the meaning of the expression and how it is evaluated.

In block-based languages, that hierarchical structure becomes visible because the blocks are visually nested. Here is a piece of a Snap! program that is equivalent to the above Java source code:

Some curricula stress the understanding of that hierarchical structure. For example, the Bootstrap curriculum (which involves functional programming) uses the metaphor of "circles of evaluation" to help students understand in which order an expression is evaluated. This is made possible thanks to the Lisp-like functional programming language Bootstrap is based on, where every subexpression is surrounded by parentheses. Thus, the hierarchy is explicitly given by the nesting of parentheses. Here is the equivalent expression in Bootstrap's language:

```
(join                                        BSL / Lisp / Scheme / Racket
  (cond
    [
      (< position (length message))
      (letter position message)
    ]
    [
      else
      "?"
    ]
  )
  " Yeah!"
)
```

▶ Visually Representing Expression Trees

To clearly bring out the hierarchical structure of an expression, one can use nested circles (à la Bootstrap) or node-link diagrams of trees.

Here is a simple expression in Java:

```
3 - 1 + a                                                          Java
```

Even though the expression is simple, understanding it requires some insight into the order of evaluation. The expression is evaluated from left to right. First 3 - 1, and then 2 + a.

Here is the equivalent expression in Scheme:

```
(+ (- 3 1) a)                                BSL / Lisp / Scheme / Racket
```

The Scheme expression can naturally be converted into circles of evaluation, simply by turning each pair of parentheses into a circle. This structure is obvious in Scheme, but it is harder to see in the (equivalent) Java source code, because Java does not force us to surround each subexpression with parentheses.

Figure 1a shows the circles of evaluation visually representing the nested structure of the expression. Figure 1b shows the corresponding node-link diagram showing the nesting as a tree structure (as is common in computer science, trees are drawn with the root at the top).

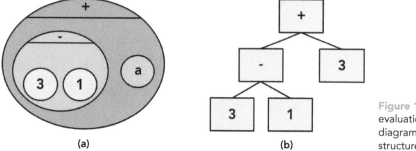

(a) **(b)**

Figure 1a and b. 'Circles of evaluation' and a node-link diagram showing the nested structure of expressions

▶ Trees Help in Evaluating Expressions

Given a visual representation of an expression as a tree, either as nested blocks in languages like Scratch or Snap!, as circles of evaluation, or as node-link diagrams makes it easier to explain (and for students to understand) the evaluation order: Evaluation always proceeds inside out (for nested blocks or circles of evaluation) or bottom up (for node-link diagrams).

Bootstrap uses the metaphor of an ant or worm moving through the circles of evaluation, entering each circle on the left, going to the operator at the top, then entering each inside circle from left to right. When explaining the evaluation of an expression with a node-link diagram, one draws upward arrows from each node. It's possible to annotate each arrow with the value produced by the subexpression that node represents. In the following example, we assume that variable a contains the value 17.

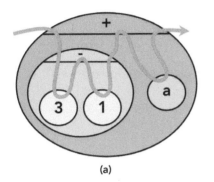 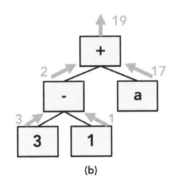

(a) (b)

Figure 2a and b. Evaluation in 'circles of evaluation' and in node-link diagram

EXPRESSIONS AND TYPES

When you evaluate an expression, you get a value. Each value has a type. For example, in Java the value 19 has type int, the value 3.14 has type double, the value true has type boolean, the value "Hello" has type String, and the value 'x' has type char.

Due to space constraints, we will not go in-depth into dynamically and statically typed languages and expressions in this section.

To determine the type of an expression, one proceeds inside out, or bottom up, similar to how one determines the value. The *leaves* of the expression tree, the innermost or bottom-most nodes, are nodes like a **literal** value (the type of literal values are known; e.g., in Java the literal 1234567890 has type int) or **variables** (and variables have to be declared with a type; e.g., in Java one could declare int a; to say that variable a stored values of type int).

The *internal nodes* of the expression tree have well-defined types. They are nodes like **operators** (e.g., in Java the + operator produces values of type int if both arguments are of type int) or **function calls** (e.g., in Java the function Integer.parseInt(String) takes an argument of type String and returns an argument of type int).

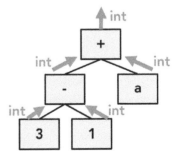

Figure 3 is a node-link diagram of our example expression, showing how the type of the expression is determined. To be able to determine the type, we do need the type of all involved variables and methods. Here, there's only the variable a, and we assume that that has been declared as an int.

The type of the expression is int. This means that no matter what value is stored in variable a when we evaluate the expression, the result of the expression is a value of type int.

Figure 3. Determining the type of the expression in a node-link diagram

Among block-based languages, Scratch does not require you to specify the type of values that can be stored in a variable. Here, the expression 19 / x is not well typed. The statement `set x to "Hello!"` stores a value of type String into variable x. Later, the statement `say 19 / x` will try to evaluate the expression 19 / x, which will try to divide the number 19 by the string "Hello!".

In conclusion, in dynamically typed languages like Scratch, it is **not** generally possible to determine the type of an expression. A given expression could produce a different type of value each time it is evaluated. And thus one has to evaluate the expression, look at the value it produces, and then determine the type of that value.

IDEAS FOR THE CLASSROOM

Following are a set of classroom activities that help in teaching expressions.

▶ Non-programming and Unplugged/Offline Activities

The following activities do not require programming or a computer.

▶ "Boole Says" Game

This is played exactly like the game *Simon Says*, except that the instructions use the special words and, or, and not. For example, you may say something like

- "Boole says put your left hand on your head or tap your stomach with your right hand."
- "Boole says raise your right foot and wave your right hand."
- "Boole says clap your hands and do not march your feet."

Have the entire class stand up for this, and you can read the instructions one by one. Students sit down if they make a mistake (or they come up front to announce the instructions). Have a long list of such instructions ready, and read them out faster and faster to make the game more exciting.

▶ Dice Game

The game presented in the VELA non-programming learning activities designed by Grover et al. (2019) can be played with online or physical die. The players roll the die and Player 1 or 2 gets a point based on the outcome of evaluating an expression involving written arithmetic and relational operators e.g., IF `Dice1 + Dice2 < 12`, THEN Player 1 gets a point (Figure 4).

The teacher could bring the class together after the game to discuss the core underlying ideas and to ensure students understand the difference between IF-THEN and IF-THEN-ELSE statements. They could also solve worksheets individually in which students need to create conditional statements and expressions that involve real-world situations, for example, deciding whether there is enough pizza for a party based on the number of guests and the number of slices for each guest (as shown in Example 1 in the next section).

Dice Game - Worksheet

Instructions: For each round follow the instructions in rolling dice and write down the expression (i.e. if it says Roll 2 dice and add their values together, and you roll a 1 and a 5, write 1+5 in the "expression" column).

Then look at the **instructions** and decide whether the IF-THEN evaluates to TRUE (T) or FALSE(F), then follow the scoring directions.

Both players start with a score of 0.

[You can roll the dice virtually here: http://tinyurl.com/7rbusyk]

PLEASE TAKE TURNS FILLING OUT THE WORKSHEET

Round	Instructions	Expression using dice values	T/F	Player 1 Score	Player 2 Score
1	Roll 2 dice and add them together IF **Dice1 + Dice2** < 12, THEN player 1 gains a point				
2	Roll 2 dice and add them together IF **expression > 2**, THEN player 2 gets a point				
3	Roll 2 dice and add them together IF **expression = 7**, THEN player 1 gets a point				
4	Roll 1 dice and then roll a 2nd, subtract the 2nd dice from the 1st dice IF **expression = a negative number**, THEN player 1 gets a point, ELSE player 2				

Figure 4. Section of worksheet accompanying the *Dice Game*

▶ Constructing Expressions for Use in Conditionals

As mentioned in **Chapter 19** on conditionals, students can be provided off-screen activities that require them to construct the expression for use in a conditional. You can use everyday scenarios for such activities. The following examples are drawn from the VELA curriculum designed by Grover and colleagues.

Example 1:

You are planning a party!

- There are **12 guests** and you want **2 slices** of pizza <u>for each</u> guest.
- `TotalPizzaSlices` is the variable for the total number of pizza slices you have.
- Write the expression that checks if you have enough pizza.
- If you have enough pizza, you can *"set the table"*; otherwise, you need to *"order more pizza"*.
- Write an `IF-THEN-ELSE` statement to describe this situation.

IF _____ THEN

        `Set the table`

ELSE

        `Order more pizza`

Example 2:

Tom's parents lay down the following rules for him:

Rule 1: If homework is done and chores are complete, Tom can play video games.

Rule 2: If there is an exam the next day, Tom does not get to play video games, even if he does his homework and chores.

Tom can play video games `IF` _____

▶ Programming-Based Activities

The following activities explicitly use programming languages.

▶ Fill-in-the-Blank Activity

Provide students with incomplete programs, where some expressions are left out. This works particularly well for expressions that are conditions, like in the next example.

▶ Identify Expressions Activity

Ask students to identify expressions in snippets of programs provided to them. This can be a pencil-and-paper activity, or you can do it in a programming environment (where students are required to add comments where they find expressions) or in an online document where they can annotate programs through highlights or boxes or text comments.

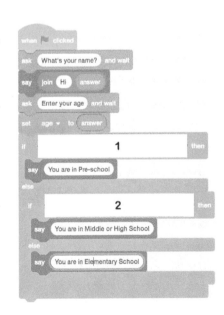

Here are two examples, one in Scratch and one in Java.

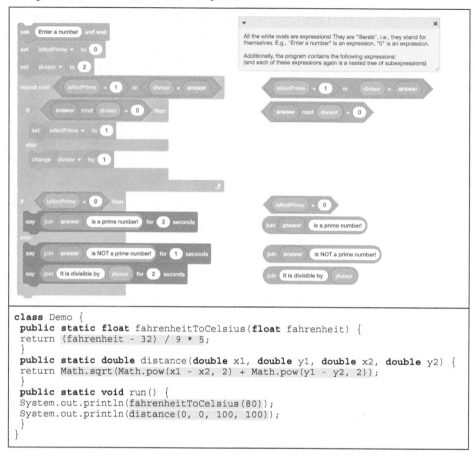

```
class Demo {
  public static float fahrenheitToCelsius(float fahrenheit) {
    return (fahrenheit - 32) / 9 * 5;
  }
  public static double distance(double x1, double y1, double x2, double y2) {
    return Math.sqrt(Math.pow(x1 - x2, 2) + Math.pow(y1 - y2, 2));
  }
  public static void run() {
    System.out.println(fahrenheitToCelsius(80));
    System.out.println(distance(0, 0, 100, 100));
  }
}
```

COMMON MISTAKES AND NAÏVE CONCEPTIONS

There are many naïve conceptions students may hold when learning about expressions. The Programming Misconceptions website (progmiscon.org) contains an extensive curated list. Each misconception has a unique name and is connected to a specific programming language. At the time of this writing, most misconceptions are specific to Java; however, misconceptions for other languages (e.g., Python and JavaScript) are being added. Also check out **Chapter 14** on naïve conceptions across this and other programming topics.

Here is a selection of the most relevant misconceptions about expressions, with descriptions from progmiscon.org.

▶ NoAtomicExpression

Misconception: **Expressions must consist of more than one piece.**
An individual literal, like **19**, or a variable, like **x**, or a method call, like **m()**, or a constructor invocation, like **new Point()**, is not an expression. An expression must involve multiple operands combined with operators.

Correction:
Even 1 is an expression. The same applies to a, or m(), or new Point(). There is no need for an operator. Of course, an expression *can* involve operators, like 1+3, or 1+a.

The leaves of an expression tree (atomic expressions) are expressions, too.

▶ VariablesHoldExpressions

Misconception: An expression is stored in a variable.
For example, `int a = v/2` stores the expression `v/2` in the variable a.

Correction:

First, the expression is evaluated. Then the assignment operator (`=`) stores the resulting value in the variable.

Variables hold *values*. An expression is *not* a value. Thus, variables cannot store expressions. However, an expression can be evaluated, producing a value. That value can then be stored in the variable.

Note that once a value is produced, there is no more connection between that value and the expression that produced it.

▶ ComparisonWithBooleanLiteral

Misconception: To test whether an expression is true or false, compare it to `true` or to `false`.
To determine whether an expression evaluates to `true` or `false`, one should use a relational operator (`==` or `!=`) to compare with a Boolean literal (`true` or `false`).

Correction:

Such a comparison is entirely unnecessary. Such an expression can (and should) be simplified.

Expression	Equivalent Simplified Expression
e == true	e
e == false	!e
e != true	!e
e != false	e

▶ OutsideInMethodNesting

Misconception: Nested method calls are invoked outside in.
When nesting method calls, like with `a(b())`, calls are invoked from the outside in (first `a()`, then `b()`).

Correction:

This misconception manifests itself when drawing expression trees, such as the tree for `a(b())`, where the inner piece of the expression (here, `b()`) is drawn as the root of the expression tree.

The correct way to execute nested method calls is inside out (from the bottom to the top in the expression tree). For the example expression, first `b()` is called, producing a value, then `a()` is called, receiving the return value of `b()` as an argument. The fact that the call `a()` needs the return value of `b()` as an argument implies that `b()` has to be called before `a()`, and thus that these calls evaluate from the inside out.

Another variation of the nesting error is caused by misplaced parentheses that result in an incorrect order of precedence in a Boolean expression. This sometimes happens when learners are converting from an English sentence to a Boolean expression that involves multiple Boolean operators as in the following example from Cacefo et al. (2017).

OPERATORS AND EXPRESSIONS

Consider the following definition of leap year

"A leap year is exactly divisible by 4 except for century years (years ending with 00). The century year is a leap year only if it is perfectly divisible by 400."

Write a function that receives an integer and returns 1 if it corresponds to a leap year, and 0 otherwise.

```c
int isLeapYear(int year) {
  if ( (year%400==0 || year%4==0) && year%100!=0 )
    return 1;
  else
    return 0;
```

The correct condition above should be

```c
if ( year%400==0 || (year%4==0 && year%100!=0) )
```

BIBLIOGRAPHY

1. Bootstrap curriculum. https://www.bootstrapworld.org

2. Caceffo, R., de França, B., Gama, G., Benatti, R., Aparecida, T., Caldas, T., & Azevedo, R. (2017). An antipattern documentation about misconceptions related to an introductory programming course in C. *Technical Report 17–15 (p. 42)*. Institute of Computing, University of Campinas.

3. Grover, S., Jackiw, N., & Lundh, P. (2019). Concepts before coding: Non-programming interactives to advance learning of introductory programming concepts in middle school. *Computer Science Education, 29*(2–3), 106–135.

Peer Collaboration and Pair Programming

Shannon Campe & Jill Denner

INTRODUCTION

> *Alone we can do so little; together we can do so much.*
> – Helen Keller

Put simply, is when two or more people work together toward a shared goal. Extensive research shows the benefits of collaborative learning for students' problem-solving and cognitive development. Interactions that involve working with a peer support, challenge, and require students to explain the subject matter, reflect on another person's contribution, and lead to deeper learning. Collaboration is increasingly important in introductory programing classrooms. Computer science (CS) is increasingly being introduced as a new subject, and more teachers are expected to teach programming as part of introductory CS curricula. Collaborative computing is described in the US K–12 CS Framework as "the process of performing a computational task by working in pairs and on teams," which "requires individuals to navigate and incorporate diverse perspectives, conflicting ideas, disparate skills, and distinct personalities." Similar to the Framework, the Computer Science Teachers Association (CSTA) standards recommend that students learn how to seek and incorporate feedback from team members and users to refine a solution that meets user needs. A strategy that can be used with primary and secondary school students to facilitate and practice collaboration is *pair programming*.

> **Pair programming** is a pedagogy where two people work side by side with one computer, monitor, keyboard and mouse, each trading roles as *driver* and *navigator*. The driver controls programming actions with the mouse and keyboard, and the navigator provides input to programming actions, looks for mistakes, and accesses resources.

Practicing pair programming (PP) driver and navigator roles builds in an opportunity to collaborate by giving and receiving feedback and discussing varied perspectives. Beyond students building essential collaboration skills, PP has the potential to impact students by increasing their interest in computer science (e.g., show that it's not necessarily a solo endeavor), learning programming skills (e.g., solve challenges together), and fostering creativity (e.g., bounce ideas off of each other). Teachers can use this strategy to increase interest and engagement in programming to address a greater range of students and their varied styles of interacting and learning.

Educators can benefit from what has been learned about what collaboration looks like when children are programming together. This includes how and about what the pairs are interacting and how interactions between partners support or undermine their problem-solving. Children negotiate their roles in different ways—some contribute more by driving, whereas others contribute more by making suggestions to the driver. Effective pairs give and receive input, exchange driver and navigator roles to build on each other's expertise, and help each other think through problems. They are not always overtly interacting, and often they interact about other things besides their programming tasks (e.g., favorite game character, what they are doing after school) as they build rapport with one another or take breaks from working.

Pair programming requires careful planning and preparation to build strong partnerships, as well as support and scaffolding to persist when challenges occur. It can be used for a range of tasks, including exploring new software, debugging, performing closed-ended tasks with explicit directions, and taking on open-ended design projects. Tasks that include explicit directions (e.g., make a character move and say something) have a more defined role for the navigator, who can guide the driver through the steps. More open-ended tasks (e.g., create an interactive game) may require additional support from the teacher to help pairs work together successfully. PP can be used sporadically for specific tasks or as often as every day.

This chapter takes teachers through the steps of implementing PP in their classroom. This includes guidance in how to pair students, how to teach PP roles and responsibilities, a description of what strong collaboration between pairs looks like, what it looks like when pairs are struggling, and ways to help those pairs become more effective. Also see **Chapter 26, Zestful Learning**, for ideas on how to create a classroom culture that fosters peer collaboration more broadly, and **Chapter 6, Feedback With Formative Check-Ins**, for rubrics and other tools that can scaffold the process of peer feedback.

▶ How to Pair Students

The first step after deciding to use PP to foster collaboration within a group of students is pairing them. For this is it helpful to consider potential partners' compatibility. Pairing students who have similar attitudes toward collaboration and a perception that they have an equal or higher level of programming skill than their partner (not one partner thinking they are less skilled) not only makes for more effective partnerships but can also increase their interest in computing. Also, pairs who are more positive about their partnership and friendship can be more compatible.

Try these activities with your class as a way to gather information on students' attitudes toward collaboration and their level of programming skill and experience, as well as give them the opportunity to partner with peers they feel close to.

1) Have individual students take a brief survey.
2) Have them pair program for a short time with three or four trial partners.
3) At the end of trial, have them write down their top three partner preferences.
4) Review survey and preferences along with your observations, and assign permanent pairs.

Because most students choose peers they feel closer to and are friends with at the start of class, the information about their attitude toward collaboration (from survey) can be useful for deciding when to, and when not to, pair close friends.

As pairs work together over time, teachers may find instances when they need to reorganize pairs due to a partner's excessive absences or to a conflict the pair cannot resolve to stay on task. The teacher needs to assess which students would work well together and which original pairs would be least hindered when making changes. It's important to focus on what students can bring to the new pair and emphasize the value in learning how to work collaboratively with more than one person.

TEACHING PAIR PROGRAMMING

A common misunderstanding is that children will learn to collaborate on their own when they are placed in pairs or teams. For students to be successful at PP, they need to be explicitly taught the basics about the roles, come up with their own description of those roles, and then practice how to communicate so they can collaboratively program together with adult guidance and support. The Pair Programming Activity Map in Figure 1 shows the three broad areas involved with implementing PP in the classroom: pairing students, teaching the basics of PP and the partners' roles and responsibilities, and providing support to pairs. Detailed descriptions of each area and sample activity plans can be found in the K–12 Pair Programming Toolkit (see the link at the end of the chapter).

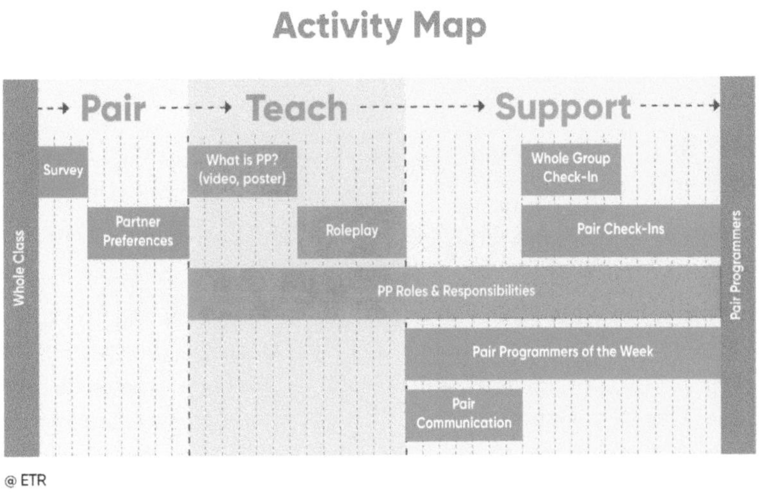

Activity Map
Pair
Teach
Support
Whole Class
Survey
Partner Preferences
What is PP? (video, poster)
Roleplay
Whole Group Check-In
Pair Check-Ins
PP Roles & Responsibilities
Pair Programmers of the Week
Pair Communication
Pair Programmers
@ ETR

Figure 1. Pair Programming Activity Map (Source: ETR Pair Programming Toolkit)

Running throughout all activities should be principles of PP that are emphasized throughout teaching and supporting the strategy. As a basis for these principles are the driver and navigator roles and responsibilities, shown in Figure 2.

Driver
Controls the mouse and keyboard
Talks about thoughts and actions
Moves monitor so that both partners can see it
Both
Switch roles regularly
Take breaks
Respect roles (e.g., no grabbing tools or materials without consent)
Update partner on project work if they've been absent
Navigator
N
W
E
S
Uses help resources (printed or online, other peers)
Gives direction & makes suggestions
Catches mistakes
Keeps the big picture of the project goal in mind
@ ETR

Figure 2. Driver and Navigator roles described (Source: ETR Pair Programming Toolkit)

Besides the basic roles of each partner, both students should be actively cooperating, talking about ideas and solutions, listening and responding to each other in a respectful way, and switching roles in a way that builds upon each other's expertise as well as enables each partner to control the mouse and keyboard. One way to emphasize this is for teachers to cocreate a poster with their students that includes PP roles and responsibilities and incorporates existing classroom norms and elements of teamwork that build a collaborative partnership.

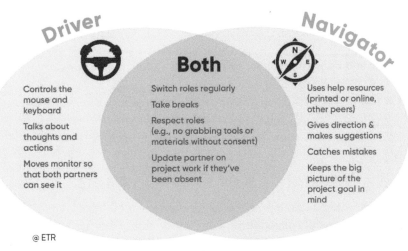

- Listen
- Compromise
- Share ideas
- Give feedback
- Check for agreement
- Respectfully disagree
- Check in with you partner (about roles, engagement, and programming decisions)
- Step back sometimes if you tend to take over
- Step in by speaking up if you tend to be quiet

Also help create buy-in to the strategy by discussing and reminding students of the value of PP: built-in help, fun, two-heads-are-better-than-one, increase in communication skills, learning real-life "teamwork" skills.

▶ Switching Roles

There is some debate about whether partners should routinely switch navigator and driver roles. Sometimes more structured switching can help ensure equity between the partners, but letting partners switch on their own, depending on their individual expertise during a given task, can be another effective approach. When pairs are free to switch roles on their own, they may switch less frequently as they work together more, but when they do switch, they engage in part of the collaborative process by negotiating about the switch. It's important to remember that just because one partner has the keyboard more often, there's not necessarily an imbalance. Pairs could be dividing tasks based on a previous discussion only they were privy to. Whether a more rigid role-switching structure is implemented only at the beginning of pairs working together, throughout all of their time together, or if pairs are left to regulate their role switches with periodic reminders, teachers need to be intentional about their expectations and check in with pairs regularly.

Be intentional and transparent about what is expected with regard to switching roles and how the switching will take place.

Check in regularly with pairs to increase engagement and equity and reduce problematic conflict (e.g., why are each staying in a particular role more often?).

SUPPORTING COLLABORATIVE PAIR PROGRAMMING

The principles and activities noted in the previous section are essential for laying the foundation and providing the support for successful collaborative pair programming. But per usual, some pairs will naturally fall into a rhythm of working together, and others will need more scaffolding to be successful.

The nature of collaboration in paired students can vary greatly. Some partners talk a lot, whereas others rely heavily on nonverbal communication (e.g., head nodding, smile, pointing at monitor). Partners are not always talking with one another—sometimes they need time to think independently or take a short break, so they can reengage more effectively. Some focus primarily on the task, and others talk about their friends, family, movies, or schoolwork. Productive interactions can appear to be serious and focused, as well as playful and fun. Partners often have disagreements, and although some argue about what they want to do or how to fix something in their program, others allow the driver to make the decision. It's important to be open to all the ways it can look, depending on the students and the task they are completing. Educators should observe how partnerships evolve over time, which will help identify what aspects of PP need support, recognize any disengagement and conflict early enough to intervene effectively, reinforce partners' positive behaviors, and assess their progress on their programming project.

After teaching students how to pair program, it's important to continually gather information about what is going on within the pair and then work with them to implement elements of the principles of PP (roles, responsibilities, teamwork) to support the partnership. See these key suggestions of what to emphasize to support pairs in becoming collaborative, effective programming partners regardless of where they are on the continuum of being less or more collaborative.

Tips for Talking With Pairs

- Reiterate PP roles and responsibilities by affirming students for specific PP behaviors.
- Emphasize teamwork and communication. Remind them to say "we" and "us," not "I" and "me."
- Encourage more assertive students to "step back" in the pair—to listen and respond to their partner. Encourage less assertive students to "step in"—to talk about their ideas and help solve programming challenges.
- Remind pairs to switch navigator and driver roles to build upon each other's expertise and monitor for imbalances in time or power in the driver role.
- Challenge pairs to work together effectively. Ask students to come up with ideas on how to improve their partnership.
- When pairs encounter a challenge, encourage them to rely on their partner and their other peers to foster a collaborative classroom. Teach them steps to take before asking teacher for help (e.g., identify and talk about what the challenge is, revisit programming instructions for the task, ask other classmates for help, try something new).

▶ Collaborative Interactions

To teach and support PP, it's important to be familiar with what collaborative and non-collaborative behaviors and interactions look like for primary and secondary-age students (see Figures 3a and b). There is an increased understanding of the types and quality of interactions that make for collaborative, effective pair programming at this age. Pairs who collaborate more effectively move their programming goals forward by each giving and receiving feedback, which is often acted upon. They tend to have more fluid roles that are exchanged to build on each other's expertise, and they use each other as a sounding board for ideas and problem-solving. Even when the driver can code without a navigator, having a navigator present seems to help the driver think through problems they encounter. Additionally, humor is sometimes used between partners to reduce tension when programming challenges or differences in opinions surface.

Figure 3a and b. Pair programming may or may not involve engaged and productive collaboration

Besides the basics of the driver and navigator roles are the following examples of effective PP behaviors and interactions that facilitate collaborative learning:

NAVIGATOR

- Directs the driver (verbally and/or nonverbally) through the steps of how to code something.
- Narrates what driver is doing, even if not giving instructions.
- Stays engaged by watching monitor, leaning into monitor, making comments, asking questions, identifying bugs, and so on.
- Manages support materials/resources (i.e., programming directions).
- Asks (verbally or nonverbally) to take control of mouse to do something, driver consents, and navigator returns it afterward.
- Offers affirmations and suggestions.

BOTH

- Share nonverbal acknowledgment (e.g., look at each other, nod heads, point at screen).
- Comment about what they like and don't like about their project.
- Talk back and forth about what they want to do in their programming project.
- Stay in conversation when there is disagreement.
- Give thorough explanations of what is not working and how they want to fix it.
- Asks questions related to ideas and solving problems.

DRIVER

- Talks out loud about what they want to do or are doing.
- Asks navigator for input on design ideas and coding decisions.
- Gives mouse/keyboard to partner when discussed and agreed upon between partners.
- Shows responsiveness to navigator by listening, discussing, affirming, and so forth.
- Acknowledges (verbally or nonverbally) navigator's suggestions.
- At least sometimes implements navigator's suggestions.

▶ Non-collaborative Interactions

Not all pairs are going to automatically work together collaboratively. It is important to observe pairs to gather information about their interactions. For example, what might look like conflict across the classroom may actually be an intense exchange where partners are challenging each other in ways that ultimately lead to successful, mutual problem-solving. But there are plenty of obvious and subtle conflicts where pairs fail to find compromise and their partnership deteriorates. Below are examples of behaviors within a pair that can undermine collaboration and set a pair back from completing their programming goals. These actions encourage or play into power struggles, facilitate disengagement, and can result in a partner or pair giving up and/or the driver dominating the design and programming.

NAVIGATOR

- Unresponsive to driver, who is attempting to engage verbally or nonverbally.
- Consistently unfocused and not tracking programming goal.
- Does not contribute design or problem-solving ideas.
- Takes control of the mouse and/or keyboard without consent or explanation.
- Verbal and nonverbal actions that divert focus from programming task (e.g., consistently not talking about programming goal, talking with neighbors, making noise that appears to annoy driver).
- Nonverbal disengagement (e.g., leaning back on chair, wiggling in chair and around workstation, walking away).

BOTH

- Not listening to each other—ignoring or rejecting suggestions.
- Lack of clarity in communication.
- Moving in and out of their roles without communicating about it (often a result of "giving up").
- Stopping communication and giving up when there is disagreement.
- Using "me"/"mine"/"my" instead of "we"/"ours" teamwork language.
- Asking for help from teacher or peer before partner.

DRIVER

- Ignores or rejects navigator's attempts to contribute with suggestions and ideas.
- Does not talk about what they are doing while programming.
- Does not ask navigator for input or guidance.
- Shows no effort toward coaching navigator into their role.
- Takes support materials/resources from navigator without consent.
- Consistently resists switching roles upon navigator's request.
- Leans in close to monitor to physically block the view for navigator who is attempting to engage.

▶ Additional Support for Non-collaborative Pairs

To support pairs who exhibit multiple, consistent non-collaborative actions, implement the aforementioned strategies to move them toward a more successful partnership. In addition, when observing these pairs, pay special attention to either partner's repeated disengagement as a form of silent conflict within the pair. A typical example is when the navigator is disengaged (e.g., looking around, not paying attention to the screen or partner, talking to others or looking upset). To stay involved, the navigator needs to learn how to co-construct and implement design and programming ideas since the driver is the only one touching the mouse and keyboard. Drivers can work on encouraging their partner to speak up and contribute by asking questions and talking about what they are doing. Here are some examples of behaviors and questions for pairs to help solicit more information about what is going on, encourage discussion between the two of them, and help shape the kind of support teachers can provide.

Teacher Observations	Questions for Pairs
The navigator is disengaged (e.g., appears to be bored, getting up from work station a lot).	• How are you deciding who does what? Is it related to what task you are doing or based on time? Are you talking about it with each other? • Are you [driver] responding to your partner when they make comments and suggestions to show them you are listening?
The partners are not communicating with one another.	• Are you talking about your design and programming tasks with each other? • Are you helping each other by asking questions or respectfully directing your partner? • Are you speaking up about your own ideas?
The navigator does not appear to be tracking what is going on.	• Do you both understand that an important role of the Navigator is that they pay attention to the "big picture" of the task (i.e., what final product are you working toward and how are you moving toward it)? • Is your driver talking enough about what they are doing so the navigator can follow what's going on?
One partner is getting much more time as the driver than the other.	• Is there a reason the same person seems to be getting much more time as driver than the other (e.g., splitting tasks, won't give up control)? • Do you need more reminders to switch roles?

RESEARCH AND READINGS

We (Shannon and Jill) have conducted extensive research on pair programming over the years along with our colleagues at ETR. This chapter draws on our own research (e.g., Campe, Denner, Green, & Torres, 2019) as well as other scholarly research in the field (see the papers in the Bibliography). For more details on how to get the most out of pair programming in your classroom, check out the K–12 Pair Programming Toolkit we created, available at https://www.etr.org/areas-of-focus/it-diversity/. For more about equitable pair programming, refer to Lewis and Shah (2015). In addition to our Campe et al. (2019) paper, also check out Tsan, Lynch, and Boyer (2018) for research findings on how middle school students interact while pair programming. Code.org's video on pair programming, available on YouTube, is also worth watching to get a short, quick introduction to pair programming. **Chapter 26, Zestful Learning**, shares ideas on how to fosters peer collaboration in the classroom more broadly, and **Chapter 6, Feedback With Formative Check-Ins** shares rubrics and other tools that can scaffold the process of peer feedback.

BIBLIOGRAPHY

Barron, B. (2000). Achieving coordination in collaborative problem-solving groups. *The Journal of the Learning Sciences*, 9(4), 403–436.

Bernard, M., & Bachu, E. (2015). Enhancing the metacognitive skill of novice programmers through collaborative learning. In *Metacognition: Fundaments, applications, and trends* (pp. 277–298). Springer, Cham.

Campe, S., Denner, J., Green, E., & Torres, D. (2019). *Pair programming in middle school: Variations in interactions and behaviors.* Computer Science Education. DOI: 10.1080/08993408.2019.1648119

Kuhn, D. (2015). Thinking together and alone. *Educational Researcher*, 44(1), 46–53.

Lewis, C. M., & Shah, N. (2015). How equity and inequity can emerge in pair programming. In *Proceedings of the 11th Annual International Conference on International Computing Education Research* (pp. 41–50). ACM.

Tsan, J., Lynch, C. F., & Boyer, K. E. (2018). "Alright, what do we need?": A study of young coders' collaborative dialogue. *International Journal of Child-Computer Interaction*, 17, 61–71.

Tsan, J., Rodríguez,- F. J., Boyer, K. E., & Lynch, C. (2018). I think we should...: Analyzing elementary students' collaborative processes for giving and taking suggestions. In *Proceedings of the 49th ACM Technical Symposium on Computer Science Education* (pp. 622–627). ACM.

Werner, L. L., Hanks, B., & McDowell, C. (2004). Pair-programming helps female computer science students. *Journal on Educational Resources in Computing (JERIC)*, 4(1), 4.

Zhong, B., Wang, Q., & Chen, J. (2016). The impact of social factors on pair programming in a primary school. *Computers in Human Behavior*, 64, 423–431.

Zhong, B., Wang, Q., Chen, J., & Li, Y. (2017). Investigating the period of switching roles in pair programming in a primary school. *Journal of Educational Technology & Society, 20*(3), 220–233.

Questions and Inquiry

Shuchi Grover and Steven Floyd

THE WHAT AND WHY OF QUESTIONS IN A THINKING CLASSROOM

I have six honest serving horses

They taught me all I knew

Their names are What, and Where and When;and Why and How and Who.

– Rudyard Kipling

Questions are central to learning and problem-solving. Not only are they integral to the process by which teachers guide their students in developing their understanding of a topic, they are deeply intertwined with the process through which students extend their learning while exploring concepts. Student and teacher questions can also guide the process of student reflection and 'self-explanation'. Self-explanation has been shown to be valuable to student learning.

> Programming is essentially about problem solving. George Pólya's famous problem-solving methodology or technique is book-ended with a series of questions—initially, to understand the problem, and in the end to look back at the process and solution for verification and reflection.
>
> Questions at the beginning—
>
> * *Do you understand all the words used in stating the problem?*
> * *What are you asked to find or show?*
> * *Can you restate the problem in your own words?*
> * *Can you think of a picture or diagram that might help you understand the problem?*
> * *Is there enough information to enable you to find a solution?*
>
> Questions at the end—
>
> * *Did you answer the question?*
> * *Is your result reasonable?*
> * *Is there another way of doing the problem that may be simpler? (This promotes flexibility in thinking. There usually is not one right way.)*
> * *Can the problem or method be generalized to be useful for future problems?*

The influence of good questions in an introductory programming classroom cannot be overemphasized. In this chapter, we focus on two aspects of inquiry, the first related to how teachers can use questions to prompt discussion and/or promote deeper engagement with aspects of programming beyond the procedural—conceptual or pragmatic. The second relates to how teachers could respond to student questions. Questions are also a key part of the formative assessment process for the teacher, and for student to get feedback on their learning, and improve their learning and understanding from the process. But first, we start with a set of questions teachers may ask *themselves* as they plan a curriculum or a lesson for the day.

Questions, as you will see, truly are at the heart of all teaching and learning.

▶ Part 0. Questions Teachers Ask Themselves and of the Lesson Plan

Often teachers use an existing curriculum that has been designed and made available to them. However, even the best curriculum cannot be designed for every classroom, every student group, and every situation. A first step in any classroom is for a teacher to get to know their students better. (In fact, an "About Me" project as the first project in any introductory programming classroom is a good way to achieve this.) With that knowledge, teachers can customize a curriculum to make it engaging, relevant, and inclusive in its implementation in their curriculum. Here is a list of suggested questions that teachers could pose to themselves regardless of curriculum:

- Can I improve on this lesson plan to make it more appropriate for my students?
- How can I make this lesson more inclusive for both girls and boys in my classroom?
- How can I make this lesson more inclusive for other underrepresented groups in my class and in the field of computer science?
- How can I ensure that this lesson has a low floor and a high ceiling—that it can be entered into by all students, and interested students can extend the activity by adding depth or connecting to other concepts?
- How can I ensure that the examples accommodate students' backgrounds better?
- How can I ensure that opportunities exist for creativity and innovation on the part of the student to provide them with voice and choice and to increase engagement?
- What examples would be most interesting or relevant to my students?
- How does this build on prior work?
- What example(s) best serve(s) to illustrate this work?
- Can I connect to other subjects or topics students are learning?
- Do students have the required prior knowledge—of programming and other subjects (such as mathematics)—to tackle the programming assignments in this lesson?

▶ Part 1. Questions to Foster Inquiry, Prompt Discussion, and Deepen Understanding

Due to the inherent problem-solving nature of programming, introductory programming classrooms lend themselves well to inquiry. A good example of an inquiry-based curriculum is Exploring Computer Science (ECS)—an introductory CS high school curriculum popular in the United States. One of the strategies used in ECS is to start each lesson with a "journal entry" activity that prompts learners to ponder on and respond to a question, such as the following, relevant to the lesson at hand:

- *How is solving this kind of problem the same as/different from how you solve a problem in "real life"?*
- *Imagine that you are attending a sporting event, a movie, or concert. Your ticket shows seat H16. Describe how you would find your seat.*
- *How do the programs on the computer know what the user wants to do next? In other words, if you are surfing the web, how does the computer know what page to go to next?*
- *What does it mean to broadcast something (e.g., the radio station is broadcasting music right now)? If a radio or television station is broadcasting something, does that mean that everyone is listening to it?*
- *What comes to mind when you hear the word "if"? What are some ways we use the word "if" in English?*
- *What's the difference between "and" and "or"?*

- *What does the word "random" mean in English?*
- *When you are told to brush your teeth, list the steps that you follow. What does the command "Brush your teeth" actually mean to do?*

Reflecting on code orally or through journals in relation to prior and current understandings represents a form of formative assessment called "ipsative assessment." Such reflection encourages learners to engage in the process of self-explanation that helps them connect the code they are writing with abstractions in the problem. Journal entries also help students develop skills in communicating their perspectives and ideas related to computing and programming. In addition to a general inquiry focus in the classroom, teachers could use specific types of questions to push students' thinking in various situations. The following examples serve to bring to light the use of questions to probe their thinking during programming, deliberating on alternate solutions, and asking for explanations. They all help build student understanding of programming and programming practices.

▶ Example 1. Questions to Help Students Plan a Solution

Our first couple of examples come from earlier chapters in this book. **Chapter 2, Before You Program, Plan!**, shares how questions can help guide young learners plan their program solution based on an idea for a program they wish to create. For example,

Student: "I want to make a zoo. When you touch the animals, they make their noise and move around."

Teacher: A good follow-up question would be, "Are you making that for your classmates or for younger/older children?" This query would start students thinking about audience in their ideas level.

In a similar vein, **Chapter 5, Events**, suggests that when students are planning their event-based programs, ask guiding questions such as *"How will the user know what to do?"* or *"How will the user tell the program to do X?"* so that students can explain their thinking about the program events and event handlers.

▶ Example 2. Probing Questions About a Code Snippet

A teacher is introducing how variables can be updated in a loop. She works with students to program a "counting cat" who counts up from 0. Figure 1 shows the code snippet.

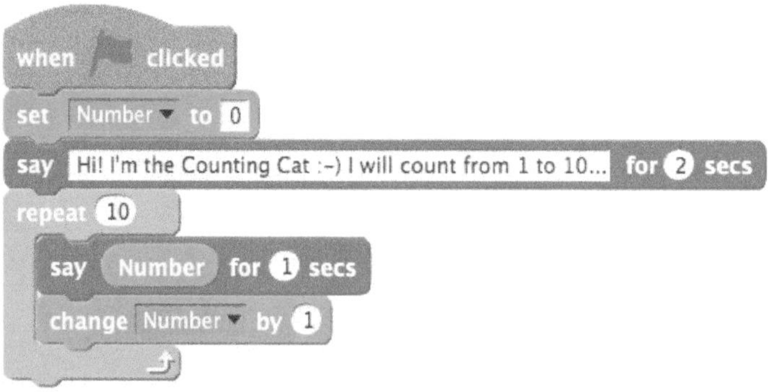

Figure 1. A simple code snippet can be a vehicle for pushing for deeper understanding

The code looks straightforward, right? What kinds of questions can you pose to learners to push them to think more deeply about changing variable values and how a loop works? Here are some that we have used in the past.

1. What is the value of `Number` when we enter the loop? What is the value when we leave the loop?

2. What if we swapped the change block and the say block? What will the cat say? What will the values of `Number` be upon entry into and exit from the loop?

3. What if we initialized the variable to 1 instead of 0? How would you change the code to make it work?

4. How would we change the code so that the cat counts from 1 to 100? From 50 to 100?

5. How would we change the code so that the cat counts by 2s, or by 3s, or by 5s (like in multiplication tables?)

Do you think the probing questions pushed students' thinking about the importance of sequence of commands inside or outside a loop, about the starting value of variable, or about how the variable changes within the loop? We like to think so!

▶ Example 3. **Evaluating Alternative Solutions**

One of the enduring attributes of problem-solving in an introductory programming classroom is that a problem is rarely characterized by a single, definitive correct solution. Often, in fact, multiple pathways lead to a solution. Asking questions that prompt students to weigh the pros and cons of different approaches (essentially evaluating different solutions) helps promote discussion and deeper understanding.

For example, in a Scratch program that used broadcast blocks to coordinate actions between two sprites, ask how well the `Wait` block might work instead. Or ask them to describe the difference between using a bunch of `IF <key pressed>` blocks in a `forever` block to navigate a sprite on the screen versus using `When <key pressed>` event blocks. Sometimes neither solution is better or worse, but asking such questions helps learners develop an appreciation for the fact that we have multiple ways to think about a problem and its solution(s).

▶ Example 4: **Artifact-Based Questions (ABQs)**

Programming curricula typically include programming projects and creation of artifacts. Artifact-based interviews, first used by Brigid Barron and her colleagues in 2002, have been an invaluable tool to elicit student explanations by cueing student memory and perspectives using their projects. Teachers can use ABQs to ask students to explain the goal of the project and how they got there or to justify their choices by asking questions such as *"How do you know?" "How did you decide?" "Why do you believe that?"* Such questions around code are also viewed to be part of ipsative assessment, or assessment *as* learning (O'Leary, 2019). Table 1 describes how students' understanding can be nudged further based on their comments about a piece of code. ABQs can also be part of the process of summative reflection on the entire class and experience, as shown in this set of questions used in Grover (2014) around students' final projects.

- How did you decide on your project?
- What does it do? How did you do it? (Student controls the mouse to points things on the screen while talking.)
- What was it like working on this project? (Offer suggestions such as fun/challenging/difficult/creative/boring.)
- Overall, how did you feel about this course?
- How does it feel to know more about CS?
- Thinking back on the course, what did you enjoy the most? What was the hardest part?

Table 1. Artifact-based questions (Source: O'Leary, 2019)

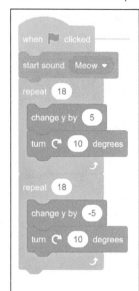

Scenario 1 (Very basic explanation)

• **Student response to 'What does this code do?'**
  ○ *This code makes the cat move.*
• Follow-up questions might include:
  ○ Can you walk me through each step of the algorithm?
  ○ What do you think the first repeat does?
  ○ What about the second repeat?
  ○ What happens if you change this (point) number to a larger or smaller number?

Scenario 2 (Some detail in explanation)

• **Description or prediction:**
  ○ *When the green flag is clicked, this code makes the cat make a sound, then do a flip.*
• Follow-up questions might include:
  ○ Can you walk me through each step of the algorithm?
  ○ What do you think the first repeat does?
  ○ What about the second repeat?
  ○ What happens if you change this (point) number to a larger or smaller number?
  ○ When might you use code like this in a project?
  ○ What happens if we change the order of these blocks?

Scenario 2 (Detailed explanation)

• **Description or prediction:**
  ○ *When the green flag is clicked, this code makes the cat meow. The first repeat makes the cat jump in the air and do half a flip. The second repeat makes the cat fall to the ground and finish the flip.*
• Follow-up questions might include:
  ○ What happens if you change this (point) number to a larger or smaller number?
  ○ When might you use code like this in a project?
  ○ What happens if we change the order of these blocks?
  ○ What could you add or change to this code, and what do you think would happen?
  ○ How might you use code like this in everyday life?

▶ Example 5: Questions Based on Buggy Programs

Mistakes are often excellent learning instruments. As mentioned in **Chapter 6, Feedback Through Formation Check-Ins** and **Chapter 20, Testing and Debugging**, students can learn a lot about programming through debugging exercises. A teacher could present an example of buggy code and ask *why* something does not work or why the code does or does not behave as desired. Teachers can use such questions to engage with common naïve conceptions of novice learners and prompt students to deepen their understanding. Table 2 demonstrates two such scenarios that highlight common errors students make related to loops and conditionals.

Table 2. Questions based on buggy programs can highlight common errors students make (Grover, 2014)

Scenario 1	Scenario 2
Will the following code reach the say block? Why or why not? If not, how can this be fixed?	What grade does the following program give for a score of 75? Why does it do this? How can you fix it?

Scenario 1 code:

```
when [flag] clicked
set [TouchedColorRed] to [0]
set [Flag] to [-1]
repeat until <TouchedColorRed = Flag>
    point in direction (pick random [1] to [360])
    move [100] steps
    if <touching color [ ] ?>
        change [TouchedColorRed] by [1]
say (join (join [I touched the color red] [TouchedColorRed]) [times]) for [2] secs
say [Bye!] for [2] secs
```

Scenario 2 code:

```
when [flag] clicked
ask [Tell me your score, and I will tell you your grade..] and wait
set [score] to (answer)
if <score > [86]> then
    set [grade] to [A]
    say [You got an 'A'!] for [2] seconds
if <score > [70]> then
    set [grade] to [B]
    say [You got a 'B'!] for [2] seconds
if <score > [55]> then
    set [grade] to [C]
    say [You got a 'C'!] for [2] seconds
if <<score < [55]> or <score = [55]>> then
    set [grade] to [D]
    say [You got a 'D'!] for [2] seconds
```

▶ Part 2. Responding to Student Questions

Although questions posed by teachers are important in an introductory programming classroom, it's also important to recognize the importance of student questions. When students engage in coding activities, they often ask many questions, and the way in which the teacher responds to these questions can have a dramatic impact on the learning that takes place in the classroom.

When should teachers provide the students with direct answers, and when should they guide students toward finding the answer themselves? When guiding students toward independent solutions, how much information should the teacher provide?

The following three scenarios explore ways in which teachers might consider responding to different types of student questions.

SCENARIO 1:
A student asks the teacher to help them with their program. Their program is generating incorrect output, and the teacher notices that the student has mixed up their "greater than" and "less than" symbols.

How should the teacher respond?

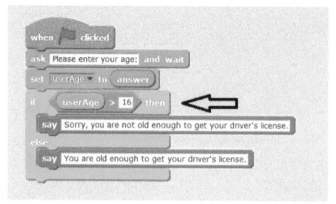

Figure 2. How should a teacher help a student with this buggy code?

- "You've mixed up your greater than and less than symbols. They need to be switched around."
- "I wonder if it has something to do with the greater than and less than symbols?"
- "There must be something wrong with your conditional statements. Take a closer look."
- "Looks like a logic error. Get your elbow partner to take a look."

SCENARIO 2:

A student has incorrectly placed a semicolon at the end of their conditional statement.

How should the teacher respond?

```
public static boolean isPrime (int num)
{
    for(int i = 2; i * i<= num; i = i + 1)
        {
            if(num % i == 0);   ⬅
            {
                return false;
            }
        }
    return true;
}
```

Figure 3. How should a teacher help a student with this syntax error in the code?

- "You don't need semicolons at the end of conditional statements."
- "Double-check to make sure that the if statement is executing properly. Maybe add some output statements in there."
- "It must be the conditional statement. Take a closer look."

SCENARIO 3:

A student's program is not setting the position of the character correctly when the level changes. The following Q&A is drawn from a real classroom example between a teacher and a student in which the teacher guides the student toward a solution for fixing a bug instead of giving the solution outright.

Student: And see when you touch the first red, it will take you to Level 2. [Backdrop changes to Level 2 of maze at this point] Here you see when you touch the black, it'll start you down here instead of up there, and we don't know why. We tried to fix it but . . . but we couldn't fix it. I don't know what was going on.

Teacher: Right. What about the fact that you . . . when you told color black, you go to this spot . . . So, how would you fix it? Over here when you're touching black. This is with respect to the first screen, right?

Student: Uh-huh.

Teacher: And that's why you come here. So, how do you think you would fix this bug if it's on the second level?

Student: Uh, switch the x and y to the one up here?

Teacher: But then if the black was touched in the first screen, then it would be wrong for that one. So how would you add some way of identifying which level you're at?

Student: Oh, IF . . . ELSE? Have the IF in the first level and the ELSE for the second one?

Teacher: Yes! That way you could tell it where to go.

The scenarios above explore a few examples of the types of questions students might ask in an introductory programming activity. Occasionally, teachers neglect to realize the value of these questions and the different ways in which they can respond to help students begin to develop their own understanding of concepts.

When responding to student questions during an introductory programming activity, teachers would be well advised to consider the following:

1. **Consider the type of question that is being asked:**

   Students might have questions related to the syntax of a command or in block coding where a command is found. On the other hand, students might have questions related to the logic or algorithms involved in their program. Syntax questions can be answered quickly, whereas logic and algorithm questions depend on higher-order thinking and may require more time from the teacher for a response. Teachers should carefully consider what type of question is being asked. Students might also be able to respond to their own questions when prompted to reflect on it further.

2. **Consider the learning goals of the lesson:**

   Imagine teaching a lesson where the goal is to have students develop an algorithm to determine whether a number is prime. It might be wise to quickly respond to student questions related to syntax errors so that they can focus on the problem-solving and algorithm-design components of the lesson.

3. **Consider the student themselves:**

   Each of our students has different needs and strengths. It might be prudent to respond to students in a manner that allows them to use their strengths to further remedy their weaknesses. For example

   Student: "The program runs, but the answer makes no sense. It seems to be off by a factor of 100."

   Teacher: "You've really been developing your tracing and debugging skills. Why don't you output values after each step of your rounding algorithm? Maybe the problem is somewhere in there."

CONCLUSION

The introductory computer programming class is an exciting place. Often, teachers are helping students to develop new and powerful skills, and as a result, many questions arise. Teachers are asking students to answer questions related to code and algorithm design, whereas students are asking teachers questions that will help them complete their projects. Teachers should be aware of the power of the questions they ask, and they should also consider carefully the ways in which they answer student questions. Inquiry in a problem solving-based classroom contains six valuable probes in an inquiry: what, where, when, why, how, and who.

Helping students to move from "how to" (do x, y, or z) questions to "why?" "where?" "when" and "what if?" questions is a productive pedagogical strategy for deeper engagement with programming. These question starters can lead students, teachers, and entire classrooms into wonderful learning experiences within the programming context. Failing to carefully consider how to ask and respond to these questions would cost a classroom a valuable learning experience.

BIBLIOGRAPHY

Barron, B., Martin, C., Roberts, E., Osipovich, A., & Ross, M. (2002). Assisting and assessing the development of technological fluencies: Insights from a project-based approach to teaching computer science. In *Proceedings of Computer Support for Collaborative Learning (CSCL)* 2002.

DeLyser, L. A. (2015, February). Expression of abstraction: Self explanation in code production. In *Proceedings of the 46th ACM Technical Symposium on Computer Science Education* (pp. 272-277).

Goode, J., Chapman, G., & Margolis, J. (2012). Beyond curriculum: the exploring computer science program. *ACM Inroads, 3*(2), 47–53.

Grover, S. (2014). *Foundations for advancing computational thinking: Balanced designs for deeper learning in an online computer science course for middle school students* (Doctoral dissertation, Stanford University).

O'Leary, J. (2019). Introduction to Ipsative Assessment. Retrieved from https://jaredoleary.com/presentations/introduction-to-ipsative-assessment

Pólya, G.(1945) *How to Solve It*, Princeton University Press, Princeton.

Repetition and Recursion

Dan Garcia and Joshua Paley

INTRODUCTION

Computers are wonderful tools for performing repetitive tasks, usually either a fixed number of times or until a specific condition is reached. This chapter shares ideas about how to teach the concepts of iteration and recursion and what types of problems lend themselves most naturally to each. We present a series of case studies (coded in Snap! and Python) that serve to ground these ideas and highlight things to focus on or watch out for when introducing these concepts to your students.

> *There's Joy in Repetition.*
> – Prince

▶ Definitions

▶ Iteration

The *Merriam-Webster dictionary* defines *iteration* as:

it·er·a·tion | \ ˌi-tə-ˈrā-shən \ noun

the repetition of a sequence of computer instructions a specified number of times or until a condition is met

In the case of repeating instructions (i.e., iterating) a specific number of times, the programmatic constructs for control flow that students need to be familiar with are typically among the earliest taught in textbooks, and are shown in Table 1 with examples for Snap! and Python. These usually don't cause students much trouble to learn, once they practice with them a bit. Note that Python has chosen an elegant, minimalist approach, with the single `for` construct the only syntax a new programmer has to learn. The constructs `for each` (Snap!) and `for` (Python) are particularly nice, in that they allow the programmer to ignore the indices of lists (Snap!) and collections (Python) and just think about the elements themselves.

Table 1. Constructs for repetition in Snap! And Python

	Snap!	Python

Construct	**repeat 10**
	
	Semantics: Repeat the scripts inside the loop exactly 10 times.
		`for _ in range(10):`
		    `code`
		
		Semantics: Repeat the *code* inside the loop exactly 10 times.

Construct	**for i = 1 to 10**
	
	Semantics: Repeat the scripts inside the loop exactly 10 times, each time binding i to a different value, here 1 through 10.
		`for i in range(1,11):`
		    `code`
		
		Semantics: Repeat the *code* inside the loop exactly 10 times, each time binding i to a different value, here 1 through 10.

continued on next page

Table 1. Constructs for repetition in Snap! And Python (continued)

	Snap!	Python

Construct	for each (item) in ▤	```for item in collection:```
		``` code```
		
		Semantics: Go through the *collection*, each iteration binding *item* to the next unchosen element, and running the code inside the loop.

	Semantics: Go through the list, each iteration binding item to the next unchosen element, and running the scripts inside the loop.	

Example: Drawing a square of side 100	pen down
	repeat 4
	  move 100 steps
	  turn ↻ 90 degrees
		```from turtle import pd, fd, rt```
		```pd()```
		```for _ in range(4):```
		``` fd(100)```
		``` rt(90)```

Example: Displaying the numbers from 1 through 10 (inclusive)	for (i) = (1) to (10) say (i) for (1) secs	```for i in range(1,11):``` ``` print(i)```

Example: Displaying the names of the Beatles	set beatles ▾ to list John Paul George Ringo ◀▶
	for each (beatle) in (beatles)
	  say (beatle) for (1) secs
		```beatles = ['John','Paul','George',```
		```'Ringo']```
		```for beatle in beatles:```
		``` print(beatle)```

In the case of repeating instructions (i.e., iterating) until a specific condition is met, the programmatic constructs for control flow here differ significantly from language to language (Table 2). Snap! chooses to repeat the code in its `repeat until` loop while the condition is still *false*, that is, until something bad occurs. Python's `while` iterates while the condition is still *true*, that is, while we're still good. So, if both languages were attempting to simulate your life, Snap! would say "repeat 'live one day' until you die", whereas Python would say "while you are still living, 'live one day'".

Table 2. Difference between `repeat until` in Snap! and Python's `while` construct demonstrated with the 'Eating all the M&Ms from a bag' example

Snap!	Python

repeat until ⬡	```while test:```
	``` code```
	
	Semantics: Repeat the *code* inside the loop while the *test* remains true.

Semantics: Repeat the scripts inside the loop until the expression is true.	
repeat until ⟨Bag is Empty⟩ Eat one M&M	```while BagHasMandMsLeft():``` ``` EatOneMandM()```

It's worth noting that there is still one more case: What if the programmer desired the repetition to happen forever? Infinite loops are very useful if there's no reason the program should stop. Consider a web server or your computer's operating system handling your mouse and keyboard events or displaying a clock (shown below). The strict definition of iteration from Merriam-Webster doesn't include that as iteration, but it surely is.

Table 3. Forever loop in Snap! and Python with example of displaying a clock.

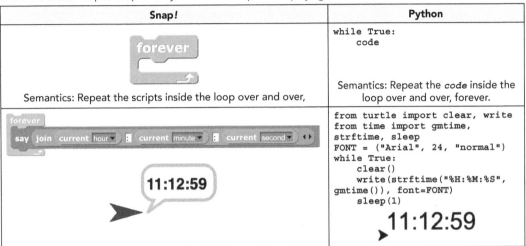

It is also worth pointing out that the ease of use of the `forever` loop block in environments like Scratch and Snap! can sometimes lead to its overuse (especially in younger grades) for *programs that do need to stop.* Often, animations in Scratch and Snap! are first introduced as never-ending programs through the use of the `forever` block. Instead of resorting to the more appropriate repeat `until` block that checks for an ending condition, students tend to continue to use `forever` blocks in games and other apps and check for a stopping condition by adding an `IF` conditional block within the `forever` block that triggers a `Stop` all if the stopping condition is met (Figure 1a). We advise students learn to use the `repeat until` construct that repeats until a specific condition is met in these cases (Figure 1b). This practice not only leads to cleaner code but the Stop all approach doesn't allow for other scripts to run afterward; it's the same as clicking the stop sign icon. Helping students learn and be encouraged to "refactor" their code from Figure 1a to Figure 1b can be motivated by asking them to do something after the Hit-Count exceeds 20.

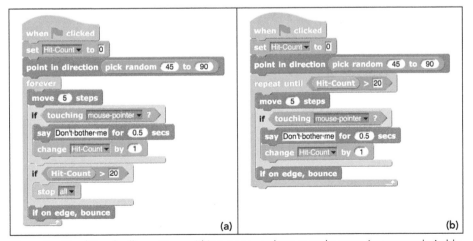

Figure 1a. Conditional calling a **Stop** within a **forever** loop to end a game (not a very desirable approach); 1b: A cleaner approach is to use a **repeat until** loop with the stopping condition.

REPETITION AND RECURSION

▶ Recursion

The *Merriam-Webster Dictionary* defines *recursion* as

re·cur·sion | \ ri-'kər-zhən \ noun

a computer programming technique involving the use of a procedure, subroutine, function, or algorithm that calls itself one or more times until a specified condition is met at which time the rest of each repetition is processed from the last one called to the first.

Note we don't need to introduce any new control flow constructs here. Whereas the control flow was *implicit* with iteration—the language somehow knew to go back to the top after it finished the loop—with recursion it's *explicit*, in that we're directly calling a function (ourselves) to continue the recursion, and we're controlling when that stops with judiciously placed `if`s.

The idea from 10 miles up is that we're going to be calling ourselves with a smaller version of the problem and stop when the problem gets small enough to answer instantly. We often use this simple example and contrast it with the M&Ms iteration example earlier. We then encourage our students to come up with other examples in their life and then design their iterative and recursive solutions, with the freedom to make up any helper procedures they need. Examples that come up include walking to class, doing their homework, talking to their friend, and doing a jigsaw puzzle.

Table 4. Recursion for eating all the M&Ms from a bag in Snap! And Python

Snap!	Python
Eat a bag of M&Ms recursively if Bag has M&Ms left Eat one M&M Eat a bag of M&Ms recursively	```def EatAllMandMsRecursively(): if BagHasMandMsLeft(): EatOneMandM() EatAllMandMsRecursively()```

A recursive procedure has two components.

1. At least one recursive call, in which the procedure calls itself (e.g., "Eat all the M&Ms recursively").
2. At least one base case, in which the procedure terminates when a condition is met (e.g., "Bag is Empty"). *A base case is necessary to terminate the recursion!*

Consider the following definition of *factorial* for positive integers[1]:

$$1! = 1$$

$$n! = n * (n-1)!$$

Table 5. The classic factorial example using recursion in Snap! And Python

Snap!	Python
+ n +!+ if n = 1 report 1 else report n × (n − 1) !	```def factorial(n): if (n == 1): return 1 else: return n * factorial(n-1)```

---

[1] We often omit 0! = 1 in the early introduction of factorial to draw connections between the recursive definition and the idea that it's the product of all the numbers 1 through n.

When teaching recursion, covering what happens when the program lacks a base case is helpful. In this example, what would happen if ⑤! were called and there were no test for ⟨ n = 1 ⟩? The program would never report a result because 5! would call 4! would call 3! would call 2! would call 1! would call 0! would call (−1)! and so on.

But wait! Can't the factorial function be written iteratively? Absolutely! See Table 6.

This raises the question of whether it makes more sense to use iteration or recursion when solving a problem requiring repetition.

Before we address this, it is worth noting that there is a solution involving a higher-order function (Table 7). One way to think about *factorial* is this: How can we take the numbers from 1 to N and multiply them together?

Table 6. Programs for calculating Factorial using iteration (for loop) in Snap! and Python

Snap!	Python
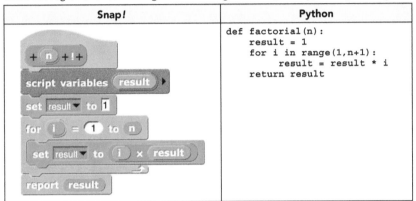	```def factorial(n):
result = 1
for i in range(1,n+1):
result = result * i
return result```

Table 7. Programs for calculating Factorial using higher-order functions in Snap! and Python

Snap!	Python
+ n +!+ report combine numbers from 1 to n using (×)	```def factorial(n):
reduce(lambda x,y: x*y,
range(1,n+1))```

In Snap!, the `combine` block takes a list of data and a procedure and combines those data using the procedure. In Python, the same thing is called `reduce`.

Note that even though this is an idea not necessarily taught in high school, map-reduce is at the core of search engines: map some search function over massive amounts of data, and reduce the results into something humans consume. Imagine how hard that would be if the programmer could not think so abstractly!

A central concept—arguably *the* central concept—of computer science is abstraction. Higher-order functions are a great way to hide details of computation, allowing the programmer to think about problem-solving with a 10,000-foot view.

WHEN TO USE ITERATION OR RECURSION

In practice, given a choice of iteration (loops) or recursion, iteration is at least as efficient and usually better. This has to do with the mechanics of how recursion works, which involves keeping information about a program in the computer's stack every time a recursive call is performed. For example, calculating 1000000! recursively will cause many systems and languages to "stack overflow" on a typical personal computer, but calculating it iteratively just takes a little time. Feel free to look up tail call optimization (TCO) to learn about how you can optimize certain recursive routines so as not to grow the stack.

There are times, however, when an iterative solution would involve quite a bit more effort! Problems that tend to split themselves into two or more parts at each level (and require us to process each of those parts) tend to be easier to write using recursion. Otherwise, the programmer has to have the code explicitly remember when the program is done with one of those parts to renew computation on another part, at every place the subproblem splits! Recursion takes care of this for us, which is delightful. One category of problems that are screaming for a recursive (vs. iterative) solution is any computation that involves trees, particularly binary trees. An example is the Parking Problem, addressed by the mathematician Rényi (Wolfram, 2019) and Wirth (2008), described later.

It's important to note that anything that can be done with iteration can be done with recursion (and vice versa)! It's just that some problems lend themselves to one approach or another. They're like salt and sugar on foods—sure, you can eat a meal with either, but, boy, will it be more enjoyable if you choose the right one.

▶ The Parking Problem

A city creates space for parking on a curb 10 units long. In this city, all cars have the same length, 1. That means there is enough room for 10 cars to fit perfectly, front to back. (Assume they can just slide right in sideways and don't have to turn their wheels, rocking back and forth, to get into a space.) That doesn't mean that they will. See Figure 2.

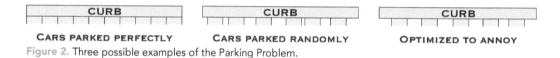

Figure 2. Three possible examples of the Parking Problem.

In each case, there is no longer space for another car to park.

Problem: Assume that cars park randomly within some space along a curb (again, initially set to 10). Write a program, park(space), that runs this parking simulation within a given space and returns the number of cars that would be parked when room runs out (e.g., the return values for the three placements shown above would be 10, 6, and 5, respectively).

We don't offer an easy way to think about this problem iteratively; it's hard to think about trees that way.

Trees? This may not look like a tree problem at first blush, but it is one! Figure 3 shows a standard binary tree visualization.

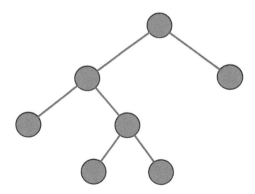

Figure 3. An example binary tree

Think of each circle as representing a parked car, with lines to the left and right representing the remaining space where cars can park to the left and right.

- If there isn't space to park a car, then the number of cars parked is 0. Easy enough.
- Otherwise, park the car. This creates two smaller parking lots, one on the left and one on the right. The total number of cars that get parked will be 1 (for this car) plus the number of cars that get parked in the smaller parking lots.

The diagram below helps to demonstrate the solutions we'll present. There is another way to solve this, which involves sending in 2 parameters to park representing the front and the back of the given curb on some absolute grid, like park(back, front), shown in Figure 4. That isn't as elegant as our solution, which just looks at the total space left.

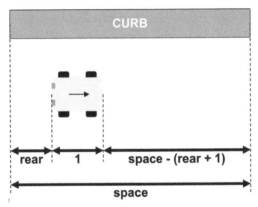

Figure 4. Using 2 parameters to park

Our solutions follow, first in Snap! and then in Python. Note: Whenever a single random number is going to be used multiple times in any code, it's important to assign it to a variable; naïve implementations might involve multiple calls to random-number generators, which aren't correct. In Snap!, the "pick random" operator, when given integer inputs, returns only integer random values, so we have to make the car just a little bit bigger so the computer will think it's a floating-point number. See Figure 5.

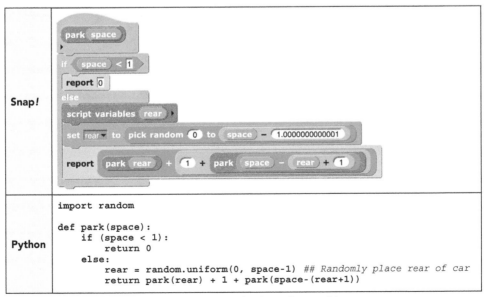

Figure 5. Recursion solutions in Snap! and Python for the Parking Problem

When you run the simulation 10 million times, you get a distribution that looks something like Figure 6. The average was 7.2235337 for this run.

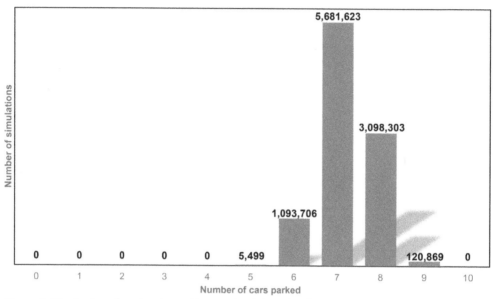

Figure 6. Distribution of running the parking car simulation 10 million times.

HOW TO WRITE A RECURSIVE PROCEDURE

The key strategy we share with our students is to *trust the recursion*. A degree of faith is involved when authoring recursive solutions. You're writing a procedure, and you call yourself with a smaller version of the problem to create your solution. But your procedure isn't written yet, so the helper call (to yourself) won't yet work! That's what we mean when we say you need to *trust* that it will work, and then you use that result in your overall result. So, here's a handy-dandy 4-step guide. (Note that some educators prefer to start with the easier one, Step 4, first.)

1. **Divide:** Think about how to break the problem down into smaller parts.

2. **Invoke:** Call yourself recursively with the appropriate smaller parts.

3. **Combine:** Think about how to combine those smaller parts to solve the original problem. Think about domain and range here—what are you returning (your *range*) and how that fits into the *domain* of the combining operator?

4. **Stop Dividing:** Set up the base case as a conditional whose sole job is to stop Step 1 ("Make it smaller") from going on forever, and figure out what should happen in that case.

LINEAR RECURSION CASE STUDIES

We've found it useful to show a series of examples to our students, with each example different in a small, subtle way from the previous one. These all have one recursive call and make the problem smaller by 1 at each step, so they're called *linear recursion*.

▶ Length of a Sentence

You're given a sentence (in some languages, that means a string) and asked to compute the length. There's a built-in utility for that, certainly, but by rewriting it, you can test it, as shown in Figure 7.

- **Divide:** Cut off a letter.
- **Invoke:** Call yourself on the sentence that's smaller by one letter.
- **Combine:** If you're asked to find the length of "computer" and someone hands you the length of "omputer", what will you do with it to find the length of computer? You just add 1 for the "c", right?
- **Stop Dividing:** We can stop with one letter (and return 1) or no letters (and return 0). We prefer the latter.

Snap!	![Snap! blocks] my length (sentence) / if (sentence = ☐) / report 0 / else / report (1 + my length (all but first letter of (sentence)))
Python	```def my_length(sentence):\n if sentence == "":\n return 0\n else:\n return 1 + my_length(sentence[1:])```

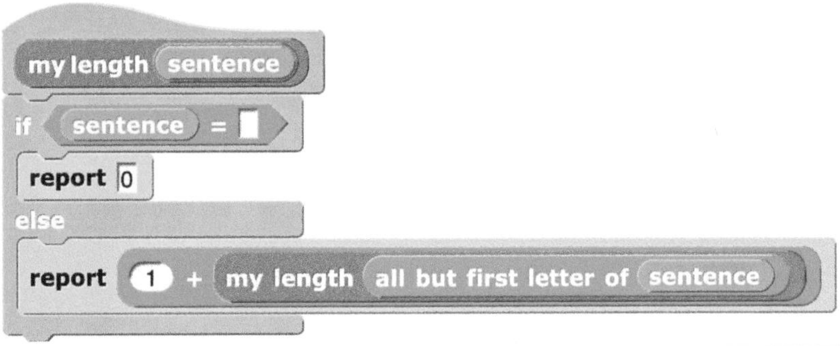

Figure 7. Recursion solutions in Snap! and Python for calculating the length of a sentence.

TREE RECURSION CASE STUDIES

These examples all have more than one recursive call and make the problem smaller by one at each step, so they're called *tree recursion*.

▶ All Subsets

You're given a list of elements and asked to return a list of all the subsets of that list. For example, given the list (A B C) all the subsets are (), (A), (B), (C), (A B), (A C), (B C), and (A B C).

- **Divide:** Cut off the first list element.
- **Invoke:** Call yourself on the list that's smaller by one element.
- **Combine:** If you're asked to find the all the subsets of (A B C) and someone hands you the subsets of (B C), what will you do with it to find all the subsets? The clever thing is to realize that the first element A can either *be* in each of the sublists of the subsets of (B C) or *not*.
- **Stop Dividing:** We stop when the list is empty, but we don't return an empty list—we return a list of a single entry, the empty subset (here also an empty list). See Figure 8.

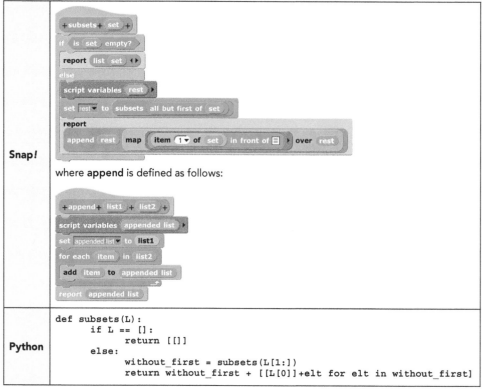

Snap!	
| Python | ```
def subsets(L):
    if L == []:
        return [[]]
    else:
        without_first = subsets(L[1:])
        return without_first + [[L[0]]+elt for elt in without_first]
``` |

Figure 8. Recursion solutions in Snap! and Python for returning all the subsets of a list.

▶ Count Change

How many ways can you make change for some amount of money, given some set of coin denominations, where you have an infinite number of coins in each denomination? For example, if you had the usual American coins (dimes = 10 cents, nickels = 5 cents, and pennies = 1 cent) and needed to make change for 10 cents, there are four solutions.

- 1 dime
- 2 nickels
- 1 nickel and 5 pennies
- 10 pennies

In this problem, we write an algorithm that computes the number of ways to count change as follows: Look at the first coin. We either make change with it or not. If we do, the amount we need to make change from gets smaller, and we recurse. If we don't make change with it, we remove it from consideration and never use it again and recurse. The total ways to make change are the sum of those two recursive calls, as shown in Figure 9.

- **Divide (use the coin):** The amount gets smaller by that coin, and the list of coins stay the same.
- **Divide (don't use the coin):** The list of coins gets smaller by that coin, and the amount stays the same.
- **Invoke:** Call yourself on both of the cases above.
- **Combine:** Add the number of ways together from the two cases.
- **Stop Dividing:**
  - If the number of cents remaining goes negative, there is no way to make change; return 0.
  - If there are no more coin types to process, there is no way to make change with no coins, so return 0.
  - If there are 0 cents left, then change has been made, and return 1.
```

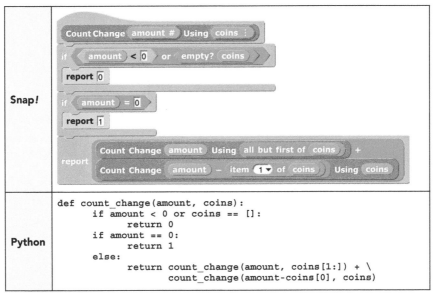

Figure 9. Recursion solutions in Snap! and Python for the Count Change (or Coin) Problem.

Figure 10 shows the call tree for Count Change(10, (10 5 1)): Each light gray node is labeled with the amount and list of coins. The blue nodes are the base cases that return 0, and the red nodes are the base cases that return 1. The "right branch" path to each of the red nodes are the change returned. From top to bottom: (10), (5 5), (5 1 1 1 1 1), and (1 1 1 1 1 1 1 1 1 1).

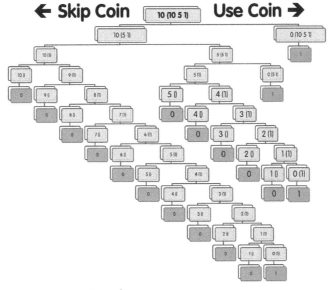

Figure 10. The call tree for Count Change(10, (10 5 1))

▶ Fractal Tree

To demonstrate how starting with the base case can be a good way to go, we offer a lesson plan for fractal trees, shown in Figure 11.

1. Draw a Level 1 tree by going forward and backward.

2. Draw a Level 2 tree: Forward, turn left, Level 1 tree, turn right twice, Level 1 tree, turn left, backward.

3. Draw a Level 3 tree: Forward, turn left, Level 2 tree, turn right twice, Level 2 tree, turn left, backward.

4. Ask the students to draw a Level 4 tree.

5. Ask the students to draw a Level 100 tree. (This is not feasible by hand because the order of growth for the fractal tree is exponential, but it's often fun to show them how big 2^{100} really is. Bring this up on a web calculator—typing "2^{100}" in Google will do.) You then tell the students you can do it (they usually gasp). Walk up and write

   a. Forward, turn left, draw a cloud, and say, "Here would be a Level 99 tree," turn right twice, draw a cloud, and say, "Here would be a Level 99 tree," turn left, backward.

6. Ask the students to draw a Level N tree. (Hopefully they see the idea—the two clouds become "level N-1 trees.")

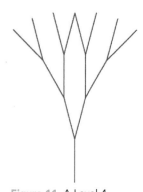

Figure 11. A Level 4 fractal tree—notice that this is a Level 1 tree (bottom branch) with two Level 3 trees, one to the left and one to the right

- **Stop Dividing (base case):** What is the smallest tree? A tree with 1 branch (Level 1 tree).
- **Divide:** A level N tree is a tree with 1 branch with 2 level N-1 trees attached.
- **Invoke:** Call Level N-1 tree twice
- **Combine:** Connect the Level N-1 trees by drawing.

Note that there's some duplication. The first thing both `if` and else cases do is "move (size) steps" and the last thing both cases do is move (-size) steps, so we can remove that. See Figure 12.

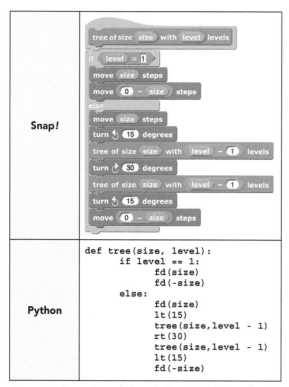

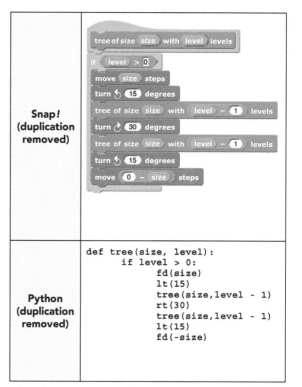

Figure 12. Recursion solutions in Snap! and Python for drawing a fractal tree as shown in figure 11.

COMMON MISTAKES STUDENTS MAKE

This chapter seeks to explain how to introduce the foundational ideas of repetition and recursion, but it is also helpful to be aware of common pitfalls documented in the research literature (e.g., duBoulay 1989, Robins, Rountree, & Rountree, 2003; Soloway & Spohrer, 2013) and teachers' anecdotal experiences. Although such struggles are more common among younger learners in upper elementary and middle school, novice learners in high school (and even in college) may also make mistakes. These mistakes often point to a lack of a robust mental model of the notional machine and foundational programming constructs (as described in **Chapter 12**). *Most of these misconceptions can be mitigated with code tracing, stepping through code, and variable inspection.*

▶ How Looping Constructs Work

1. Though the fixed repeat loop may seem simple and straightforward, novice learners in primary and middle grades sometimes assume that each action with the loop is repeated individually rather than as a unit. For example,

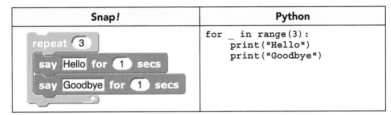

...is misunderstood to result in the program saying (or printing)

```
Hello
Hello
Hello
Goodbye
Goodbye
Goodbye
```

rather than

```
Hello
Goodbye
Hello
Goodbye
Hello
Goodbye
```

2. Students sometimes assume that the `repeat until` or `while` condition is *constantly checked* (rather than at the top of the block), so the loop terminates the instant a variable is updated to exit the loop. For example, they assume that the moment `counter` is incremented to 3, the loop will terminate immediately, and the last `after` will not be output, so

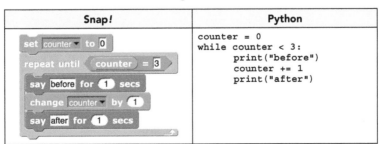

...is misunderstood to result in the program saying (or printing)

```
before (counter = 0)
after (counter = 1)
before (counter = 1)
after (counter = 2)
before (counter = 2)
(counter = 3, and the loop exits without saying/printing the last after)
```

rather than

```
before (counter = 0)
after (counter = 1)
before (counter = 1)
after (counter = 2)
before (counter = 2)
after (counter = 3)
```

3. Novice learners often find the for construct hard to understand (and more challenging than the while construct). Research suggests that this is because of the implicit (behind-the-scenes) incrementing of the controlling variable (duBoulay, 1986; Robins, Rountree, & Rountree, 2003).

▶ Variables Controlling Loops and Updated Within the Loop

1. Errors related to the previous issue sometimes result in infinite loops or loops that never terminate, like the one below, which attempts to add the numbers from 1 to 10 together.

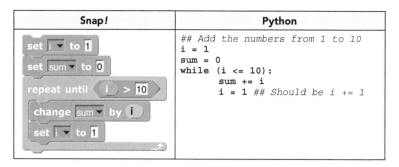

Snap!	Python

set i to 1
set sum to 0
repeat until (i > 10)
    change sum by i
    set i to 1
	``## Add the numbers from 1 to 10

i = 1
sum = 0
while (i <= 10):
sum += i
i = 1 ## Should be i += 1```

2. **Fence post and off-by-1 errors.** Such errors are common and occur when the loop iterates one time too many or too few. For example, when calculating the sum of the numbers from 1 to 10 (inclusive), the code snippets below sum the numbers only 1 to 9.

Snap!	Python

set i to 1
set sum to 0
repeat until (i = 10)
    change sum by i
    change i by 1
	``## Add the numbers from 1 to 10 (inclusive)

i = 1
sum = 0
while (i < 10): ## Should be i <= 10
sum += i
i += 1```

3. **Constructing the Boolean expression to control the loop.** Students struggle with creating the expression or understanding how the loop will terminate, especially when a compound expression is involved. English expressions to describe loop termination are often not as easily translated to the Boolean expression. For example, the pseudocode

while a or b are 0

...is often translated as

```
while (a or b) == 0
```

when it should be

```
while (a == 0) or (b == 0).
```

This results in younger learners struggling with conceptualizing and using variable-iteration `while` and `repeat until` loops (controlled by a Boolean expression) after initially working with fixed-iteration `repeat` loops or infinite-iteration `forever` loops. This issue is compounded when the controlling expression involves a variable that is updated within the loop.

▶ Recursion-related Issues

It is also helpful to keep in mind what trips up novice learners when it comes to recursion.

1. **Poor understanding of the stack and how it works in recursion.** We have found it helpful to use the "subcontractor" unplugged activity (e.g., to simulate factorial), in which students stand when they are called, hire others who stand and help them compute their value, and sit only when they have computed the return value and told the result to the person who hired them.

2. Students often end up coding an infinite recursion.

   a. Sometimes students assume that the recursive function that it will automatically stop at a given time.

   b. Figuring out the base case is key. If the recursion fails to *converge to its base case*, it leads to an infinite recursion. Sometimes an incorrect expression in the recursive call results in an infinite loop, or the base case is skipped. For example, the following code for the Fibonacci sequence runs forever because `fib(1)` *skips over* the base case test.

```
def fib(n):
   if n == 0:
      return 0
   else:
      return(fib(n-1) + fib(n-2))
```

This base case test and return value would fix the error:

```
if n <= 1:
   return n
```

BIBLIOGRAPHY

du Boulay, B. (1986). Some difficulties of learning to program. *Journal of Educational Computing Research, 2*(1), 57–73.

Robins, A., Rountree, J., & Rountree, N. (2003). Learning and teaching programming: A review and discussion. *Computer Science Education, 13*(2), 137–172.

Soloway, E., & Spohrer, J. C. (2013). *Studying the novice programmer*. Psychology Press.

Wirth, M. (2008). Introducing recursion by parking cars. *ACM SIGCSE Bulletin, 40*(4), 52–55.

Wolfram Mathworld (2019). https://mathworld.wolfram.com/RenyisParkingConstants.html

Selecting Pathways with Conditionals

Shuchi Grover

INTRODUCTION

Consciously or not, humans constantly engage in the "if this, then that" type of reasoning and logic. If an obstacle is in our path, we walk around it; if a beverage is too hot, we wait for a while before we sip it; if it's raining (and we don't want to get wet), we carry an umbrella or wear a raincoat. These are just some simple examples of decisions made day to day. This type of thinking is the foundation of reasoning and what we often refer to as "conditional thinking." Conditional thinking is a fundamental piece of logical thinking.

Conditional—and logical—thinking involves analyzing situations to make a decision or reach a conclusion about a situation. Another everyday example of such thinking might involve analyzing whether it is worthwhile to go to *Shop A* to buy a dress for $30 or *Shop B* where it's available for $20. Such a decision would involve taking into account the distance to the two shops, how busy one is on that day, and the traffic to get to the farther shop. It may not make *logical* sense to go to *Shop B* if it is farther away than *Shop A* and the cost of traveling to *Shop B* is greater than the $10 price difference or if you have only a limited amount of time to spare to pick up the dress due to other time commitments.

STRUCTURE OF CONDITIONALS IN PROGRAMS

In programming, conditional logic (along with sequence and repetition is an inherent part of algorithms and code (see **Chapter 1, Algorithms**). It usually takes the form of `IF-THEN` or `IF-THEN-ELSE` statements. It involves evaluating a "condition"; if the condition is TRUE then the code in the `THEN` part is executed; if the condition evaluates to FALSE, then the `ELSE` block of code is executed. If there is no `ELSE` part, then the program continues from the command after the `IF-THEN` block (see Figure 1).

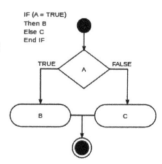

Figure 1. A simple flowchart of the `IF-THEN-ELSE LOGIC`.

So imagine a program with the following set of commands:

```
Action 0;
IF (condition)
THEN
    Action 1;
    Action 2;
ELSE
    Action 3;
ENDIF
Action 4;
```

If *condition* is TRUE, then the following actions are executed in sequence: `Action 0`, `Action 1`, `Action 2`, `Action 4`.

If *condition* is FALSE, then the following actions are executed in sequence: `Action 0`, `Action 3`, `Action 4`.

Now suppose the program was essentially the same as above but with no `ELSE` part.

```
Action 0;
IF (condition)
THEN
   Action 1;
   Action 2;
ENDIF
Action 3;
```

If *condition* is TRUE, then the following actions are executed in sequence: `Action 0`, `Action 1`, `Action 2`, `Action 3`.

If *condition* is FALSE, then the following actions are executed in sequence: `Action 0`, `Action 3`.

All popular programming languages provide the logical "if-then" and "if-then-else" constructs though they may have varying syntax rules about how to demarcate chunks of code in each part. Sometimes languages have their own unique versions of these constructs. In Python, for example, we have the **if-elif** construct in addition to the **if-else**.

```
if boolean_expression:
    indented block of statements

if boolean_expression:
    indented block of statements
else:
    indented block of statements
```

```
if boolean_expression_1:
    indented block of statements
elif boolean_expression_2:
    indented block of statements
else
    indented block of statements
```

▶ The Condition in the Conditional

Conditions checked in the `IF` statement may be a simple statement that is True or False (e.g., "it is raining"), or a simple relational expression (e.g., "age >= 18") or compound relational expressions or other expressions combined by Boolean operators like OR, AND, or NOT (e.g., "customer is a senior citizen" OR "customer is a veteran"), which evaluates to True or False. Refer to **Chapter 15, Operators and Expressions**, for more on relational and Boolean operators.

In addition to relational expressions that usually involve variables, conditional statements in environments like Scratch may also involve evaluating conditions such as `touching <other sprite>?` or `key <specific key> pressed>?` Scratch and other visual programming languages also use blue color-coded blocks with a specific shape and the question mark, as shown in Figure 2, to cue the learner to the fact that these are conditions that are used in `IF-ELSE` commands.

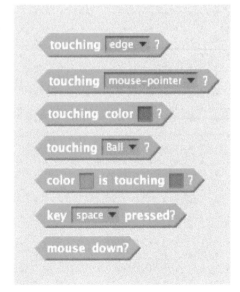

Figure 2. Pre-packaged conditions that can be used in `IF-ELSE` blocks in Scratch

It is important to help students *visualize* the alternate pathways or branching. Be sure to include different examples with—
(a) statements before and after the conditional block;
(b) different options with or without an ELSE part;
(c) multiple commands in the IF and/or ELSE blocks; and
(d) use beginning and ending block markers to make the blocks of code more apparent (especially when working with examples in text or pseudocode).

Blocks with multiple commands are easy to deal with in Scratch, Alice, and other block-based languages, but they need parentheses or indentations or other block-beginning and -ending syntax in text-based languages. Remember to use similar techniques like indentation or bullets and sub-bullets or numbered lists when representing IF-ELSE blocks in pseudocode.

```
if someCondition:
    do_something      # could be a single statement or a series of statements
  else:
    do_something_else # could be a single statement or a series of statements
```

TEACHING IDEAS

Regardless of classroom context, flowcharts such as the one in Figure 1 are excellent ways of visualizing conditional flow in a program. Pseudocode is also useful for helping children think through their conditional logic. Actually writing out the expressions that form the condition to be evaluated is also very helpful. Having students enact the code that will be executed through tracing the code with various inputs is also useful.

It is important for students to understand the flow of control and the commands in the code that will be executed (and importantly, not executed) when the code contains conditional statements.

Examples of activities that could be used at various grade levels follow. Also highlighted are concepts that are more relevant in secondary grades than in primary.

▶ Primary Grades

Unplugged activities using everyday examples that involve the evaluation of a condition are great for helping young learners think through conditionals. When working in programming environments like Scratch, students could use prebuilt conditions such as those in Figure 2 above.

▶ Example Activity 1:

Have students evaluate the conditionals and write all the steps executed.

Suppose we have the following set of steps we follow before getting ready to leave the house:

1. Put on hat;

2. IF (weather is sunny) THEN

    a. Put on sunglasses;

    b. Apply sunscreen;

3. ENDIF

4. Put on shoes;

A. What items of clothing will we put on (a) when weather is rainy (b) when weather is sunny?

B. Change the algorithm above to show that you will take an umbrella if it is rainy.

    a. Create one version with an ELSE part.

    b. Create another version with 2 separate IF statements.

▶ Example Activity 2:

Have students create their own everyday IF-THEN situations. They could create their own from scratch or use a few fill-in-the-blank starters. For example

1. IF I step out and it feels cold,

    THEN _____

    [*I will come back in and get a jacket*]

2. IF the weather forecast predicts rain for the day

    THEN _____

    [*I will carry an umbrella with me*]

3. IF we need to make pizza for dinner

    THEN

{

    _____

    _____

    _____

}

ELSE

{

    _____

    _____

    _____

}

▶ Secondary Grades

In secondary school students must learn two additional key skills related to conditionals. The first is the construction of nested conditionals, and the second is the use of complex expressions—relational, arithmetic, and Boolean, as well as combinations of these—in the condition that must be evaluated in the conditional. Both these concepts are sometimes challenging for students, so it is worth spending time and effort (with several examples and programming exercises that require the construction of these skills). Also see **Chapter 15, Operators and Expressions**, for consonant ideas relevant to teaching conditionals.

Nested Conditionals

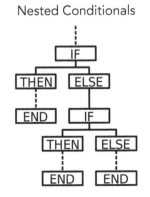

Recall the leap year algorithm from **Chapter 1, Algorithms**. It is an excellent example of a program/ algorithm with nested IFs (Figure 3a). For students to understand nested loops and control flow, have them trace the algorithm for various values of `year` such as 2000, 2010, 2008, 2020.

```
if (year is not divisible by 4) then          int isLeapYear(int year){
{                                                 if (year % 400 == 0 || (year
        (it is a common year)                     % 4 == 0 && year % 100 != 0))
}                                                         return 1;
else                                              else
{                                                         return 0;
        if (year is not divisible by 100)then   }
        {
                (it is a leap year)
        }
        else
        {
                if (year is not divisible by 400) then
                {
                        (it is a common year)
                }
                else
                {
                        (it is a leap year)
                }
        }
}
```

Figure 3a and 3b. Two versions of the leap year algorithm, one using nested IFs and the other using a chained conditional with a compound Boolean expression in Java.

Nested conditionals can also be combined into a single conditional using a compound expression, as shown in Figure 3b. Order of precedence in the evaluation of such expressions is important. Python also provides ways to **chain** expressions. For example, x < y < z is equivalent to x < y and y < z, *except that y is evaluated only once (but in both cases, z is not evaluated at all when x < y is found to be false).*

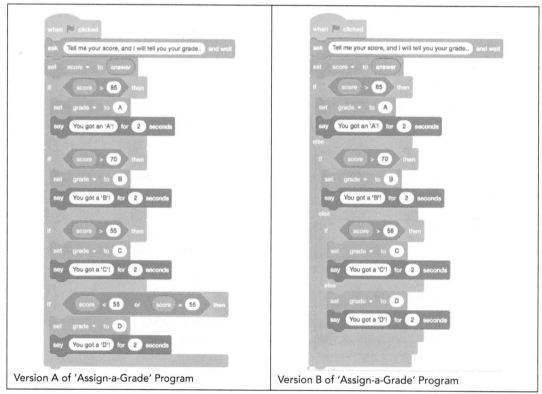

Version A of 'Assign-a-Grade' Program | Version B of 'Assign-a-Grade' Program

Figure 4. Which version of the Assign-a-Grade program works? Why or why not?

▶ Compound Expressions to Be Evaluated in Conditionals

You can also discuss a third solution for the Assign-a-Grade program that uses ranges of scores. Such a program requires Boolean operators combined with relational expressions, for example, a grade of 'B' is assigned if `score > 70` and `score < 85`. *Be sure to discuss the boundary cases in this form of the solution.*

Several other examples can be used to demonstrate the use of compound expressions requiring relational and Boolean operators. These could be drawn from everyday examples.

1. The following is the car seat law in California—*"Children under 2 years of age shall ride in a rear-facing car seat unless the child weighs 40 or more pounds OR is 40 or more inches tall."*

2. Travis's parents say that he can go out and play with his friends if he has finished his homework and made his bed in the morning.

3. We will go on a hike if it is not raining.

4. Keisha can watch a movie if she finishes her mathematics homework or her computer science project.

5. A car gives a warning beep if the driver's or the passenger's seat belt is not locked when the car is being driven.

"Car will give a warning beep" is true `IF` (driver's seat belt is not locked `OR` passenger's seat belt is not locked) `AND` (car is being driven).

▶ Interesting Projects Requiring the Use of Conditionals

Games usually require the use of conditionals where one has to check for collisions or reach certain objects in the game, and keep track of scores or lives or levels. Stories, too—especially the "choose-your-adventure" kind, require the use of conditional to create different pathways in the story.

Here are popular ideas for fun challenges and games that require conditionals and that can also be coded in block-based programming environments.

Example 1: Rock-Paper-Scissors where a user and a computer select one of three options (rock, paper, or scissors) independently, and the result could be a win, lose, or draw. To solve the problem, students are expected to consider all possible results based on the selections.

Example 2: FizzBuzz is a popular programming challenge for introductory programmers. The challenge is as follows:

For every number from 1 to 100, output Fizz if the number is divisible by 3, output Buzz if the number is divisible by 5, and output FizzBuzz if the number is divisible by both 3 and 5. If none of these conditions match, then just output the number.

Students need to be familiar with the *modulo* operator to tackle this program. The pseudocode and Scratch solution are shown in Figure 5.

```
FOR num = 1 TO 100 DO
{
IF (num is divisible by 3 AND num is divisible by 5)
THEN
        Print "FizzBuzz"
ELSE
        IF num is divisible by 3
        THEN
                Print "Fizz"
        ELSE
                IF num is divisible by 5
                THEN
                        Print "Buzz"
                ELSE
                        Print num
}
```

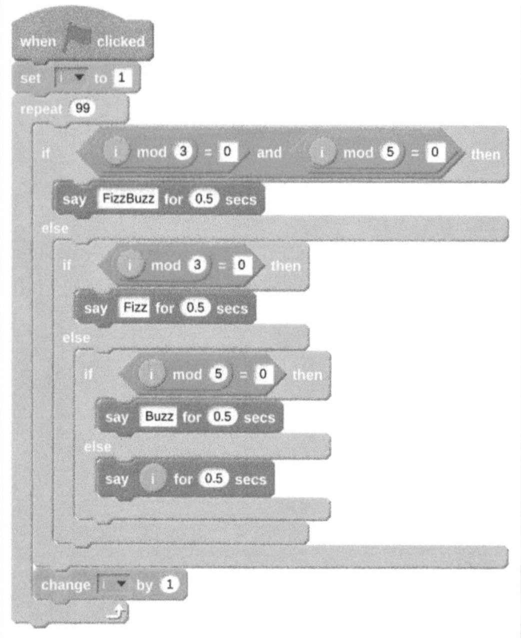

Figure 4. Pseudocode and Scratch code for FizzBuzz

THINGS TO WATCH OUT FOR!

Even though conditionals are a relatively simple concept, some students struggle with various aspects of using conditionals. Often these struggles are related to multiple conditionals (that may or may not be nested) or combining multiple Boolean expressions in the condition. Some of these difficulties are discussed in **Chapter 14, Naive Conceptions of Novice Programmers**. Here are additional pitfalls related to conditionals that teachers can watch out for.

- Redundancy—checking for both x>y as well as y>x.

- Unnecessary use of a conditional—taking the same action in the IF-THEN and ELSE part of the code.

- Use of multiple IF-THENs instead of nested IF-THEN-ELSEs.

- Incorrect order of precedence in compound conditions—expression evaluation in a condition with multiple Booleans is a common source of student struggles. For example, in the leap year example earlier (Figure 1b), it has been found that students incorrectly express the leap year logic as ((year%400==0||year%4 ==0)&& year % 100 != 0). To avoid such errors, students should be encouraged to break down the compound Boolean logic using nested IFs as shown in Figure 1a.

BIBLIOGRAPHY

Examples in this chapter have been drawn from my past research (Grover, 2014; Grover, Jackiw, & Lundh, 2019).

Grover. S. (2014). Foundations for advancing computational thinking: Balanced designs for deeper learning in an online computer science course for middle school students. (Dissertation). *Stanford University*.

Grover, S., Jackiw, N., & Lundh, P. (2019). Concepts before coding: Non-programming interactives to advance learning of introductory programming concepts in middle school. *Computer Science Education*, 29(2–3), 106–135.

Testing and Debugging

Kathryn M. Rich and Carla Strickland

INTRODUCTION

Debugging is the process of identifying and correcting errors in code. As programmers develop and test programs, they often find their code is not working as intended. It may be that the program does not run at all—instead, the computer produces an error message when it is being compiled (what is called a compilation error). A program could also crash or terminate when it is run. This is called a runtime error. It may also be that the program does run, but the result of the code—its output—is not what the programmer intended or planned for. This is called a logical error.

Imagine, for example, that you were trying to write a program that would convert a numerical score into a letter grade. You intend for a score above 85 to be an A, a score from 70 to 85 to be a B, and so on. You produce the code in Figure 1a. To test your program, you enter a numerical score of 92, and the program tells you that you got a C. You did not receive an error message, but nonetheless you know something in your code is not working as you hoped. You have just discovered a bug in your code. (In this case, you have written a faulty set of conditions.)

Having an idea of what you hope or expect your code to do is important to debugging. It is challenging to test whether your code is working when you do not have a sense of what to expect.

> The most effective debugging tool is still careful thought, coupled with judiciously placed "print" statements
> – Brian W. Kernighan

> It is often not obvious *why* a particular unexpected outcome is being produced, where in the code the problem lies, and *how* the code can be adjusted, or debugged, so that the desired outcome is produced. Debugging is the process that allows a programmer to answer these questions.

WHY IS DEBUGGING IMPORTANT?

Regardless of the skill level of the programmer, debugging is an unavoidable and integral part of coding - it is almost impossible to write a non-trivial program correctly the first time around. Although programmers become better able to avoid certain kinds of bugs as their knowledge and experience increase, programming is an inherently creative and complex activity. Testing and debugging are also inextricably a part of iteratively programming a solution.

> Debugging is a necessary part of fine-tuning and iteratively refining computational solutions to problems.

▶ Why Is It Important to Teach Testing and Debugging Explicitly?

As students matriculate through their education, they gradually develop their analytical skills in many areas. For example, children enter school with oral language but learn to codify it as they begin to read and express this language in written form. Making errors is a natural and expected part of this learning process, but is swiftly followed by the recognition of errors and an eventual desire to correct them. Proofreading is cultivated as an important and widely applicable habit for students to employ as they use written language to communicate with others in increasingly sophisticated forms. As students develop skills and habits in editing and proofreading, they improve their writing products, learn new language skills, and come to appreciate and appropriately deal with errors.

Testing and debugging serve a similar role in programming as proofreading serves in writing. Debugging may be even more crucial to learn as part of learning programming due to a strict distinction between human-to-human communication and human-to-computer communication. Although proofreading may improve the quality of written communication, students can use imprecise written language and still communicate meaning, because the human recipient can infer meaning as they read. Computers can only literally execute the instructions given to them through specific "commands" in a programming language. Thus, novice programmers must learn to debug programs to effectively communicate with computers. If a program or algorithm does not correctly perform the task a student intends, they need strategies to figure out how the message is different from the one they intended to communicate to the machine. Students may naturally take a trial-and-error approach to debugging, but explicit instruction in other strategies is critical to improving debugging skills. Table 1 provides a few of the common types of errors made by novices. Some of these are a result of naïve conceptions novice programmers harbor about how computers work (as described in **Chapter 14**). This list is not comprehensive, and the categories are not mutually exclusive, but they may help to frame your thinking about the bugs students may encounter when learning to program.

Table 1. Common types of errors (bugs), drawn from McCauley et al., 2008

Name	Description	Example
Natural language problems	Students expect a programming construct to behave a certain way based on their understanding of the way a word is used in natural language.	In natural language, *while* implies continuous checking of a condition, but in programming a *while* condition is only checked when the control flow is at the *while* loop.
Human interpreter problems	Students expect a computer to be able to interpret what they intend to do.	It is intuitive to expect a human to proceed to the next row after finishing a row, so students may not explicitly direct a computer to do so.
Boundary problems	Students forget to code conditions that account for edge or anomalous cases.	When using a division function, it is common for students to omit code that handles division by 0.
Errors in control flow	Students make control-flow errors when implementing a correctly designed solution (e.g., faulty set of conditions, loops off by 1, unreachable code).	If the initialization of a counter variable is placed inside a loop, the value will never increment more than once. Other examples are shown in the figure below.
Design or algorithmic problems	Students write the code for their designed solution perfectly, but the design does not (completely) solve the original problem.	A program to calculate the median of a data set may instead be designed and written to calculate the mean.
Typos	Students make small mistakes when writing code that are not directly related to a misunderstanding of the problem or constructs.	In text-based languages, it is quite easy to misspell a command, forget colons or semicolons, and so on. These result in errors during compile time.

```
score = input("Tell me your score,
and I will tell you your grade..")
if score > 85:
        grade = "A"
        print("You got an 'A'!")
if score > 70:
        grade = "B"
        print("You got a 'B'!")
if score > 55:
        grade = "C"
        print("You got a 'C'!")
if score <= 55:
        grade = "D"
        print("You got a 'D'!")
```

Figure 1a and b. Two control-flow bugs: (a) A faulty set of conditions that overwrites the correct grade for some numerical scores; (b) a loop that will never terminate because the `TouchedColorRed = Flag` condition will never be true [Source: Grover (2014)].

STRATEGIES AND TIPS FOR TEACHING DEBUGGING

▶ Strategies for Finding and Fixing Errors

Debugging is driven by errors and difficulties programmers encounter as they create computational solutions. Thus, it is impossible to provide a formulaic way to teach debugging. To a certain extent, helping students become competent debuggers always requires teachers to be responsive to issues that arise as students work. However, there are some techniques that you and your students can use to structure and streamline your debugging activity.

As noted in the chapter introduction, the first step in debugging is realizing there is an error. This happens only when students test their code. It is important that students test with a range of inputs. They should be encouraged to create and use good "test cases." (See **Chapter 25** on good habits of programming.) The next steps are *finding* the error within the code and then *fixing* the error. It can be difficult for students to know where to start in either of these steps. We provide a few concrete strategies for each below, illustrating with examples. We use Scratch as an example of a block-based language and JavaScript as an example of a text-based language. When possible, we also refer back to the nature of the error as described in Table 1.

▶ Locating Errors

Once a programmer knows there is a bug in their code, the next step toward correcting the bug is finding it. We describe three strategies for finding errors below, with notes about when each strategy might be most useful.

Examining Outcomes Line by Line

For short programs, a simple and efficient strategy for locating an error is examining the effects of the code line by line. Programmers can often find an error by considering whether the outcome after each line is what they expected or wanted. If not, that line may contain a bug. Using this strategy requires the programmer to either run the code one line at a time or slow down execution of the code enough to be able to see the outcome after each line. Many text-based environments allow programmers to "step through" the code, or run it line by line. Other environments execute the entire program, highlighting or marking the active line as the program is running. Alternatively, students can "code trace," or simulate execution of the code by hand using pen and paper.

Example

The JavaScript program below calculates the average of three numbers. As the programmer traces this code or watches it being executed, they would likely realize a bug: The output is attempting to print the average before it is calculated (and before the variable "result" is defined). This could be a human interpreter problem—students may assume the computer will search for a way to calculate "result" if it does not yet have a value to report.

```
1    console.log("I can find the average of three numbers!");
2    var number1 = 4;
3    var number2 = 3;
4    var number3 = 9;
5    console.log("The average of three numbers: " + result);
6    var result = (number1 + number2 + number3) / 3;
```

In some block-based programming environments, such as Scratch, users cannot run a script line by line. However, they can slow down the execution of code by inserting wait blocks between commands. Another popular technique involves adding print or "say" commands at strategic places in the code to get feedback on control flow and whether/when a certain portion of the code was executed.

Example

The Scratch script below is intended to have the cat draw a square. Without the wait blocks (left), the user will see the buggy output (center) instantaneously. With the wait blocks (right), the cat will pause after each motion block is executed, making it easy to pinpoint the typo in the second turn block.

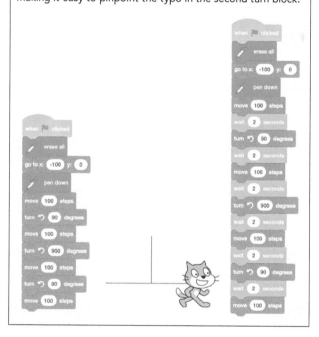

Watch Out!

For this strategy to be effective, the programmer needs to be able to evaluate some sort of outcome after each, or at least most, lines of code are executed. When students are creating animations, as is often the case in environments like Scratch and Alice, visible changes in the animation after most commands allow students to consider whether the command did what they intended. In other kinds of programs, many of the effects of individual lines of code are (intentionally) not made visible. For example, a program may calculate values that are not reported to the user of the program. When attempting to find bugs, it can be useful to add code that makes some of these intermediate results visible to the programmer (e.g., by printing the values of variables to the screen after each line). All popular block-based programming environments, including Scratch, Alice, Snap!, and App Inventor, allow the user to view the values in each variable in real time (also called "variable inspection"). Many text-based IDEs (Integrated Development Environments) also have similar features for inspecting variables during runtime. Once the bug is found and corrected, this extra code can be deleted. Alternatively, if students are code tracing in a text-based language, they can simulate execution of each line of code, keeping track of the values of variables and how they change after each line is executed.

Decomposing the Code Into Sections and Testing in Parts

When programs are long or complex, it can be inefficient to locate an error by examining every line of the code. Instead, programmers can break down, or decompose, their program into sections (generally more than one line of code long) and determine which one of the sections contains the bug. Once the bug has been located within a section of the program, line-by-line strategies can be used within that section as needed.

There are many different ways to decompose code into sections to find an error, some of which depend on the kind of program you are creating. If a program is designed to complete a multipart task, one strategy is to *test in parts*—run the parts of the code corresponding to each of the parts of the task separately. For example, if a program is intended to first ask for and store user input and then use the input in a calculation, a first step toward finding a bug might be to consider whether the error seems to be happening during the input phase or during the calculation phase. To help determine this, students can run just the section of code handling one part of the problem and check if the output, variable values, or other outcomes are as expected. Some text-based environments allow a programmer to highlight a specific section of code to run. Block-based environments, like Scratch and Alice, allow users to easily pull apart or comment sections of code, so that parts of code can be run in isolation—a feature that is helpful for testing in parts.

If the program is a simulation controlling the behavior of multiple objects, another way to decompose the code is to consider one object or script at a time. Running individual scripts can be helpful for determining if each one is working as intended.

Watch Out!

Although decomposing can be a helpful strategy, sometimes bugs occur in the coordination between sections of code. For example, focusing on one sprite at a time in Scratch code can make it difficult to find errors involving synchronization between sprites. Similarly, breaking a section of code that accepts user input from the section of the code that calculates based on that input could make it difficult to find a bug related to passing the user input values into the calculation. If students cannot locate a bug in any of the sections into which they broke their code, a next step can be to consider whether the bug might involve interaction between the sections.

Example
Scratch programmers write scripts for individual sprites, initiated by specific events. The interface allows programmers to run just one script at a time by clicking on it. A script is highlighted when it is running (as in the example at right, below).

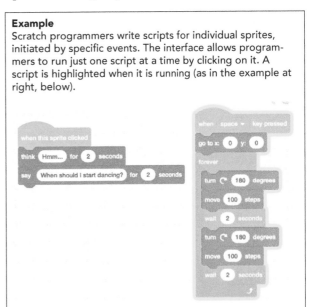

Utilizing Error Codes

In many programming environments, especially those that are text-based, built-in tools such as compilers or debuggers produce error messages that can help students find errors. Often students can use the error codes in messages to find out more about the bug in online forums.

Example
The JavaScript program below tries to use a variable before it is defined. In this environment, code is not compiled in advance, but interpreted one line at a time as the program is running. Although the program does contain a line later defining the variable "result", the interface identifies the error by flagging its use in the earlier line.

```
1   console.log("I can find the average of three numbers!");
2   var number1 = 4;
3   var number2 = 3;
4   var number3 = 9;
5   console.log("The average of three numbers: " + result);
6   var result = (number1 + number2 + number3) / 3;
```

Watch Out!

It is important to keep in mind that automated debugging tools usually find only syntax errors, or errors in the structure or spelling of the code. Examples of syntax errors are missing semicolons, misspellings of commands, or using a variable before it is defined. Syntax is the grammar of programming. If a computer cannot run a piece of code as written, there is a syntax error, and usually automated debugging tools help programmers isolate these errors. The built-in debugging tools do not, by contrast, detect semantic errors, or errors in meaning or design. An example of a semantic error is using the wrong command.

▶ Fixing Errors

The last step in debugging is to fix the error. This can sometimes be the most challenging part of debugging. Determining *what* is going wrong is often easier than determining *why*. In this section, we offer four strategies for deciding how to fix errors.

Scrutinizing Existing Code

Sometimes, the easiest way to fix an error, when you know where to find it, is simply to scrutinize the code for something irregular. Most programming languages have very particular syntax, and something as small as a misplaced semicolon or a letter written in lowercase rather than uppercase can cause a bug. Especially when students are first learning a new programming language, encouraging them to scrutinize their code and pay attention to small details can be an effective way to help them fix bugs.

Considering Omissions

On the other hand, sometimes errors are not visible to even the most scrutinizing eyes. Another potential cause of a bug is not an error in the code that has already been written but rather *code that is missing*. As discussed earlier, computers do not make inferences. Everything the programmer wants the computer to do has to be explicitly written into the code. Students new to programming may forget to code directions that humans are likely to infer. If all the code in the program seems to be correct, students might next consider if adding code could fix the bug.

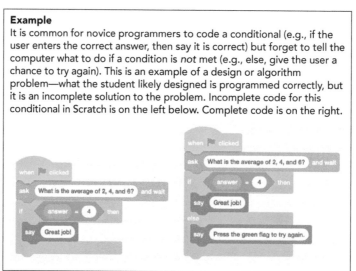

Example
It is common for novice programmers to code a conditional (e.g., if the user enters the correct answer, then say it is correct) but forget to tell the computer what to do if a condition is *not* met (e.g., else, give the user a chance to try again). This is an example of a design or algorithm problem—what the student likely designed is programmed correctly, but it is an incomplete solution to the problem. Incomplete code for this conditional in Scratch is on the left below. Complete code is on the right.

Compare to Similar Working Code

When scrutinizing the code and considering omissions does not lead to a solution, another strategy for determining how to fix code is comparing it to other code, written in the same programming language, that solves a similar problem. In short, when a student is having difficulty writing something the computer understands, adapting the code to match something the computer *does* understand can be an efficient strategy for fixing an error. In fact, often programmers begin developing a new solution by working from a similar, existing example. For example, novice programmers find it difficult to construct loops that involve Boolean conditions and variables whose values are updated in the loop—a design pattern that is common to many games. Students could benefit from drawing on similar programs as examples.

Stepping Away From Code to Find Design Errors

Lastly, sometimes a bug may not be in the code at all but rather in the design of the program. Because debugging requires programmers to dig into the fine details of code, it is not uncommon for them to forget the bigger picture. When the fix for a bug is elusive, it can be helpful for students to step away from the code and return to the algorithm to reexamine the larger problem they are trying to solve with their program and how they have designed their solution. Not only can this 'moving between levels of abstraction' (see **Chapter 2, Before You Program, Plan!**) help students to see mistakes in the code they had overlooked, sometimes they may also discover that the bug is not in the code but rather in their approach to the problem.

FOSTERING A PRODUCTIVE DEBUGGING CULTURE

Teaching debugging in your classroom requires you to devote time to discussion and dissection of buggy programs or snippets of code. Such discussions can be uncomfortable and unfamiliar to students, as formal school culture tends to focus on correct and complete solutions that do not include errors. Students may therefore sense a tension between making errors and producing a correct final product. However, in programming and elsewhere, errors are inevitable and play an important role in the process of learning.

Inspiration for fostering such a culture can be taken from pedagogies commonly used in elementary school.

> Appreciation of debugging as an important and necessary process can be supported and enhanced by a wider classroom culture that frames errors as productive.

In secondary school, where the culture is less forgiving of mistakes, there is a focus on producing a product judged as correct compared to some external standard. For example, there is one correct spelling for a word, and students are expected to learn and apply that spelling. By comparison, in early elementary school, invented spelling is often valued as a stepping-stone in the literacy journey. A first grader's final written product may be technically incorrect, but it represents progress in a child's literacy development. Students and their teachers appreciate the incorrect writing, recognize that it attempts to communicate meaning, and build from it to work toward standard spelling and writing.

One instructional strategy for increasing appreciation of errors and discussion of in-progress work is group reengagement. Typically, for individual reengagement, students attempt a problem, then look at their own work again. In group reengagement, the class examines a selected student's work, which may be presented anonymously, and discusses what is good or interesting and what may be improved. Reengagement can focus students' attention on recognizing the value in the code students have created, clarify their intention for the program, and identify the errors that are preventing the computer from accomplishing the desired objective. Through these discussions, students can learn that elements in their code that are not necessarily correct are still useful and productive. This in turn encourages them to salvage their in-process work, instead of starting over each time, which is an untenable programming habit.

You might also consider *celebrating mistakes* (as described in **Chapter 8, Hard Fun With Hands-On Constructionist Project-Based Learning**) by posting examples of common errors and their fixes as a sort of "bug museum" or "hall of bugs," or having individual students keep a debugging log, to remind them of what they have learned about bugs and the value of errors. See also **Chapter 11** and **Chapter 15** on creating a supportive classroom culture. In addition, learning programming must include giving students targeted programming exercises that require them to fix faulty code (as seen in **Chapter 6** on formative feedback). This practice can be particularly useful for exposing students to errors that result from common misconceptions (detailed in **Chapter 14, Naïve Conceptions of Novice Programmers**). Students may also use different strategies to debug sample code than to debug their own code. When debugging sample code, students may be more likely to mentally execute the program to find the error. With their own code, students may be more likely to focus on the symptom of the problem (the output) to find the error. (See the Fitzgerald et al. (2008) article in the reading list for more information.) It is important that students learn to consider both what a buggy program is actually doing (by simulating execution) and what it is intended to do (by comparing the actual output to the intended output).

Bugs are inevitable in the course of coding, and students should learn to expect and embrace them. Even the most experienced programmers spend much of their time debugging code. Though debugging can be a frustrating process for novice programmers, it is critical to provide students with plenty of opportunities to practice debugging and discuss bugs and their fixes. No matter what grade level you teach, you should foster productive attitudes toward debugging in your students by making discussion of the utility of errors a regular part of your classroom programming culture.

BIBLIOGRAPHY

Carver, S. M., & Klahr, D. (1986). Assessing children's Logo debugging skills with a formal model. *Journal of Educational Computing Research, 2*(4), 487–525.

Ettles, A., Luxton-Reilly, A., & Denny, P. (2018). Common logic errors made by novice programmers. In *Proceedings of the 20th Australasian Computing Education Conference (ACE '18)* (pp. 83–89). ACM.

Fitzgerald, S., Lewandowski, G., McCauley, R., Murphy, L., Simon, B., Thomas, L., & Zander, C. (2008). Debugging: finding, fixing and flailing, a multi-institutional study of novice debuggers. *Computer Science Education, 18*(2), 93–116.

Grover, S. (2014). *Foundations for advancing computational thinking: Balanced designs for deeper learning in an online computer science course for middle school students* (Doctoral dissertation, Stanford University).

Klahr, D., & Carver, S. M. (1988). Cognitive objectives in a Logo debugging curriculum: Instruction, learning, and transfer. *Cognitive Psychology, 20*(3), 362–404.

Lee, M. J., Bahmani, F., Kwan, I., LaFerte, J., Charters, P., Horvath, A., Luor, F., Cao, J., Law, C., Beswetherick, M. et al. (2014). Principles of a debugging-first puzzle game for computing education. In *Proceedings of the 2014 IEEE Symposium on Visual Languages and Human-Centric Computing (VL/HCC)* (pp. 57–64).

McCauley, R., Fitzgerald, S., Lewandowski, G., Murphy, L., Simon, B., Thomas, L., & Zander, C. (2008). Debugging: a review of the literature from an educational perspective. *Computer Science Education, 18*(2), 67–92.

Rich, K. M., Strickland, C., Binkowski, T. A., & Franklin, D. (2019). A K–8 debugging learning trajectory derived from research literature. In *Proceedings of the 2019 ACM SIGCSE Technical Symposium on Computer Science Education* (pp. 745–751). ACM.

Universal Design for Learning: Reaching All Students

Maya Israel and Todd Lash

INTRODUCTION

Beginning in the very early grades, when considering how to teach programming, we focus on providing meaningful, inclusive experiences to all students. This commitment to all learners means that today's classrooms are more academically, culturally, and linguistically diverse than they have ever been. This diversity provides us with an opportunity to consider how to provide meaningfully engaging, accessible, and personally relevant programming experiences.

A primary method of proactively planning instruction for the widest range of learners is through the **Universal Design for Learning (UDL)** framework designed by the Center for Applied Special Technology (CAST). This instructional focus increases access and engagement for all learners. This chapter aims to provide an overview of UDL-based approaches to teaching programming to young learners as well as real examples of how UDL has been implemented in practice.

▶ UDL: Maximizing Students' Strengths and Reducing Instructional Barriers

The UDL framework offers a practical way for teachers to plan instruction in a way that accounts for the wide range of learner differences in their classrooms. Two fundamental concepts underlie this framework.

1. **Learner variability is the norm, not the exception**: Each of us approaches learning differently. Although it is necessary to consider characteristics such as disability status to meet students' individual needs, when we look at students only within categories (e.g., gifted, learning disability), we oversimplify differences between learners and do not fully acknowledge the diversity among them.

2. **(Dis)ability is contextual**: Instructional tools, materials, and curricula can disable students' learning. Imagine that you use a wheelchair for mobility, but a building you want to enter does not have a ramp. The lack of a ramp would disable your ability to enter the building. When we view disability as contextual (the challenge may be native to instruction and tools and not the individual), we can begin to consider ways to add supports, scaffolds, and flexibility to minimize instructional barriers.

Thus, a UDL approach takes into account learner variability from the very beginning when considering goals, methods of instruction, assessments, and materials.

THE THREE UDL PRINCIPLES

The UDL framework is organized around three primary principles developed by CAST (http://cast.org): (1) **Multiple means of engagement (the "why" of learning)**, (2) **multiple means of representation (the "what" of learning)**, and (3) **multiple means of expression (the "how" of learning)**. These three principles provide a way for us to design instruction based on students' strengths and challenges (see Figure 1).

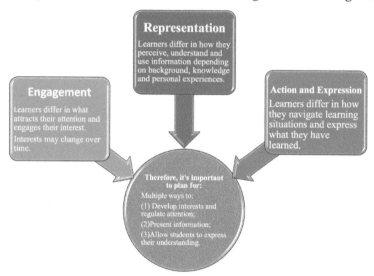

Figure 1. The three UDL Principles

These principles were derived from neuroscience research on learning and delineate how we can proactively support all learners in becoming expert learners (learners who are motivated to learn and take ownership of their own learning).

A word about maximizing student strengths and minimizing barriers. Programming can be extremely engaging for a diverse range of learners, including those with disabilities. However, programming can also pose multiple challenges, including

1. <u>Accessibility barriers</u>: Most programming languages (both block-based and text-based) have limited or no accessibility for text readers. If a student has a visual impairment or print-based learning disability, they will benefit from a programming environment that works well with text readers such as the *Quorum* programming environment (https://quorumlanguage.com/) and *Bootstrap* (https://www. bootstrapworld.org/), both of which have invested a great deal of effort into accessibility features.

2. <u>Cognitive load barriers</u>: Many students, especially those with learning disabilities, struggle with complex, multistep problem-solving when faced with open-ended computational tasks. Most CS-education curricula do not have a great deal of instructional supports to account for these cognitive load challenges. Therefore, as a teacher, you will need to evaluate the tools, curricula, and other materials for concepts and activities that need additional scaffolding.

Despite these challenges, when given the support they need, most students, including those with disabilities, experience success. By considering students' interests, areas of strength, and motivations alongside instructional barriers, we can maximize opportunities to help students take ownership of their learning of programming.

▶ UDL for Programming Instruction

The three UDL principles are broken down into nine guidelines that provide ideas for how to apply UDL in an instructional context. You can learn more about these by going to http://udlguidelines.cast.org/. Figure 2 provides suggestions for applying these guidelines to programming instruction. Additional examples can be found in the *Universal Design for Learning Guidelines + Computer Science/Computational Thinking* resource here: https://tinyurl.com/y244kkd6.

Multiple Means of **Engagement**	Multiple Means of **Representation**	Multiple Means of **Action & Expression**
Affective Networks The "WHY" of learning	Recognition Networks The "WHAT" of learning	Strategic Networks The "HOW" of learning
Access — Provide options for **Recruiting Interest** • Give students choices (choose project, software, topic) • Allow students to make projects relevant to culture and age	Provide options for **Perception** • Model computing using physical representations as well as through an interactive whiteboard, videos • Give access to modeled code while students work independently	Provide options for **Physical Action** • Provide teacher's codes as templates • Include CS Unplugged activities that show physical relationship of abstract computing concepts
Build — Provide options for **Sustaining Effort & Persistence** • Remind students of both computing and content goals • Provide support or extensions for students to keep engaged • Teach and encourage peer collaboration by sharing products	Provide options for **Language & Symbols** • Teach and review content specific vocabulary • Teach and review computing vocabulary (e.g., code, animations, computing, algorithm) • Post anchor charts and provide reference sheets with images of blocks or with common syntax when using text	Provide options for **Expression & Communication** • Give options of unplugged activities and computing software and materials (e.g., Pseudocode, Scratch, code.org, Alice) • Give opportunities to practice computing skills and content through projects that build prior lessons
Internalize — Provide options for **Self Regulation** • Communicate clear expectations for computing tasks, collaboration, and help seeking • Develop ways for students to self-assess and reflect on own projects and those of others	Provide options for **Comprehension** • Activate background knowledge by making computing tasks interesting and culturally relevant • State lesson content/ computing goals	Provide options for **Executive Functions** • Guide students to set goals for long-term projects • Record students' progress (have planned checkpoints during lessons for understanding and progress for computing skills and content)

Figure 2. Programming instruction within the UDL Framework (Israel, Lash, & Ray, 2018; adapted by B. Marsland, San Francisco Unified School District)

In teaching programming, instructors can apply these guidelines to planning in four areas: goals, barriers, methods/materials, and assessment (see Table 1).

Table 1. UDL instructional planning process

UDL-Based Planning Questions	Programming-Specific examples
What are my instructional **goals**?	Goal 1: Students will collaboratively create a program in Scratch to animate a comic strip. Goal 2: Students will use the "wait" block to synchronize the sprites' actions.
What **barriers** could interfere with students achieving those goals?	Students may have difficulty deciding on the value of the "wait" blocks. Students may struggle with the collaborative aspects of this activity
What **methods** and **materials** can I use to address the instructional barriers in this activity?	Methods: Modeling the use cases for the "wait" block; practice opportunities; teach children about collaboration expectations. Materials: Project planning guide and checklist of expectations; multimodal tools for project explanation.
How might I **assess** learning in a flexible manner?	Project-planning guides (with a checklist that includes the "wait" block and other required components). Use this for both formative (throughout development process) and summative feedback. Students can create video, audio, or pictorial explanation of their final Scratch project, their design process, and successes/challenges.

▶ Scaffolding Programming Instruction: Multiple Means of Engagement, Action, and Expression

Providing choice as part of programming project planning can engage students' interests, persistence, and self-regulation. However, choice without guidance and scaffolding can lead to frustration and limited learning opportunities. Examples of project scaffolding guides may include the following:

1. *Scaffolded CS projects.* Scaffolded programming projects balance instructional support with opportunities for creative problem-solving. Structuring "base" activities with flexible extensions allows for a great deal of instructional flexibility. For example, after modeling, provide students with checklists of base project components and extensions. The students will have a clear understanding of the basic tasks but will also have opportunities to extend their projects beyond those base expectations. Example "base project" components in Scratch may include (a) at least two sprites who are programmed to have a conversation, (b) at least one background in the project, and (c) at least one user input component. Extensions can include adding additional animations, sounds, and so on.

2. *Project checklists.* As part of scaffolded projects, checklists can provide explicit directions about expectations for project completion. These checklists are extremely helpful for unpacking directions for students who might struggle with projects that have multiple elements. Table 2 provides an example of a programming-specific checklist.

Table 2. Project planning checklist

Project Component	Checklist Elements	✓
Game Elements	• Game should have a start and an end. • Game should have a control mechanism (e.g., mouse or keyboard controlling the main sprite).	
Sprites	• At least one MAIN sprite controlled by the player. • At least TWO other sprites that interact with the main sprite.	
Feedback	• Share your game with at least TWO people. Ask what they like about the game and what improvements they recommend. • Give feedback to at least TWO peers about their games.	
Extensions	• •Import images. • Add sound to your project.	

3. *Project storyboards.* Because complex, multistep problem-solving can be challenging for many learners, storyboards can offer a planning tool to help students think about their projects, elements within the projects, and the order of events within the projects. The teacher can model how to use storyboards to record the elements of a projects. Table 3 shows an example of a simple storyboarding scaffold that can be modified for any grade level, giving students options to track project progress and self-learning goals.

Table 3. Project brainstorming and storyboarding

	Scene _1__ Background:	Scene _2__ Background:
Describe and/or draw project scen		
Sprite 1 **Sprite 2**	**Actions:**	
Dialogue:		
#___	#___	

4. *Multiple entry points.* Another UDL-based strategy is to create programming activities with multiple entry points. Rather than all students completing the same project, we can design projects with different participation. For example, one project can have multiple options that students can explore. Such options can include (a) complete code that the students can remix and redesign, (b) code that is "buggy" that the students can debug by finding the errors in the code, (c) "exploded" code that the students need to sequence in order (e.g., similar to Parsons problems; see Figure 3), (d) partially completed code that the students can construct and add to, and (e) extension activities that go beyond the initial computing task.

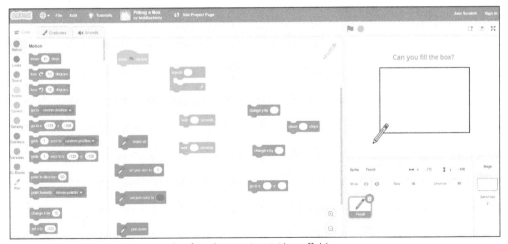

Figure 3. "Exploded code" example of student project with scaffolds

The clear expectations within each of these strategies can provide students with multiple ways of engaging and understanding the computing knowledge and tasks that they encounter.

▶ Strategies for Unpacking K–12 Programming Instructional Implementation: Multiple Means of Representation and Engagement

Providing multiple ways for students to access knowledge is a critical component of the UDL framework. Three ways of doing so when teaching programming to young learners include teacher modeling, providing video tutorials, and providing academic language supports.

1. *Balancing explicit instruction into open-inquiry activities.* Explicit instruction with modeling can proactively address instructional misconceptions and other barriers that the teacher anticipates during computing activities. It is important to note that the goal of explicit instruction is to teach students how to be independent thinkers, so it's important to phase out this type of instruction and use it only when students require additional support. Teachers can use several stages of explicit instruction when teaching programming: (a) Modeling and demonstrating, (b) guided practice for students with corrective feedback, and finally, (c) withdrawal of teacher support. For example, when teaching about *"sequencing"* the steps to draw polygons in Scratch, the teacher can model with an unplugged activity such as drawing a square using pseudocode (a simplified notation of code designed to show the steps in a program). The teacher can write out: Move 10 steps forward, turn 90 degrees to the left, move 15 steps backward, and so forth and then act out this code. The teacher can then have the students act out their own pseudocode to see if they all get the same result prior to attempting to independently create their own polygon in Scratch. This explicit modeling and follow-up activity promotes understanding of sequencing by enabling students to visualize how and in what order each line of code is executed and how that contributes to the final result.

2. *Video tutorials.* One way to provide reinforcement of teacher modeling is through the use of video tutorials. A student can watch and re-watch a video for steps and processes if they need additional reminders. Making these resources available and easily accessible to students allow them to independently problem-solve rather than needing to always seek an adult or peer. These video tutorials, for example, can help address software-related issues that students commonly face. Students often spend a long time trying to figure out non-computing problems. For example, in the context of Scratch, students may spend a great deal of time logging in or finding a specific sprite within the interface. Therefore, how to navigate software (e.g., set up an account, log in, save/share/upload a project) should be modeled by the teacher and then demonstrated through video tutorials so that students can access this information independently.

3. *Academic language support.* The goal of providing academic language support is to enable students to unlock their capability and creativity in computing activities without being restricted by syntax or vocabulary. Academic language support includes

- Providing background knowledge of the content area and (if applicable) how it relates to any subject areas in which programming is integrated. For example, students can be introduced to the concept of an algorithm and how it relates to both programming and the students' mathematics instruction.

- Providing reference and explanations of code, blocks, and/or common syntax. Often, even when the academic language of programming is taught in general, it helps to teach it as related to specific programming tasks to help students generalize that academic language to the task at hand.

▶ Unpacking Debugging Strategies

Debugging is an important skill for novice programmers to learn. Yet while many, if not most, curricula introduce debugging, few actually provide systematic instruction in debugging strategies. Without this systematic strategy instruction, students may become overly frustrated. As novices, students often use "guess and check" when their code ceases to work. For example, in block-based programming environments such as Scratch, they often pick blocks without knowing either what they do or where they should be placed in a script and then try these blocks to see if they work. Though this practice may succeed on occasion, it is not systematic. Instead, we can think about debugging in terms of having knowledge of strategies and self-monitoring for the use of those strategies (see Figure 4). Teaching students to effectively use debugging tools helps them self-assess and even record their own debugging behaviors. (Also see **Chapter 20, Testing and Debugging**.)

THINGS TO CONSIDER: INDIVIDUALIZATION IN THE CONTEXT OF UDL

UDL can proactively leverage students' strengths and remove learning barriers. Even when done well, however, UDL does not remove the need to individualize learning for some students. Class-wide UDL implementation may reduce the need for individualization, but it does not substitute for individualization. For example, students with Individualized Education Programs (IEPs) that require text-to-speech as an accommodation will no longer need specialized planning for text-to-speech if that is already offered as part of instructional planning. However, if the same student also requires a specialized assistive technology (such as a modified mouse) to interact with the computer, that form of individualization will still be necessary. Utilizing the UDL framework does not, therefore, discount the need for providing student-specific accommodations or modifications.

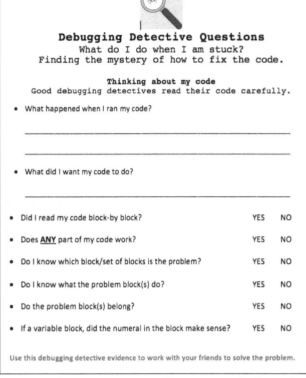

Figure 4. Debugging Detective—self-monitoring and self-recording debugging strategy use

UNIVERSAL DESIGN FOR LEARNING

Lastly, applying UDL to one's computing instruction may seem daunting at first and perhaps doubly so for teachers new to programming. The key is to begin small. Begin planning by considering the most important components of the lesson or unit and then determine what might make that content or practice(s) most difficult for your students. By focusing on the three broad UDL principles along with the four questions laid out earlier, one can then begin to explore UDL implementation incrementally. Do not attempt to address all nine guidelines in any one lesson. Start with a few and build up as necessary.

RESEARCH, RESOURCES, AND READINGS

This chapter draws on research on UDL more generally and UDL in computer science education, more specifically. The UDL framework was originally designed by Anne Meyer and David Rose, who cofounded CAST in 1984 and introduced the first set of UDL principles in 1998. Key publications on UDL aimed at educators include Rose and Meyer (2002), Meyer, Rose, and Gordon (2014), and Meo (2008). General UDL resources can be found at

- CAST: http://www.cast.org/
- The UDL guidelines: http://udlguidelines.cast.org/
- UDL: What do you need to know: https://www.understood.org/en/learning-attention-issues/treatments-approaches/educational-strategies/universal-design-for-learning-what-it-is-and-how-it-works

Our own research has focused on UDL in computer science and programming in primary classrooms (e.g., Israel, Lash, & Ray, 2017; Ray et al., 2018; Snodgrass et al., 2016).

ACKNOWLEDGMENTS

Our gratitude to Wei Yan, Ruohan Liu, and Feiya Luo for their contributions to this work and chapter.

BIBLIOGRAPHY

Israel, M., Lash, T., & Ray, M. (2017). Universal Design for Learning within computer science education. Adapted by B. Marsland. *Creative Technology Research Lab*. University of Florida. Retrieved from https://docs.google.com/document/d/1V7qsDUgrE6_L7xGF3CuPLs7BhuBwp4P-EIGqio27rxo/edit?usp=sharing.

Meo, G. (2008). Curriculum planning for all learners: Applying Universal Design for Learning (UDL) to a high school reading comprehension program. *Preventing School Failure: Alternative Education for Children and Youth, 52*(2), 21–30.

Meyer, A., Rose, D. H., & Gordon, D. (2014). *Universal Design for Learning: Theory and practice.* CAST. Retrieved from http://udltheorypractice.cast.org/login

Milne, L. R., & Ladner, R. E. (2018, April). Blocks4All: Overcoming accessibility barriers to blocks programming for children with visual impairments. In *Proceedings of the 2018 CHI Conference on Human Factors in Computing Systems* (p. 69). ACM.

Ray, M., Israel, M., Lee, C., & Do, V. (2018). A cross-case analysis of instructional strategies to support participation of K–8 students with disabilities in CS for all. In *Proceedings of the Association for Computing Machinery (ACM) Technical Symposium on Computer Science Education.* SIGCSE ACM.

Rose, D. H., & Meyer, A. (2002). *Teaching every student in the digital age: Universal Design for Learning.* Association for Supervision and Curriculum Development.

Snodgrass, M. R., Israel, M., & Reese, G. C. (2016). Instructional supports for students with disabilities in K–5 computing: Findings from a cross-case analysis. *Computers & Education, 100*, 1–17.

Stefik, A., & Ladner, R. (2017, March). The quorum programming language. In *Proceedings of the 2017 ACM SIGCSE Technical Symposium on Computer Science Education* (pp. 641–641).

Variables

Philip Bagge and Shuchi Grover

(*Equal contribution)

CHAPTER 22

INTRODUCTION

Generally speaking, **variables** represent quantities or things that change over time. In programming, we often need to work with data that are stored, manipulated, displayed, and, operated on by the program. Variables are named entities that have a value (that can change over the course of program execution). From a computer architecture perspective, *a variable is a named storage location in a computer's memory (identified by a memory address) that holds a value*.

> One man's constant is another man's variable
> – Alan Perlis

Variables are used to represent data in a program. Depending on the type of data represented by a variable, its values might be numbers, names, directions, colors, or true/false (to represent a flag or "yes/no" situation).

Additional relevant concepts and ideas related to variables include types, range, initialization, naming, assignment (when creating and updating variables), and scope. Operators and expressions are also closely related to variables (in that they usually involve variables). Check out **Chapter 15, Operators and Expressions**, as a companion chapter to this one.

▶ Variables Afford Data Abstraction

Variables help *parameterize* the solution so that a more general solution that works for a range of inputs can be created. For example, in Figure 1a, the pseudocode for a Scratch program draws a hexagon, and that is all it is good for. The program in Figure 1b can be used to create a range of polygons based on input from the user.

```
goto (0,0)
pen down
repeat (6) {
      move 75 steps
      turn 60 degrees
}
```

```
ask user for number of sides in polygon
save input in num_sides
goto (0,0)
pen down
repeat (num_sides) {
      move 75 steps
      turn 360/num_sides degrees
}
```

Figure 1a and b. Variables can be used to create a generalized solution, a key idea of abstraction

Additionally, variables can be used to hide complexity and detail. A variable can stand for a complex expression. For example, using a single Boolean variable isWeekday is better than using the entire expression (isMonday OR isTuesday OR isWednesday OR isThursday OR isFriday) many times in a program. Once we execute the following statement, isWeekday can stand in for the entire expression on the right-hand side:

isWeekday = isMonday OR isTuesday OR isWednesday OR isThursday OR isFriday

In a similar vein, in some programming languages, one can create a compound data object such as "**person**" that could comprise various other variables such as **name**, **age**, **address**, and **email id**.

ESSENTIAL IDEAS OF VARIABLES

▶ Variables Consist of a Name and a Value

Variables have two parts (1) a name that we can use to refer to them in algorithms and programs and (2) a value.

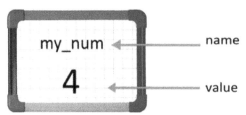

Figure 2. Whiteboard metaphor for variable

Beware of the "Box" Analogy!
Many teachers use the "box with a label on the side and objects inside" metaphor to explain the idea to learners. The concreteness of this analogy is appealing because boxes store things, but other boxlike traits don't apply. For example, a box can accept different types of objects at the same time, but a variable accepts only one type of object at a time. A potentially better introductory analogy is a whiteboard, where you erase the previous value to enter a new one (Figure 2).

▶ Variables Have "Types" Based on the Kinds of Values They Store

A variable's type suggests the data type that the variable stores, such as names, numbers (of various kinds), and alphanumeric strings. Common data types in programming are shown in the table below.

Type	Associated keyword(s)	Description (To represent...)
Character	char	A single character data, e.g. a currency symbol "$"
String	string	Textual data e.g. a name "Philip"
Numeric	int float double long	Numbers. In some languages numeric data types could be more specific for the type of number stored such as 'int' for integers or 'float' for floating point numbers, or the size of number they can store (which is driven by the number of bits allocated by the system for storing that value)
Boolean	bool	True/false or 1/0 (can only be one of two values)

Note: Often we need to store collections of data such as a list of students enrolled in a class or a matrix (or two-dimensional array) of numbers to represent cartesian coordinates. In such cases, we use *data structures* such as lists, arrays, stacks, or trees (among others). **Chapter 4, Data Structures**, deals with these *collections or containers of variables.*

The data type of a variable determines what operations can be conducted on a variable. For example arithmetic operators for numeric types, concatenation ("join" in Scratch) for string types, and Boolean operators such as NOT, AND, OR, XOR, and such for Boolean types. These are discussed in detail in **Chapter 15, Operators and Expressions.**

Strong vs. weak and static vs. dynamic typing. Some languages are strongly typed, meaning that they require the data type to be explicitly stated in the variable declaration (or creation). The variable type strictly determines which operations can be conducted on the variable. Other languages, such as Scratch and JavaScript, are weakly (or loosely) typed. The variable type does not have to be specified when the variable is created. The following example in JavaScript demonstrates this.

```
let foo = "Philip"; // foo is a string
foo = 27; // foo is now a number
foo = true; // foo is now a Boolean
```

Another differentiating factor in the way various programming languages treat variable types is whether they are static or dynamically typed. In static typing, type-checking of variables happens at compile time, whereas dynamically typed languages do type-checking at runtime. Both paradigms have advantages and disadvantages. Static type-checking allows for more error detection at compile time, whereas dynamic checking allows for more abstract data handling that can be robust for varied inputs but places a higher onus on runtime testing.

Examples of Common Types of Variables, Operations, and Their Use

String and numeric variables are used to store text values. Numeric variables are used to store numbers— integers, floating numbers, and such. Although Scratch and many block-based programming languages do not require students to declare different variables types differently, the operations on string variables are different from those one would normally use with numeric variables. For example, arithmetic and relational operations are appropriate for the `Score` numeric variable in this code, but a concatenation operation such as "join" is appropriate for the string `ResultMessage` variable.

It is important to note that languages like Python "overload" operators like "+" that can be used to concatenate string variables or add numeric variables, as the case may be. However using "+" with a numeric and string variable will result in an error.

`x = "awesome"`
`print("Python is " + x)`
	`x = 5`
	`y = 10`
	`print(x + y)`
		`x = 5`
		`y = "John"`
		`print(x + y)`

Text-based languages such as Java require specifying different types of numeric variables in the variable declaration process, which often also involves initializing the value (see the following examples).

```
int myNum = 15;
System.out.println(myNum);
float myFloatNum = 8.39f;
```

Boolean variables hold only one of two values, **1 (true)** or **0 (false)**, and can be used in the same way that Boolean or relational expressions are—to control conditions or loops (Figure 3).

Consider the code segment below.

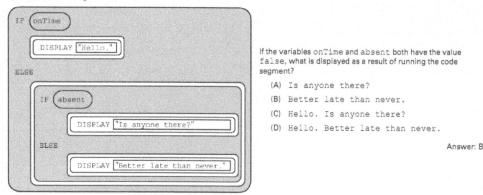

If the variables `onTime` and `absent` both have the value `false`, what is displayed as a result of running the code segment?

(A) `Is anyone there?`

(B) `Better late than never.`

(C) `Hello. Is anyone there?`

(D) `Hello. Better late than never.`

Answer: B

Figure 3. Example of the use of Boolean variables in a sample assessment for the CS Principles Exam (Source: https://apcentral.collegeboard.org)

Which Is Better to Start With for Younger Learners—Number or String Variables?

For elementary school learners, we can reduce the cognitive load by starting with just one type at a time. At some point in their learning journey, we want them to understand that variables can have different types of data assigned but only ever one type at a time. Typically, numeric and string are the simplest types to introduce to learners.

If you choose to use numeric variables for introductory examples, make sure to keep to low values to not make mathematics a gatekeeper to understanding programming and to reduce cognitive load; and if you choose textual values, remember to keep writing to a minimum for those who find writing difficult.

▶ Variable Range

Though this is not a concept often taught in introductory programming classrooms, it is nonetheless an important concept for students to understand. If a program deals with school students' age, a logical range for the Age variable might be 5 to 18 (or 19). Negative values have no meaning for the Age variable, and neither do values above 19 or 20. A string variable Tee-Size representing size of youth T-shirts may likely hold only 5 logical values: "XS", "S", "M", "L", and "XL". Understanding a logical range or set of values for a variable would be helpful in creating validation rules for user input in a program. Variable range should be a consideration when coding and also when testing for boundary or edge cases. Additionally, the numeric variable types in many languages have a specified range of possible values that is determined by the amount of memory allocated to that variable type (e.g. 32 bits in the case of integers in C++).

▶ Variable Assignment

When a value is linked to a variable, we call it "variable assignment" or "assigning a value" to a variable. It is wise to use the word "assign" right from the beginning when variables are introduced to students. "Assign" has no unwanted connotations—it implies something linked to something else but that this might not always be the case. A value may be linked ("assigned") to a variable at a given point, but at some other point in the program, the value might change. The set block in Scratch and Snap! (similar to set value to in Alice) is used to assign values to variables, as shown next.

In text-based languages, assignment often happens with the '=' sign but it's important to point out the distinction from the "equal to" operator in mathematics that denotes equality. That said, assignment can look different in different languages (i.e. it does not always use the = sign). However it always happens from right to left.

The following examples show forms of syntax for variable assignment (in various languages):

```
Score := 0
Counter ← Counter + 1
area = area * 5
thisScore = thatScore
FinalScore = QuizScore + TestScore
```

> **Key aspects of variable assignment**
> - '=' does not represent equality (like in mathematics)
> - Variable assignment happens from right to left
> - Assignment results in replacing the current value of the variable with the value on the right hand side (which may result from the evaluation of an expression)
> - Often this involves taking the old value of the variable and adding / subtracting / multiplying / dividing and putting the new value back into the variable (memory location)

▶ Naming Variables

Variables usually play a certain role in programs, as shown in Table 1. In primary grades, we find that students usually use variables for aggregating a score, to hold and use input by the user, and to iterate through a loop to count.

Table 1. Commonly used roles for variables (adapted from Kuittinen & Sajaniemi [2004]).

Role	Description
Fixed value or constant	A variable that is initialized without any calculation and whose value does not change thereafter (e.g., a variable for holding the value of pi)
Stepper	A variable stepping through a succession of values that can be predicted as soon as the succession starts
Most-recent holder	A variable holding the latest value encountered in going through a succession of values
Most-wanted holder	A variable holding the "best value encountered so far in going through a succession of values" (e.g., a max variable)
Aggregator	A variable accumulating the effect of individual values in going through a succession of values. (e.g., a score variable)
Transformation	A variable that always gets its new value based on an expression containing one or more other variables
Flag	A two-valued variable that holds a true or false value based on whether or not something has happened
Temporary	A variable holding some value for a short time only

It is important to inculcate good habits in naming variables. Encourage students to name variables sensibly according to their role in the program. It makes their algorithms and programs much more comprehensible and aids the finding of errors (bugs). In mathematics, variables are typically represented as letters (such as x or y) rather than a description of what it represents. (Note that most students do not really encounter a variable in mathematics until the middle grades, which means that students in primary grades likely have never encountered the idea of a variable.) For the novice programmer, their language understanding is far in advance of any programming logic understanding, so readability is important. So, if a variable is used to collect a user's score, then `score`, `points`, or `total` would be good names. If there are multiple scores we need to keep track of, then `player_score`, `team_score`, or `user_points` are good names because they further specify what the variable is being used for. Using examples that link multiple words with using Pascal Case convention (such as `MaxScore` or `NumberOfRounds`), underscores (such as `player_score`), or dashes (such as `player-name`) helps to encourage good practice among students as well.

> It is a good habit of programming to give variables meaningful names based on their role in an algorithm or program

Here is a set of guidelines related to naming of variables from Grover et al.'s work that students may find helpful.

What are best naming practices? Use this list to guide your discussion with students. Cover as many of these as possible while keeping up momentum and an authentic discussion.

- Short—ideally one word or a short noun phrase (when writing in most programs, words will need to be concatenated `TeacherName` or spaces will be an underscore `Teacher_Name`.
- Most environments do not allow variable names to start with a number.
- Identifiable for its role (you should be able to identify what role it is being used for).
- Isn't confusable with other variables in the program.
- Almost always nouns (`speed` rather than `how_fast`).
- Fits in a sentence like *"Right now the <variableName> is <variableValue>."* For example "Right now, the `priceOfThePen` is $3.00."
- Somehow suggests appropriate values (`temperature` = 45° is better than `howHot` = 45°).
- When we say "The temperature is 80°F," the variable is `temperature` because it answers the question "what is changing?" ("The TEMPERATURE is changing" not "80°F is changing."). And 80°F is the VALUE that the variable has at the given moment. So a single VARIABLE, when it changes, takes on new and different VALUE. Likewise, a single VALUE might be the same for multiple different variables. ("The `outsideTemperature` is 80°F AND the `poolTemperature` is 80°F.")

▶ Assigning Initial Values to Variables (Variable Initialization)

What will the starting position of the characters be at the start of the game? What value will the score have before the quiz starts? What number will we start with when we start a loop counter? Setting a variable's initial value, or "initialization," is important for all objects in an algorithm or program. It typically happens at the start of programs in block-based environments like Scratch or Snap! or wherever a variable is created (or declared) in text-based languages. Encouraging novice programmers to think about initialization in their planning improves their projects and leads to fewer frustrations in the programming and execution stages. Initializing all variables is essential in most programming languages, so teaching this early establishes good practice.

In programs like Scratch, rerunning a program without initialization means starting with the last value associated with a variable. Setting up a program with initial state and variable values to ensure a correct starting point for programs is a key idea.

Uninitialized values are usually unknown (garbage) values, or default values (like 0, or the empty string), depending on the language.

▶ Updating Variable Values in the Algorithm or Program

Fortunately, the very name "variable" implies "changeable." However, while most variables change values when a program execute, the values of some can remain constant. It is important to highlight to students that sometimes a variable may be a **constant** and its value never updated throughout the program.

Some students struggle with the idea of variable update and understanding when exactly variables are updated (see Figure 4). For example, many middle school students pick C to be the answer to the following question, also shared in **Chapter 6, Feedback Through Formative Check-Ins**.

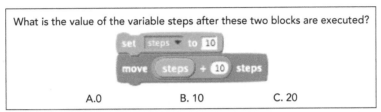

Figure 4. A simple question that reveals students' struggles with understanding when variables get updated

It is important to help learners understand the difference between changing the value of a variable by assigning a number or value to it and using the current value of the variable to change it through an expression. For example, if foo=12, then the command foo = foo + 10 and foo = 22 have the same end result. What is the advantage of using one over the other? When would one need to use one or the other? It is important for students to understand these distinctions. This confusion has been seen in the use of set versus change blocks in Scratch.

▶ Variable Scope

The scope of a variable refers to the places that you can see or access a variable. Usually, a variable has local or global scope in a program. A variable defined and used within a function is local to that function and cannot be accessed outside the function, whereas a global variable can be accessed and changed anywhere in the program. Function parameters are always local to that function.

The following JavaScript code explains the difference between global and local variables of the same name.

```
<html>
<body onload = checkscope();>
<script type = "text/javascript">
<!--
var myVar = "global"; // Declare a global variable
function checkscope( ) {
var myVar = "local"; // Declare a local variable
document.write(myVar);
}
//-->
</script>
</body>
</html>

The code above will produce the following output:
local
```

In Scratch too, variables can be local or global—a local variable can be used by just one sprite; a global variable can be used by all the sprites in the project. Elementary (primary) school classrooms usually do not worry about variable scope; however, in secondary school, where functions and methods are more commonly taught, variable scope becomes a relevant concept for learners to understand. (Refer to Sorva's chapter on misconceptions [**Chapter 14**] to see some of the common areas of difficulty learners have about parameters and variable scope as it refers to functions.)

IDEAS FOR TEACHING VARIABLES

▶ Introducing Variables in Elementary (Primary) Classrooms

The simplest introduction for working with numeric variables with young learners involves role-play using everyday algorithms while tracking the changes using the "whiteboard" variable metaphor.

Assign 5 to variable called my_num

Stand up

Bow my_num times

Subtract 2 from my_num

Say my_num

Sit down

Wave my_num times

Add 1 to my_num

Say my_num

> my_num
> 5

> my_num
> 3

> my_num
> 4

When we follow this algorithm, we would update the values of the variable and perform other actions based on the value of the variable, like so.

Assign 5 to variable called my_num

Stand up

Bow 5 times

Subtract 2 from my_num

Say 3

Sit down

Wave 3 times

Add 1 to my_num

Say 4

Pupils enjoy writing their own examples and challenging their peers to act them out (see Figure 5).

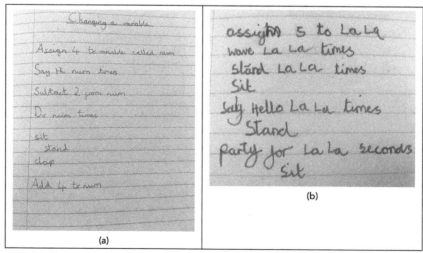

Figure 5. Examples of primary school pupils learning to use variables (*Well done if you spotted that the name in (b) doesn't follow the naming convention! Spotting something like this can be an opportunity for a brief conversation about next steps to improve their work.*

▶ Read the Name, Get the Value

It is easy to forget that many novices won't understand the relationship between the variable name and its value unless it is explained and demonstrated. When we read an algorithm and we get to a variable, we read the name but should act on the value. When a program gets to a variable, it also reads the name and acts on the value.

Number example

> *Assign 3 to variable called my_num*
>
> *Stand up*
>
> *Bow my_num times*
>
> *Sit down*
>
> *Wave my_num times*
>
> *Say my_num*

When the algorithm is executed, students would read the name but act on the value.

> Stand up
>
> Bow 3 times
>
> Sit down
>
> Wave 3 times
>
> Say 3

We know that the harder we are forced to think about something, the more it will be likely to make it into our long-term memory, so after acting out the teacher's everyday algorithms with variables a great next step is to write their own (as in Figure 5b).

▶ Introducing the Idea of Variables from Everyday Examples

A great way of exploring variables researched by Grover and colleagues, and successfully used by Bagge, involves engaging students with the idea of variables through short everyday scenarios or stories. In the *Story Variables* activity, students can work in pairs to complete the activity sheet in Figure 6. Following a whole-class discussion on students' responses, the teacher and students collectively come up with a definition for a "variable" as a quantity that changes over time and discuss the characteristics of variables. Through the activity, try to capture the following ideas:

- Variables are quantities that can change over a story or program.
- A variable's value is its quantity at one specific time in the story or program.
- At any given moment in time, a variable has a specific value—even if we don't always know what it is (e.g., OurScore at halftime!). In fact, one of the main reasons we use variables—in stories and in computer programs—is so we can describe situations even when we don't know their exact values. "It's hotter than yesterday" doesn't tell you what "it"(the temperature variable) is, but instead tells you how its value today relates to whatever value it had yesterday.
- Likewise, a variable's name lets us talk about it even without knowing its value at a specific moment.
- Variable values don't have to be numbers, the way they are in mathematics class (e.g., shirt size, temperature).
- Values of variables tend to be in a range or drawn from a set of reasonable possibilities. For example, T-shirt size will never be a negative number and a team's basketball score will never be 10 million.

Story 1 "Excuse me --- last week I bought one of these pens here for $1.50. Are you really telling me they now cost $3?" 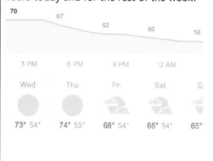	**Story 2** "We sell t-shirts in all sizes - extra-small (XS), small (S), medium (M), large (L), and extra-large (XL)" 
Story 3 "Here is the temperature forecast for the next few hours today and for the rest of the week." 	**Story 4** "I watched the basketball game last night. At halftime we were tied, but in the end they beat us, 34-30."

Figure 6. *Story Variables* uses everyday examples to introduce the idea of variables. [Source: Grover, et al. (2019)]

Next, have students complete the worksheet in Figure 7. The questions prompt thought and discussion before planning how to use these in a program.

With a partner fill out the following table about variables in these stories				
Story:	Describe a specific element or quantity in the story that is changing	What would be a good, meaningful name for the variable?	What are some of the *specific values* of the variable within the story?	How would you describe *all possible values* this variable might take?
1				
2				
3				
4				

Figure 7. *Story Variables* activity worksheet [Source: Grover, et al. (2019)] Pictures on the left include a display of drinks that a customer is purchasing, T-shirts for different ages, weather patterns over a day, and a basketball match.

In a version of this idea used by Bagge in the UK, 9- and 10-year-old students are presented with a story and asked questions to draw out their understanding of variables while planning before creating a simple program using Scratch (Figure 8). Pupils were able to concretize the complex idea of a value that changes but retains the same name through the everyday known medium of a story, linking the new to the known.

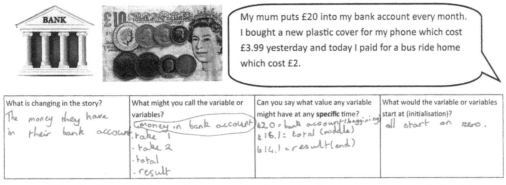

Figure 8. Using the *Story Variables* worksheet as a planning tool before creating a program in Scratch.
[Image source: Phil Bagge]

SUMMARY

The following list summarizes the foundational aspects related to variables that novice programmers need to comprehend to understand variables in both text-based and block-based programming languages. Note that primary students are usually introduced to the idea of variables in block-based environments for one of three reasons—**(1) to collect a score, (2) to hold and use user input, and (3) to use as a loop iterator.**

- A variable consists of a name and a value.
- Variables should be named based on their **role** in the program.
- In many text-based languages, there are variable naming conventions. For example, there are *reserved* words in a programming language that can't be used for naming user-defined variables.
- In many programming languages, the programmer has to decide the **scope** of the variable— if the variable is local or global.
- Variables have '**types**' based on the data they represent.
- Common variable types are numeric and text. These variables can be used in place of numbers or text (respectively) in any part of an algorithm or program.
  - Number values can be assigned to numeric variables. In most text-based programming languages, number values are further divided into floats or integers. Number values can be retrieved from variables, combined using mathematical operations, and the results can be stored back in variables.
  - Text values can be assigned to string variables. These are strings of characters that include text, digits, and/or symbols.
- In some text-based programming languages, the type of variable value has to be decided and stuck to at the time of variable creation or **declaration**.
- Variable **assignment** involves giving a value to a variable. (We also refer to this as **assigning** a value to a variable).
- Values are usually assigned to variables at the beginning of a program. This is called **initialization**.

- Variables can be also assigned values by the user through a keyboard input. *Some languages like Scratch and Snap! automatically store the most recent keyboard input in a system variable called* **answer**.

- The value stored in a variable can be changed in the program. Variables can be repeatedly changed each time a loop iterates.

THINGS TO WATCH OUT FOR!

Throughout the chapter, we have highlighted cautions related to student difficulties or sources of difficulty related to variables. We summarize them here. Also check out **Chapter 14, Naïve Conceptions of Novice Programmers** and **Chapter 15, Operators and Expressions** in this book. **Chapter 25** on good habits of programming also offers guidance on initializing and naming variables.

1. Students often believe a variable can hold multiple values. This is often reinforced by the 'variable as a box' metaphor. Use caution when you use this metaphor!

2. Students in higher grades sometimes bring preconceived notions of variables from their mathematics classrooms. Variables in programming are treated differently than in mathematics, even though in both subjects they stand for named quantities that can hold different values. Key differences have to do with the idea of variable assignment, how we name variables, and the idea of state related to the temporal nature of code execution in programming.

3. Students sometimes struggle with variables associated with loops—constructing expressions with variables that control a `while` or `repeat until` loop and/or with understanding how variables may be updated in every iteration of a loop.

4. The idea of "constant" variables can be confusing. For example, one can define a variable `pi` to hold the value 3.14 and then use `pi` for various mathematical operations in the program. A "constant" variable (or simply "constant") is a named quantity that has a value that does not change over the life of the program. Figure 9 demonstrates a `user_name` variable that does not change in the program.

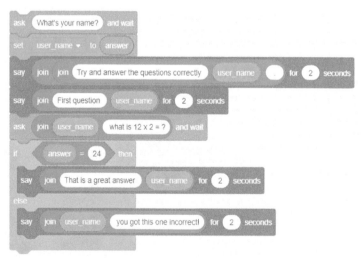

Figure 9. In this quiz example, the value of `user_name` does not change in the program

RESEARCH AND READINGS

This article draws on Grover's research related to variables in middle and high school classrooms in the United States and Bagge's work in primary classrooms in the UK. The main sources of inspiration (and examples) for this chapter are as follows:

- Grover's dissertation research at Stanford University (Grover, 2014; Grover, Pea, & Cooper, 2015).

- Grover et al. (2019)'s paper on *Concepts Before Coding: Non-Programming Interactives to Advance Learning of Introductory Programming Concepts in Middle School.*

- *What Is in the Box?* An article by Waite, Hermans, and Aivaloglou in *Hello World*, 7th edition.

- Sue Sentence and Jane Waite's work on PRIMM.

- Jane Waite et al.'s 2017 article, *Abstraction in Action: K–5 Teachers' Uses of Levels of Abstraction,* particularly the design level, in teaching programming. Jane names the levels as shown in this chapter but calls the last level "running the code."

BIBLIOGRAPHY

Grover, S. (2014). *Foundations for advancing computational thinking: Balanced designs for deeper learning in an online computer science course for middle school students* (Doctoral dissertation, Stanford University).

Grover, S., Pea, R., & Cooper, S. (2015). Designing for deeper learning in a blended computer science course for middle school students. *Computer science education, 25*(2), 199-237.

Grover, S., & Basu, S. (2017). Measuring student learning in introductory block-based programming: Examining misconceptions of loops, variables, and Boolean logic. In *Proceedings of the 2017 ACM SIGCSE Technical Symposium on Computer Science Education* (pp. 267–272).

Grover, S., Jackiw, N., & Lundh, P. (2019). Concepts before coding: Non-programming interactives to advance learning of introductory programming concepts in middle school. *Computer Science Education, 29*(2–3), 106–135.

Kuittinen, M., & Sajaniemi, J. (2004). Teaching roles of variables in elementary programming courses. In *Proceedings of the 9th annual SIGCSE Conference on Innovation and Technology in Computer Science Education* (pp. 57–61).

Samurcay, R. (1989). The concept of variable in programming: Its meaning and use in problem-solving by novice programmers. *Studying the Novice Programmer*, 161–178.

Sentance, S., & Waite, J. (2017). PRIMM: Exploring pedagogical approaches for teaching text-based programming in school. In *Proceedings of the 12th Workshop on Primary and Secondary Computing Education* (pp. 113–114).

Waite, J. L., Curzon, P., Marsh, W., Sentance, S., & Hadwen-Bennett, A. (2018). Abstraction in action: K–5 teachers' uses of levels of abstraction, particularly the design level, in teaching programming. *Online Submission, 2*(4), 14–40.

CHAPTER 23

Worked Examples & Other Scaffolding Strategies

Jane Waite & Shuchi Grover

INTRODUCTION: THE WHY AND WHAT OF SCAFFOLDING

▶ Why Scaffolding?

> Scaffolding situations are those in which the learner gets assistance or support to perform a task beyond his or her own reach if pursued independently when "unassisted"
> – Roy Pea (paraphrasing Wood, 1976)

Learning to program is known to be non-trivial. It is a complex cognitive activity that is often difficult for novice learners regardless of age and programming environment. One of the reasons programming is considered difficult is due to the high cognitive load imposed by the concepts that learners need to master as they learn to code. They have to make sense of the task at hand, conceptualize a design, implement and evaluate a programmed solution.

Although we strive for hands-on engagement with programming, activities that rely on open-ended programming with minimal guidance may result in a lack of explicit engagement with, and understanding of, programming concepts and patterns. In order to develop a deep sense for computational problem-solving, young learners should be artfully shepherded through meaningful learning activities with *high-quality* examples of coded solutions before they begin writing programs.

This chapter presents teaching approaches and sequences of approaches that teachers can use to reduce students' cognitive load while learning to program. All these teaching approaches scaffold learning, thereby making lessons more cognitively manageable. The approaches are code reading, worked examples, live coding, Use-Modify-Create, and PRIMM, or sensible combinations thereof.

Chapter 7, Guided Exploration Through Unplugged Activities, Chapter 14, Naïve Conceptions of Novice Programmers and **Chapter 21, Universal Design for Learning** constitute excellent companion reading to this chapter. **Chapter 7** highlights the importance of deliberate and careful knowledge building and elucidates how guided exploration and unplugged activities are essential techniques to the development of deep conceptual understanding. Without the deliberate planning of rich concept-building experiences, students are left to grapple with key learning in haphazard ways. **Chapter 14** details how things can go wrong, how students form weak or incorrect mental models peppered with misconceptions, and how to deal with specific conceptual targets of difficulty. Compromised understanding and bad habits are hard to detect, can have far reaching impact, and are difficult to overcome. Therefore, it is a good idea to get things right from the start, to work out what skills and concepts need to be taught, and to construct learning experiences that manage learner cognitive load, making them manageable for all. **Chapter 21** details why, how and when various kinds of scaffolds must be used to support neurodiversity and learner variability in the classroom.

▶ What Is Scaffolding, and How Is It Used?

Scaffolding is the use of instructional techniques to support students' learning until they are able to tackle learning activities on their own. Some scaffolding techniques tightly constrain the learning experiences; the teacher is very much in control. Other techniques are loose, giving learners more autonomy over both what they are learning and how. Teaching activities, as shown in Figure 1, scaffold or constrain the skills and concepts being taught through the task, people, or resources involved in the learning experience.

> It is important to remember that as students make progress, scaffolding must **fade away**, giving more responsibility to the learner, so that learners become more independent and take more ownership of their learning process. As educational theorist, Thomas Carruthers, famously quipped, "a teacher is one who makes himself (or herself) progressively unnecessary."

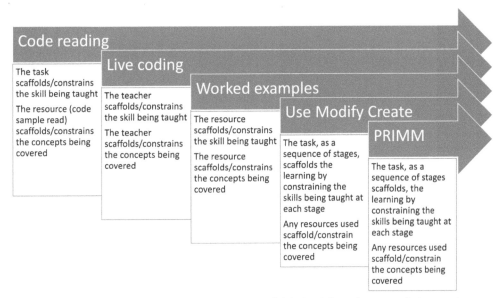

Figure 1. An overview of how each teaching activity scaffolds the skills and concepts being taught

APPROACHES FOR SCAFFOLDING PROGRAMMING ACTIVITIES

Several scaffolding techniques are available for teaching programming. In this chapter, we outline a selection of the most popular and promising ones, with illustrative examples.

> **A CAUTIONARY NOTE:** Some scaffolding approaches are specific techniques, others are general frameworks, and yet others are collections of techniques that fade support over time. As such, lists of scaffolding techniques may come across as messy, interrelated, overlapping items, and, in fact, they are.

▶ Worked Examples and Subgoal Labeling

Worked examples are a well-used and important pedagogical strategy for helping students deal with the cognitive load related to conceptual learning in STEM subjects including mathematics, physics, and, yes, computer programming. Having students work with well-designed and well-chosen examples helps them encounter conceptual ideas in use and ultimately acquire the desired cognitive skills related to learning programming. Typically, a worked example presents learners with a problem or a goal, a solution (or multiple solutions, because there are often many ways to approach a solution), and an explanation of how the solution was developed. Presenting multiple examples for each concept to be learned is also useful to highlight different situations of use or multiple facets of the concept. Worked examples have also been shown to be more effective when used in worked-example practice pairs. In these pairs, students study a worked example solution and immediately practice by solving a similar problem.

In worked examples for programming problems, subgoal labels are names given to a set of steps in the solution process, allowing the user to "chunk" the information to ease learning. Including explanations and labeling sections of the code are also a useful strategy—this not only helps students understand the program as they work through it but it also supports understanding when they later reuse or examine the example code. Such subgoal labels could be provided (passive learning) or generated by the learner (constructive/active learning) by providing a placeholder for a label. See the example in Figure 2. Related work has shown that learners should receive guidance and training for generating such explanations and labels and that subgoals also help learners solve Parsons problems (described in **Chapters 6 and 13**).

No Label	Given labels (passive)	Placeholder for label (constructive)

`sum = 0`
`lcv = 1`
 	
`WHILE lcv <= 100 DO`
`lcv = lcv + 1`
 	
`ENDWHILE`
	Initialize Variables
	`sum = 0`
	`lcv = 1`
	
	Determine Loop Condition
	`WHILE lcv <= 100 DO`
	
	    Update Loop Variable
	    `lcv = lcv + 1`
	`ENDWHILE`
		Label 1: _____.
		`sum = 0`
		`lcv = 1`
		
		Label 2: _____.
		`WHILE lcv <= 100 DO`
		
		    Label 3:_____.
		    `Lcv = lcv + 1`
		`ENDWHILE`

Figure 2. An example of worked examples with passive and constructive subgoal labeling
(Source: Morrison, Margulieux, & Guzdial, 2015).

▶ Modeling How to Code or "Live/Shared" Coding

Live coding is an approach wherein the teacher or a selected learner demonstrates the design and implementation of a program for a 'live' classroom audience. During this session, the demonstrator talks through the decisions they are making, thinking aloud and sharing their internal dialogue. In such live-coding scenarios, teachers may invite the class to contribute to the development process. This technique of modeling the process of problem-solving or completing a task is a common approach used in other subjects, such as when teachers demonstrate how to write a story, how to solve a mathematics problem, or how to undertake a science experiment. In writing classes, this can be called shared writing. When modeling, teachers often give the illusion to pupils that they, the students, are shaping the process of production and that the teacher is thinking things through on the spot. This is not the case; in reality, the teacher has a clear plan of teaching points to cover. Teachers often incorporate mistakes for formative assessment (and entertainment), they introduce key ideas, address misconceptions, and assess specific pupils needs. Essentially, a teacher should use the opportunity to not just highlight conceptual ideas and uses of constructs but also to demonstrate practices such as problem decomposition, debugging, testing (with a range of inputs, including invalid inputs), and constructing a program through a process of iterative refinement.

Another approach, termed "**live/shared coding with worked examples**," combines the two approaches of worked examples and modeling how to code. It involves providing learners with a programming task, and then the teacher and class examine a worked example together. The solution could be projected on a screen so that the teacher can examine the steps along with the class, question or discuss the strategy, discuss alternatives, or add comments and labels on subsections of code to highlight the structure of the code. The teacher could also demonstrate tracing the code with a particular set of inputs. Or the teacher could call upon volunteers to help do that. In essence, worked examples can become a whole-class activity in the vein of shared coding.

▶ Code Reading/Code Tracing/Code Comprehension

Reading and writing code go hand in hand. It has been shown conclusively that the two skills are highly correlated. But which should students learn first? Many scaffolding techniques draw upon the importance of learning to read code before writing code. Students who can accurately read code do better at writing code than their peers who cannot. This seems obvious—when learning a new spoken language, we would expect to learn to read a word before being expected to write it.

> There are two "types" of code comprehension. Code comprehension is both the ability to predict what a program will do when it is run, saying what the output or outcome will be, line by line as the code executes, as well as being able to explain in plain English the overall purpose of the code. Saying what each line will do, including what the values of variables will be when the program executes, is called tracing. Explaining the purpose of parts of a program can be seen as a separate skill to tracing because learners have to remember not only what the individual commands will do but also what they will achieve when combined.

Figures 3–5 show systematic approaches to teaching students how to trace code involving conditionals.

```
cost = 1.25
if(cost <= 1.00):
    print("buy the soda!")
else:
    print("do NOT buy the soda.")
    print("I repeat, do NOT buy it!")
```

```
cost = 0.75
if(cost <= 1.00):
    print("buy the soda!")
else:
    print("do NOT buy the soda.")
    print("I repeat, do NOT buy it!")
```

Figure 3. When teaching students the skill of tracing for conditionals, visualizations can be used to show how the control flow is different based on different inputs.(Source: Xie et al., 2019)

```
friend = "juan"
temp = 30
if(temp <= 40 and friend == "sue"):
    print("Bring 2 jackets.")
elif(temp<=35):
    print("Bring 1 jacket.")
else:
    print("You don't need a jacket!")
```

```
num_people = 11
seats_per_table = 4
extra_chairs = 0
max_chairs = 2

if(num_people % seats_per_table > 0):
    extra_chairs = num_people % seats_per_table
else:
    print("No extra chairs needed.")

if(extra_chairs>0 and extra_chairs <= max_chairs):
    print("We'll need extra chairs")
else:
    print("We don't have enough chairs.")
```

Figure 4. Practice exercise for tracing skill for conditionals. Students read the code, cross out the lines of code that do not execute, and then determine what the code would output. (Source: Xie et al., 2019)

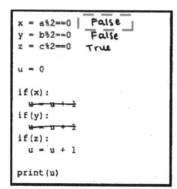

```
x = a%2==0   False
y = b%2==0   False
z = c%2==0   True

u = 0

if(x):
    u = u + 1
if(y):
    u = u + 1
if(z):
    u = u + 1

print(u)
```

A) Given the variable values a = -2, b = 3, c = 4, determine the output of the code and write the output in the box below:

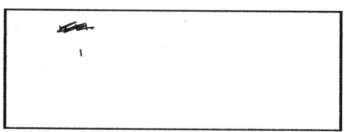

Figure 5. An exercise that provides students with a code snippet (left) and initial values for variables a, b, and c. The student is then required to trace the code and write the output. (Source: Xie et al., 2019)

▶ Use-Modify-Create

Use-Modify-Create is a progression for engaging learners in computational activities (Figure 6). In the first phase, learners are consumers as they use a product that someone else made, such as a game, program, or simulation. Learners explore what the product does and how it works. For example, pupils might be asked to play a two-player game, where the teacher has chosen or created the game to exemplify the underlying concepts that are about to be learned. The teacher might demonstrate to students how to spot and record some of the main features of the game and then ask them to find more features. Students might notice instructions on how to play the game or two characters, each of which is controlled by a player. They might spot obstacles to be avoided, rewards, and a score for each player. To take this further, the teacher could ask students, in groups, to reenact the game unplugged. To begin with, she might encourage learners to do this without requiring that the rules being followed are recorded. Subsequently, as they struggle to remember what to do, she might guide them toward the idea of a drawn or written representation of the game. The teacher could show learners a design for the game, such as a concept map with annotations, such as "If a player's character touches an obstacle, then they lose a point from their score." Groups of pupils could then use the design as an unplugged game with a view that they should next modify it. In the second stage, the ownership of the program starts to transition to the learners as they begin to modify the program. The degree of complexity of changes will vary, but over time the learners develop new skills and understanding with successive refinements.

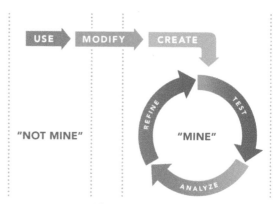

Figure 6. Use-Modify-Create Learning Progression (Image source: k12cs.org)

Consider our games example— students might next modify features that they have noticed. Sometimes learners may have no notion of exactly what they are trying to achieve and may through trial and error make relatively random changes, discarding modifications they don't like and keeping those they do like. Or teachers may carefully constrain the modification task and ask learners just to change one feature, such as the instructions for playing the game, the keys used to control the movement of a player, or the number of points awarded when an obstacle is touched. These modifications might increase in difficulty and are likely to guide pupils to learn about particular concepts that the teacher is aiming for them to learn about. If a drawn or written design has been introduced, the teachers might ask learners to change the design first and then to implement the change.

In the final stage, learners create a new product using the concepts and techniques they have studied in the preceding phases; the product is now "all theirs." With our games example, learners have gained experience of working with game instructions, characters, obstacles, and scores. As they move to creating their own new product, the teacher will be looking for them to apply this new expertise. The degree of freedom given to learners in their Create activity can vary and may be controlled by the teacher to further scaffold learning. For example, some learners might be given complete freedom to develop a new product, whereas for others a familiar context might be suggested so that they can reuse ideas from the Modify phase. One learner might create a simulation that on the surface looks very different from a game but that uses the same underlying concepts, whereas another pupil might create a very similar-looking game but set in a new context.

This progression is not advocated as a single experience for a single concept; it is more of an overarching flow of experiences that transpires across projects and the entire career of learners. Students accumulate understanding and expertise as they engage in multiple experiences, moving back and forth as users, modifiers, and creators.

▶ TIPPSEE - An Adaptation of Use-Modify-Create

Use-Modify-Create has been used in the Scratch Encore curriculum (for grades 4-6) created at CANON Lab at the University of Chicago. They have adapted it into TIPPSEE— a learning strategy for 'learning through example' in Scratch inspired by reading comprehension learning strategies. TIPPSEE (Figure 7) gives students a roadmap for taking a pre-created Scratch project and focusing on how to use it for learning. It begins with familiarizing them with the title and instructions, reminding them of the purpose, and then playing the project itself. Once they have figured out which sprite(s) they need to modify, then go inside the code and find the sprite and script they want to change. Then it's time to explore. According to the project website— in order to support this learning strategy, it is important for the teacher to first model the strategy (I DO), then have students do it along with the teacher (WE DO), then finally provide reminders for the students so they can do it themselves (YOU DO). A poster in the classroom can help students remember the steps to keep them on track.

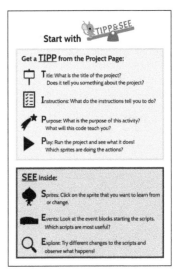

Figure 7. TIPPSEE strategy to scaffold conceptual learning in Scratch (Source: CANON Lab)

▶ PRIMM

PRIMM (**predict, run, investigate, modify,** and **make**) combines code reading and the Use-Modify-Create framework. It is a carefully ordered sequence of instructional phases used to introduce and apply a programming concept or set of concepts. For example, PRIMM might be used to teach about using variables in Scratch or using file handling in Python. Figures 7 and 8 show examples of PRIMM in Scratch and Python.

Each phase of PRIMM has a set of pre-prepared learning activities, and each phase builds on the learning presented in the preceding stage. Most PRIMMs take several lessons to complete.

▶ Predict

PRIMM starts with the teacher creating (or finding) a starter or sample program that exemplifies the features of the concept they are introducing. Teachers do not ask pupils to type the sample code, nor do they model how to create this program; instead, they always start by asking the learner to predict what the presented code does. This phase builds the habit of reading your code first.

It is advised at this stage that pupils talk to their peers about their prediction. Some teachers in trials of PRIMM asked pupils to predict independently. However, most found the social aspect of code reading very motivational (if not transformative) to their class. Most importantly, each pupil is asked to write their prediction before they run the code. Otherwise, learners are likely to say, "That is what I thought anyway."

> Writing down predictions can cause problems to start with, because some learners may not like to be seen to get it wrong, but this can be overcome by careful modelling and pupil support.

▶ Run

Following *prediction*, the code is *run*. It is advised that pupils take ownership and run the code themselves. However, in trials, some teachers reported building learner anticipation and excitement by the teacher withholding running the code until everyone had made a prediction.

▶ Investigate

Then, what is essential is to reflect on what was predicted and what the outcome of running the code was and to start to address any gaps in knowledge and misconceptions. In anticipation of this, the *investigate* phase is a series of pre-prepared questions and tasks that learners undertake. These tasks can be performed independently or by students in pairs. Teachers can add much value as they provide a carefully scaffolded series of experiences. Some questions or tasks might address the syntax of code, others might consider what combinations of commands achieve together, and still others tackle the understanding of the whole program. Code-tracing activities, guided exploration, and direct questions can be seen in the *investigate* phase. At this point, learners are required to make some small changes to the code and to rerun it, sometimes several times.

> In trials, some teachers spent much time on the *investigate* phase, asking many follow-up questions and adapting tasks to learner outcomes, whereas other teachers moved quickly to the next phase. More research is needed to find out what is most effective.

▶ Modify

The *modify* phase is, again, carefully planned by the teacher ahead of the lesson. This phase includes further guided exploration of the code. Students are given challenges to extend the program, advancing the learning to highlight key points and again address anticipated misconceptions. At this point, the ownership of the starter sample is transferred from the teacher to the learner. More choices are introduced here, but the tasks are relatively closed. Hints might be included to further scaffold learning.

An example *modify* phase might be to extend an additional quiz to include subtraction questions.

▶ Make

The final phase passes ownership to the learners, where they are asked to use what they learned in the early phases to make a new product.

> In trials, many teachers found they did not get onto the *make* stage for all learners. This is a potential problem, because we want to see all learners apply their new knowledge and skills in a more creative context.

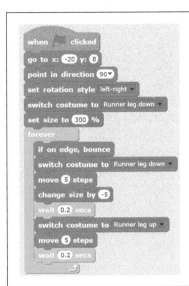

Run

https://scratch.mit.edu/proj
ects/164555770/#player

Investigate

1. What type of loop is being used?
2. What happens if you change the rotation style?
3. What will happen if you change the 'move 5' to 'move 500'?
4. What if you change the 'change size' to a positive number? What might this link to?

Modify

1. Make the sprite appear from very far away and move towards you.
2. Change the animal and its movement.

Make

Task: Make a nocturnal animal scene.
Or
Task: Make a scene about your favourite animal.

Figure 1. Example of a PRIMM activity that teaches a common design pattern of making an object appear to be getting smaller or larger (The example has been used in K–5 teacher training.)

Activity sheet 9: Using functions

Task 1: In pairs, look at the program below and write out what you think might happen when it runs

```
def add():
    answer=num1+num2
    print(answer)

def subtract():
    answer=num1-num2
    print(answer)

num1 = int(input("Enter the 1st number: "))
num2 = int(input("Enter the 2nd number: "))

calcType = input("Do you want to add or subtract?: ")

if calcType=="add":
    add()
elif calcType=="subtract":
    subtract()
```

What would you expect the computer to do? Write it out exactly.

Task 2: Download and run the program and see if it does what you think it might do. You will find it at <insert your shared drive link here>

Did the program run as you predicted? _____

Task 3: In pairs, work out the answers to the following questions by examining the code and running it a few times.

1. Name a variable that is defined in this program _____

2. Name a function that is defined in this program _____

3. Give an example of an assignment used in this program

_____

4. What would happen if you entered "Add" as the calculation type?

_____

5. Give an example of how selection is used in this program

_____
_____

6. What is the difference between input() and int(input())?

_____

Now add comments (beginning with #) to the program to make sure everything you understand is included in your program for future reference. When you think you understand how this program works then go on to the exercises.

Task 4: Exercises

In pairs, try these challenges:

1. Extend the program to include the full calculation in the output for each calculation, for example "2 + 2 = 4".

```
Enter the 1st number: 2
Enter the 2nd number: 2
Do you want to add or subtract?: add
2 + 2 = 4
```

2. Now extend the program to enable multiplication and division. You will need to add a new function for each operation and update the if statement to allow the user to choose the new options.

3. Now update the if statement to accept calculation types written in title case (e.g. "Add") and uppercase (e.g. "ADD"). You can use the "or" operator to combine conditions.

Challenge
Write a new program for a guess the number game. The user should be asked to enter their name at the start of the program. Create a function that asks the user to input a number between 1 and 10 and uses an if statement to compare their answer with the real number.
If they guess the number correctly it should display a well done message which includes their name.
If they guess a number that is higher than the actual number output "Too high".
If they guess a number that is lower than the actual number output "Too low".
Ensure you add comments explaining your code.

Make a note of any errors that you come across in your exercise book and how you fix them.

Figure 8. Example of a PRIMM activity that teaches functions in Python (The example was used in PRIMM research.)

RESEARCH AND READINGS

Roy Pea's paper on scaffolding (2004) draws on Vygotsky's framework of social learning (1978) and has been influential in understanding the dimensions of scaffolding in learning.

The idea that discovery learning does not fare well for deeper understanding of conceptual topics has been repeatedly borne out in several research studies in various contexts and presented in seminal reading such as Kirschner, Sweller, & Clark, (2006) and Mayer (2004). Roy Pea and Midian Kurland conducted extensive studies on the cognitive demands of learning programming in the 1980s around the use of Logo and BASIC in elementary and high school classrooms (such as Pea & Kurland, 1984). Their papers, in addition to an anthology of research papers from extensive research in the 1980s that were published in Soloway and Spohrer's 1988 book, *Studying the Novice Programmer* (now in its second edition, released in 2013), remain deeply influential and relevant today even though the context of learning introductory programming has changed with the advent of "low-floor" block-based programming environments, which offer an easier entry point into programming.

Research on the reading of text-based languages has a long history in university settings, with notable work by Raymond Lister and Donna Teague. This work has evidenced a strong link between the ability to trace and explain programs on the ability to write programs (Lister et al., 2009). This research continues today and includes studying strategies such as those in Amy Ko's research lab at the University of Washington, Seattle (e.g., Xie et al., 2019). However, research on the reading of block-based programs is limited. Early research indicates that reading code in such environments is complex and that learners may need explicit instruction on how to read code (Dwyer et al., 2015).

The Use-Modify-Create framework (Lee et al., 2011) has been very influential in CS classrooms and was outlined by a group of computer science education academics (Irene Lee, Fred Martin, Jill Denner, Bob Coulter, Walter Alla, Jeri Erickson, Joyce Malyn-Smith, and Linda Werner). It has since become a popular approach to scaffold learning, which is often referenced in research work. It has influenced curricula such as Scratch Encore designed by the CANON Lab (led by Diana Franklin at the University of Chicago ; https://www.canonlab.org/scratchencorematerials). Scratch Encore has adapted the Use-Modify-Create to TIPPSEE as described in this chapter.

The PRIMM approach was developed by Sue Sentance as a synthesis of the way she had taught programming to pupils in English secondary schools and to teachers in teacher training. Sue and her team have investigated PRIMM with over 500 students in grades 6-8 in over a dozen secondary schools in the UK. Teachers and pupils have found many benefits from the approach, including both teachers and pupils liking the clearly defined routine structure for lessons, teachers seeing benefits from increased speaking and listening about programming, improved accessibility for all pupils, as well as improved learning outcomes. Overall teachers found PRIMM to be a very effective scaffolding technique that increased their confidence to teach programming (Sentance et al., 2019).

Worked examples as a strategy (with or without explanations or labeling) for reducing cognitive load have been hugely influential in many STEM fields, especially mathematics and physics (Atkins, Derry, Renkl, & Wortham, 2000). Similar research in the context of programming demonstrating the benefits of worked examples and subgoal labeling continues, though mostly in university settings (Morrison, Margulieux, & Guzdial, 2015; Margulieux, Guzdial, & Catrambone, 2012).

Grover's successful work on live coding and modeling with worked examples (Grover, 2014; Grover, Pea, & Cooper, 2015) was based on modeling of mathematical problem-solving as outlined in Alan Schoenfield's 2014 paper, Mathematical Problem Solving. This approach builds conceptual understanding using the learning theory of cognitive apprenticeship. Although there is evidence of the success of live coding in university settings (Rubin, 2013), the research in primary and secondary school settings is limited, as yet, much like the research on worked examples.

BIBLIOGRAPHY

Atkinson, R. K., Derry, S. J., Renkl, A., & Wortham, D. (2000). Learning from examples: Instructional principles from the worked examples research. *Review of Educational Research, 70*(2), 181–214.

Du Boulay, B. (1986). Some difficulties of learning to program. *Journal of Educational Computing Research, 2*(1), 57–73.

Dwyer, H., Hill, C., Hansen, A., Iveland, A., Franklin, D., & Harlow, D., 2015. Fourth-grade students reading block-based programs: Predictions, visual cues, and affordances. In *Proceedings 11th Annual International Computing Education Research Conference*. ACM, pp. 111–119.

Kirschner, P. A., Sweller, J., & Clark, R. E. (2006). Why minimal guidance during instruction does not work: An analysis of the failure of constructivist, discovery, problem-based, experiential, and inquiry-based teaching. *Educational Psychologist, 41*(2), 75–86.

Kurland, D. M., & Pea, R. D. (1985). Children's mental models of recursive Logo programs. *Journal of Educational Computing Research, 1*(2), 235–243.

Lee, I., Martin, F., Denner, J., Coulter, B., Allan, W., Erickson, J., Malyn-Smith, & J., Werner, L. (2011). Computational thinking for youth in practice. *ACM Inroads 2*, 32–37.

Lister, R., Fidge, C., Teague, D., 2009. Further evidence of a relationship between explaining, tracing and writing skills in introductory programming. *ACM SIGCSE Bulletin*. ACM, pp. 161–165.

Margulieux, L. E., Guzdial, M., & Catrambone, R. (2012, September). Subgoal-labeled instructional material improves performance and transfer in learning to develop mobile applications. In *Proceedings of the Ninth Annual International Conference on International Computing Education Research* (pp. 71–78). ACM.

Margulieux, L.E., & Catrambone, R., 2016. Improving problem-solving with subgoal labels in expository text and worked examples. *Learning and Instruction 42*, 58–71.

Mayer, R. E. (2004). Should there be a three-strikes rule against pure discovery learning? *American Psychologist, 59*(1), 14.

Morrison, B. B., Margulieux, L. E., & Guzdial, M. (2015, August). Subgoals, context, and worked examples in learning computing problem solving. In *Proceedings of the 11th Annual International Conference on International Computing Education Research* (pp. 21–29).

Pea, R. D. (2004). The social and technological dimensions of scaffolding and related theoretical concepts for learning, education, and human activity. *The journal of the learning sciences, 13*(3), 423-451.

Pea, R. D., & Kurland, D. M. (1984). On the cognitive effects of learning computer programming. *New Ideas in Psychology, 2*(2), 137–168.

Sentance, S., Waite, J., & Kallia, M., 2019. Teaching computer programming with PRIMM: A sociocultural perspective. *Computer Science Education*. 1–41.

Schoenfeld, A. H. (2014). *Mathematical problem solving*. Elsevier.

Vygotsky, L. S. (1978). *Mind in society: The development of higher mental processes* (M. Cole, V. John-Steiner, S. Scribner, & E. Soubeman, Eds.). Cambridge, MA Harvard University Press.

Xie, B., Loksa, D., Nelson, G. L., Davidson, M. J., Dong, D., Kwik, H., ... & Ko, A. J. (2019). A theory of instruction for introductory programming skills. *Computer Science Education, 29*(2–3), 205–253.

CHAPTER 24

X-ing Boundaries With Physical Computing

Sue Sentance and Katharine Childs

WHAT IS PHYSICAL COMPUTING?

Physical computing (also called tangible computing) refers to the use of both software and hardware to build interactive physical systems that sense and respond to the real world. It includes building tangible interactive objects or systems, designing with creativity and imagination, and engaging physically as well as mentally. From a learning perspective, physical computing intersects a range of activities often associated with design technology, electronics, robotics, and computer science. But perhaps more importantly, physical computing provides a means to explore the use of technology in a wide range of subjects.

Physical computing can be used for digital making projects that cross curriculum subjects. In digital making projects, children have a project as an end goal and need to use design, programming, and "making" skills to create something functional. Some examples are given later on in this chapter. These kind of activities are well suited to clubs or nonformal settings where children can work on projects over a number of weeks, but can also be used in the classroom using ideas presented in this chapter. Physical computing also provides a link to other subject areas, such as science, music, and physical education.

Physical computing is associated with the learning of programming, something that children (and adults!) can find difficult. Nonphysical computing is screen-based, so the success (or not!) of the program is indicated by something happening on the screen. With a physical device, instant feedback from the device shows whether the program code works as desired. This can be rewarding as well as accelerate learning.

Physical computing is often associated with constructionism, an influential theory introduced by Seymour Papert, which supports the importance of doing . Within this theoretical perspective, children learn by building a personal world-view piece by piece, adding onto what they already know and can do. Papert believed that making things in the real world cemented children's knowledge. Drawing on this approach, learning takes place by exploring and as a product of experience. **Chapter 8, Hard Fun With Hands-on Constructionist Project-Based Learning**, also shares guidelines and principles for employing constructionism in a programming classroom.

Physical computing has become very popular with hobbyists and educators in recent years with a plethora of devices. Table 1 shows examples of different devices that can be used. A range of sophisticated modular kits and programmable toys at prices up to many hundreds of dollars are popular, including packaged components and modules like LittleBits, robotic turtles like Sphero, and programmable construction sets like Lego.

However, in recent years a large range of board-level devices have become well-established, and arguably it is these that are currently driving the adoption of physical computing. These board-level devices are extensible with basic electronic interfacing and/or via readily available pluggable modules. Some embedded devices require a PC or tablet for programming but can then be used as stand-alone projects; some of these, such as Crumble and Micro:bit, can be used with students aged from primary school upward. Despite their ease of use, many have plenty of headroom for teaching quite advanced programming concepts, if appropriate. Finally, general-purpose board-level products, such as Raspberry Pi, are essentially stand-alone PCs in their own right and naturally provide the greatest flexibility, albeit with a little added complexity.

BENEFITS OF PHYSICAL COMPUTING

Recent educational research is beginning to highlight several benefits associated with physical computing. First, the most obvious benefit is **increased motivation** for students, including those from diverse backgrounds, because the learning experience and the outcome are visible, not virtual. This is especially true when a programming task delivers a practical, meaningful device.

One of the reasons that physical computing is motivating relates to the **interactivity** often associated with programming physical devices, which can take a number of different inputs. For example, physical games can be developed that respond to button presses or sound and light inputs.

Another benefit of physical computing is the ability to be **creative**. There is no limit to the possibilities for different projects when working with the devices shown in Table 1. This practice can encourage students to think creatively and independently, rather than being limited by what can be displayed on the screen.

A third benefit is the opportunity for **collaborative work**. Research in computing education has already shown us that pair work is effective in solving programming problems, and when young people are working around a project rather than a screen, there is the potential for different roles as well as larger groups working collaboratively together. There is some indication that collaborative learning environments create a more balanced gender take-up of computing, with emerging evidence that girls enjoy physical computing. Working with devices lends itself to group work—different roles include enclosure design, hardware interfacing, algorithm design, and user interaction.

> Examining these benefits more deeply provides evidence that the **tangible nature** of physical computing provides the motivation and also improves learning outcomes. The ability to use a variety of senses, receive feedback through touch, and hold the device you are programming may assist learning. We need more research to establish this. Another explanation may be that we *learn by doing* and that physical computing allows children to practice new skills repeatedly on practical projects.

The benefits of physical computing go beyond learning computer science and programming through the many links that can be made to other subjects. For example, in other STEM subjects, physical computing can have a multitude of applications, including simulation of behavior in biology, collection and analysis of measurements in physics, and developing logic gates in electronics. It has applications in many other subjects too—making step counters for sport activities, digital jewelry designed in art lessons, and solar systems designed and built in geography lessons. **Chapter 8** on constructionist project-based learning also shares examples of activities involving creation of tangible e-textile artifacts.

continued on next page

Table 1. Commercially available physical computing devices and kits (adapted from Hodges, Sentance, Ball & Finney [in press]).

Categorization	Type of product	Examples	
Packaged electronics. No programming	Kits of packaged components and modules	Snap Circuits, basic LittleBits, Circuit Stickers	
Consumer products (not boards), programmable via PC or phone Often battery powered	Robot turtles	Sphero, Ozobot, Kibo, Dash and Dot, BeeBot, Cubetto, Finch, Robot Mouse	
	Programmable construction sets	Lego WeDo, Lego Mindstorms, Vex Robotics, Pico Cricket	
Board level programmable devices, need PC during use	Integrated I/O devices for PCs	Makey-makey, PicoBoard, BlinkM, Sense Board	
	Modular I/O devices for PCs	Phidgets	
Board level embedded devices Need PC to program but operate standalone. Can be battery powered	Microcontroller boards with integrated I/O devices	micro:bit, Light Blue Bean, Arduino Esplora, Circuit Playground, Calliope	
	Microcontroller boards with low-level I/O	Crumble, BASIC stamp, ARM mbed, Chibi Chip	
	Microcontroller boards with support for modular I/O	Arduino variants (Uno, Lilypad, Pro, Pro Mini, Fio, etc)	
		.NET Gadgeteer, TinkerKit, Hummingbird	
Board level general-purpose devices. Often use wired power.	Often used without PC. I/O available through accessories	Raspberry Pi, BeagleBone, Intel Galileo	

TEACHING EFFECTIVELY WITH PHYSICAL COMPUTING

Despite the motivational nature of physical computing, students still need to understand key concepts, which can be challenging. Therefore, teaching with physical computing requires the same skills and techniques from the teacher as any other computing activity, particularly involving programming. Children need support to learn effectively and can become discouraged. In encouraging diversity and inclusion, we need to ensure that physical computing lessons are accessible to all students. Here are some top tips:

1. Use scaffolding: When teaching new principles, break then down into tiny steps.

2. Provide working programs to play with first (following Use-Modify-Create or PRIMM as described in **Chapter 23, Worked Examples and Scaffolding Strategies**).

3. Plan group work so that everybody is involved. Use pair-programming (following ideas in **Chapter 16, Peer Collaboration and Pair Programming**) or give your students roles such as designer-programmer-tester-builder.

4. Encourage students to design and plan projects in advance (following ideas in **Chapter 2, Before You Program, Plan!**). Ask students to identify what they want to do that they don't know how to do and research the skills they will need first.

5. Investigate: Get students to work with existing physical computing projects and look at the code—debug it, explain it, annotate it, pull it apart, and so on.

In the next section we look at some examples that you can use in the classroom.

▶ Examples for the Classroom

The following examples encourage primary and secondary learners to solve real-world problems in a creative learning environment. Suggested strategies to assess these activities include self-assessment via a learning journal and peer assessment via oral feedback to focus attention on what has been learned rather than what has been achieved. These example projects would integrate well with social science, science, and/or geography curricula. Many teachers of other subjects have found that physical computing projects can make topics come alive.

▶ Example 1 (Primary Grades): Who Walks the Farthest in a Day?

Overview:

The BBC Micro:bit (http://microbit.org) contains a sensor called an accelerometer, which can detect motion. In this activity, children work in pairs to create a pedometer then use it to collect data about how many steps they have taken.

Learning objectives:

- To program the Micro:bit to detect an input and to output information using the LED display
- To use a variable to store, change, and display a value

Equipment:

- BBC Micro:bits and battery packs
- Micro USB cables and laptops
- Microsoft MakeCode for Micro:bit (https://makecode.microbit.org/)

Introduction:

Have a class discussion about the question, "Who in our class walks farthest in a day?" If pedometers are unfamiliar, explain what they are and how they might help find an answer to the questions.

Model how a pedometer works using a volunteer holding a sign that says "Steps" and the number 0. Ask the volunteer to walk step-by-step across the classroom. Every time they take a step, tell them to add 1 to the current number and write the new number on the sign. This is an "unplugged," or offline, version of the activity to help children understand the code they write.

Main activity:

Demonstrate the MakeCode editor to the whole class and point out features such as the color-coding of the code blocks and how to drag, drop, and connect blocks together to create a script. Show how to download code as a *.hex file (i.e., a format that the Micro:bit understands) and how to transfer this to the Micro:bit, noting that the flashing light on the back of the device shows that the program is downloading.

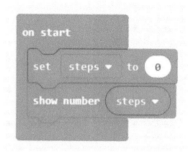

Figure 1a. Example code to set the pedometer to 0

Show the code in Figure 1a in the editor, and ask the children to discuss with a partner what they think it will do. Elicit that this code will set the pedometer to 0 at the start, then demonstrate this is correct by running the code on the emulator. Explain that steps is a variable—a way that computers store, change, and retrieve important pieces of information in a computer program.

Children then work in pairs to work out how to control the incremental increases on the stepometer using the on shake block, which detects the motion input from the accelerometer (Figure 1b). Reference the starter activity as required.

Encourage children to test their code by walking around with the Micro:bit. Can they modify their code so that the steps variable is reset to 0 when Button A is pressed?

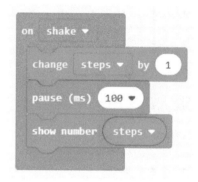

Figure 1b. Example code to increment the step count

Extension:

The data collected from the Micro:bits can be used in a data-handling activity, for example, to create a graph of the number of steps walked by each child.

▶ Example 2 (Secondary Grades): Creating a Weather Sensor

Overview:

The Raspberry Pi computer can be combined with a Sense HAT add-on board to detect inputs from the various sensors. In this activity, students work in small groups to design and create a weather sensor that will measure temperature and humidity and display a message to the user if they can take action. The activity assumes students have had a basic introduction to Python.

Learning objectives:
- To design a weather sensor that detects one or more inputs and use these to produce an output
- To use programming constructs such as conditional statements and Boolean expressions in a text-based programming language

Equipment:

- Raspberry Pi computers with Sense HAT add-on boards (one per group); alternatively, the Sense HAT emulator on the Raspberry Pi, or the Trinket Sense Hat emulator can also be used (https://trinket.io/sense-hat)

- Python 3 either through IDLE or trinket.io

Introduction:

Discuss as a class some real-world scenarios where programming can help solve a problem. An example of this could be a greenhouse that needs to have an air vent opened when a particular temperature is reached and closed if the temperature drops or if it is raining. Split the class into smaller groups, and ask them to decide on a scenario for their group to work on. Encourage them to break this down into specific parts: the weather information do they need to detect, and the message(s) to display.

Main activity:

Students work in small groups (suggested size: three to four students) and look at some examples of existing code off-screen to predict what they will do. They can then try them out and modify values in the code. The examples in Figures 2a,b and 3a,b have been written in trinket.io.

```python
#!/bin/python3

from sense_hat import SenseHat
from time import sleep

sense = SenseHat()
sense.clear()

while True:
  if sense.temp > 30:
    sense.show_message("Too hot")
    sleep (1)
```

```python
#!/bin/python3

from sense_hat import SenseHat

sense = SenseHat()
sense.clear()

while True:
  if sense.humidity > 70:
    sense.clear([0, 255, 255])
  elif sense.humidity < 70:
    sense.clear ([255, 0, 255])
```

Figure 2a. Example code to display a message saying "Too hot" if the temperature is over 30 degrees
Figure 2b. Example code to turn the Sense HAT LED matrix a different color, depending on whether the humidity is above or below 70%

```python
from sense_hat import SenseHat
import time

sense = SenseHat()
sense.clear()

R = (255, 0, 0)
X = (0,0,0)

warning=[
  X,X,X,R,R,R,X,X,
  X,X,X,R,R,R,X,X,
  X,X,X,R,R,R,X,X,
  X,X,X,R,R,R,X,X,
  X,X,X,R,R,R,X,X,
  X,X,X,R,R,R,X,X,
  X,X,X,X,X,X,X,X,
  X,X,X,R,R,R,X,X
  ]

while True:
  if sense.humidity > 80 and sense.temp > 30:
    sense.set_pixels(warning)
```

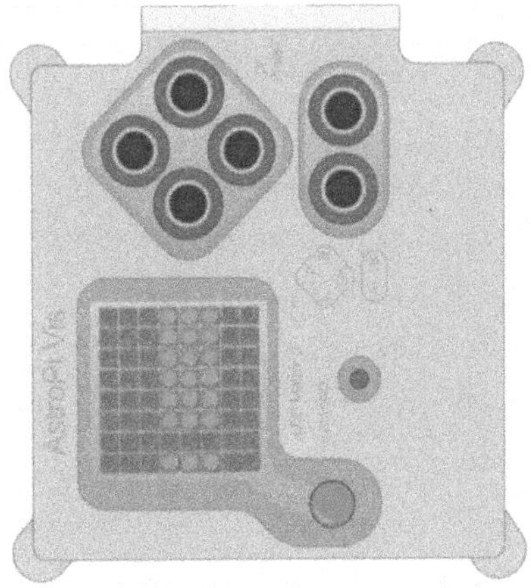

Figure 3a & 3b. Example code (3a) to display an exclamation mark on the Sense HAT interface (3b) if both the temperature is over 30 degrees and the humidity is above 80%

In a whole-class discussion, discuss the commands used to collect the weather readings (`sense.humidity` and `sense.temp`). Elicit three different ways to program the Sense HAT LED matrix. If appropriate, provide online resources to look up additional commands available for programming the Sense HAT, such as pythonhosted.org/sense-hat/api/.

Project work:

This part of the activity is open ended, depending on the scenario that groups have chosen to work on. They can use the examples as the basis for their project, and they may need to investigate and use additional resources (see, for example, on the Raspberry Pi projects website, the Interesting Links and Reading section).

Your role as a teacher is to actively support the groups to make sure they are setting challenging problems, facilitate any disagreements to reach a resolution, and monitor activity to make sure groups stay on task. If groups encounter bugs in their code, encourage them to use debugging strategies such as referring back to the initial examples, using the error message to guide them, or reading their code out loud in the group.

Extension:

Some groups can be stretched by encouraging them to write functions that detect and react to different weather conditions. A show-and-tell presentation session where groups explain what they have learned as well as what they have made is a good reflection session and provides the opportunity to reinforce any key learning points.

BARRIERS AND TIPS ON HOW TO OVERCOME THEM

We all worry that the technology will let us down, and for this reason some teachers may tend to avoid physical computing! Some obstacles can make physical computing difficult to implement in the classroom.

Obstacles that teachers may be conscious of include technical issues, such as the need for software installation for certain physical devices. We know that this can be a real barrier in some schools where technical staff are unwilling to allow individual teachers to install software. Similarly, some schools disable USB ports for security reasons, and they are likely to be needed for physical computing applications. An internet connection may be needed for some web-based applications, including the Micro:bit simulator.

Even without any technical problems, some teachers may be wary of working with physical computing because of the perceived need for an understanding of electronics. At a very practical level, physical computing may include small parts that can be fragile and difficult for children without good fine-motor skills to manage. There is also the additional time that a teacher may need to get the construction kits ready for the class, which can require extreme organization in a busy school day.

Finally, the question of cost cannot be avoided. In a time when we are used to free software and web-based environments, anything physical has a cost. Manufacturers have been working hard to minimize these costs, with the Raspberry Pi Zero and BBC Micro:bit being good examples of kits that don't need to take up the whole year's budget.

Many of these barriers can be overcome by being well organized and encouraging students to be tidy and organized as well. Here are some useful tips to help you survive physical computing lessons:

1. Organize the kit
   a. Train students to put the kit away in your very organized boxes and tell you when something is not working.
   b. Have a place where a nonworking kit can go so it doesn't get mixed up with the working bits!
   c. Have spares, including batteries and leads, in a clear place where students can find them when they need them.

2. Encourage independent learning

   a. Give students a few resources that they can use to troubleshoot problems. Even a few video links can be very helpful and save some disasters.

   b. Get students working in groups so that they get used to troubleshooting between them.

   c. Keep a list of common things that may go wrong—over time you can turn these into a poster on the wall.

3. Timing

   a. Allow time for other activities in the lesson as well as building the project, including getting kit out and putting it away and drawing designs on paper.

   b. Have backup activities for the worst possible scenario, for example, using emulators if the devices don't work.

Work with other teachers to try out the same activities. That way you can share experiences because managing physical computing in a busy classroom can take practice!

RESOURCES AND READINGS

A lot of reading material is available to help you find out more about physical computing. Here are some suggestions for starters. Links are correct at the time of printing.

Websites

https://projects.raspberrypi.org/en/	A range of physical computing projects developed by the Raspberry Pi Foundation team
http://microbit.org https://microbit.org/ideas/	Links involving the Micro:bit
http://physicalcomputing.co.uk/	Example STEM projects involving physical computing
https://education.lego.com/en-gb/primary/intro/c/ computational-thinking	Projects for the Lego WeDo

Books About Physical Computing and Constructionism

Invent to Learn, Sylvia Libow Martinez and Gary Stager

Adventures in Raspberry Pi, Carrie Anne Philbin

Programming the BBC Micro:Bit, Simon Monk

Mindstorms, Seymour Papert

BIBLIOGRAPHY

Blikstein, P. (2013). Gears of our childhood: Constructionist toolkits, robotics, and physical computing, past and future. In *Proceedings of the 12th International Conference on Interaction Design and Children* (IDC '13). ACM, 173¬–182.

Hodges, S., Sentance, S., Ball, T., & Finney, J. (in press). Physical computing: A key element of modern computer science education. *IEEE Computer.*

Horn, M. S., Crouser, R. J., & Bers, M. U. (2012). Tangible interaction and learning: The case for a hybrid approach. *Personal and Ubiquitous Computing, 16*(4), 379–389.

Jin, K., Haynie, K., and Kearns, G. (2016). Teaching elementary students programming in a physical computing Classroom. In *Proceedings of the 17th Annual Conference on Information Technology Education*. Boston.

Marshall, P. (2007). Do tangible interfaces enhance learning? In *Proceedings of TEI'07*, 15–17 Feb 2007, Baton Rouge, LA.

Martinez, S. L., & Stager, G. (2013). Invent to learn. In *Making, Tinkering, and Engineering in the Classroom. Torrance, Canada: Constructing Modern Knowledge.* Constructing Modern Knowledge Press.

Papert, S. (1980). *Mindstorms: Computers, children, and powerful ideas.* Basic Books.

Philbin, C. A. (2017). *Adventures in Raspberry Pi.* John Wiley & Sons.

Przybylla, M., & Romeike, R. (2015) Physical computing and its scope—towards a constructionist computer science curriculum with physical computing. *Informatics in Education, 13*(2), 241–254.

Sentance, S., Waite, J., Hodges, S., MacLeod, E., and Yeomans, L. (2017). Creating cool stuff: Pupils' experiences of the Micro:bit. SIGCSE 2017. *Proceedings of the 48th ACM technical symposium on Computer Science Education.* ACM

Stiller, E. (2009). Teaching programming using bricolage. *Journal of Computing Sciences in Colleges, 24*(6), 35–42.

Yay, My Program Works! Beyond Working Code... Good Habits of Programming

Shuchi Grover

> *Programs must be written for people to read, and only incidentally for machines to execute.*
> – Hal Abelson and Gerald Sussman

INTRODUCTION

One of the uniquely euphoric experiences in an introductory programming classroom is observing students' unbridled joy on seeing their programs work. Anybody who has taught coding can relate to that experience of watching kids cock-a-hoop on getting their first program to work.

However, the goal of teaching introductory programming is to not merely help students write working programs but to also help them develop an appreciation for finer elements of program design and elegance. This implies writing readable and elegant code, and having an understanding of the way the program or algorithm works (yes, novice learners often don't entirely understand why their programs work!) that is deeper than the typical introductory programming experience affords; and. All too often beginners write code that, while being technically functional, is poorly designed and incomprehensible (even to the student). Any teacher who has survived manual grading of student programs can testify to this. As Donald Knuth famously said, "The best programs are written so that computing machines can perform them quickly and so that human beings can understand them clearly."

This chapter presents a list of good programming habits that can be viewed as "programming pearls" (similar to those famously written and compiled by Jon Bentley) that you should encourage your students to keep in mind.

> Teaching students to write efficient and readable programs is a key goal of teaching introductory programming. Note that teaching good habits need not be preceded by instruction in the basic concepts. Teaching good habits of programming is like inculcating good manners or hygiene in children - it is never done too early.

As a teacher, you are in a position to find creative ways to actively encourage these good habits (through showcasing exemplary work, modeling good habits, or even bonus points on projects). It is imperative that this learning be addressed in the classroom early on with sufficient rigour, and be woven in as foundational concepts are introduced to children.

▶ Code Comprehension and Good Habits of Programming

Coding has been likened to a literacy skill. Many liken writing code to writing prose in language arts. Coding provides learners with a way of expressing themselves just as writing does. As Knuth puts it, "A programmer is ideally an essayist who works with traditional aesthetic and literary forms as well as mathematical concepts, to communicate the way that an algorithm works and to convince a reader that the results will be correct." Learning to write code must therefore have parallels to learning to write in a traditional human language.

> As in writing prose, style matters in code as well. It is not enough to merely write code that works. There is more to correctness than working code, and helping students write programs that others (and they themselves) can read and figure out without difficulty should be a key goal of teaching introductory programming.

Good habits of programming are cultivated over time, and thus, it is worthwhile to push learners to practice and perfect writing well-structured readable code that others—and they themselves—can understand. The remainder of the chapter shares practical tips—do's and don'ts—that contribute to helping students develop good habits of programming.

TIPS FOR DEVELOPING GOOD HABITS OF PROGRAMMING

▶ Naming of Variables and Language Constructs

A variable name can seem like a deceptively harmless element of a program. In reality, giving variables meaningful names is a crucial habit of programming that must be inculcated from the moment variables are presented to learners.

In general learners should choose names that are specific and convey their purpose. If a function calculates a tax amount, it should have a name that reflects its intent. If a variable holds a running total of scores of a certain sports team, it should be named accordingly. Naming it merely "score" may not be specific enough. Generic labels such as "func" or "var" only obscure the purpose, as do letters such as x, y, or z, that are commonly used to denote variables in mathematics.

Meaningful variable names are especially advantageous for novices. Joni and Soloway observe,

> When program readers see new code, they ask the questions "Why is this code here? What purpose is it serving in helping to accomplish the overall program tasks?" The experienced program reader will generally assume that there is a useful purpose for all program constructs, and therefore will attempt, when reading code, to find meaning from all parts of the code.

Think of information roles when naming variables. Every information role should have one corresponding variable. A potential problem in text-based programming (that has been solved in the way block-based programs are designed to deal with variables) is that novice programmers use the same name for two different variables because *they* know the different roles of them. These were termed *egocentrism* bugs by Roy Pea in his 1980s research with K-12 students, and they occur when novices design programs only from their perspective and attribute their understanding of things to how the computer "understands" them.

▶ Initializing Variables

Novice programmers tend to incorrectly initialize variables, by either failing to initialize them or initializing them more than once. This habit of programming must be addressed in lock-step with an introduction to variables. Variables are initialized in three basic ways: assignment to a value through I/O (when an input value is assigned to a variable); assignment to a specific (hard-coded) value; or assignment to a value that results from a computation. Ergo, variables should be initialized in only one place. If a variable gets its initial value through user input, it need not necessarily be initialized to another value through an assignment command elsewhere. Variables initialized multiple times usually do not cause the code to fail to work;

---

however, they do lead to false expectations about the code and difficulty in comprehension from the perspective of the program reader. **Chapter 22, Variables,** has more on variable naming and initialization.

▶ Commenting Code

The importance of code comments cannot be overstated. Code comments are imperative for ensuring code readability. Comments may also effectively serve as a record of the algorithm and the logic conceived by the coder. Comments at the beginning of the program should give a brief, broad explanation of what the program does. Comments at the beginning of functions should provide a brief idea of what that code chunk or function does. Such comments may also state the return value and its type so that a reader of the program knows how to use the function if they need to (as part of a different program). Comments for individual commands—especially for small programs— should be encouraged so that the teacher (or a fellow student) understands the purported behavior of that command.

Furthermore, *comments are a form of self-explanation*. Self-explanation is a technique wherein learners are asked to explain with clarity the meaning of passages of text or, in the case of programming, what a command (or set of commands) is achieving. In programming, as in other subjects, extensive evidence from research shows learners accrue concrete benefits from self-explanation.

> Code comments are a form of self-explanation that are beneficial to both the student and to the teacher and to anyone else who may (re)use or read the code.

Often, students are averse to having to add comments to their code. Again, this habit of programming can be encouraged by underscoring its benefits and also by adding extrinsic motivation in the form of commenting awards or extra points in the scoring rubric

▶ Modularizing Code and Using Functions

▶ Avoiding Duplication of Code

A good habit of programming is to eliminate redundancy and duplication of code within the program. Duplicate chunks of code in a program present a perfect opportunity to help students see the value of—and need to—create functions (or "user-defined blocks" in block-based programming languages like Scratch and Snap!). See **Chapter 14, Modularity With Methods And Functions**, for more ideas on instilling sound habits of modularizing code.

▶ Avoiding Merging Functional Plans and Goals of a Program

The *Rainfall problem* is an enduring research exercise used to examine novice programmers' understanding in introductory programming courses (at the undergraduate level): *Write a program that reads in integers and outputs their average. Stop reading when the value 99999 is input.* The seemingly simple problem that requires programmers to take in input, sum the inputs, compute the average (which involves counting the number of inputs), and output the average has often caused programmers in introductory classes to stumble, and has revealed several difficulties that novices face in learning to program. The problem illustrates the semantics of coherently weaving together disparate components of a problem into a program. It turns out that interleaving the goals of the program (reading the input and adding and checking for the sentinel value, all interleaved in the looping structure) tripped up most programmers. Here are the salient takeaways from the Rainfall problem:

1. **Minimize having merged goals in your program.**
   Try to use a separate plan to realize each program goal. The complex issues novice learners face in the Rainfall problem related to merged plans.

2. **Don't merge validation of input with any other goal.**

Recent research in an introductory functional programming class using Racket (and a slightly different wording of the problem (to include a list of numbers instead of I/O) finally succeeded in making progress on the Rainfall problem.

▶ Avoiding Unreachable Code

Unreachable or extraneous code is simply poor programming. Encourage students to make sure that all portions of their code are useful to the task at hand. Unreachable code is an undesirable quality of programs, even when it doesn't cause the program to be buggy.

> *Extraneous code tends to lead program readers to expect program plans that are inappropriate for the program actions the programmer is attempting to realize, and therefore can be misleading during program comprehension*
> —Joni & Soloway (1986).

▶ Cleaning Up Extraneous Code

Children are taught from an early age to tidy up their physical play and workspaces after they are done with an activity, even though messiness may be absolutely fine while they are actively engaged in the activity. Tidying up our programs is another good habit of programming that helps others (and the student) to understand a program. Extraneous code that does not play a role in the program is confusing and sometimes misleading. Leaving extraneous blocks of code is a poor habit of programming that is unfortunately a by-product of the design of environments like Scratch and Snap!. As teachers, we need to actively discourage this practice and make sure kids clean up the scripting area of all extraneous blocks of code. (Perhaps scoring rubrics or other incentives can help with this). Even in text-based programming, we often have chunks of code that may have been commented out in the course of debugging or iterative program design that are left in at the end, even when there is no longer a use for them in the program. Be sure to delete them!

▶ Iteratively Building and Refining Programs

Iterative refinement is the process of developing a program by starting with a simplified version of a problem and adding detail and functionality to it bit by bit, or decomposing a problem into subparts, and tackling it in phases. A key aspect of iterative refinement is that the program is built in chunks with frequent rounds of testing and debugging in between. This helps with identifying bugs—if one tests a large portion of code with various components and functions, it is harder to identify the source of an error. Also see **Chapter 2, Before You Program, Plan!** for ideas on problem decomposition, and **Chapter 20, Testing and Debugging**.

▶ Testing With a Range of Inputs (and Error Handling)

Students typically exult if their program works with their inputs. But in reality, their testing is often biased to the use of valid inputs. Inculcating the habit of testing the program for a range of inputs—valid, invalid, and even "illogical"—helps them realize the need for robust tightening of conditionals that regulate input values. Attending to the program's response to wrong input is as important as testing with valid input. Testing with invalid and illogical inputs is also a good opportunity to impart sensitivity to error handling (how one can make a program react appropriately to bad inputs) and error messages.

Below are examples in Scratch that demonstrate these issues.

Example 1 (Figure 1): Checking against a "divide by 0" error in a program that calculates the average of a certain number of scores. In Program B below, the additional `IF` statement checks if `NumScores` is greater than zero before performing the division of `SumofScores` by `NumScores`.

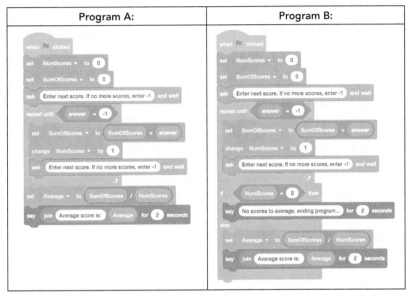

Figure 1. Checking for division by 0 when computing the average of a set of scores

Example 2 (Figure 2a): Validating user input to restrict input to a certain desired range in a program. Below is the code for a "generic polygon-maker" program. It is also a good example to demonstrate use of the `Repeat Until` loop construct for such purposes—to keep asking for an input until a valid value is entered by the user.

Example 3 (Figure 2b): Guarding the program against "illogical" inputs. Ask your students for "illogical" values for age if this program responds with a "You Are in Middle or High School" and how it can be fixed. Such an example is a good demonstration of the perils of using a catch-all `ELSE` statement when the code must work for only a fixed ranges of values.

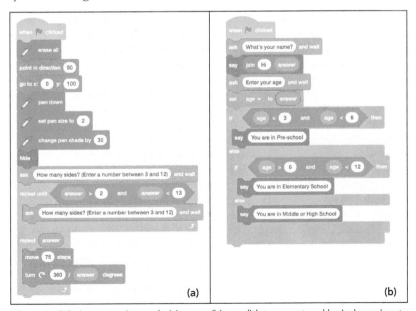

Figure 2a & b. Incorporating code (a) or not (b) to validate correct and logical user inputs

▶ Avoiding Fine-Grained and Bottom-Up Coding

(This section has been drawn—along with examples—from a well-cited research paper by Orni Meerbaum-Salant along with coauthors Michal Armoni and Mordechai Ben-Ari that documents this issue in detail.)

We often notice a troubling trend in students' block-based code in Scratch and other similar environments like Snap!. It is the creation of multiple, separate chunks of code that are all attached to different start blocks (usually when green flag clicked, but it could also be other event triggers). Even if not actively encouraged, this issue is usually ignored (because teachers assume it's OK). Teachers should, however, actively dissuade students from engaging in this poor or bad habit of programming that is sometimes referred to as *fine-grained coding*. Although Scratch supports convenient decomposition into multiple scripts for multiple sprites, this ease of decomposition fosters a habit of extreme fine-grained coding.

This fine-grained approach is not necessarily the fault of the teacher but a practice encouraged by tinkering approaches to programming espoused by the design of several popular block-based programming environments. It involves a bottom-up development process that starts at the individual block level rather than a more wholesome top-down approach that begins with a learner planning the algorithm. Having a good algorithm before starting programming will usually end with the desirable, cleaner program structure.

As a case in point, here are two scripts written in Scratch for the same sprite (Figure 3).

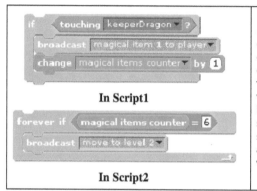

"Although the three steps *as a whole* form a logically coherent unit, this student decomposed it further, creating a separate script for the third step of deciding whether to move to the next level. Furthermore, this script was for a *different* sprite, one that had nothing at all to do with the event of winning a fight!"

Figure 3. Example of fine-grained decomposition of program tasks that leads to suboptimal code [Source: Meerbaum-Salant, Armoni, & Ben-Ari (2011)]

This fine-grained decomposition also adversely affects the use of control structures into suboptimal code that is inefficient and inelegant. For example, in Script 2, the forever if causes a busy wait loop instead of the use of a simple IF block structure. Similarly, to implement if <cond> do <op1> else do <op2>, it has been observed that students will often decompose the problem into two IFs to handle the two outcomes of the <cond> condition —if <cond> do <op1> and an if <not cond> do <op2>. We need to help students to realize the operational distinction between these two options. In the former, <cond> is evaluated once, and if it is true the else code is ignored. In the latter, <cond> is evaluated twice in succession.

The use of loops is similarly suboptimal in fine-grained coding. In the next example all three scripts could be combined into one repeat until loop that works with no busy wait loops.

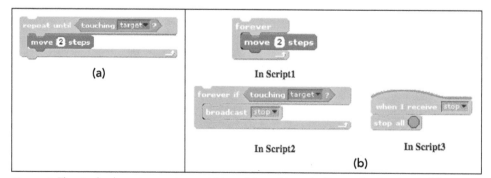

Figure 4. The single elegant repeat until loop (a) combines the fine-grained scripts in (b). [Source: Meerbaum-Salant, Armoni, & Ben-Ari (2011)]

It has been widely observed that the `repeat until` loop construct is not introduced to children until much later, with `forever` loops and `if` conditions taught as the preferred way to code the checking of conditions that terminate a loop. In reality, a `repeat until` loop is a coherent logical looping concept that closely mimics the `while` loop where the body of the loop and the condition for its termination are co-located and easy to understand. Anecdotal evidence suggests that Scratch code created by students is often unstructured, spaghetti-like, and so full of multiple scripts that it almost loses any semblance of logical coherence.

> A good habit of programming to instill in children using Scratch and Snap! would be to use structured constructs like `repeat-until` loops unless there is a special reason not to!

Modularity is indeed desirable in code as explained earlier, but taking that principle to the extreme as in environments like Scratch and Snap! can be extremely problematic.

▶ Avoiding Inappropriate Use of Conditionals and Loops

1. **Don't use a while loop when it will execute at most once**. Students should use an `IF` instead. This is essential from a code readability perspective as well—when a reader encounters a `WHILE` loop, one of the expectations that is set up is that the body of this loop will repeat, with a looping action, some number of times and terminate when the conditional clause becomes false.

2. Do not place identical code into both branches of an `IF-THEN-ELSE` construct (or all branches of a multiple branching). This is inappropriate conditionalization, because the code is invariant with respect to the outcome of the conditional `IF` test. The code thus created may not be incorrect; however, doing so makes the code confusing. The unnecessary conditionalization of code makes it difficult for the program reader to distinguish code in the branch body that is dependent on the conditional test from code in the branch body that is independent of this test. As teachers, we need to insist that students place only code that is dependent on the outcome of the `IF` test inside the scope of the `IF` block. In doing so, we also give our students the opportunity to systematically sort out the scope of their conditionalizations for themselves.

READINGS AND RESEARCH

Joni and Soloway's 1986 paper, *But My Program Runs! Discourse Rules for Novice Programmers*, provided the inspiration for both the title and the content of this chapter. *Programming Pearls* by Jon Bentley is also an ageless, relevant classic, even though several ideas are in the context of to yesteryear programming languages. Meerbaum-Salant, Armoni, and Ben-Ari's 2011 paper reflects many of the concerns of K-12 CS teachers related to learning programming in environments like Scratch and Snap!, which encourage fine-grained, bottom-up programming. Grover's research at Stanford revolved around how to create a middle school curriculum that used Scratch but consciously mitigated such influences of the programming environment. Several Scratch examples in this chapter are drawn from that research. Bugs related to variables and variable naming that reflect egocentrism biases are described in Roy Pea's research (Pea, 1986). Finally, Soloway's research on the Rainfall problem inspired some of the tips. Check out Soloway's 1986 paper and also Kathi Fisler's recent research on their success with the problem using functional programming and scaffolds suggested in *How to Design Programs* by Felleisen, Findler, Flatt, and Krishnamurthi.

When students develop good habits of programming, they write cleaner, less cluttered code that has a coherent logical structure. Such "clean code" in turn, makes the code easier to read, debug, and maintain (add or make changes). I close this chapter with one more quote on "clean code" by Grady Booch, a guru in the field of software engineering.

Clean code is simple and direct. Clean code reads like well-written prose. Clean code never obscures the designer's intent but rather is full of crisp abstractions and straightforward lines of control. —Grady Booch

BIBLIOGRAPHY

Bentley, J. (1986). *Programming pearls.* Addison-Wesley Professional. (First Edition).

Grover, S., Pea, R., & Cooper, S. (2015). Designing for deeper learning in a blended computer science course for middle school students. *Computer science education, 25*(2), 199-237.

Felleisen, M., Findler, R. B., Flatt, M., & Krishnamurthi, S. (2018). *How to design programs: An introduction to programming and computing.* MIT Press.

Fisler, K. (2014). The recurring rainfall problem. In *Proceedings of the 10th Annual Conference on International Computing Education Research* (pp. 35–42).

Joni, S. N. A., & Soloway, E. (1986). But my program runs! Discourse rules for novice programmers. *Journal of Educational Computing Research, 2*(1), 95–125.

Meerbaum-Salant, O., Armoni, M., & Ben-Ari, M. (2011). Habits of programming in scratch. In *Proceedings of the 16th Annual Joint Conference on Innovation and Technology in Computer Science Education* (pp. 168–172).

Pea, R. D. (1986). Language-independent conceptual "bugs" in novice programming. *Journal of Educational Computing Research, 2*(1), 25-36.

Soloway, E. (1986). Learning to program—learning to construct mechanisms and explanations. *Communications of the ACM, 29*(9), 850–858.

Zestful Learning

Bryan Twarek

INTRODUCTION

Zest is the feeling of spirited satisfaction associated with the intrinsic joy of learning. Both the process and the outcome of learning involves curiosity, collaboration, fun, and pride. *Zestful learning* (synonymous with *joyful learning*) positively influences students' attitudes, engagement, self-efficacy, and consequently, all learning outcomes. When students are motivated, engaged, and unimpaired by stress, they are better able to process information and make connections critical to the learning at hand. San Francisco Unified School District (SFUSD) computer science (CS) specialist Irene Nolan notes, "If you construct a classroom environment that is joyful, it creates intrinsic rewards and leads to positive feelings about CS. Students think about CS as something that they want to continue learning and exploring."

> *True happiness comes from the joy of deeds well done, the zest of creating things new.*
> – Antoine de Saint-Exupery

A zestful class more closely resembles a writer's workshop in elementary school than a college introductory CS classroom. Students spend the majority of time creating and working, rather than listening to lectures. They are deeply engaged in content and ask lots of questions. They create things they care about and receive targeted feedback as guidance; they are proud to showcase and celebrate their work. It is clear that students want to be there; they lose track of time, and they are reluctant to pause their work when the class ends.

Author and curriculum writer Grant Smith illustrated joyful learning through an unexpected example: A group of seventh-grade girls created a project to memorialize a student at their school who passed away. They were driven by a meaningful purpose and worked together to create an animation project to celebrate the student, support from their teacher and peers, and the opportunity to showcase it to the school community. Even in a tragic situation, their experience demonstrates important qualities of joyful learning.

TENETS OF ZESTFUL LEARNING

This chapter describes the tenets of zestful learning and explains how K–12 teachers can create such learning environments in their introductory computer science classes. To create zestful learning environments, teachers of all grade levels should create opportunities for their students to explore and discover, create relevant projects, showcase their work, and be supported and validated by their teachers and peers.

▶ 1. Create Relevant Projects

Teachers need to create relevant learning experiences for their students. When students find the content relevant (culturally and otherwise), they are more engaged, less stressed, and better able to learn. But how can teachers do this while still meeting standards and addressing the varied interests within one class?

First, they can select examples and make connections that their students will understand and appreciate. However, this first requires that teachers develop relationships with and seek to understand their students.

> Elementary CS specialist in the San Francisco Unified School District (SFUSD) Michelle G. Lee asks her students on the first day of CS class to write about or draw their interests. Then, she creates a word cloud to represent the variety of interests in the class, which include pop culture references, activities like drawing, and favorite subjects. Michelle then references these interests frequently while creating analogies and modeling. She frequently utilizes interactive coding ("code-alongs") to demonstrate a new concept while drawing suggestions from the class or referencing interests from the word cloud. She makes her examples relevant and students engaged by having different students pick the character, record the sounds, decide how many times to repeat, and determine what happens next.

Second, teachers can create greater relevance by allowing students to have choice in both what they create and how they create it. CS is a beautiful medium for self-expression, and teachers can help students develop a new way to express themselves and explore their interests and passions. Michelle notes, "CS is a place where students can integrate their interests and work on projects they care about. They have not only daily permission but a wholehearted invitation for them to make their learning meaningful to them." Rather than designing or assigning projects they think students will like, teachers should ask them what they want to create and support them in creating those projects. This leads not only to joy but also self-efficacy. Students are more motivated, accepting of errors, able to persevere, and confident in asking questions.

Allowing students to make some choices in how they work also improves engagement. Teachers could allow students to choose their partners, decide whether they listen to music, and select the method or order in which they approach their work and how they demonstrate their understanding.

▶ 2. Scaffolded Creativity

Although teachers should help students create meaningful projects, this does not mean they should create a free-for-all environment. In fact, fully open-ended projects can lead to a wide range in engagement across the class; whereas some may be very motivated to implement their ideas, many students may struggle to make steady progress or even get started. A lack of structure can also lead to inconsistent learning outcomes. If students can create whatever they want, some projects naturally lean toward specific concepts and structures, and teachers will likely struggle to support and measure students' progress toward meeting all course standards.

Scaffolding the creative process supports students to learn through creating, while also leading them toward common learning outcomes. That is, students are not following stepwise directions; they have sufficient but constrained choice. For example, in an elementary unit focused on loops, a teacher may prompt students to animate a character's motion in a scene, with action before and after. Students choose the character(s), background, and what happens in the scene. This allows students to create original projects based on their interests but still demonstrate mastery of the focal standard. In his Processing-based AP Computer Science A class (a computer science course for advanced high school students in the US), Art Simon challenges his students to create a fireworks-like ("starfield") animation to demonstrate their understanding of inheritance and encapsulation (see Figure 1). Although all students followed the same basic requirements, they each chose their own way to creatively apply their learning, with projects ranging from abstract art to exploding volcanoes, cotton candy, and what is in Taylor Swift's mind.

Figure 1. Student creativity and artwork using Processing demonstrating object-oriented programming concepts in an advanced high school CS class

A useful structure to provide scaffolding with creative projects is the *Use-Modify-Create* progression (described in **Chapter 23, Worked Examples and Scaffolding Strategies**). In SFUSD, we designed our curricular units to first introduce a concept using unplugged activities or other ways to connect to prior knowledge. Then, students jump right into exploring a pre-built project. They work to understand how it works and how a focal concept is integrated. Next, they make adjustments to customize an existing project before they design and implement their own original project. The unit culminates with students showcasing their work and reflecting on their learning. (See Figure 2.)

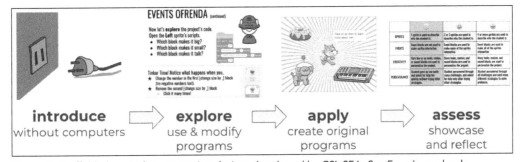

Figure 2. Scaffolded curricular progression designed and used by CSinSF in San Francisco schools

Teachers should support students during each stage, but this is especially important during the Create stage, and different students need different types of support. The Universal Design for Learning (UDL) framework (described in detail in **Chapter 21**) provides guidance on how teachers can support their students' individual learning needs in a variety of ways. Providing multiple entry points to a project is a common strategy to prepare students and alleviate frustration. Though some students will create their projects from scratch, others may benefit from selecting a starter project with media assets preloaded or with "exploded code" (i.e., teacher-curated snippets of code that can be assembled together, like a "word bank" for writing) or creating a storyboard. See **Chapter 2** on more ideas for planning before programming. Figure 3 shows a student's storyboard before coding. For more ideas on scaffolding learning of programming, see **Chapter 23**.

> *The joy comes from students being prepared to actually create the project relevant to their interests.*
> —SFUSD CS specialist Bill Marsland

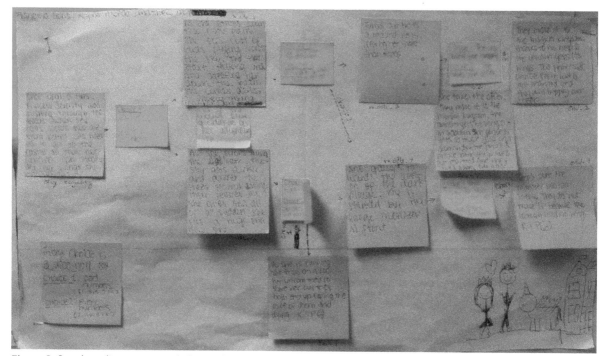

Figure 3. Storyboarding a program helps students plan before coding the project [Image courtesy: Meg Ray]

▶ 3. Showcasing and Authentic Audience

Students' voices shine in zestful classrooms. Teachers should create regular opportunities for students to share their voice and showcase their work and what they have learned. Having an audience inspires authenticity. Students are motivated by the opportunity to present work to their peers, families, and community members. They can also learn new skills and gain inspiration by seeing each other's work. Seeing diverse ways to approach a problem adds to the fun.

There are many different methods for showcasing student work. Teachers can randomly select (using equity sticks or a random name selector) one to three students to project their projects and quickly share progress and learnings to the full class. They can also involve all students at once through online review and commenting (each student comments on an assigned table's work), a gallery walk (students walk around to review work displayed on peers' computers), or a musical chairs–like rotation. Older students can provide targeted feedback based on focal concepts. Even the youngest students can and should showcase their work. An effective technique is having students sit in a circle, pass tablets in a clockwise direction when prompted, and note out loud things they like using sentence frames. Teachers could also use other showcase techniques: rotating concentric circles to match students one to one to give each other feedback; inviting families, other teachers, or community members to view presentations; and displaying student projects in the cafeteria during lunch or in the hallways during parent teacher conferences (see Figure 4).

It is useful to dedicate the last 5 to 10 minutes of every class period, or at least several times per week, to showcasing. Doing so creates urgency and a sense of purpose during each class period. It also normalizes sharing one's work and receiving feedback. When this practice becomes a regular routine, students look forward to the opportunity to showcase and are more invested, knowing that they will show their peers what they have created. **Chapter 6, Feedback Through Formative Check-Ins**, also shares specific ideas and worksheets on organizing student showcases so that students can be guided on how to present and provide feedback, and thus learn from this process.

Figure 4. Project showcases provide an opportunity for students to share and demo their creations. [Image courtesy: Meg Ray]

▶ 4. Supportive Classroom Culture

Scaffolded creativity and showcasing are effective only when teachers first establish a safe and supportive classroom culture. Many students are scared to try, fear failure, may be reluctant to share their work, don't persist when encountering bugs in programs, and are wary of asking questions or volunteering answers in front of peers. Teachers should help students develop strong practices and dispositions of creative professionals, such as being resilient and taking reasonable risks; knowing how and when to seek help, as well as how to help oneself; being collaborative and supportive of teammates; and thinking flexibly. Teachers can achieve this through thoughtful modeling, clear outcomes and deliverables, ongoing feedback and reinforcement, and consistent and equitable classroom rules, norms, and procedures. In addition to the ideas presented below, check out **Chapter 17, Questions and Inquiry**, as well as **Chapter 6, Feedback Through Formative Check-Ins**, for specific and practical ideas on supporting students through creative projects.

To support students with creative projects, teachers should act as a coach and mentor. They should frequently check in and provide feedback. Meg Ray, an author, instructional coach, and consultant, describes how she coached students in the classroom: "I ask critical questions, help brainstorm solutions, suggest resources, and provide targeted feedback. The goal is to support students in owning their work, persevering, and being proud in the end. I create structures to support students in setting daily and weekly goals, monitoring progress toward goals, and making adjustments when off-track toward goals."

A supportive culture enables students to feel comfortable with the vulnerability involved in sharing their work. It is helpful to establish clear guidelines and protocols for showcasing and feedback so that students know what to expect. For example, elementary teachers may use the two stars and a wish peer feedback structure, so students come to expect two compliments and one constructively worded suggestion, rather than criticism. Encouraging students to share works in progress, rather than finished or polished projects, helps others feel more comfortable sharing work that is not complete or perfect. They can describe their process and invite peers to interact with their project and ask questions.

When first starting showcases, it can be helpful for teachers to ask one or a few students during work time if they are willing to share their work at the end of class. They can prime students and help them prepare or practice what they will say in front of the class. Once routines are established and showcasing is normalized, it is preferable to randomly select students or create a calendar for the showcase so that participation is more equitable. Teachers can build confidence by debriefing

PEER FEEDBACK: TWO STARS AND A WISH

Share **two** things you like about a classmate's project.

Share **one** way to improve their project.

	My favorite part was _____.
⭐ ⭐	I like the way you _____.
	I'm excited to learn how you _____.
	What if _____?
🤞	Next time, try _____.
	An idea I had is _____.

with students after showcasing and providing specific feedback (e.g., "I noticed how Desiree reacted when you ___. You inspired her to ___!").

Michelle G. Lee is an expert at creating safe and joyful classroom environments where student voices shine. This requires building relational trust with students. Teachers do this by learning more about students and their individual interests and strengths. Her success in establishing strong relationships and an inclusive, positive classroom environment allows all students to feel comfortable sharing. She shared this story about a student who was once reluctant to share: "One of my third-grade students, who was two grade levels behind in reading, struggled to get started with Scratch. One day, she was really excited to have taught herself how to change the size of an apple sprite. I asked if she wanted to teach the class at the end of the day. She slid right into my chair and confidently explained her process. The class erupted into cheers for her!"

▶ 5. Discovery and Exploration

Students need time for exploration because they better understand and retain what they find interesting and have figured out for themselves. This is supported by a long line of research, including Piaget's "constructivism" and Papert's "constructionism" as discussed in **Chapter 3, Creative Coding** and **Chapter 8, Chapter 8, Hard Fun With Hands-on Constructionist Project-Based Learning.** Teachers face very real challenges around time and priorities, but it is important to create time and space to support students' curiosity and discovery.

One simple method to support discovery is through tinkering. When introducing a new concept or learning tool (e.g., programming language, robot, data analysis tool), teachers can give students (limited) time to play and dig right in, with minimal instructions. Students will naturally test, ask questions, and learn through their hands-on exploration. This is even more effective when students work collaboratively and discuss their observations and learnings.

Teachers should spotlight what students have discovered, by asking them to share out or through positive narration (e.g., "I see that Gloria discovered how to turn on the LEDs with a button press"). Students become motivated and inspired by trying to figure out how to do similar things that their peers did. Some teachers dedicate time at the beginning or end of a class to allow a student to demonstrate something new they learned recently.

Teachers can also expand on this showcasing of student discovery by creating "classroom experts." All students have talents and strengths from which their peers can benefit. When teachers help students identify these and make these visible, they validate students' abilities and build confidence. A simple way to do this is putting students' names on a poster, pocket chart, or spreadsheet, next to something they are willing to help their peers with. For some, this will be specific programming or technical skills, but for others, it may be designing characters or user testing. Students often learn more effectively through peer instruction, and this also eases the burden of the teacher having to answer all questions. Less formally, teachers can also suggest that a student teaches another peer (e.g., "I know that Javon was also trying to import his own music. Could you teach him?"). Teachers can support students in using language rather than taking over the computer or just showing them. This helps both students learn more effectively, because having to clearly communicate deepens understanding for the student who is explaining, too. This may not come naturally to students, so teachers can help build their skills by modeling and providing suggested language (e.g., "If you want to ___, first you should ___, and then ___.").

Another strategy is designing learning experiences that inspire just-in-time learning as suggested in **Chapter 3, Creative Coding** and **Chapter 8, Hard Fun With Hands-on Constructionist Project-Based Learning**. For example, if a teacher wants to introduce variables, she may prompt students to create a catch or chase game. This type of project will lead many students to want to learn how to keep score to improve their games. When students have a need for a concept, it becomes more concrete, and they are more likely to learn it effectively.

▶ 6. Physical Activity

Learning to program can be challenging and frustrating, and pausing work to allow for a quick conversation, exercise, or dance party can reduce stress, heighten focus, and improve creativity. A "brain break" allows students to rest and reset, so they are prepared to jump back in. Even a short amount of time can result in a significant impact. At the secondary level, this may be allowing students a 3-minute break to get out of their seat and chat with a friend, and at the elementary level, a great tool to use is GoNoodle.com, which has lots of fun, short videos that inspire movement. Some physical movement during a lesson is important because sitting for an entire 40- to 90-minute period can be taxing for people of all ages, and physical activity improves attention. Even rotating seats or table groups is helpful in introducing some movement.

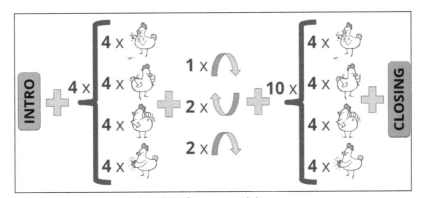

Figure 5. Creating visual algorithms for songs and dances

Additionally, as described extensively in **Chapter 7, Guided Exploration With Unplugged Activities**, teaching CS concepts without computers is effective because it helps make the concepts more concrete. In addition to that chapter, you can check out CS Unplugged (CSUnplugged.org) and Code.org for a range of unplugged activities. Also, the Mozilla Learning Center has a lesson involving relay races to sequence common tags in a webpage. Teachers can also create their own unplugged activities using simple manipulatives; for instance, they can give students printed code blocks or have them write commands on cards and put them in order to reverse-engineer a displayed program. They can also play games; charades can be used to act out what happens before, during, and after a loop block, and *Simon Says* can be used to practice conditionals and Boolean logic (as described in **Chapters 7 and 15**). Another example is creating visual algorithms to represent instructions for songs and dances (like the chicken dance—see Figure 5). Unplugged activities are relevant even in higher grades with advanced programming courses, like using LEGO blocks to model software engineering concepts. The tangible nature of these activities not only leads to greater understanding of concepts but are a lot of fun.

ACKNOWLEDGMENTS

We would like to extend our gratitude to Meg Ray, Grant Smith, Michelle G. Lee, Bill Marsland, Irene Nolan, Art Simon, Andrew Rothman, and the entire CSinSF community for shaping this chapter and contributing ideas, examples, and artifacts.

READINGS AND RESOURCES

Many classroom examples, ideas, and experiences presented in this chapter are drawn from CSinSF (https://www.csinsf.org/)—an effort to bring computer science to every school, classroom, and student in the San Francisco Unified School District that was launched and shaped for 5 years by author Bryan "BT" Twarek. The CSinSF team worked closely with and borrowed from other collaborators to create their curriculum, including the ScratchEd team at Harvard University and the Computing for ANyONe (CANON) lab at the University of Chicago. The CSinSF K–12 computer science curriculum is accessible at CSinSF.org/curriculum.

Art Simon's Processing-based AP CS A course available at https://apcslowell.github.io has lots of great projects and examples. The Central Connecticut State University created a comprehensive set of playful activities to teach software engineering concepts using LEGO (Kurkovsky, Ludi, & Clark, 2019). Check out https://web.ccsu.edu/lego-se/ for more. Check out CS Unplugged (CSUnplugged.org) and Code.org for fun lesson plans and activities that introduce CS and programming concepts. Gonoodle.com has a treasure trove of fun physical classroom activities.

BIBLIOGRAPHY

Ackermann, E. (2001). Piaget's constructivism, Papert's constructionism: What's the difference? *Future of Learning Group Publication, 5*(3), 438.

Bell, T., Alexander, J., Freeman, I., & Grimley, M. (2009). Computer science unplugged: School students doing real computing without computers. *The New Zealand Journal of Applied Computing and Information Technology, 13*(1), 20–29.

Kurkovsky, S., Ludi, S., & Clark, L. (2019, February). Active learning with LEGO for software requirements. In *Proceedings of the 50th ACM Technical Symposium on Computer Science Education* (pp. 218–224).

Willis, J. (2007). The Neuroscience of Joyful Education. *Engaging the Whole Child* [Online]. Available from http://www.ascd.org/publications/educational-leadership/summer07/vol64/num09/The-Neuroscience-of-Joyful-Education.aspx

Index

Index

C++ xix, 2, 105, 106, 230
Callback 38, 39
   See also *Events*
CANON lab 245, 248, 274
Celebrating mistakes 79, 81, 119, 217
   See also *Growth mindset*
Center for Applied Special Technology (CAST) 219, 220, 225, 226
Chained expressions 208
Character 15, 77, 105, 139, 172, 186, 228, 244, 268
Circles of evaluation 164, 165
Circuit 2, 76, 78, 80, 91, 163, 252
Circuit Playground 76, 252
Class (object) 146, 149
Classroom culture
   See *Culture*
Clean code
   See *Habit(s) of programming*
Clojure 109
CODAP 109
Code comprehension 52, 54, 243
   See also *Code reading*
Code Jumper 110
Code.org 46, 47, 107, 178, 273, 274
Code reading 61, 66, 115, 151, 240, 243, 245, 246, 248, 260
Code tracing 51, 61, 66, 70, 72, 141, 142, 143, 151, 201, 208, 213, 214, 243, 244, 246, 248
Cognitive load 27, 96, 100, 149, 220, 230, 240, 242, 248
Coin change problem 86
   See also *Count Change Problem*
Collaboration xviii, 12, 24, 58, 75, 91, 95, 122, 171–179, 221, 251, 253, 271
   See also *Peer collaboration*
Communication 50, 80, 81, 82, 101, 113, 122, 123, 127, 174, 175, 177, 212
Community xii, xiv, 26, 27, 56, 75, 76, 81, 91, 101, 104, 121, 123, 124, 126, 126–128, 127, 128, 267, 270, 274
   See also *Scratch: community*
Computability 10
Computational thinking (CT) xvi, 10–12, 17, 21, 23, 51, 62, 73, 74, 81, 83, 91, 96–98, 108, 113, 115, 124, 155, 188, 210, 218, 239, 249
Computer science xiii–xvii, 9, 48, 73, 74, 85, 97, 98, 112, 124, 171, 239, 266, 274
   definition xiv
Computing
   See also *Computer science*
   definition xiv
Computing education xiii–xv
Conceptual understanding 52, 64, 66, 143, 150, 153, 240, 248
Condition 53, 68, 158, 163, 170, 189–192, 201, 204–207, 205, 210, 212, 213, 216, 242, 264, 265
Conditional 4, 50, 52, 67, 77, 108, 131, 132, 136, 158, 163, 166, 167, 186, 191, 196, 204–210, 216, 254, 265
Constant (programming) 88, 145, 227, 231, 233, 238
Constraints 20, 55, 70, 76–78, 81, 165

Constructionism 22, 26, 27, 76, 81, 97, 153, 250, 272, 274
   See also *Papert, Seymour*
Construction kit 76, **256**
Constructivism **153**, **155**, **272**, **274**
   See also *Constructionism*
Content knowledge xvii, 114, 155
Control flow 64, 142, 189, 190, 192, 208, 212, 214, 243
Control structure 106, 264
Count Change Problem 198, 199
   See also *Coin change problem*
Crazy Characters 73
Creative coding 7, 22–27, 76, 85, 272, 273
   See also *Creativity*
Creative computing 25, 77, 81, 90, 251
   See also *Creative coding*
Creativity xv, 22, 23, 26, 27, 29, 44, 50, 56, 58, 76–78, 81, 90, 98, 108, 171, 181, 224, 250, 268–269, 271, 273
Critical thinking 114, 117
CSinSF 269, 274
CS Teaching Tips 121, 124
CS Unplugged 10, 72, 273–274
   See also *Unplugged activities*
Cultural xxi, 23, 101, 125–129
Culturally relevant pedagogy (CRP) xviii, 121, 125–129, 268
Culturally responsive approaches
   See *Culturally relevant pedagogy (CRP)*
Culture 22–26, 51, 75, 119, 120, 124, 127, 172, 217, 218, 268, 271

Dash and Dot 107, 252
Data science 25, 84, 91, 109, 127, 253–254
Data structure xv, xvii, xviii, 23, 28–37, 85, 90, 106, 108, 163, 228
Data type 31, 106, 147, 154, 227, 228
   See also *Variables: Types*
Debug(ging) 19, 23, 31, 46, 47, 51, 53, 55, 56, 60, 64, 77, 79, 84, 89, 104, 108, 117, 119, 130, 136, 138, 146, 172, 184, 187, 211–218, 223–225, 242, 253, 256, 262, 265
Decision-making 4, 16
Decomposition 12, 15, 17–19, 21, 51, 56, 108, 115, 116, 138, 242, 262, 264
   See also *Modularity*
Design xvii, xviii, xix, 7, 11, 12, 17, 23, 38, 39, 44, 72, 73, 76, 78, 80, 91, 99, 107, 113, 115–118, 120, 122, 127, 133, 136, 150, 151, 153, 155, 156, 172, 176–178, 187, 192, 212, 216, 217, 220, 221, 223, 225, 239, 240, 242, 244, 247, 250, 251, 253, 254, 259, 260, 262, 264, 266, 269
   See also *Universal Design for Learning*
     algorithm 19–24
     culturally responsive 125, 127, 128, 129
     design pattern 217, 247
     design principles 7, 109, 117, 155
     design thinking 118
     (of) programming languages 100, 103, 108, 109, 110
Dice Game 67, 68, 73, 166
Dictionary 36, 189
   See also *Data structure*

Index

Index

Index